THE ACUPUNCTURE HANDBOOK

Of Sports Injuries & Pain

A Four Step Approach to Treatment

Whitfield Reaves
With Chad Bong

Illustrations by Deborah Kelley

Hidden Needle Press
Boulder, Colorado

THE ACUPUNCTURE HANDBOOK
Of Sports Injuries and Pain
A Four Step Approach to Treatment

Whitfield Reaves
With Chad Bong

Publisher:
Hidden Needle Press
P.O. Box 2067
Boulder, Colorado, 80306 USA

First Edition, July, 2009
Second Printing, March, 2011
Third Printing, October 2013

ISBN: 9780615274409
Library of Congress Control Number: 2009921450

Copyright ©2009
Whitfield Reaves, Hidden Needle Press

All rights reserved. No part of this publication may be reproduced, stored in a retrieval system, or transmitted in any form by any means, electronic, photocopying, recording, or otherwise, without the written permission of the publisher.

Printed in the USA

www.whitfieldreaves.com
www.theacupuncturehandbook.com

Table of Contents

Acknowledgments IX

Disclaimer XI

Injury Quick Reference XIII

Section I: *The Four Steps*

Summary of the Four Steps 3-8

STEP ONE: INITIAL TREATMENT
Technique #1: The Tendino-Muscle Meridians 9-12
Technique #2: Opposite Side (contra-lateral) 13-15
Technique #3: Opposite Extremity (upper/lower) 17-20
Technique #4: Empirical Points 21-22

STEP TWO: MERIDIANS & MICROSYSTEMS
Technique #5: The Shu-Stream Point Combination 23-25
Technique #6: Traditional Point Categories 27-29
Technique #7: The Extraordinary Meridians 31-34
Technique #8: Microsystems 35-37

STEP THREE: INTERNAL ORGAN IMBALANCES
Technique #9: Qi, Blood, and the Zang-fu Organs 39-43

STEP FOUR: THE SITE OF INJURY
Technique #10: Local and Adjacent Points 45-49

Section II: *The Injuries*

HEEL PAIN
1 Achilles Tendonitis 53-62
2 Plantar Fasciitis 63-73

FOOT PAIN
3 Lateral (Inversion) Ankle Sprain 75-83
4 Pain of the First MTP Joint (The Big Toe) 85-92
5 Metatarsal neuroma (Morton's neuroma) 93-99

LEG PAIN
6 Shin Splints (Anterior Tibial Stress Syndrome) 101-109
7 Shin Splints (Medial Tibial Stress Syndrome). 111-120

ANTERIOR KNEE PAIN
8 Patello-femoral Joint Dysfunction 121-132
9 Patellar Tendonitis 133-141

MEDIAL KNEE PAIN
10 Acute: Injury to the Medial Collateral Ligament
   or the Medial Meniscus 143-152
11 Chronic: Degenerative Arthritis of the Medial Compartment. 153-161

LATERAL KNEE PAIN
12 Ilio-tibial Band Syndrome. 163-174

POSTERIOR THIGH PAIN
13 The Hamstring Muscle Group. 175-183

HIP PAIN
14 Trochanteric Bursitis of the Hip 185-194
15 Arthritis of the Hip 195-203

LOW BACK PAIN
16 The Quadratus Lumborum Muscle 205-215

HAND PAIN
17 Carpal Tunnel Syndrome. 217-226

ELBOW PAIN
18 Lateral Epicondylitis (Tennis elbow). 227-237
19 Medial Epicondylitis (Golfer's Elbow) 239-247

SHOULDER PAIN

20 The Supraspinatous Muscle 249-261

21 The Infraspinatous Muscle 263-273

22 Frozen Shoulder 275-284

23 The Biceps Muscle Group 285-294

24 The Acromial-Clavicular Joint 295-302

NECK PAIN

25 The Levator Scapulae Muscle 303-313

Section III: *The Appendices*

Appendix A: References 317-319

Appendix B: R.I.C.E., Application of Ice, Application of Heat 320-322

Appendix C: Anti-inflammatory Medications 323-324

Appendix D: Biomechanical Imbalances 325-327

Appendix E: Cross Training 328-329

Appendix F: Physical Therapy 330-333

Appendix G: Orthopedic Assessment 334-335

Appendix H: Orthopedic Tests 336-341

Appendix I: Grading System for Sprains and Strains 342-343

Appendix J: Electrical Stimulation 344-346

Appendix K: Activation of the Tendino-Muscle Meridian 347-349

Appendix L: Topical Applications 350-352

Appendix M: Acupuncture Points 353-355

Appendix N: The Extraordinary Acupuncture Points 356-358

Appendix O: Myofascial Trigger Points 359-360

Appendix P: Wrist-Ankle Acupuncture 361-362

Index 363-365

Biography of the Authors 367-368

Acknowledgments

BOOK DESIGN:	Patricia Appelfeller/Appelfeller Arts
	www.AppelfellerArts.com
	Whitfield Reaves
TEXT FORMATTING:	Patricia Appelfeller/Appelfeller Arts
	George Roche/Roche Design
	www.RocheDesign.com
ILLUSTRATIONS:	Deborah Kelley
	deborah.kelley@msn.com
PRIMARY EDITOR:	Rachael Niehaus
	www.rachwrites.com
PRODUCTION/RESEARCH:	Chad Bong
	Martin Reaves
PRINTING:	Wayne Johnson
	www.GrubStreetPrinting.com

Let us begin by dedicating *The Acupuncture Handbook of Sports Injuries and Pain* to Grace Liu, MD (China). I first met Dr. Liu in 1977, at the acupuncture clinic of Dharma Rhealm Buddhist University, in Ukiah, California. As I left her office from my first-ever acupuncture treatment, I knew without question that Chinese medicine would be my life's work. I subsequently spent a year and a half studying with Dr. Liu in a formal acupuncture apprenticeship. I am grateful for her willingness to teach, but more importantly, for the opportunity to experience her compassion. The impact of our first meeting has stayed with me for over 30 years.

I would like to acknowledge Llewellyn Vaughn-Lee, and his influence in the writing and publication of this book. Several years ago he had the insight that the next stage in my professional development as an acupuncturist was to teach my work to apprentices. Llewellyn's encouragement led to my formal apprenticeship programs that started in 2006. Out of this one-on-one teaching, the *The Acupuncture Handbook* emerged.

I would also like to give my huge heartfelt thanks to my wife Mary Saunders and our son Martin Reaves. They tolerated my absence from the family for two long years as I was involved in the intricate tasks of writing this book. And when production was interrupted by my back surgery, they were wonderful caregivers and essential in my rehabilitation and recovery. Without them, the momentum of the book would have stalled.

My contributing writer Chad Bong assisted in both the writing and the production of this handbook. I would never have continued the long and tedious process without his gentle prodding. And his research, editorial opinion, and common-sense assistance was invaluable.

I would also like to acknowledge my colleagues. Jake Fratkin and his burning love of Chinese medicine has always been an inspiration to me. His advice on writing and publishing this handbook needs acknowledgement. My friend and colleague Matt Callison understands the intricacies of acupuncture sports medicine more than any other individual I have met. He has been a pillar for me, and I am both grateful and awed by his continuous contribution to orthopedic acupuncture.

Over the last several decades, there have been numerous other practitioners that have been involved in the shaping and texturing of Chinese medicine into a clinical tradition for treating sports injuries and pain. David Nickel, John Steinke, John Stebbins, Jim Skoein, and others too numerous to name ... to you all, I am appreciative.

This book would never have been written without my apprentices. They have reflected the power and efficiency of the student-teacher relationship in traditional Chinese medicine. Their application of the teachings to clinical practice confirmed to me that the points and techniques discussed in *The Acupuncture Handbook* indeed could to be put into writing.

And finally, I acknowledge all those unnamed individuals on the journey of integrating traditional Chinese acupuncture with western orthopedic and sports medicine. I am in gratitude to you all.

Whitfield Reaves
June, 2009

Disclaimer

The Acupuncture Handbook of Sports Injuries and Pain is written for licensed practitioners of acupuncture and traditional Chinese medicine. However, it may serve as a guide for other licensed health care providers whose scope of practice includes the insertion of acupuncture needles. This includes physical therapists, chiropractors, physicians, and other health care providers who have been properly trained and are licensed by the medical board in the state where they practice. *The Acupuncture Handbook* is intended to give the practitioner additional insight into the diagnosis, assessment, and treatment of sports injuries and pain. The information in this book should not be used as a substitute for a proper medical diagnosis and evaluation.

Additionally, the insertion of acupuncture needles is a potential risk. The practitioner who follows any of the techniques in this book should do so with full medical knowledge of the anatomy and physiology of the tissues being treated, as well as any medical contra-indications for acupuncture treatment of a patient. The author and the publisher can not take responsibility for improper use of techniques or avoiding timely medical advice.

The information in this book is written and published in good faith, as a contribution to the medical profession. The author and the publisher are not responsible for printed or perceived errors or omissions.

Injury Quick Reference

HEEL PAIN

Achilles tendonitis 53-62
Pain in the heel localized at the achilles tendon

A repetitive stress injury characterized by pain, inflammation, and swelling of the achilles tendon and its sheath. Pain is of gradual onset, and usually starts after a change in activity level, such as increased mileage, hills, or speed. Acute onset due to trauma is possible.

- Pain and stiffness localized at the achilles tendon
- Symptoms often experienced upon taking first steps in the morning or after prolonged sitting or rest
- Symptoms relieved as the heel "warms up" with moderate activity, but pain returns again during or after exercise
- Tenderness with "pinching" palpation of the tendon

Plantar Fasciitis 63-73
Pain and stiffness in the heel and the plantar aspect of the foot

A repetitive stress injury characterized by inflammation and irritation of the plantar fascia. Pain is of gradual onset, and usually starts after a change in activity level, such as increased mileage, hills, or speed. Acute onset due to trauma is possible.

- Heel pain and stiffness, which may extend down the arch
- Symptoms often experienced upon taking first steps in the morning or after prolonged sitting or rest
- Symptoms alleviated as the heel "warms up" with moderate activity, but pain returns again during or after exercise

FOOT PAIN

Lateral (Inversion) Ankle Sprain... 75-83
Pain, swelling, and bruising of the lateral ankle and foot.

This injury results in ligament sprain and joint inflammation from inverting or inward rolling of the ankle.

- Pain, swelling, and bruising
- Trauma to the ligament may range from a mild grade I sprain to a serious grade III injury

Pain of the First MTP Joint (The Big Toe)....................................85-92
Pain, stiffness, and decreased range of motion of the first metatarsal-phalanges joint of the big toe

Osteoarthritis and degeneration of the articular surface of the first MTP joint associated with repetitive stress or prior injury. Pain is of gradual onset. Acute onset due to trauma ("turf toe) is possible.

- Pain, stiffness, and decreased range of motion
- Swelling, inflammation, and signs of heat may be present
- Aggravated from exercise and weight-bearing activities, and relieved with rest

Metatarsal neuroma (Morton's neuroma) 93-99
Pain in the metatarsal region of the foot, on either the dorsal or plantar surfaces

A repetitive stress injury characterized by inflammation and irritation of the inter-digital nerves between the metatarsal bones. Pain is of gradual onset, and is usually related to activity level.

- Pain may be accompanied by numbness and tingling
- Pain is aggravated during exercise and weight-bearing activities
- Aggravated from exercise, and relieved with rest
- Pain is worsened by tight and restrictive shoes
- The 2nd/3rd and the 3rd/ 4th spaces are the two most common sites
- Pain may result from compression of the nerve bundle by the bony metatarsal heads

LEG PAIN

Shin Splints (Anterior Tibial Stress Syndrome)............................... 101-109
Pain and tenderness along the anterior lateral aspect of the leg just lateral to the tibia

A repetitive stress injury characterized by strain or inflammation of the anterior tibialis or other anterior compartment muscles of the leg. Pain is of gradual onset, and usually starts after a change in activity level, such as increased mileage, hills, or speed.

- Pain upon palpation along the lateral border of the tibia, and possibly along the anterior compartment muscle group
- Aggravated from exercise, and relieved with rest
- May have pain with resisted dorsiflexion of the ankle

Shin Splints (Medial Tibial Stress Syndrome).................................111-120
Pain and tenderness along the medial aspect of the leg at the medial border of the tibia

A repetitive stress injury characterized by strain or inflammation of the posterior tibialis or other medial compartment muscles of the leg. Pain is of gradual onset, and usually starts after a change in activity level, such as increased mileage, hills, or speed.

- Pain upon palpation along the medial border of the tibia, and possibly along the medial compartment muscle group
- Aggravated from exercise, and relieved with rest
- May have pain with resisted plantar-flexion, or with resisted inversion of the foot

ANTERIOR KNEE PAIN

Patello-femoral Joint Dysfunction..121-132
Pain in the anterior knee in the region of the patella and the patello-femoral groove

A repetitive stress injury characterized by inflammation and irritation of the undersurface of the patella. This may progress to chondromalacia or anterior compartment arthritis. Pain is of gradual onset, and is usually related to activity level.

- Pain aggravated with exercise, going up and down stairs, and various positions like squatting
- Pain may radiate to the posterior knee in the region of the popliteal fossa
- Creaking (crepitus) under the knee cap
- Patello-femoral joint syndrome is pain caused by dysfunctional tracking of the patella
- Chondromalacia is a softening of the cartilage on the posterior aspect of the patella

Patellar Tendonitis 133-141
Pain in the anterior knee anywhere along the tendon, from the inferior border of the patella to its attachment at the tuberocity of the tibia

Called "jumper's knee," patellar tendonitis is usually a repetitive stress injury characterized by inflammation and irritation of the patellar tendon. Pain is of gradual onset, and usually starts after a change in activity level, such as increased mileage, hills, or speed. Acute onset due to trauma is possible.

- Pain aggravated with exercise, especially jumping and going up or down stairs
- Sharp pain is reported during exercise, while dull pain is present even during rest
- Often seen with patello-femoral joint dysfunction
- In adolescents during a growth spurt, Osgood-Schlatter's disease is the common diagnosis

MEDIAL KNEE PAIN

ACUTE
Injury to the Medial Collateral Ligament or the Medial Meniscus............143-152
Acute pain, inflammation, and swelling in the medial knee experienced after injury or trauma

Acute injury commonly occurs with a twisting motion when the foot is planted, or from being hit on the lateral side of the knee. This results in acute injury to the MCL or the medial meniscus.

- General pain in the medial aspect of the knee, with swelling and stiffness
- Possible "giving out," locking, clicking or catching in knee
- May have the feeling of instability of the knee joint

CHRONIC
Degenerative Arthritis of the Medial Compartment of the Knee.............153-161
Chronic pain, inflammation, swelling, and stiffness of the medial knee

Chronic knee pain due to medial compartment osteoarthritis. May be associated with prior injury or from chronic degeneration of the articular surface due to repetitive stress.

- General pain in the medial aspect of the knee, with swelling and stiffness
- May have other symptoms characteristic of chronic arthritis, such as aggravation from cold weather and relief from warmth
- Aggravated from exercise and weight-bearing activities, and relieved with rest

LATERAL KNEE PAIN

Ilio-tibial Band Syndrome...163-174
Pain in the lateral knee and thigh

A repetitive stress injury characterized by inflammation and irritation of the ilio-tibial (IT) band just proximal to the lateral knee. Sometimes referred to as "runner's knee". Pain is of gradual onset, and usually starts after a change in activity level, such as increased mileage, hills, or speed. Acute onset due to trauma is possible.

- Pain and stiffness may radiate up ilio-tibial band to the greater trochanter
- Aggravated from exercise, and relieved with rest
- May have "popping" or "snapping" during activities involving knee flexion and extension
- Pain with palpation on the IT band just proximal to the lateral joint space of the knee

POSTERIOR THIGH PAIN

The Hamstring Muscle Group 175-183
Pain, spasm, and stiffness of the posterior thigh along the course of the hamstring muscle group

An acute injury with strain to one or more of the hamstring muscles, the muscle-tendon junction, or the attachments to the ischial tuberocity. Strain usually occurs during activities involving fast acceleration or deceleration. Chronic cases may be due to repetitive stress disorder.

- Pain may be accompanied by muscle spasms and stiffness
- In acute cases, pain may be accompanied by bruising and swelling
- May have heard a "popping" noise or felt a "tearing" sensation
- Pain reproduced with resisted knee flexion

HIP PAIN

Trochanteric Bursitis of the Hip 185-194
Pain in the hip and lateral thigh which may radiate down the ilio-tibial band

A repetitive stress injury characterized by inflammation of the trochanteric bursa of the hip. Sometimes it may occur from acute trauma, such as a direct blow to the thigh or a fall on the hip. Hip bursitis usually involves the gluteal muscles and the ilio-tibial band.

- Pain is usually experienced during lower-extremity activities, such as running and hiking
- Pain lying on the affected side at night
- May have audible popping or snapping with hip flexion and extension
- Pain with pressure directly over the greater trochanter

Arthritis of the Hip 195-203
Pain, stiffness, and limited range of motion of the hip. Pain may radiate to the inguinal and groin region

A repetitive stress injury or osteoarthritis characterized by chronic degeneration of the articular surface of the hip joint

- Aggravated from exercise, and relieved with rest
- Often seen as a chronic condition in patients over 50
- Pain with passive internal rotation of hip, and frequently, limited hip flexion

LOW BACK PAIN

The Quadratus Lumborum Muscle 205-215
Acute or chronic low back pain and spasm due to the quadratus lumborum (QL), which may radiate to the gluteal region. Pain is often one-sided.

Acutely is seen in acute sprain/strain of the low back, but may be a source of chronic or lingering lumbo-sacral pain. The QL is involved as a secondary lesion in many cases of back pain from other causes.

- Pain upon palpation at the superior attachment of the quadratus lumborum in the region of the extraordinary point *Pigen* about 3.5 cun lateral to the first lumbar vertebrae
- Elevated pelvis on the side of pain
- Lumbar region may be slightly flexed laterally to the side of pain
- Acute injury often accompanied by lifting and twisting movements
- The quadratus lumborum is involved in many cases of acute and chronic back sprain and strain, degenerative spine disorders, and disc disease

HAND PAIN

Carpal Tunnel Syndrome 217-226
Pain, tingling, and numbness in the palmar aspect of the hand and wrist

A repetitive stress injury characterized by entrapment, compression or irritation to the median nerve in its narrow passageway of the carpal tunnel at the wrist.

- As the condition worsens, the patient may report weakness, and grasping objects can become difficult
- Repetitive stress from hand motions is usually the suspected cause
- Symptoms follow the distribution area of the median nerve, which includes the first three digits and radial side of fourth digit
- Progressed cases may present with muscle atrophy in the thenar eminence in the region of Lu 10

ELBOW PAIN

Lateral Epicondylitis (Tennis elbow) 227-237
Pain in the elbow at the lateral epicondyle and distally along the extensor tendon and muscles of the forearm

A repetitive stress injury characterized by inflammation and irritation of the forearm extensors and possibly the supinators. This injury is often referred to as "tennis elbow", and pain is usually of gradual onset.

- Hand and wrist activities usually aggravate the condition
- Inflammation of the common extensor tendon, with the possibility of micro-tears at the site of the attachment
- Tenderness with palpation at the lateral epicondyle and distal to the attachment following the extensor tendon
- Pain with resisted wrist extension, radial deviation, and/or hand supination

Medial Epicondylitis (Golfer's Elbow, Climber's Elbow) 239-247
Pain in the elbow at the medial epicondyle and distally along the flexor tendon and muscles of the forearm

A repetitive stress injury characterized by inflammation and irritation of the forearm flexors and possibly the pronators. This injury is often referred to as "golfer's elbow" as well as "climber's elbow", and pain is usually of gradual onset.

- Hand and wrist activities usually aggravate the condition
- Inflammation of the common flexor tendon, with the possibility of micro-tears at the site of the attachment
- Tenderness with palpation at the medial epicondyle and distal to the attachment following the flexor tendon
- Pain with resisted wrist flexion and/or hand pronation

SHOULDER PAIN

The Supraspinatous Muscle...249-261
Pain in scapular region of the shoulder, with a referral pattern to the area of the deltoid. Possible sudden, sharp pain is due to shoulder impingement syndrome

An acute or chronic injury characterized by inflammation of the tendon and possible strain or muscle tears at the attachment to the humerus.

- Tenderness with palpation in the supraspinatous muscle, in the region of SI 12
- Pain and/or weakness with resisted abduction and a positive "arch of pain"
- Patient may have history of repeated or strenuous overhead motions, or of prior accident involving the shoulder

The Infraspinatous Muscle..263-273
Pain in scapular region of the shoulder, with a referral pattern to the area of the deltoid and the shoulder joint

An acute or chronic injury characterized by inflammation of the tendon and possible strain or muscle tears at the attachment to the humerus.

- Patient may report the feeling of pain "in the shoulder joint"
- Tenderness with palpation in the infraspinatous muscle, in the region of SI 11, or at the muscle-tendon junction at SI 10
- Pain and/or weakness with resisted external rotation
- Patient may have history of repeated or strenuous arm motions, or of accidents involving the shoulder
- The infraspinatous often accompanies other rotator cuff injuries

Frozen Shoulder..275-284
Decreased range of motion of the shoulder, often accompanied by pain and stiffness

Frozen shoulder may be associated with known etiology, such as capsular lesions, rotator cuff injury, or other trauma. It may also occur post-surgically, however it sometimes has no defined cause.

- Decreased or restricted range of motion
- Loss of normal function occurs with both active and passive movements
- More commonly seen in female patients
- May develop after trauma to the shoulder, after immobilization, and post-surgery

The Biceps Muscle Group..285-294
Pain in the anterior and the anterior-lateral aspect of the shoulder, which may radiate down the biceps muscle

A repetitive stress injury characterized by inflammation and irritation of the biceps tendon as it passes through the bicipital groove of the anterior shoulder. Injury to the biceps may occur acutely, with strain or tears to the muscle or tendon.

- Aggravated from exercise, and relieved with rest
- May have "popping" or "snapping" in the anterior shoulder (subluxation of the biceps tendon in the bicipital groove)
- Tenderness with palpation is noted directly over the bicipital groove
- Overuse injury is usually from overhead arm activities, such as tennis and throwing
- May occur as an acute traumatic injury

The Acromial-Clavicular Joint..295-302
Pain and inflammation on the top of the shoulder at the acromial-clavicular (AC) joint, often called shoulder separation

An injury due to separation of the AC joint and/or sprain to the acromial-clavicular ligament, characterized by pain, inflammation, and swelling. Joint laxity is possible in moderate to severe injuries.

- Called a shoulder separation, injury is almost always the result of a sudden traumatic event
- Arm movements may be painful and not tolerated
- Tenderness with palpation at the AC joint between LI 16 and LI 15
- AC joint injury usually produces pain with lateral abduction of the arm that may continue past 120 degrees
- Some patients may report chronic arthritic pain in the AC joint

NECK PAIN

The Levator Scapulae Muscle 303-313
Pain in the neck and the scapular region of the shoulder

Acutely is seen as torticollis ("stiff neck"), but may be a source of chronic or lingering neck and shoulder pain. The levator is involved as a secondary lesion in many cases of neck pain from other causes.

- Pain is often one-sided
- Pain upon palpation at the attachment just above the superior angle of the scapula at SI 14 and SI 15
- Elevated scapula on the side of pain
- Neck may be slightly flexed laterally to the side of pain
- Discomfort when laterally flexing or rotating to the side of pain

SECTION I
The Four Steps

The Four Steps

STEP ONE: INITIAL TREATMENT

Technique #1: *The Tendino-Muscle Meridians*

Technique #2: *Opposite Side (contra-lateral)*

Technique #3: *Opposite Extremity (upper/lower)*

Technique #4: *Empirical Points*

STEP TWO: MERIDIANS & MICROSYSTEMS

Technique #5: *The Shu-Stream Point Combination*

Technique #6: *Traditional Point Categories*

Technique #7: *The Extraordinary Meridians*

Technique #8: *Microsystems*

STEP THREE: INTERNAL ORGAN IMBALANCES

Technique #9: *Qi, Blood, and the Zang-fu Organs*

STEP FOUR: THE SITE OF INJURY

Technique #10: *Local and Adjacent Points*

SUMMARY OF THE FOUR STEPS

The Four Steps is a systematic approach to selecting points and techniques during treatment. As acupuncturists, we are always searching for "key" points that balance the patient and effectively treat his or her current condition. In sports medicine acupuncture, this is no exception. This Four Step approach is simple, systematic, and allows the practitioner flexibility to utilize his or her skills of diagnosis and assessment in the selection of appropriate points and treatment techniques.

Treatment of each sports injury in Section II is divided into this simple Four Step approach. There should be no surprises – each technique is well articulated in the current acupuncture texts and should be familiar to practitioners in North America, Europe, and Asia. I suggest using this step-by-step approach to make treatment of the athlete and the injured patient systematic, and therefore, more clinically effective. And while these techniques need to be performed with skill and precision, it is my hope that they will instill in the practitioner both enthusiasm and a sense of confidence.

Consider the Four Steps as a "template" used in the treatment of each injury. They are not a complete set of acupuncture techniques and treatment protocols. And it is far from a perfect list for the practitioner. During the 20-plus years I have been teaching sports medicine acupuncture, these steps have been altered and changed in order and content. So please view the Four Steps as a process, not as a fixed system of points and techniques.

One intention of the Four Steps approach is to "make conscious" the points and treatment techniques the practitioner has already studied and uses in clinical practice. Because of the wide diversity of styles and lineages, some of the outlined techniques may not be commonly practiced by acupuncturists. Hopefully the techniques list will assist the practitioner to "remember" some of those less-common points and often-overlooked treatment protocols.

The Four Steps also provides the practitioner with a strategy that guides treatment from the most superficial aspect of the body tissues to deep internal organ imbalances. For example, in Step One, the jing-well point is treated in order to activate the tendino-muscle meridians. These meridians are often considered the most superficial and yang portion of the body. Step Two utilizes techniques that treat points on the primary and extraordinary meridians. These pathways access a deeper level of qi and blood in the body. In Step Three, the internal organs are assessed and treated, which are considered the deepest and most yin portions of the body.

The Four Steps also guides the practitioner in treatment, beginning with the distal points and ending at the site of the injury. Step One starts with the most distal treatment, the jing-well point. Step Two considers the shu-stream and other antique points along the course of the affected meridians. The protocol ends with Step Four, treating points local and adjacent to the injured site. Whether in the muscles, tendons, ligaments, or the joint capsule, this is the primary stagnation of qi and blood.

Viewed from another perspective, the Four Steps resembles a treatment flow chart. I hope this will assist practitioners who are still defining their treatment strategies for sports injuries and pain. However, the Four Steps do not necessarily need to be viewed as a linear process. Some practitioners may use only some of the points and techniques for a specific injury. They might choose to use them in a different order or sequence. Points and techniques may even be selected for different reasons than articulated in this handbook.

In the chapters that follow in Section I, each of the techniques of the Four Steps will be discussed and summarized. Hopefully this will provide a basis for understanding these steps when applied to the sports injuries covered in detail in Section II. But first, let's summarize each of the Four Steps.

STEP ONE: INITIAL TREATMENT

Initial treatment encompasses a group of four techniques that are the first to consider with acute injuries. However, chronic and lingering pain syndromes may also respond to one or more of these techniques. The treatments are simple and straightforward, and do not necessarily depend upon a precise diagnosis of the cause of injury.

In Step One, points are selected with the intention of obtaining immediate improvement in the signs and symptoms of the patient. With each of the four techniques of Step One, a point or points are selected for treatment. After needle insertion, the most common procedure is to have the patient perform active movements of the affected area. If active movement is not possible, the site of injury may be massaged. Allow two minutes after insertion and manipulation of the needle to determine if there is an immediate effect. Then palpate the site of injury for pain to determine if there is improvement. Also, observe if an increase in range of motion is achieved.

To repeat: The objective of Initial Treatment is an immediate change in pain and an increase in range of motion. While this is not always achievable, and it might not be a complete solution, we must at least attempt this for the patient! Simply use palpation and range of motion to determine if there is, in fact, improvement.

In Step One, the practitioner must determine which of the four techniques is appropriate for the patient. These techniques are summarized as follows:

Technique #1: *The Tendino-Muscle Meridians*
Activate the tendino-muscle meridian by treating the appropriate jing-well point on the same side as the injury.

Technique #2: *Opposite Side (contra-lateral)*
Treat a corresponding point on the opposite (unaffected) side of the injury. This point may be an *ahshi* point or a defined acupuncture point, anatomically mirrored on the contra-lateral side of the body.

Technique #3: *Opposite Extremity (upper/lower)*
Treat a corresponding point on the opposite extremity of the site of injury. The points should be on the same paired Six Division meridian. It may be an *ahshi* point or a defined acupuncture point. In general, the corresponding upper/lower point is treated on the opposite side when the injury is acute and the same side when it is chronic.

Technique #4: *Empirical Points*

Treat an empirical point based upon the signs and symptoms of the patient. Empirical points may be defined acupuncture points or extraordinary points, and are used for their specific clinical effect.

These four simple techniques of Step One may be used as the primary treatment, or combined with other points and techniques, depending on the clinical result. Remember, immediate feedback from the patient is all-important in Step One.

STEP TWO: MERIDIANS & MICROSYSTEMS

Step Two encompasses four more techniques to consider in the treatment of sports injuries and pain. These techniques include virtually all the major points on the body, excluding those at the site of injury or adjacent to it. Point selection often depends upon a precise diagnosis of the cause of injury as well as an accurate determination of which meridians are affected.

Step Two focuses on the meridians and the microsystems of acupuncture. The points utilized in this step are not located at the site of injury. Frequently, these points are distal to where the patient experiences the pain, and are chosen according to which meridian or meridians are affected. The most important techniques in Step Two are the use of the shu-stream points and the other antique points. Also included in this step are the extraordinary meridians and auricular therapy.

The possibilities of points and point combinations in Step Two are numerous. In this step, the practitioner is simply looking for the points that activate the meridian and dispel stagnation in the tissues at the site of injury. Choosing among these four techniques is not always obvious, and point selection must be appropriate for the signs and symptoms of the patient.

Step Two includes the following techniques:

Technique #5: *The Shu-Stream Point Combination*

Treat a shu-stream point on the affected meridian, distal to the site of injury. This point is on the same side of pain. Couple the point with the shu-stream point of the same paired Six Division meridian on the opposite extremity. This point is on the opposite side of pain.

Technique #6: *Traditional Point Categories*

Treat a point based on its actions and indications. The antique points are all-important for this technique, but other categories include the xi-cleft, luo-connecting, and the back-shu and front-mu points. Use palpation as well as analysis of the signs and symptoms of the patient for point selection.

Technique #7: *The Extraordinary Meridians*

Activate an extraordinary meridian based on the signs and symptoms of the patient as well as the location of the injury. Both the master point and the coupled point of the affected extraordinary meridian are usually treated.

Technique #8: *Microsystems*

Auricular therapy is an effective microsystem approach in sports medicine acupuncture. Treat auricular points that correspond with the site of injury and the tissues affected by the trauma. Internal organ imbalances as well as general systemic points for pain may also be included. Wrist-ankle acupuncture may also be included in this technique.

The only common denominator for the points in Step Two is that they are not located at the site of injury. Fortunately, all of these points and techniques should be familiar to the acupuncturist. Palpation may be used to select which point or point combinations might be effective for any given injury. Analysis of the specific signs and symptoms of the patient may also assist the practitioner in their choice of points. The objective is to choose the points that work! And obviously, you can't use them all, so change the points as needed according to clinical results.

STEP THREE: INTERNAL ORGAN IMBALANCES

Treat the zang-fu organs that may contribute to the injury or pain syndrome. Additionally, treatment may be designed for internal organ imbalances of the patient even if they are not directly causative to the condition.

Technique #9: *Qi, Blood, and the Zang-fu Organs*

In Step Three, internal organ imbalances are considered. With some patients, the function of the zang-fu organs plays a significant role in the mechanism of the injury and its resulting pain syndrome. This is especially true for chronic and lingering conditions where the qi and blood are not properly assisting the healing process of the injured tissues. Sometimes, treating excess or deficiency of the internal organs is essential for relief of pain and improvement in function.

In the injuries covered in Section II, Step Three may appear brief and over-simplified to the reader. This is due in part to the considerable and unpredictable number of internal organ imbalances that may contribute with any individual patient. It is assumed that the practitioner will use his or her skills in diagnosis and assessment to create more precise treatment strategies for the complexity of the internal organ system of each case.

STEP FOUR: THE SITE OF INJURY

Treat the site of injury in order to dispel stagnation of qi and blood. In addition, other pathogens such as wind (feng), heat (re), cold (han), and damp (shi) should be assessed and treated. The objective is to normalize the function of the muscles, tendons, ligaments, and other tissues affected by the trauma or injury. Points may be determined by palpation, orthopedic testing, and analysis of the signs and symptoms of the patient.

Technique #10: *Local and Adjacent Points*

Treating the site of injury is the most comprehensive step covered in this handbook. The techniques in Step One and Step Two clearly follow the language of traditional Chinese medicine (TCM) and the meridian systems of acupuncture. Step Three uses the same viewpoint in assessing internal imbalances of the zang-fu organs. Important to Step Four is the emphasis on western anatomy, physiology, and orthopedic medicine. After assessing the site of injury from this perspective, the practitioner may then translate into the more familiar language of TCM if appropriate.

In Step Four, the site of injury is treated with local and adjacent points. Needling is often at the precise site of the trauma or injury. They may be *ahshi* points, trigger points, or motor points of a muscle. The obvious objective of local treatment is to dispel the stagnation of qi and blood. Some injuries require treatment to release taut bands of muscle, fascia, and other soft tissue at the site of injury. These are usually adjacent points, and this technique assists in the healing of the local stagnation. It may also be necessary to treat secondary muscle groups that contribute to or perpetuate a pain pattern. Whether due to compensation or muscle guarding patterns, treatment to these secondary tissues is often beneficial. These secondary points are often "above" and "below" the site of injury.

In Step Four, numerous points and needle techniques will be suggested to treat local stagnation and to normalize tissue function. Remember, points may be determined by orthopedic testing, palpation, and analysis of the signs and symptoms of the patient. It is assumed that the practitioner will use his or her clinical skills to make this determination. Be patient, and don't try to treat too many local points in a treatment session. Hopefully the patient will experience improvement from the techniques of Step One and Step Two, allowing time to experiment with local treatment in Step Four.

STEP ONE: INITIAL TREATMENT

Technique #1
The Tendino-Muscle Meridians

Activate the tendino-muscle meridian by treating the appropriate jing-well point on the same side as the site of injury. After treatment, carefully determine if there is an immediate decrease in pain or an increase in range of motion.

Technique #1 is based upon the tendino-muscle meridians (jin mai, jin jing), and is the first place to start in treating patients with pain from acute trauma or repetitive stress injuries. The tendino-muscle meridian (TMM) is often overlooked and frequently under-utilized by the practitioner of acupuncture. The activation of these important pathways can be crucial in effectively treating pain and sports injuries. And treatment of the TMM is simple, as the primary way to activate the meridian is by treating the jing-well point.

The tendino-muscle meridians are described as a channel network that circulates qi over the superficial aspect of the body. This includes the skin, the muscles, and the tendons. As described in *The Secondary Vessels of Acupuncture*, they travel in the "depressions and planes between muscles and tendons".[1] Furthermore, the muscle meridians are comprised of wei qi ("protective" qi), which is not "contained" within a vessel. Thus, their pathways have a bit more freedom and flexibility. I suggest that the reader view the tendino-muscle meridians as a general pathway of qi in the muscles, the fascia, and the tendons. They are responsible for many functional activities of the musculo-skeletal system, and are therefore involved in many sprains, strains, and other traumatic injuries.

The jing-well point is the only acupuncture point directly shared by both the primary meridian and the tendino-muscle meridian. After the jing-well point, the TMM follows the path of the primary meridian past the first, second, and third joints of the extremity (i.e., the ankle or wrist, the knee or elbow, the hip or shoulder). Because the wei qi of the meridian is not contained within a vessel, its pathway is superficial, broad, and diffuse. If we think of the primary meridian as a freeway, then the tendino-muscle meridian is the frontage road that parallels it, where so much of the business activity occurs.

The texts refer to the "insertion" or "binding" points of each tendino-muscle meridian. This is where the TMM has a functional connection with the primary meridian at or near a joint. For example, the Large Intestine muscle meridian binds in the shoulder at LI 15, in the elbow at LI ll, and in the wrist at LI 5. After the third joint (the hip or shoulder), the course of each TMM varies somewhat. They often connect to various parts of the body's trunk, including the spine, neck, and scapula. The tendino-muscle meridians terminate at a specific region or zone, translated as a "convergent point" or a "meeting point". This is where they unite with the two other yin or yang meridians that traverse the extremity of origin. For example, the three leg yang muscle meridians – the Stomach, Bladder, and Gall Bladder – converge at the region of SI 18.

Most texts describe the pathology of the tendino-muscle meridians as syndromes of either excess (shi) or deficiency (xu). For the purpose of this exploration, we will cover the excess syndromes, as this is the primary diagnosis in trauma and injury. As expected, an excess syndrome of the TMM produces pain! It is usually described as diffuse and distending, and frequently found at multiple *ahshi* points in the affected muscle, fascia, or tendinous areas. Most sources emphasize that pain is elicited by light palpation and pressure. Remember, the tendino-muscle meridians are superficial and the qi is not contained within a vessel. Thus the pain will not manifest as fixed, localized, and deep. Other accompanying symptoms include stiffness, swelling, spasm, and contraction. You may observe inflammatory signs of a yang nature, including heat and redness.

A typical clinical picture is the downhill skier who has been on the slopes all day long. He or she complains of pain, tightness, and a feeling of fullness in the quadriceps muscle group – that typical and predictable ache after a good hard workout. Upon palpation, there are numerous *ahshi* points on the anterior thigh, with pain being elicited using relatively light pressure. These painful points are found in the superficial layers of the muscle, along the Stomach channel. This may be diagnosed as an acute excess condition of the tendino-muscle meridian of the Stomach. Simply bleeding St 45, the jing-well point, should improve the condition significantly, possibly without any further treatment.

If, however, our ambitious skier had taken a hard fall, the quadriceps could have sustained a slight strain or tear in the muscle tissue. This case would present quite differently. Palpation would reveal fixed pain at the site of the tear, elicited with deep pressure. While the TMM may also be involved, the primary lesion is in deeper tissues of the muscle, and treatment to the jing-well point would not be sufficient to fully heal this case. You would undoubtedly need additional points and techniques in the treatment protocol for the patient.

NEEDLE TECHNIQUE

Bleeding technique is the preferred way to treat a jing-well point. Generally, it is simple, and needs to be done quickly, without hesitation. Using sterile lancets and surgical gloves, swiftly needle-prick the point while holding firm pressure on the finger or toe. I use "pinching pressure" at the distal aspect of the digit, with my fingers proximal enough that I don't needle prick myself. Try to get 10 large drops of blood to drain from the point. If the quantity of blood is not sufficient, a simple trick is to lower the patient's foot or arm off the table. Gravity works wonders, and this will often produce the necessary drops of blood.

While bleeding appears to be the most effective way to treat this distal point, you may also consider needling for 20 to 30 minutes. Use a one-inch body needle or half-inch ear needle. Some practitioners apply thread moxa, especially with patients where the bleeding technique or needling the fingers or toes may be contraindicated; however, this is a technique I rarely employ.

Activating the tendino-muscle meridian by bleeding the jing-well point is the first technique I use with most injuries presenting with pain, inflammation, and swelling. Even if the primary lesion is in the deeper tissues, such as with muscle strain, ligament sprain, and joint inflammation, the TMM may still be affected. There are, however, additional points used for the treatment of TMM disorders. These details are covered on page 347 for those practitioners who think the jing-well point is just not enough!

Keep in mind that immediate change is the objective of Step One. After treating the jing-well point, palpate for pain at the site of injury. You might also have the patient actively move the affected area, observing for an increase in range of motion. This treatment may give immediate relief, which hopefully you will come to expect. My experience is that up to 80 percent of patients with musculo-skeletal pain due to injury or trauma will have some degree of improvement from the simple technique of bleeding the jing-well point. Patients with qi stagnation and blood stasis in the deeper tissues – conditions like sprained ankle, shoulder tendonitis, or joint pain – will often experience a 15 to 25 percent improvement. Not bad for a few minutes of work! And you still have more techniques in Step One to try.

OTHER CLINICAL COMMENTS

- Jing-well points are treated on the same side as the site of injury.
- Treatment to the jing-well point may be repeated, even daily, up to six times.
- The yang tendino-muscle meridians are usually more responsive and clinically effective than those of the yin meridians.
- Treatment may include more than one jing-well point when the site of injury extends to multiple meridian pathways.
- If treatment to the jing-well point benefits the patient, it may indicate that other points on the same meridian may be clinically effective.
- If treatment to the jing-well point does not benefit the patient, it may indicate that the stagnation of qi and blood is in deeper tissues of the body.
- Care should be taken in bleeding yin meridian jing-well points, considering all of their contra-indications.
- Remember to always use gloves and proper sterile procedures.

CLINICAL EXAMPLES

I recently treated a runner from a local high school track team. He had a slight tear of the quadriceps tendon at its attachment to the ilium at the anterior superior iliac spine. Manual muscle testing of both hip flexion and knee extension reproduced pain and weakness. As this injury is likely on the tendino-muscle meridian of the Stomach, the jing-well point St 45 was treated with bleeding technique. After performing this simple procedure, I immediately retested hip flexion and knee extension. These tests revealed both a strong muscle and significantly reduced pain at the tendinous attachment. This was the first acupuncture treatment for this young athlete, and he was amazed to see such an immediate change. Within several treatments and a week or so of rest, he was back to full training and competition. The jing-well point was used along with other local and distal points on the Stomach meridian.

Several weeks later, I had another patient with pain at the anterior hip in the region of the attachment of the quadriceps tendon. Confidently, I used bleeding technique on St 45 to activate the tendino-muscle meridian. However, manual muscle testing of the quadriceps after the treatment produced no change in either muscle weakness or pain. Although the patient did not immediately respond, I was not discouraged. I concluded that the pain was probably due to some cause other than quadriceps tendonitis. After a more complete assessment of the patient, it was determined that her problem was caused by the ilio-psoas muscle, requiring a completely different set of points and techniques. Importantly, the lack of clinical results from a treatment can be used to assist the practitioner in diagnosis, assessment, and choice of additional points to treat.

REFERENCES

[1] Low, R: *The Secondary Vessels of Acupuncture*. Thorsons Publishers, United Kingdom, 1983 (pages 77-81).

STEP ONE: INITIAL TREATMENT

Technique #2

Opposite Side (contra-lateral)

Treat a corresponding point on the opposite (unaffected) side of the injury. This point may be an *ahshi* point or a defined acupuncture point, anatomically mirrored on the contra-lateral side of the body. After treatment, carefully determine if there is an immediate decrease in pain or an increase in range of motion.

The technique of treating the opposite (unaffected) side of the injury works well for many acute injuries, including sprains, strains, and trauma. However, don't rule out contra-lateral treatment for chronic or lingering cases, as this sometimes results in improvement. The treatment is simple, and most acupuncturists have used this technique at one time or another.

POINT SELECTION

The first step of this technique is selecting a corresponding point on the unaffected side. Generally, there are two possibilities to consider; palpation is usually reliable in determining which point or points to treat.

- *Ahshi* point(s) on the opposite (unaffected) side

  Palpation often reveals a painful point on the opposite side of the body that is a precise anatomical mirror of the site of injury. With some injuries, the body will mirror multiple points on the contra-lateral side. These painful *ahshi* point(s) are selected for treatment.

- Acupuncture point(s) on the opposite (unaffected) side

  Sometimes palpation reveals point sensitivity at a defined acupuncture point on the unaffected side. Often, if an acupuncture point is "reasonably close" to a precise anatomical mirror of the injury, it may be selected for treatment.

A lateral (inversion) ankle sprain is a good example of this technique. Some patients will present with a painful *ahshi* point mirrored on the unaffected side. With other patients, the point GB 40, also on the unaffected side, will be painful on palpation. Treating either the corresponding *ahshi* point or GB 40 will often result in improvement in both pain and range of motion of the ankle. Medial shin splints are a good example of a "zone" of pain, where multiple *ahshi* points may be found along the posterior border of the tibia on the contra-lateral side. Several needles in these *ahshi* points can potentially result in an improvement of symptoms.

NEEDLE TECHNIQUE

Remember, with all the techniques in Step One, we are looking for an immediate change in the signs and symptoms of the patient. The technique is simple: the practitioner stimulates the needle while the patient performs active movement of the area affected by the injury. First, needle the corresponding point or points on the opposite (unaffected) side. Then, use mild to moderate stimulation to the point continuously for two minutes. If active movement is not possible, the injured area may be massaged. After two minutes, palpate the site of injury for pain to determine if there is improvement. Observing the patient's movement will also reveal if an increase in range of motion has been achieved.

I usually find that mild to moderate needle stimulation is sufficient for this technique. However, precise location and needle depth is required. Some practitioners suggest "pecking and rotating" using moderate to strong stimulation. Pecking and rotating increases the probability of achieving correct depth of insertion. The "price" is more pain and discomfort to the patient. We are not looking for strong needle sensation as the result. We are looking for an improvement of signs and symptoms, and a point needled with precision is preferable.

There are generally three possible outcomes of treatment to the opposite side:

- There is no immediate change. Don't be discouraged, as I have treated opposite side points for years with no immediate change. It takes only several minutes of treatment time, and there are more points to try! Remove the needle and proceed to the next technique.

- There is moderate change. If some degree of relief is achieved, retain the needle, and proceed to the next technique. Every three to five minutes during the treatment session, use mild to moderate stimulation on the point for 30 to 60 seconds. If further treatment includes points on the affected extremity, obviously active movement will not be possible.

- There is significant change. Occasionally a corresponding point on the opposite side may result in significant improvement of symptoms. I have had this technique completely eliminate pain and restore normal motion to an ankle sprain. Although the practitioner is usually inclined to proceed with other local and adjacent treatments, sometimes this may be a mistake. Needling at or near the site of injury may potentially aggravate the condition. It is "practitioner's greed", and we have all done it, because we don't believe treatment can be so simple as one needle in the unaffected side!

OTHER CLINICAL COMMENTS

- Treatment to the opposite side may be repeated as long as clinical improvement is observed.

- Optimally, treatment should be limited to only one or two corresponding points on the opposite side.

- Opposite side treatment is more likely to work for one-sided symptoms. If the patient has bilateral pain, other techniques are more likely to benefit.

- The probability that opposite side treatment will benefit increases when the corresponding points are significantly point sensitive.

- Corresponding points on a "yang" surface (i.e., the extensor muscles of the forearm) are usually more effective than those on a "yin" surface (i.e., the flexor muscles of the forearm).

- Frequently, the opposite side treatment will be combined with other points on the affected side and at the site of injury. After the removal of all other needles, retain those on the opposite side. Use mild stimulation for two minutes while the patient once again moves the affected area. This may assist in reducing or avoiding aggravation from local and adjacent treatment.

Notes

STEP ONE: INITIAL TREATMENT

Technique #3
Opposite Extremity (upper/lower)

Treat a corresponding point on the opposite extremity of the injury. This point may be an *ahshi* point or a defined acupuncture point. Upper-extremity injuries are anatomically mirrored on the lower extremity, and lower-extremity injuries on the upper extremity. The upper/lower point correspondences should be located on the paired Six Division meridian. After treatment, carefully determine if there is an immediate decrease in pain or an increase in range of motion.

The technique of treating the opposite extremity benefits many acute conditions, including sprains, strains, and localized trauma. However, don't rule out upper/lower treatment for chronic or lingering injuries, as this sometimes results in improvement. The treatment is based upon this simple concept from the classics: "If the upper is diseased, treat the lower. If the lower is diseased, treat the upper."[1]

POINT SELECTION

In general, upper-extremity lesions are treated on the lower extremity, and lower-extremity lesions on the upper extremity. The correspondences are described as follows:

1. Treat the wrist for ankle lesions, and the ankle for wrist lesions

2. Treat the elbow for knee lesions, and the knee for elbow lesions

3. Treat the shoulder for hip lesions, and the hip for shoulder lesions

In addition to the anatomical mirror, treating the opposite extremity is based upon the paired Six Division meridian pathways. Simply stated, stagnation on a meridian of one extremity may be treated on its Six Division paired meridian on the opposite extremity. For example, pain on the elbow at LI 11 (upper extremity Yang ming) may be treated at the knee on point St 36 (lower extremity Yang ming).

The upper/lower correspondences are summarized as follows:

Six Division Pairing	Upper Extremity	Lower Extremity
Tai yang	Small Intestine	Bladder
Shao yang	San Jiao	Gall Bladder
Yang ming	Large Intestine	Stomach
Tai yin	Lung	Spleen
Shao yin	Heart	Kidney
Jue yin	Pericardium	Liver

The technique is simple. Start with the anatomical relationships of the wrist to the ankle, the elbow to the knee, and the shoulder to the hip. Use the meridian relationship of the Six Divisions to precisely locate where the upper/lower mirrored point may be found.

Keep in mind that some practitioners use anatomical mirroring without regard to the Six Division pathways. An example is the use of St 41 in the center of the ankle to treat carpal tunnel syndrome, where the nerve entrapment is in the center of the wrist at the region of P 7. This is a precise anatomical mirror. However it is not a Six Division correspondence, as the Stomach and Pericardium pathways are not paired meridians. The protocols that follow will insist upon a Six Division pairing for this technique. The reader is encouraged to experiment with both variations for this technique.

The only issue left to determine is whether the upper/lower corresponding point to be used is on the same side or opposite side of the site of injury. The general rule is to use the corresponding point on the opposite (contra-lateral) side when the injury is acute and on the same side when chronic. However, rules are meant to be broken! Check both sides of the body, choosing the more point-sensitive location. If one side does not achieve results, try the other.

Like opposite side treatment, there are two general possibilities to consider when selecting an upper/lower mirrored point. Palpation is usually reliable in determining which point or points to treat.

- *Ahshi* point(s) on the opposite extremity (upper/lower)

  Palpation often reveals a painful point on the opposite extremity that is a precise anatomical mirror of the site of injury. With some injuries, the body will mirror multiple points on the opposite extremity. These painful *ahshi* point(s) are selected for treatment.

- Acupuncture point(s) on the opposite extremity (upper/lower)

  Sometimes palpation reveals point sensitivity at a defined acupuncture point on the opposite extremity. Often, if an acupuncture point is "reasonably close" to a precise Six Division anatomical mirror of the injury, it may be selected for treatment.

Tennis elbow is a good example of this technique. It may present with a corresponding *ahshi* point on the opposite extremity of the injury. This may be at either St 35 or St 36. Either one of these points can potentially result in a relief of symptoms. And while results are not always lasting, I try to accept that sometimes "a little better" is acceptable while experimenting with other points and techniques.

NEEDLE TECHNIQUE

As with the other techniques of Step One, we are looking for an immediate change. The technique is simple: the practitioner stimulates the needle while the patient actively moves the area affected by the injury. First, needle the corresponding point or points on the opposite extremity. Then, use mild to moderate stimulation to the point continuously for two minutes. If the practitioner is inclined and the patient is willing, stronger stimulation to the point with "pecking and rotating" may be considered. While the point(s) are being stimulated, the patient performs active movement of the affected area. If active movement is not possible, the injured area may be massaged while the points are being stimulated.

After two minutes, palpate the site of injury for pain to determine if there is improvement. Observing the patient's movement will also reveal if an increase in range of motion has been achieved.

There are generally three possible outcomes of treatment:

- There is no immediate change. Remove the needle(s) and proceed to the next technique.

- There is moderate change. If some degree of relief is achieved, retain the needle, and proceed to the next technique. Every three to five minutes during the treatment session, use mild to moderate stimulation on the point for 30 to 60 seconds. If further treatment includes points on the affected extremity, obviously active movement will not be possible.

- There is significant change. Retain the needle, and every three to five minutes during the treatment session, use mild stimulation on the point for 30 to 60 seconds. Further treatment with other points may be considered. Be cautious, as it might not be necessary!

OTHER CLINICAL COMMENTS

- Treatment to the opposite extremity may be repeated as long as clinical improvement is observed.

- Optimally, treatment should be limited to only one or two corresponding points on the opposite extremity.

- Opposite extremity treatment is more likely to work for one-sided symptoms. If the patient has bilateral pain, other techniques may be more effective.

- The probability that opposite extremity treatment will benefit increases when the corresponding points are significantly point sensitive.

- Corresponding points on a "yang" surface (i.e., the extensor muscles of the forearm) are usually more effective than those on a "yin" surface (i.e., the flexor muscles of the forearm).

- Frequently, opposite extremity treatment will be combined with other points on the affected side and at the site of injury. After the removal of all other needles, retain those on the opposite extremity. Use mild stimulation for two minutes while the patient once again moves the affected area. This may assist in reducing or avoiding aggravations from local and adjacent treatment.

CLINICAL EXAMPLE

This is a story I frequently tell and will never forget. During the 1984 Olympics in Los Angeles, I was treating a tennis player from the United Kingdom. He complained of wrist pain on the dorsal surface, in the region of SJ 4. He had surgery several years earlier to debride the extensor tendons due to chronic inflammation. I had ignored the techniques of Step One, choosing instead to needle at the site of injury. I was convinced that post-surgical scar tissue was to blame, and local needles would benefit. However, after a half-dozen sessions, there was no change in his pain or the function of his wrist.

So I had to return to the techniques of Step One, as local treatment had failed to make any change. Choosing the technique of opposite extremity, I needled GB 40, the Shao yang corresponding point on the ankle for wrist pain at SJ 4. Within two minutes of mild stimulation to the point and some active wrist movements, the "immediate" change was there! This simple treatment eliminated most of the pain and increased range of motion to almost normal. After experiencing this success, the patient pleaded with me on the next visit to treat "that point in the ankle". He was sure if I tried local points it would not work. So, he did a great job of telling me travel stories to assure that I would not get over-zealous and try needling locally in his wrist! This patient required several more visits to treat this upper/lower corresponding point, and then I never saw him again as a patient.

REFERENCES

[1] Flaws, B: *Statements of Fact in Traditional Chinese Medicine*. Blue Poppy Press, Colorado, 2007 (page 232). *Note: Shang bing xia zhi, xia bing shang zhi.*

STEP ONE: INITIAL TREATMENT

Technique #4
Empirical Points

Treat an empirical point based upon the signs and symptoms of the patient, using the point for its known clinical effects. The empirical point may be a defined acupuncture point or an extraordinary point. After treatment, carefully determine if there is an immediate decrease in pain or an increase in range of motion.

I have been quoted by students as saying, "There is no treatment like one that works!" This statement clearly applies to the use of empirical points. Empirical is defined as an outcome or result that is verifiable by means of observation and guided by practical experience.[1] The empirical points of acupuncture likely developed from the needling of *ahshi* points. Over time these points were clinically observed to be effective for specific signs, symptoms, or conditions. Through this process, this category of points slowly found its way into the knowledge base of the many different lineages of acupuncture.

CATEGORIES OF EMPIRICAL POINTS

Empirical points fall into two categories. They may be defined acupuncture points or "extraordinary" points. These empirical points may be summarized as follows:

1. Defined acupuncture points with actions or indications that differ from traditionally documented clinical uses. For example, SI 1 is sometimes considered an empirical point for lactation deficiency because many of the actions of this point do not clearly explain this specific clinical use.

2. Extraordinary points that are located on a meridian pathway, but not at the location of a defined acupuncture point. An example is Ling gu, which is located on the Large Intestine meridian, .5 cun proximal to the point LI 4.

3. Extraordinary points not located on one of the 12 primary meridian pathways. An example is *Luozhen*, located between the second and third metacarpal bones of the hand. This empirical point for stiff neck does not lie on one of the primary channels.

Many empirical points have developed from the integration of western anatomy and physiology. For instance, with scalp acupuncture, "point zones" of the scalp are treated based upon the anatomical location of the motor, sensory, and other regions of the brain. Other empirical points are located at significant anatomical sites of the musculo-skeletal system. For example, the extraordinary point *Heding* lies over the attachment of the quadriceps tendon at the superior border of the patella.

The empirical points from the lineage of Master Tong are perhaps the most widely known. These points and point prescriptions have a long tradition of use, and comprise a system of treatment rather than a collection of clinically effective points. There are various sources on his work, including *Master Tong's Acupuncture* published by Blue Poppy Press.[2] Miriam Lee, L.Ac., and Richard Tan, L.Ac., have published various works that outline the principles of treatment using the empirical points of Master Tong.

NEEDLE TECHNIQUE

As with the other techniques of Step One, we are looking for an immediate change. First, needle the appropriate empirical point for the patient's signs, symptoms, or condition. Then, use mild to moderate stimulation to the point continuously for two minutes. If the practitioner is inclined and the patient is willing, stronger stimulation to the point with "pecking and rotating" may be considered. While the point is being stimulated, the patient performs active movement of the affected area. If active movement is not possible, the site of injury may be massaged.

The technique for empirical points is the same as opposite side and opposite extremity treatment. The practitioner stimulates the needle while the patient moves the area affected by the injury. After two minutes, palpate the site of injury for pain, carefully determining if there is improvement. Observing the patient's movement will also reveal if an increase in range of motion has been achieved.

Empirical points may be incorporated into a treatment plan that includes distal, adjacent, and local points. In the sports injury treatments of Section II, it is assumed this can be accomplished with clinical success. However, the reader will find that many of these injuries do not include empirical points. In this handbook, I have chosen not to include points or techniques that are not a part of my personal clinical experience. I encourage the practitioner to consider any empirical points they have studied, and use them in Step One.

The extraordinary points referred to in Section II are listed in the Appendices on page 356.

REFERENCES

[1] *The American Heritage Dictionary of the English Language*, Third Edition. Houghton Mifflin Company, New York, 1992 (page 604).

[2] Lee, M: *Master Tong's Acupuncture*, Second Edition. Blue Poppy Press, Colorado, 1998.

STEP TWO: MERIDIANS & MICROSYSTEMS

Technique #5
The Shu-Stream Point Combination

Treat a shu-stream point on the affected meridian distal to the site of injury. This point is on same side of pain, and is distal to the site of injury. Couple this point with the shu-stream point of the same paired Six Division meridian on the opposite extremity (upper/lower). This point is on the opposite side of pain.

The shu-stream points are among the most interesting and widely used category of acupuncture points. They can work wonderfully for many acute injuries, including sprains and strains, tendonitis, and other soft tissue trauma. But don't rule out shu-stream points for chronic or lingering cases, as sometimes these antique points are beneficial. If unsure which distal points to treat, I often select the shu-stream as the first option. In general, they have a high probability of success in treating sports injuries and pain.

The texts are quite clear in describing the primary meridians as a "well" at the distal point (jing-well) and a "sea" at the elbow or knee (he-sea). As the third point proximal to the jing-well, the shu point is a "stream", insinuating that the qi of the meridian is active as it begins to "flow". Clinically, this is observed in the use of the shu-stream points for the treatment of pain due to obstruction anywhere along the course of the channel. The classic texts also suggest the shu-stream points are beneficial for *Bi* syndromes and the treatment of "pain in the joints".

POINT SELECTION

Choosing a shu-stream point is usually based upon the signs and symptoms of the patient. However, palpation is also quite reliable in determining which point or points to treat. If the shu-stream point is sensitive, that may be reason enough to use it. The point selected for treatment must be distal to the site of injury and on the affected meridian. If there is more than one meridian involved, the shu-stream points of each of the affected meridians may be used. Examples are obvious, as most practitioners have used SI 3 for neck pain or SJ 3 for earache at one time or another. And using both GB 41 and Bl 65 demonstrates the use of two shu-stream points with an acute ankle sprain where pain and swelling involve both the Shao yang and the Tai yang channels.

However, using shu-stream points as a combination is a more complete approach to treatment. First, select a shu-stream point on the affected meridian distal to the site of injury. This point is on the same side as the pain. Then, couple this point with the shu-stream point of the same paired Six Division meridian on the opposite extremity (upper/lower). This point is on the opposite side of pain. The combination is simply two shu-stream points, one on the affected side, one on the unaffected side. One shu-stream point is located on the upper extremity, one on the lower extremity. And both shu-stream points are always on the same paired Six Division meridian.

The following is a summary of the shu-stream point combinations:

Meridian	Affected Side	Opposite Side
Large Intestine	LI 3	St 43
San Jiao	SJ 3	GB 41*
Small Intestine	SI 3	Bl 65
Stomach	St 43	LI 3
Gall Bladder	GB 41*	SJ 3
Bladder	Bl 65	SI 3
Lung	Lu 9	Sp 3
Pericardium	P 7	Liv 3
Heart	H 7	Kid 3
Spleen	Sp 3	Lu 9
Liver	Liv 3	P 7
Kidney	Kid 3	H 7

For many sports injuries and pain syndromes, GB 42 is frequently more sensitive than GB 41, and should be considered as an alternative shu-stream point for the Gall Bladder meridian.

NEEDLE TECHNIQUE

First, needle the two shu-stream points. Remember, with this combination, one point is distal to the site of injury, and is on the affected side. The paired point is on the opposite side and on the opposite extremity. Mild to moderate stimulation is usually sufficient for clinical improvement. When the shu-stream points are located on yang meridians, I frequently use electrical stimulation between the two paired points. I encourage the reader to try this technique, as it often results in significant improvement.

My affinity for this shu-stream point combination is due in part to the skillful teaching I received years ago from Frank Chung, L.Ac.[1] A skilled and seasoned practitioner, Dr. Chung suggests simultaneous stimulation of both paired shu-stream points. Some patients respond well to this needle technique. And it should be noted that some practitioners report favorable results using ion pumping chords between the shu-stream points. The reader should determine which needle technique is appropriate for their clinical style as well as for the specific needs of the patient.

I remember one year teaching my weekend sports medicine seminar in my hometown of Boulder, Colorado. As we got started, I noticed a number of unfamiliar faces in the group, and inquired where they were from. This group of acupuncture students were studying in Santa Fe, and had driven a full day to come to the seminar. There are many great teachers in New Mexico, and I questioned why they had decided to attend. One student told a story of a patient in the student clinic with chronic hip pain. They had tried all the techniques in the texts, such as the local points GB 30 and GB 29 and the commonly used distal points GB 31 and GB 34. He then remembered the shu-stream point combination of GB 41 and SJ 3, which he saw in a teaching video of mine from the college's library. It ended up being the only treatment that worked!

This story demonstrates the potential clinical effectiveness of the shu-stream point combination. I use it every day in my practice, and it is one of the most important techniques in the chapters that follow in Section II.

OTHER CLINICAL COMMENTS

- Shu-stream points selected for treatment are distal to the site of injury.
- Shu-stream points on the yang meridians are generally more effective than those on the yin meridians.
- Treatment to the shu-stream points may be repeated as long as clinical improvement is observed.
- Treatment can include up to three shu-stream points distal to the site of injury on the affected extremity.
- Electrical stimulation between the two paired shu-stream points, especially on the yang meridians, often enhances the clinical outcome. Don't be afraid to use this technique.
- Don't overlook the possibility that GB 42 may be used as an alternative shu-stream point to GB 41. It took me years of clinical experimentation to discover this. I encourage the reader to try it.

REFERENCES

[1] *Notes from the Annual Convention of the National Sports Acupuncture Association. Special Points for Pain and Injuries, Frank Chung, L.Ac., Berkeley, California, 1992.*

Notes

STEP TWO: MERIDIANS & MICROSYSTEMS

Technique #6
Traditional Point Categories

Treat a point based on its actions and indications. The five antique points are all-important for this technique, but other categories include the xi-cleft, luo-connecting, and the back-shu and front-mu points. Use palpation as well as analysis of the signs and symptoms of the patient for point selection.

There is no shortage of interesting traditional point categories. The classic texts clearly define these point groupings, as well as specify their actions and indications. This technique focuses on these categories and their use in the treatment of sports injuries and pain. The five antique points are all-important, but other categories include the xi-cleft, luo-connecting, and the back-shu and front-mu points. Fortunately, all of these points are familiar to the practitioner. However, it is important to note that texts vary as to how and when each of these points are used in treatment. The possibilities are numerous, and in the treatment chapters of Section II, points from these important traditional categories are recommended.

Palpation may be used to select which point or point combinations might be effective with a specific injury. Analysis of the specific signs and symptoms of the patient may also assist the practitioner in his or her choice of points. The objective is to choose the points that work! And obviously, you can't use them all, so experiment as needed according to clinical results.

SUMMARY OF THE TRADITIONAL POINT CATEGORIES

The following is a summary of the most important acupuncture point categories:

The Five "Antique" Points

The reader is well aware of the five "antique" points. However, it might be helpful to review these categories, as there may be some points overlooked by the practitioner. They can be summarized as follows:

1. Jing-well points

   The jing-well points are exceedingly useful in trauma and injury, and are discussed in detail as part of Step One on page 9.

27 • Technique #6 *Traditional Point Categories*

2. Ying-spring points

On the yang meridians, these are the "water" points and on the yin meridians the "fire" points. Their general action is to clear heat, and they may be used to treat injuries with signs and symptoms of inflammation and swelling. A good example is St 44 for patellar tendonitis and Liv 2 for the treatment of acute sprain of the MCL.

3. Shu-stream points

Shu-stream points, like the jing-well points, are exceedingly useful in trauma and injury, and are discussed separately in Step Two on page 23.

4. Jing-river points

On the yang meridians, these are the "fire" points with the general action of clearing heat. Thus, the yang meridian jing-river points are indicated for the signs and symptoms of inflammation and swelling. In addition, the jing-river points of both yin and yang meridians may be used to treat symptoms of the extremity, distal to the shoulder or the hip. An example is using LI 5 for treating tendonitis of the forearm extensor group.

5. He-sea points

The he-sea points are the elemental quality "earth" on the yang meridians and "water" on the yin meridians. Thus, the indications often include swelling and edema. However, the he-sea points are even more important for treating symptoms of the extremity, distal to the shoulder or the hip. "Motor impairment", pain, and weakness are common indications for he-sea points such as St 36, LI ll, and GB 34.

The Xi-cleft and Luo-connecting Points

The xi-cleft points and the luo-connecting points are two other important categories useful in the treatment of pain and injury. They are summarized as follows:

1. Xi-cleft points

Described as where the qi and blood "accumulate", the xi-cleft points are commonly indicated for the treatment of acute pain and obstruction in the channels and collaterals. However, the practitioner should not exclude their use in sub-acute or chronic conditions. A good example is the point SI 6, used for the treatment of acute shoulder pain due to stagnation in the Tai yang region of the neck and scapula.

2. Luo-connecting points

The luo-connecting points are generally indicated for obstruction in the luo vessels. They may be used for both acute and chronic pain. An example is SJ 5, used for the treatment of shoulder pain in the Shao yang region of the deltoid.

The practitioner may also consider the use of the luo point-source point combination. This treats pain along the pathway of both coupled meridians. Bl 58 + Kid 3 is an example of this point combination to treat both the Tai yang and Shao yin portions of the hamstring group. In this case, the pain is along the posterior and medial aspect of the thigh.

Tonification and Sedation Points

The tonification point may be used for pain due to deficiency in the primary meridian. The sedation point is indicated for pain due to excess in the primary meridian. Lu 9 is an example of a tonification point used to treat chronic biceps pain of the shoulder. The sedation point Liv 2 is commonly used to treat acute pain in the medial knee.

Hui-influential Points

Hui-influential points treat the functionally related tissue that they "influence", as is clearly defined in the acupuncture texts. GB 34 is the most commonly used hui-influential point for soft tissue injury. It is the influential point for tendons and may be used as a secondary point for tendonitis.

Back-shu and Front-mu Points

The back-shu and front-mu points may be included in the treatment of injuries for two reasons. First, they may be useful for treating the body tissue that corresponds to the zang or fu organ. For example, Bl 18 (Liver back-shu point) or Liv 14 (Liver front-mu point) may benefit lesions of the muscles and tendons, the corresponding tissue of the Liver. Secondly, they may be useful for treating the corresponding meridian of their respective organ. An example is Bl 20 (Spleen back-shu point) and Liv 13 (Spleen front-mu point). They treat qi and blood stagnation along the Spleen channel, as seen in a case of medial shin splints.

Lower He-sea Points

Like the back-shu and front-mu points, an uncommon but sometimes effective treatment is using the lower he-sea point to dispel stagnation in its corresponding meridian. The point St 37 (lower he-sea point for the Large Intestine) may be used in the treatment of anterior shoulder pain along the course of the Large Intestine meridian.

Crossing or Intersection Points

Most practitioners are well-versed in the use of crossing or intersection points. They treat pain and other symptoms affecting the two or more meridians that cross at that point. GB 30 (crossing point of Gall Bladder and Bladder meridians) treats low back, pelvic, and lower-extremity pain in both the Shao yang and Tai yang channels.

Miscellaneous Categories

There are numerous other point categories that could potentially be beneficial in the treatment of pain. These include beginning and ending points, "window of the sky" points, and the categories of "sea of qi" and "sea of blood". It is the task of the practitioner to determine which would be useful in the treatment of pain and sports injuries.

Notes

STEP TWO: MERIDIANS & MICROSYSTEMS

Technique #7
The Extraordinary Meridians

Activate an extraordinary meridian based upon the signs and symptoms of the patient as well as the location of the tissues affected by the injury. Both the master point and the coupled point of the affected extraordinary meridian are usually treated.

The use of the extraordinary meridians provides another important perspective in the protocol for treating pain and injury. We will keep our focus on a simple overview of these important pathways. I realize the texts articulate complex and sophisticated uses for the eight extraordinary meridians, and the practitioner is encouraged to consider them with each of the injuries in Section II. Other systems, such as the divergent meridians, will not be discussed; however, the reader may experiment with them in the treatment of pain syndromes.

Chinese Acupuncture and Moxibustion states that the eight extraordinary pathways "assume the responsibility to control, join, store, and regulate the qi and blood of each meridian".[1] The classic texts consider the extraordinary vessels as "reservoirs" for the qi and blood in relation to the 12 primary meridians. While this may appear somewhat ambiguous, my general viewpoint is that the eight extraordinary meridians play a role in the circulation of qi and blood throughout the body. Therefore, they assist in treating stagnation of qi and blood in the musculo-skeletal system.

SUMMARY OF THE EIGHT EXTRAORDINARY MERIDIANS

The Du mai, the Dai mai, the Yang Qiao mai, and the Yin Qiao mai are clearly the most important of the eight extraordinary meridians in sports medicine acupuncture. Activating one or more of these pathways often complements the other techniques of the Four Steps.

1. The Du Mai (Governing Vessel)

Master point: SI 3
Coupled point: Bl 62

Regulates the qi of all the yang meridians.[2]

Body region affected: The centerline of the entire spinal column. Luo-connecting vessels branch out to the Bladder meridian along the para-spinal muscles

Traditional uses: Pain and stiffness of the spinal column, disorders of the cervical, thoracic, and lumbar region of the neck and back

Clinical use for pain and injury:

- Pain and dysfunction of the vertebral column, including the intervertebral discs
- Pain and dysfunction of the para-spinal muscles
- Possible use for all upper and lower-extremity conditions that may be affected by spinal nerve root pathology

2. The Dai Mai (Waist vessel, Belt vessel, Girdling vessel)

Master point: GB 41
Coupled point: SJ 5

As the only horizontal meridian, the Dai mai binds the vertical paths of the primary meridians.[3] Therefore, it influences the circulation of qi and blood to the legs.[4]

Body region affected: Encircles the waist and pelvis like a "belt" at the points GB 26, GB 27, and GB 28. Includes some of the gluteal and abdominal muscles.

Traditional uses: Lumbar pain, lumbar weakness, motor impairment of the lower extremities, inguinal conditions ("shan" disorder)

Clinical use for pain and injury:

- Pain and dysfunction of the lumbo-sacral region, the gluteal musculature, and the hip
- Possible use for all lower-extremity conditions that may be affected by gluteal imbalances
- Should not be ruled out for neck and shoulder conditions involving the upper trapezius muscle[5]

3. The Yang Qiao Mai (Yang motility vessel, Yang heel vessel)

Master point: Bl 62
Coupled point: SI 3

"Dominates activity".[6] The texts state that when there is excess in the Yang Qiao mai, the muscles of the lateral leg are tight and the muscles of the medial leg are flaccid.

Body region affected: The lateral aspect of the leg and thigh. Above the lower extremity, the Yang Qiao mai also includes the shoulder points SI 10, LI 15, and LI 16.

Traditional uses: Spasm and tightness of lateral leg muscles, lumbar pain, contracted sinews

Clinical use for pain and injury:

- Pain and dysfunction of the lateral aspect of the leg and thigh
- Possible use in shoulder pain due to the Yang Qiao mai crossing points of SI 10, LI 15, and LI 16
- Possible use for biomechanical imbalances of the foot due to over-pronation

4. The Yin Qiao Mai (Yin motility vessel, Yin heel vessel)

Master point: Kid 6
Coupled point: Lu 7

Dominates "inactivity".[7] The texts all state that when there is excess in the Yin Qiao mai, the muscles of the medial leg are tight and the muscles of the lateral leg are flaccid.

Body region affected: The medial aspect of the leg and thigh, and the inguinal region

Traditional uses: Spasm and tightness of the medial leg muscles, inguinal pain ("shan" disorder), contracted sinews

Clinical use for pain and injury:

- Pain and dysfunction of the medial aspect of the leg and thigh
- Possible use for biomechanical imbalances of the foot due to supination

The remaining four extraordinary meridians are less commonly used for musculo-skeletal injuries, as their functions are primarily internal. Their clinical use for pain and injury is not definitive. They are summarized as follows:

1. The Ren Mai (Conception vessel)

Master point: Lu 7
Coupled point: Kid 6

Regulates the qi of all the yin meridians.[8]

2. The Chong Mai (Penetrating vessel)

Master point: Sp 4
Coupled point: P 6

"Sea of blood".[9] Reservoir of the qi and blood of the 12 meridians.[10]

3. The Yin Wei Mai (Yin linking vessel, Yin regulating vessel)

Master point: P 6
Coupled point: Sp 4

Dominates the interior of the body.[11]

4. The Yang Wei Mai (Yang linking vessel, Yang regulating vessel)

Master point: SJ 5
Coupled point: GB 41

Dominates the exterior of the body.[12]

NEEDLE TECHNIQUE

Needle techniques to activate the eight extraordinary vessels vary considerably within the various lineages of acupuncture. Some TCM texts suggest the use of a gold needle at the master point and a silver needle at the coupled point. Many Japanese practitioners utilize ion pumping chords, with the red lead at the master point and the black lead at the coupled point. It is stated in other texts that the master point should be needled first, followed by the coupled point. While I respect the intention of these viewpoints, I am not convinced there is clear evidence that any of these techniques are essential to the clinical outcome. The reader should use the needle technique that best fits their clinical style of practice.

However, I must mention one technique useful in cases of pain and injury: the activation of both the Du mai and the Dai mai meridians. Start with palpating GB 41, the master point of the Dai mai. Needle the point-sensitive side. Then, needle SJ 5, the coupled point, on the opposite side. For the Du mai, needle SI 3, the master point, on the same side as GB 41. Its coupled point, Bl 62, is needled on the opposite side. These four needles consist of two master points and two coupled points, with one needle in each of the four extremities. The master point and coupled point of their respective meridians are crossed; they are needled contra-laterally. With some patients, I will consider electrical stimulation between the master point and the coupled point. Ion pumping chords may also be used between the crossed master point and coupled point of both extraordinary meridians.

REFERENCES

[1] Cheng Xinnong: *Chinese Acupuncture and Moxibustion*, Third Printing. Foreign Language Press, Beijing, 1993 (page 75).

[2] Deadman, Al-Khafaji, & Baker: *A Manual of Acupuncture*. Journal of Chinese Medicine Publications, East Sussex, 2001 (page 17).

[3] Deadman, et.al. (page 17).

[4] Maciocia, G: *The Foundations of Chinese Medicine*. Churchill Livingstone, United Kingdom, 1989 (page 357).

[5] *This may be explained by hip and pelvis imbalances, controlled by the Dai mai, which may affect neck and shoulder posture and muscular compensation.*

[6] Deadman, Al-Khafaji, & Baker: *A Manual of Acupuncture*. Journal of Chinese Medicine Publications, East Sussex, 2001 (page 17).

[7] Deadman, et.al. (page 17).

[8] Deadman, et.al. (page 17).

[9] Deadman, et.al. (page 17).

[10] Maciocia, G: *The Foundations of Chinese Medicine*. Churchill Livingstone, United Kingdom, 1989 (page 357).

[11] Deadman, Al-Khafaji, & Baker: *A Manual of Acupuncture*. Journal of Chinese Medicine Publications, East Sussex, 2001 (page 17).

[12] Deadman, et. al. (page 17).

STEP TWO: MERIDIANS & MICROSYSTEMS

Technique #8

Microsystems

Auricular therapy is an effective microsystem approach in sports medicine acupuncture. Treat auricular points that correspond with the site of injury and the tissues affected by trauma. Internal organ imbalances as well as general systemic points for pain may also be included. Wrist-ankle acupuncture may also be included in this technique.

Auricular therapy is a microsystem where the entire body, including the musculo-skeletal system, is reflected in the ear. Auricular acupuncture offers a significant modern contribution to TCM, and is a convenient and effective system to treat pain and sports injuries. Terrence Oleson, Ph.D., has published excellent texts to guide the acupuncture practitioner on the subject.[1]

I began using auricular acupuncture early-on in my career out of necessity. When treating ski racers or track-and-field athletes, there simply was not a convenient way to give full-body treatments while attending a sporting event. A few ear needles in a warming hut or on the sidelines would sometimes be enough to help with the pain of a minor injury. With athletes who were away for a week or more at a time to train and race, I had to find ways to maintain the momentum of a treatment during their travels. Auricular therapy, with needles retained in the ear, was both efficient and effective. And when we figured out that auricular therapy could be used for enhancing athletic performance, patients would stop by my office at the week's end to get retaining needles in the ear before departing for a road race or a triathlon.

Auricular acupuncture as developed by Paul Nogier, MD, and his colleagues may be considered a complete system of diagnosis and treatment. However, in this handbook, it is presented as one technique to be incorporated into the Four Step approach. The reader should be advised that the auricular points listed in the treatments of Section II are quite simplified. The practitioner is encouraged to use other well-indicated ear points, and consider treatment more specific to the needs of each individual patient.

POINT SELECTION

The following is a brief overview of auricular therapy as a treatment technique for sports injuries and pain:

1. Points that correspond to the site of injury

   Start by choosing an auricular point that corresponds to the site of injury and the tissues affected by trauma. While it may seem too simple, this technique can be quite effective. For example, the ankle, knee, and shoulder points often provide fairly immediate relief of pain and improvement in range of motion. You could even consider needling these auricular points while the patient uses active movement of the affected area, much like the techniques mentioned in Step One.

   In order to get optimal results, the point has to be needled with precision and accuracy. The auricle is relatively small, yet it reflects the entire body, so a millimeter or two may make all the difference in clinical results. A point finder helps to reveal active points due to increased electrical conductivity. But the practitioner must keep in mind that increased pressure from the probe may lead to a false reading. I often prefer to palpate with a blunt probe for point sensitivity, which often leads to accurate location.

2. Points that are specific for pain and inflammation

   There are numerous auricular points that have been developed for treating both acute and chronic pain. Many of these points have correspondences with the central and peripheral nervous system. In the treatment chapters that follow, Shen men, Thalamus, Adrenal, and Endocrine are often recommended as a general combination for pain and inflammation. Terrence Oleson offers more depth and explanation of these points in his texts.

3. Somatic Auricular Therapy (SAT)

   This technique is simple, and is worth considering with some injuries. It couples an auricular point that corresponds to the site of injury with a body point located at the site of injury. An example is treatment for an inversion (lateral) ankle sprain. With a lateral ankle sprain, the technique of SAT combines the auricular point for the ankle with an *ahshi* point at the site of the sprain. Miki Shima, L.Ac., suggests using electrical stimulation between these two points, with the black lead on the auricular point and the red lead on the body point.[2]

4. Points corresponding to the internal (zang-fu) organs

   Sometimes it is efficacious to treat auricular points for the internal organs that contribute to the injury. For example, the Liver often contributes to chronic tendonitis, and thus the auricular point for the Liver may be treated.

NEEDLE TECHNIQUE

1. Ear needles (usually .5 inch) may be inserted into the auricular points for the treatment session.

2. Electrical stimulation may be applied to the auricular needles during the treatment session.

3. Needles, tacks, or "seeds" may be retained in the ear for one or more days between treatments.

WRIST-ANKLE ACUPUNCTURE

Wrist-ankle acupuncture is also considered in the microsystem approach to treating pain and sports injuries. This modern technique will not be discussed in detail in this handbook. Wrist-ankle "zones" are included in some of the injuries of Section II; their locations are described in the Appendices on page 361. And as a final note, if the practitioner uses other microsystems, they could be incorporated under this treatment technique. This would include the system of Korean Hand Acupuncture.

REFERENCES

[1] Oleson, T: *Auriculotherapy Manual,* Second Edition. Health Care Alternatives, California, 1996.

[2] *Notes from The Annual Convention of the National Sports Acupuncture Association. Lectures from Miki Shima, L.Ac.*

Notes

STEP THREE: INTERNAL ORGAN IMBALANCES

Technique #9
Qi, Blood, and the Zang-fu Organs

Treat the zang-fu organs that may contribute to the injury or pain syndrome. Additionally, treatment may be designed for internal organ imbalances of the patient even if they are not directly causative of the condition.

In internal medicine, there are numerous ways the practitioner might analyze and organize the signs and symptoms of the patient. The Eight Principles (Ba zheng), Five Elements (Wu xing), and Four Levels (Wei, qi, ying, xue) are among those commonly used in TCM. The diagnostic goal is to construct a coherent viewpoint, usually in the form of a syndrome, to better understand the patient. From this framework arises the treatment plan, as well as point selection and needle technique. In sports medicine acupuncture, treatment of internal organ imbalances is often necessary. The traditional functions of the zang-fu organs must be understood, and their dysfunction assessed and treated. However, before I continue, I must tell a story from early in my acupuncture career.

In the first few years of my practice, I had a middle-aged male patient who complained of pain in the upper extremity. It started in the shoulder, in the region of the point LI 15, and followed the Large Intestine meridian distally. Pain and numbness radiated along the forearm from LI 11 to the wrist and hand near LI 4. This patient had just been released from the hospital after having a ruptured appendix. Obviously, surgery was necessary and he spent several days recovering from the procedure. Feeling confident, I palpated the extraordinary point *Lanweixue*, which most practitioners know as the "appendicitis point". It was very sensitive to even moderate pressure. In addition, the Stomach meridian was painful to palpation extending as far inferior as St 39.

That was it... I had made my diagnosis! Appendicitis, as a damp heat pathogen in the intestines, had an "interior-exterior" relationship with the pain along the Large Intestine meridian of the upper extremity and the point sensitivity on the Stomach channel of the lower extremity. Both meridians of Yang ming were affected by this zang-fu imbalance. I first treated the obvious Stomach and Large Intestine meridian points. After several ineffective treatments, I added the back-shu and front-mu points of these two organs. So sure of my diagnostic assumptions, I continued with this treatment plan for six visits, until the patient finally cancelled because there was no improvement.

When I called the patient to check in, he had just returned from seeing an orthopedic physician, as he felt something was just not right. The doctor had diagnosed thoracic outlet syndrome, where nerve entrapment to the brachial plexus refers pain to the shoulder and the upper extremity. This had probably resulted from the extreme neck hyperextension that is required for general anesthesia during surgery several weeks earlier. I quietly cringed with embarrassment. Several weekends earlier, I had attended my first seminar with Dr. Janet Travell on trigger point therapy. I had just learned about thoracic outlet syndrome. However, my attachment to the TCM diagnosis had blinded me. What appeared to be a brilliant correlation between an internal organ imbalance and the musculo-skeletal symptoms had led to ineffective treatment. This experience early in my professional career influenced me to be ever-so-diligent when making any assumptions about cause and effect.

My advice to the reader: Never assume that internal organ dysfunction is directly related to pain and injury. Just because the patient may have symptoms on a specific meridian does not necessarily suggest that organ dysfunction is the cause of the injury, or even a contributing factor to it.

ZANG-FU TREATMENT

While my point is hopefully clear to the reader, internal organ imbalances need to be assessed in all patients we treat. The following is a summary of some important considerations in the treatment of patients with pain.

1. Treat the zang-fu organ to affect its corresponding "body tissue"

It is a common technique in TCM to treat a zang-fu organ in order to affect its corresponding body tissue. The classic texts usually agree on the following correspondences:[1]

Organ	Corresponding Tissue
Liver	Tendons, "sinews" (jin)
Heart	Blood vessels (mai)
Spleen	"Belly" of the muscle, muscles and flesh (ji rou)
Lung	Skin and body hair (pi, mao)
Kidney	Bones (gu)

In the treatment of pain and injury, the Liver is the most interesting and obvious of the zang-fu organs. It governs the tendons and the function of the muscle-tendon unit in movement and activity. As is stated with many of the injuries in Section II, Liver imbalances may result in susceptibility of the tendons to acute strain, chronic "over-use" injuries, and repetitive stress disorders.

Also important is the Spleen, which governs the "belly" of the muscles. This is sometimes translated as the "muscles and the flesh". The classic texts also state that the Spleen governs the upper and lower extremities. The practitioner may consider that pain, weakness, and other disorders of the muscles in the extremities could be associated with Spleen imbalances.

The Kidney and its relationship to the bone is also clearly stated in the classics. Some fractures, bone spurs, and lesions of the periosteum may be related to its function. However, it is my experience that treatment to the Kidney does not clearly demonstrate a more favorable healing time of bone fractures. This could be due to the slower time it takes to heal such an injury relative to other more superficial injuries, such as muscle strain and spasm.

Matt Callison, MS, L.Ac., in his brilliant text *Sports Medicine Acupuncture,* makes an important modern interpretation that should be mentioned.[2] Many TCM practitioners often consider the tendons and ligaments as similar tissue, being governed by the Liver. However, Callison suggests that ligaments, the fibrous tissue that connects bone to other bones and spans a joint space, are controlled by the Kidney. Therefore, this point of view suggests that Kidney imbalances may contribute to ligamentous laxity, increased susceptibility to sprain, and other injuries to the joints.

The remaining two zang organs will only briefly be mentioned. The Lung is associated with the skin and body hair. Other than superficial scar tissue, it is difficult to understand its role in the clinical treatment of musculo-skeletal pain. And the same is true for the Heart, which is associated with the blood vessels.

2. Treat the zang-fu organ to affect the function of qi and blood

As the classics state, organ physiology is intimately related to qi and blood, as summarized below.[3]

Organ	Corresponding Function of Qi and Blood
Liver	Stores the blood
	Harmonizes the flow of qi (and blood)
Heart	Governs the blood and vessels
Spleen	Controls, "manages" the blood
Lung	Governs qi of the entire body
Kidney	Receives, "grasps" the qi

Dysfunction of the zang-fu organs may affect both the production of qi and blood as well as their functional activities. In the diagnosis of sports injuries and pain, the stagnation of qi and stasis of blood is routine. The TCM model also commonly points to deficiency syndromes that contribute to chronic conditions. For example, Liver blood deficiency is often diagnosed in the patient with recurring tendon or joint pain. However, I question this viewpoint in the determination of a treatment plan for many of the injuries covered in this handbook. The theoretical models of qi and blood often fall short in terms of clinical results for the injured patient.

I supervise acupuncture students at the clinic of Southwest Acupuncture College in Boulder, Colorado. An elderly patient had been treated over a two-month period for shoulder pain. The ongoing diagnosis was Liver yin and blood deficiency. The patient was pale, frail, and quite weak. She had not experienced any change in her shoulder symptoms, although several other complaints had improved. I did a more thorough orthopedic assessment of the patient, as I felt sure acupuncture could help her shoulder pain. After several tests, I diagnosed shoulder impingement syndrome due to inflammation of the supraspinatous tendon.

The new plan was to direct treatment to the site of the injury. Two needles were inserted at SI 12, which are trigger points in the belly of the supraspinatous. Both LI 16 and LI 15 were also needled, which treat the tendinous aspect of the muscle. We used strong electrical stimulation between the two sets of paired points. Several of the student observers were astounded that such strong "sedating" technique was being used on such a deficient patient. We did, however, include points to tonify qi and blood, still considering Step Three and the treatment of internal organ imbalances. The patient returned in five days with a 90-percent improvement in her shoulder pain. I suggested that after the local stagnation of qi and blood was resolved, treatment to the zang-fu organs could once again be the primary objective.

41 • Technique #9 *Qi, Blood, and the Zang-fu Organs*

3. Treat the organ to affect its related meridian

Organ imbalances may result in deficiency of their related meridians, which is the interior-exterior relationship stated in the TCM texts. This may lead to increased susceptibility of the tissues along that meridian to injury. For example, tonifying the Spleen and Stomach organs is often necessary in treating qi and blood stagnation along their two related channels as seen in shin splints. And Kidney imbalances may result in deficiency in the Kidney and Bladder meridians, increasing the susceptibility of the hamstring group to injury.

4. Preventative Treatment

"Treat before the disease arises" is a practice deeply rooted in traditional Chinese medicine.[4] TCM offers the possibility of diagnosing organ imbalances before the manifestation of signs and symptoms. Treating internal organ imbalances is sometimes recommended for the patient to prevent injuries such as tendonitis and muscle strains.

5. Treatment of the "Root"

A case can be made for the treatment of internal organ imbalances based on treating the "root".[5] I use the system of Korean Constitutional Acupuncture to determine what is called the "congenital" excess or deficiency within the zang-fu system. There are many other systems used to diagnose and treat the root. In general, the assumption is that when root organ imbalances are corrected, anything and everything improves! However, from my clinical perspective, I repeat: Never assume the root imbalance has any relationship with local trauma and injury. Treating the root may not affect the signs and symptoms of the injured patient, especially during the acute stage.

CONCLUDING REMARKS

Step Three and the treatment of internal organ imbalances will vary from practitioner to practitioner. I encourage the reader to use his or her training in the diagnosis and assessment of zang-fu disorders, and proceed with the appropriate treatment. Like the other techniques in this book, points should be determined from both palpation and analysis of the signs and symptoms of the patient.

REFERENCES

[1] Flaws, B: *Statements of Fact in Traditional Chinese Medicine.* Blue Poppy Press, Colorado, 2007, and *Common Terms of Traditional Chinese Medicine in English*, Beijing Medical College, 1981.

    Note: *The Liver governs the sinews (Gan zhu jin).*
           The Heart governs the blood and (blood) vessels (Xin zhu xue mai).
           The Spleen governs the muscles and flesh (Pi zhu ji rou).
           The Lungs govern the skin and (body) hair (Fei zhu pi mao).
           The Kidneys govern the bones (Shen zhu gu).

[2] Callison, M: *Sports Medicine Acupuncture.* AcuSport Seminar Series LLC, San Diego, In Printing.

[3] Flaws, B: *Statements of Fact in Traditional Chinese Medicine.* Blue Poppy Press, Colorado, 2007, and *Common Terms of Traditional Chinese Medicine in English*, Beijing Medical College, 1981.

    Note: *The Liver stores the blood (Gan cang xue).*
           The Liver harmonizes the flow of qi (and blood) (Gan zhu shu xie).
           The Heart governs the blood and (blood) vessels (Xin zhu xue mai).
           The Spleen controls ("manages") the blood (Pi tong xue).
           The Lung governs qi of the entire body (Fei zhu yi shen zhi qi).
           The Kidney receives, "grasps" the qi (Shen zhu na qi).

[4] *Common Terms of Traditional Chinese Medicine in English*, Beijing Medical College, 1981 (page 134).

[5] Flaws, B: *Statements of Fact in Traditional Chinese Medicine.* Blue Poppy Press, Colorado, 2007 (page 230).

    Note: To treat diseases, seek its root (Zhi bing qiu ben).

Notes

STEP FOUR: THE SITE OF THE INJURY

Technique #10
Local and Adjacent Points

Treat the site of injury in order to dispel stagnation of qi and blood. In addition, other pathogens such as wind (feng), heat (re), cold (han), and damp (shi) should be assessed and treated. The objective is to normalize the function of the muscles, tendons, ligaments, and other tissues affected by the trauma or injury. Points may be determined by orthopedic testing, palpation, and analysis of the signs and symptoms of the patient.

The rationale for treating the site of injury is straightforward. When the body experiences trauma, there is an inflammatory response. This occurs whether an injury is acute, chronic, or from gradual onset, as seen in repetitive stress. The TCM diagnosis is clear: qi and blood stasis in the channels. There may be other exogenous pathogens, such as wind (feng), heat (re), cold (han), or damp (shi) at the site of injury. Treating locally is therefore necessary in order to dispel stagnation of qi and blood and to normalize the function of the affected tissues.

Techniques in Step One and Step Two, such as opposite side, the shu-stream point combination, and the extra-ordinary meridians, may be effective for some of the signs and symptoms of the patient. However, when the local stagnation is "significant", local and adjacent points may be required. For instance, if blood stagnation has "walled off" a portion of an injured muscle or tendon, techniques that move the qi in the meridians may be ineffective. After all, if the micro-circulation of blood at the site of injury is impaired, then the qi does not move through it.

Let's not be trapped by the TCM model. We have a vast amount of knowledge on the etiology of injury to such tissues as muscles, tendons, fascia, ligaments, and joints. It seems out-of-touch to make a diagnosis based solely upon the anatomy of the meridian system. Treatment guided only by which meridians are affected leads to inferior clinical results. I suggest in Step Four that acupuncturists think in terms of western anatomy and physiology during the assessment of the injured patient. Once it is determined which body tissues are involved, this can easily be translated to the terminology of the TCM model. This results in far more effective treatments.

The rationale for treating locally is clearly expressed by this story. In about my 10th year of practice, I treated a female patient with severe bilateral heel pain. She had been shoveling snow from the roof of her mountain house after a week of heavy snowfall. A strong gust of wind caused her to lose her balance. Falling to the ground, she landed on both heels, and fortunately nothing was broken. The patient had some serious foot pain, and after several days found her way to my office.

After examining the patient, I ruled out a calcaneal fracture, and proceeded with the diagnosis of a traumatic bone bruise. For the first few treatments, I tried to avoid the site of injury, as even slight pressure was painful. Treatment included points on the Kidney and Bladder meridians, as well as needle insertion to adjacent *ahshi* points on the heel. The opposite (unaffected) side as well as the opposite extremity (H 8 and P 8 in the palm) were also needled. Three treatments resulted in no change; the patient was still in pain.

With a more aggressive approach in mind, I decided to needle precisely at the site of injury. Four needles were inserted at the most painful points on the heel. With deep insertion, they reached an end point, which of course was the bone! I retracted each needle about one to two millimeters, with the intention of them "resting" in the periosteum, the membrane that covers the bony calcaneus. Electrical stimulation was used for 30 minutes on each of these four needles.

The patient hobbled out of the office, as both heels were quite aggravated from the treatment. I instructed her to rest, and call me in the morning. The next day she reported that her symptoms were 80 percent improved, although she had been quite uncomfortable the previous evening. We waited three days, and repeated the treatment. As before, there was some aggravation from local needling, but not as pronounced as after the first local treatment. After the second treatment to the heel, the patient reported that her pain was almost 100 percent recovered.

This experience is one of many that supports treatment at the site of the injury. When there is pronounced qi and blood stagnation, the micro-circulation to the area of trauma is compromised. Acupuncture treatment to well-chosen meridian and adjacent points may not be able to move the qi and the blood in these affected tissues.

CATEGORIES OF TISSUES AT THE SITE OF INJURY

The different tissues of the musculo-skeletal system must be thoroughly understood when acupuncture is used to treat sports injuries and pain. Stagnation of qi and blood may be located at the surface of the body in the skin, fascia, and the superficial aspect of the muscles. In the intermediate layers, this can occur to the belly of the muscle, the tendons, and the ligaments. And at the deepest levels the periosteum, bone, and the joint capsule can be the injured sites. It is important for the practitioner to keep in mind these numerous types of tissues, if for no other reason than to serve as a guide in needle technique and depth of insertion. The categories of tissue can be summarized as follows:

1. Trigger Points

Dr. Janet Travell published two outstanding texts entitled *Myofascial Pain and Dysfunction (Volumes I & II)*.[1] In these manuals, she gives detailed descriptions of the phenomena of trigger points for the major muscles of the body. Her work on how these points contribute to musculo-skeletal dysfunction has been a significant contribution to the treatment of pain. I studied with Dr. Travell in the 1980s, and rely on trigger points for many of the injuries described in this handbook. I have included more detailed comments on the properties of trigger points on page 330 in the Appendices.

Trigger points are always *ahshi* points, so acupuncturists frequently palpate and treat them without necessarily being trained in this system. But remember, not all *ahshi* points are trigger points! Many trigger points are located at the site of defined acupuncture points, and they present as localized qi and blood stagnation. They also have clear and defined patterns of referred pain, often radiating beyond the point of local tenderness. These pain patterns are sometimes broad areas distant to the trigger point itself. It is the pain referral patterns caused by trigger points that may often confuse the practitioner and lead to treatments that fail to target the primary stagnation.

2. Motor Points

A motor point is the "entrance site" of the motor nerve into the muscle.[2] Matt Callison, MS, L.Ac., describes the precise location and needle technique for each of these clinically useful points in *The Motor Point Index*. It is a user-friendly text that the practitioner should consider as a clinical reference.

Like trigger points, a motor point is also an *ahshi* point, many being located at the site of defined acupuncture points. When properly needled, dysfunctional patterns of the muscle, such as pain and weakness, may be relieved. Motor points are included in many of the treatments described in Section II of this handbook.

3. Other Points in the Muscles

Treating other anatomical regions of the muscle often benefits pain and restores normal range of motion. The belly of the muscle and the muscle-tendon junction are two common sites for the insertion of needles. Defined acupuncture points are sometimes located in these muscle zones. The point Bl 57 is located in the belly of the gastrocnemius muscle of the calf. And the point LI 10 is an example of an acupuncture point located at or near the muscle-tendon junction of the extensor group of the forearm. Needle treatment to these various zones of the muscles may "release" a shortened, taut muscle and contribute to an improvement of symptoms. In addition, treating these sites may facilitate the healing of tendonitis and tendinosis of the related muscle.

4. Fascia

Sometimes treatment is directed into the fascia, the connective tissue layers that surround the muscles and tendons. Fascia is composed of collagen and elastin, and has a vast supply of blood vessels and nerves.[3] Some practitioners suggest that the fascia serves as the anatomical location of the channels and collaterals of Chinese acupuncture. Certainly this simple statement is worth considering: "After injury, it is the fascia that creates an environment for tissue repair".[4] An example of a common sports injury is plantar fasciitis. It is characterized by heel pain due to inflammation of the plantar fascia. Needles inserted into precise layers of this fascia often provide relief of pain and stiffness.

5. Tendons

Tendons, the tendon sheaths, and their attachments to bone are often sites of injury. The practitioner clearly knows this from the large number of patients who seek treatment for tendonitis. There are many acupuncture points located at or near these sites. The points Bl 59, Bl 60 and Bl 61 are located along the lateral aspect of the achilles tendon. LI 15 is located at the attachment of the common tendon of the rotator cuff in the shoulder. However, sometimes it is necessary for the practitioner to use more "creative" techniques to dispel stagnation of qi and blood in the treatment of tendonitis. Threading needles along both sides of a tendon is often a useful technique in treating inflammation of a tendon.

6. Ligaments

Ligaments are the fibrous tissue that connects bones to other bones. Because they usually cross a joint, they are essential for joint stability. Some acupuncture points are located at or near major ligaments of the body. For example, Liv 8 is located on the medial joint line of the knee just posterior to the medial collateral ligament. As with treating tendons, the acupuncturist may need to develop new techniques for ligament sprains. Threading needles along the side of a ligament or actually tapping the ligamentous tissue are examples of these techniques.

7. Periosteum

The periosteum is the membrane that lines the outer surface of all bones. It can be bruised in cases of direct trauma, and is susceptible to inflammation if the ligaments or tendons are injured near the site of their attachment to the bone. Treatment includes adjacent needling as well as direct insertion into the periosteal membrane.

8. Bone

The most common lesion to the bone is a fracture, which is characterized as either "closed" or "open". Open fractures are also known as compound fractures. The practitioner should be reminded of the sometimes elusive stress fracture, a hairline fracture within the shaft of a bone. While it may be clinically difficult to diagnose, this injury needs to be considered in the assessment of many lower-extremity sports injuries. Bone fractures obviously need orthopedic medical attention; however, acupuncture may play an important role as a complementary modality. There is some research that suggests needle treatment as well as electrical stimulation may enhance the healing time of a fracture.

9. Joints and the Joint Space

Every joint in the body has the potential to be inflamed by either acute trauma, repetitive stress, or other systemic inflammatory conditions. In the chapters that follow, threading needles along a joint space will be mentioned in treating the site of injury. When I teach, I often liken the technique to "knocking on the door" of the joint. We cannot always get a needle inserted into a joint, and in many instances it is not a recommended technique. However, needles inserted adjacent to the joint space accompanied with electrical stimulation or needle-top moxa often benefits inflammation.

10. Other Sites of Injury

There are numerous other sites of injury not included in the list above, but several specific examples should be mentioned. Scar tissue in the skin or the superficial fascia is not an uncommon finding. Needle treatment to scar tissue is discussed by practitioners in numerous texts, articles, and seminars. When scar tissue is present, there is always the possibility of pain and dysfunction. Nerve entrapment is another example, with neurological symptoms caused by abnormal pressure on a peripheral nerve. This can be generated from dysfunction of muscle, tendon, ligament, or bone. For example, carpal tunnel syndrome is often due to entrapment of the median nerve by ligaments in the wrist.

CONCLUDING REMARKS

Without adequate understanding of the etiology of an injury, it is difficult to determine a treatment plan. The simple strategy of treating local *ahshi* points may sometimes benefit the patient, but truthfully it often results in sub-par clinical results. While the

TCM system may give insight into the nature of a condition, most injuries require that we include orthopedic testing and other assessment procedures from the western tradition. Integrating these two medical systems increases the likelihood that treatment is being directed to the primary lesion while still utilizing the treatment principles of traditional Chinese medicine. I have included additional comments on this subject in the Appendices on page 334.

Remember, in Step Four, we are looking for the primary stagnation of qi and blood. The objective is to normalize the function of the muscles, tendons, ligaments, or other tissues affected by the trauma or injury. Points may be determined by orthopedic testing, palpation, and analysis of the signs and symptoms of the patient. Hopefully, the practitioner will approach local treatment with a sense of confidence and enthusiasm. After almost 30 years of private practice, my excitement over treating the site of injury still exudes.

OTHER CLINICAL COMMENTS

- The "reward" of treating the site of injury is that it often produces lasting results. The stagnation of qi and blood at the injured site may require direct needling, especially when distal points result in only partial relief.

- The "risk" of treating the site of injury is that it may result in an aggravation of symptoms.

- Each of the different categories of tissues react differently to acupuncture treatment. The belly of a muscle is quite "open" to needle insertion, while the denser tissues of ligaments, tendons, and bone require different and more "creative" techniques.

- It should be remembered that some lineages of acupuncture do not treat at the site of injury, emphasizing non-local and distal points for their treatment protocols.

REFERENCES

[1] Travell & Simons: *Myofascial Pain and Dysfunction, The Trigger Point Manual*. Lippincott Williams & Wilkins, Philadelphia, 1993.
Note: Volume 1 covers the upper extremities and Volume 2 the lower extremities.

[2] Callison, M: *Motor Point Index*. AcuSport Seminar Series LLC, San Diego, 2007.

[3] Rosen, M: *Osteopathy: Art of Practice, Fascia*. At www.osteodoc.com, 2000.

[4] *Wikipedia: The Free Encyclopedia*. www.wikipedia.org. 2008.

SECTION 2
The Injuries

1
Heel Pain

Achilles Tendonitis

Pain in the heel localized at the achilles tendon

A repetitive stress injury characterized by pain, inflammation, and swelling of the achilles tendon and its sheath. The entire calf muscle group may be affected.

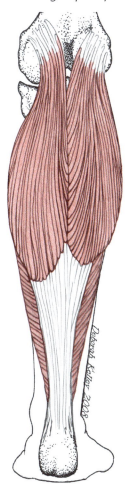

53 • Heel Pain *Achilles Tendonitis*

DIAGNOSIS & ASSESSMENT

My career in sports medicine acupuncture began in February, 1982. It was my first year of practice, and I was at the beginning stages of applying the knowledge of academic training to the day-by-day realities of the clinic. One afternoon a long-distance runner walked in my door to inquire about acupuncture for his lingering achilles tendonitis. Within minutes he was on the treatment table. It was his first-ever acupuncture experience and my first athlete with a sports injury. I treated his inflamed tendon once a day for four straight days. That weekend I accompanied him as he ran the Mission Bay Marathon in San Diego. I will never forget that foggy California morning as thousands of runners competed in this famous 26.2 mile race. And out of the fog emerged my patient as he crossed the finish line first!

I had no idea that I was treating an elite distance runner at the time. But having my patient win such a high profile race was the jump start that my practice needed. I really don't even remember which points I used; all I recall is that within days my office was filled with runners and other athletes. And it all started with achilles tendonitis.

Over the years I have treated this injury countless times, and have learned a lot about the achilles. It is the largest and strongest tendon of the body, serving as the attachment to the calcaneus for the gastrocnemius and soleus muscles of the calf. It is commonly inflamed and irritated by repetitive stress, usually in runners and other lower-extremity athletes. The occurrence of achilles tendonitis is reported to be as high as 18 percent in the running community.[1] After all, running produces forces up to 10 times the individual's body weight within the achilles tendon.[2]

The patient usually reports pain in the area of the heel, localized at the tendon. The most common inflammation site is from 2 to 6 centimeters proximal to the attachment at the calcaneus.[3] This area has a reduced amount of blood flow and therefore is less resilient to repetitive strain injuries. Some sources consider micro-tears to the tendon as the etiology. Others use the diagnostic term tendinosis, referring to inflammation without tendon strain.

In addition to pain, the patient presents with swelling of the tendon and its sheath. Crepitus may be felt on ankle movements. A common accompanying symptom is stiffness, usually experienced in the morning upon first steps or after prolonged sitting or rest. Stiffness often diminishes as the tendon "warms up", and returns again during or after activities such as hiking or running.

Begin examination with the patient lying prone (face down), with both feet on a bolster or hanging off the end of the table. The ankle should be flexed (dorsiflexion) at about a 90-degree angle. Visually examine whether the injured tendon is larger and thicker in size than the unaffected side. The more thickened the tendon, the more significant the inflammatory process has progressed. This is usually seen in chronic cases. It alerts you and the patient that in addition to acupuncture treatment, modifications to training and other activities may be necessary. After observation, palpate the tendon by "pinching" from the medial and lateral sides, starting at the calcaneus and moving upwards (proximally) towards to belly of the calf muscles. The area of maximal tenderness is usually in the mid-tendon area of the achilles.

While mid-tendon is the most common site of inflammation, palpate the muscle-tendon junction slightly inferior to Bl 57. While less common, this can be a site of injury. Also pay attention to the tendon-to-bone attachment at the calcaneus, as micro-tears can occur there. The calf muscles (the gastrocnemius and soleus group) should be

54 • Heel Pain *Achilles Tendonitis*

palpated from the popliteal fossa at Bl 40 inferiorly to Bl 57. This area of the muscle may present with *ahshi* points that are often incorporated into the treatment protocol.

You may also want to perform two simple orthopedic tests:

1. Resisted plantar flexion
   The action of the calf muscles is plantar flexion, which is "pointing the toes". Pain on resisted plantar flexion helps to confirm involvement of the achilles tendon.

2. Passive dorsiflexion
   As the practitioner flexes the patient's ankle past 90 degrees, there may be discomfort in the heel as the muscle-tendon unit is passively stretched.

Achilles tendonitis usually is of insidious onset, and is frequently associated with a change in training, such as increased mileage, hills, or speed. A change in running shoe or running surface may also be contributing to the condition. As with most lower-extremity injuries, consider having the patient evaluated for foot biomechanical imbalances. Both abnormal pronation or supination create additional repetitive strain and may need to be corrected.

In summary, achilles tendonitis is usually mid-tendon, about 2 to 6 centimeters proximal to its attachment to the calcaneus. But occasionally there may be lesions proximally at the muscle-tendon junction as you approach the area of Bl 57. Strain may also occur at the attachment to calcaneus, which may not present with the inflammation and tenderness that is so characteristic at the mid-portion of the tendon. In general, proceed with acupuncture with confidence – most patients can be helped if not totally cured with proper treatment.

SUMMARY OF THE INJURY

Clinical Features
- Repetitive stress causes pain, inflammation, and swelling of the tendon and its sheath
- Most common site is from 2 to 6 centimeters proximal to the attachment at the calcaneus
- Pain usually starts after a change in activity level, such as increased mileage, hills, or speed
- Crepitus may be felt on ankle movements
- Biomechanical imbalances usually contribute to the development of achilles tendonitis.

Common Patient Complaints
- Pain in heel, localized at the achilles tendon
- Stiffness may accompany the complaint of pain
- Symptoms often experienced upon taking first steps in the morning or after prolonged sitting or rest
- Symptoms relieved as the heel "warms up" with moderate activity, but pain returns again during or after exercise

Differentiation from Similar Injuries and Conditions
- Inflammation of the achilles bursa
- Tendon tear, tendon rupture
- Bone spur that irritates the tendon
- Plantar fasciitis occasionally refers pain to the heel
- Talar joint dysfunction of the ankle
- Referred pain from trigger points in the soleus

Typical Medical Recommendations
- R.I.C.E. (Rest, Ice, Compression, and Elevation) when acute.
- Anti-inflammatory medications
- Modify activity
  Decrease activities that aggravate the condition, especially during treatment. Cross-train, including cycling, swimming, and running in water.
- Stretching
  Stretching of the gastrocnemius and soleus muscles of the calf is usually part of the treatment and rehabilitation of achilles tendonitis.
- Biomechanics
  Correct pronation or supination with shoes and/or orthotics. Some podiatrists recommend a heel lift. For chronic tendonitis, other lower-extremity biomechanical imbalances may need to be assessed.
- Physical therapy
  Ultrasound, deep-friction massage, and other physical therapy modalities.
- Orthopedic evaluation and procedures
  If a grade II or grade III tear occurs, immobilization or surgery may be required. Chronic cases may have fibrous tissue between the tendon and sheath, which could require a surgical sheath release.

TREATMENT & TECHNIQUES

Overview Achilles tendonitis is most commonly diagnosed under the category of accident/trauma. This is usually a repetitive stress disorder due to the accumulation of micro-trauma. However, it may occur as an acute strain. The injury is at the level of the muscles and tendons, with qi and blood stagnation in the channels and collaterals. The Bladder and the Kidney are the primary meridians involved. Internal organ imbalances may contribute. The majority of achilles tendonitis cases are neither hot (re) nor cold (han)

Prognosis: Treat twice a week for three weeks, then re-evaluate. Many acute cases without complications may have good results within six treatments. With chronic cases and a thickened tendon, continue treatment at least once weekly after the first three-week period.

STEP ONE: INITIAL TREATMENT

Choose among these four techniques, carefully determining if there is an immediate decrease in pain or an increase in range of motion.

Technique #1 **The Tendino-Muscle Meridians**

Bl 67   Bleeding technique
Bleeding the jing-well point may be effective for some of the symptoms, including stiffness of the calf muscles. This may assist in relaxing the muscle group, thus easing tension at the achilles tendon.

Technique #2 **Opposite Side (contra-lateral)**

Bl 59, Bl 60, Bl 61 Corresponding points on the opposite (unaffected) side
Kid 3, Kid 4, Kid 7 Corresponding points on the opposite (unaffected) side

If "strong" needle technique is used on Kid 3, care should be taken to avoid unnecessary irritation to the posterior tibial nerve.

Technique #3 **Opposite Extremity (upper/lower)**

SI 4, SI 5   Tai yang corresponding points on the opposite extremity

These two Small Intestine meridian points are often overlooked.

In general, treat upper/lower corresponding points on the opposite (unaffected) side when acute, and the affected side when chronic. Use palpation to assist in this choice.

Technique #4 **Empirical Points**
No well known empirical points for achilles tendonitis.

STEP TWO: MERIDIANS & MICROSYSTEMS

Choose among these four techniques, selecting points that are appropriate for the signs and symptoms of the patient.

Technique #5 **The Shu-Stream Point Combination**

★ **Bl 65 affected side + SI 3 opposite side**
Use of the yin meridian shu-stream points Kid 3 + H 7 is less effective.

Technique #6 **Traditional Point Categories**

★ Palpation may assist in your choice of Bladder and Kidney meridian points.
Bl 63	Xi-cleft point
Bl 58	Luo-connecting point
Bl 40	He-sea point
GB 34	Hui-influential point of tendons

★ Point combinations to consider:
Kid 7 + Kid 8   Jing-river point + xi-cleft point of the Yin Qiao mai
Kid 4 + Kid 5   Luo-connecting point + xi-cleft point
One of these two paired-point combinations may be helpful to activate the Kidney meridian and treat achilles symptoms. Use on the affected side only, and consider electrical stimulation between the two points. Palpation may assist in your choice of points; however, if one fails, try the other set.

Technique #7 **The Extraordinary Meridians**

GB 41 + SJ 5   Activate the Dai mai
Compensating for achilles pain sometimes results in secondary hip and gluteal imbalances, which may be considered Dai mai pathology.

Bl 62 + SI 3   Activate the Yang Qiao mai
Sometimes lower-extremity biomechanics are involved in achilles tendonitis, which may be considered Yang Qiao mai pathology.

Technique #8 **Microsystems**

Auricular Therapy
Local: Heel (French), heel (Chinese), lumbar spine
Zang-fu points: Kidney, Bladder
Systemic points for pain: Shen men, Thalamus, Adrenal, Endocrine

STEP THREE: INTERNAL ORGAN IMBALANCES

Choose appropriate points to treat internal organ imbalances that may contribute to the injury or pain syndrome.

Technique #9 **Qi, Blood, and the Zang-fu Organs**

Achilles tendonitis is a repetitive stress injury and therefore internal organ imbalances are not necessarily causative. However, there are several zang-fu syndromes which may contribute to the condition.

Liver imbalances Liver qi stagnation, Liver yin deficiency, and Liver blood deficiency
Liver imbalances may result in the susceptibility of the tendons to inflammation and repetitive stress injury. Consider the following:

Liv 3   Yuan-source point; supports the Liver in its function of controlling the muscles and tendons

GB 34   Hui-influential point of tendons
Treat GB 34 on the affected side and Liv 3 on the opposite side.

Kidney imbalances Kidney deficiency
Kidney imbalances may result in deficiency in the Kidney and Bladder meridians, increasing the susceptibility of the achilles tendon to repetitive stress injury.

Points should be determined by the practitioner from both palpation and analysis of the signs and symptoms of the patient.

STEP FOUR: THE SITE OF INJURY

Choose among the local and adjacent points at the site of injury. Points may be determined by palpation, orthopedic testing, and analysis of the signs and symptoms of the patient.

Technique #10 **Local and Adjacent Points**

The achilles tendon Thread the achilles tendon with from one to three sets of
★ paired points on its medial and lateral sides

Local treatment is focused at the mid-tendon portion of the achilles from 2 to 6 centimeters proximal to the attachment at the calcaneus. This site is found by the "pinching" palpation (described in Diagnosis and Assessment). Use a set of paired points anterior to the tendon, on the medial and lateral sides. After insertion, thread them inferiorly at an oblique angle of from 45 to 60 degrees. Insertion depth is up to 1 inch. This allows the needle to pass adjacent the tendon and tendon sheath, but also to access the anterior aspect of the tendon.

59 • Heel Pain *Achilles Tendonitis*

Care should be taken that the needles are not actually inserted into the tendon. The area of inflammation should allow for up to three sets of paired points, which can be from 1 to 2 centimeters apart.

> X – Pain at mid-tendon
> O – Point variations medial and lateral to the tendon
> ⤤ – Needle insertion deep to the achilles tendon

Clinical comments For best results, each needle should be inserted toward the anterior portion of the tendon. Recent research points to lesions in this anterior region of the tendon that may contribute to chronic achilles pain.[4] Researchers have found that "neovascularisation" – the growth of new blood vessels – occurs in this inflamed area. The TCM viewpoint of blood stasis is certainly supported by these findings.

Needle Technique Electrical stimulation between the medial and lateral needles is usually effective, and fortunately this technique rarely aggravates the condition. Needle-top moxa may be considered in cold (han) cases of inflammation. However, due to the oblique angle of insertion, caution should be used to avoid burning the skin.

Tendon sheath adhesions Occasionally, a patient will have a visible and palpable lesion on the posterior aspect of the tendon. You can observe the thickening and may even see "lumps" of scar tissue from chronic inflammation. In this case, you may experiment with needles on the posterior aspect of the tendon. There is very little room between the skin and the tendon sheath, so you must use transverse insertion. And you may have to pinch the tissues to get a needle inserted. In all likelihood, the needle will pierce the tendon sheath. This will cause an aggravation, for which you and the patient should be prepared.

The muscle-tendon junction **Bl 57, "lower" Bl 57**

Strain at the muscle-tendon junction is not uncommon, and responds well to treatment. Bl 57 may be combined with "lower" Bl 57, located from 1 to 1.5 cun below Bl 57. Use perpendicular insertion, from .5 to 1.5 inches. Electrical stimulation on these paired points is often effective. Bl 57 combined with Bl 56, which is located in the belly of the gastroc muscle, is a variation to consider.

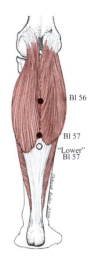

The attachment at the calcaneus **Kid 4 + Bl 60.5**
When the injury is at the attachment to the calcaneus, acupuncture may be less effective, but you must at least try treating at the tendinous attachment. Needle perpendicularly from the medial and lateral sides, on the anterior side of the tendon just superior to the attachment at the calcaneus. Insert to a depth of .5 inch. The medial side is the point Kid 4, and the lateral side we will call Bl 60.5 – halfway between Bl 60 and Bl 61. Electrical stimulation between these two needles may be used.

Kid 5 + Bl 61
You might consider using Kid 5 medially and Bl 61 laterally, also with electrical stimulation. Although these two points are not immediately at the attachment, they are adjacent and sometimes assist in the healing of the tendon strain. Use oblique to transverse insertion.

Adjacent points **Bl 40 + Bl 60**
Bl 57 + Bl 60
Various other combination of points above and below the lesion may be considered as secondary points in the treatment.

The belly of the calf muscles **The region of Bl 56**

Needling *ahshi* points in the calf may release the gastrocnemius and soleus muscle group, and assist in the treatment of achilles tendonitis. Look for these points from the popliteal fossa at Bl 40 inferiorly to Bl 57. This is the general region of Bl 56.

X – *Trigger points*
▲ – *Motor points*

61 • Heel Pain *Achilles Tendonitis*

COMPLEMENTARY PROCEDURES

- When acute, ice massage along the achilles tendon may alleviate pain and reduce inflammation.

- Alternating ice and heat after the acute stage, when the condition is "neither hot (re) nor cold (han)", may enhance recovery.

- Topical applications (herbal liniments, plasters, etc.) may benefit.

- Massage of the entire muscle group (the gastrocnemius and soleus) may benefit. Cross-fiber massage at the achilles tendon may increase local micro-circulation and enhance recovery.

★ While all techniques listed above have shown clinical relevance, the starred items are predictably effective for this specific injury. Consider them first in a treatment plan.

REFERENCES

[1] Dutton, M: *Orthopeadic Examination, Evaluation, and Intervention,* Second Edition. McGraw-Hill, USA, 2008 (page 1135).

[2] Gottschlick, L: *Achilles Tendonitis.* At www.emedicine.com, 2008.

[3] Gottschlick, L: *Achilles Tendonitis.* At www.emedicine.com, 2008.

[4] *Ultrasound guided sclerosis of neovessels in painful chronic achilles tendinosis.* The British Journal of Sports Medicine, Vol 36, 2002 (pages 173-175).

2
Heel Pain
Plantar Fasciitis

Pain and stiffness in the heel and the plantar aspect of the foot

A repetitive stress injury characterized by inflammation and irritation of the plantar fascia.

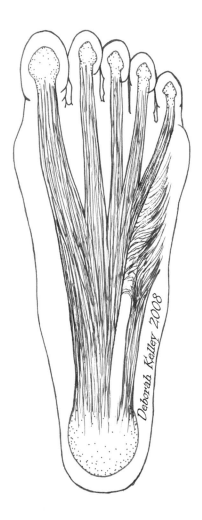

DIAGNOSIS & ASSESSMENT

Plantar fasciitis is the most common cause of heel pain, and occurs in all types of athletic and active individuals. It is commonly seen in runners, and may account for as many as 10 percent of all running injuries.[1] However, walking and standing on a hard surface may also cause symptoms. I began treating this injury in my first year of practice, and after more than 25 years of experience I am still unable to predict which patients will respond well to treatment. As I write this chapter, I am treating a 75-year-old diabetic male patient with plantar fasciitis. After three treatments over a two week period, he shook my hand and released himself from treatment, as he was totally pain-free. This was in contrast to an athletic 35-year-old patient who I referred to a physical therapist after a course of eight treatments that did not affect the condition. While I do not want to start on a negative note – I really love to treat plantar fasciitis – the practitioner should be alerted that precision in acupuncture treatment, as well as the inclusion of complementary therapies, is usually essential.

Plantar fasciitis is an inflammation and irritation of the plantar fascia, the connective tissue that supports the arch. Some orthopedic texts suggest the possibility of micro-tears in the fascia at or near its attachment to the calcaneus. Fifty percent of patients will probably also have a calcaneal heel spur.[2] Obesity is often related to non-athletic cases of plantar fasciitis. Being overweight is seen in as many as 40 percent of male and 90 percent of female patients with plantar fasciitis.[3] Although this is usually an overuse injury, it could be brought on by acute trauma in strenuous lower extremity activities.

The patient reports pain at the plantar aspect of the heel. Stiffness accompanies this pain, and symptoms may extend along the arch toward the region of Kid 1 and even as far as the toes. This injury has the characteristic of aggravation of symptoms in the morning when taking first steps, or upon standing after prolonged sitting or rest. The symptoms may be alleviated as the patient "warms up" and stretches the fascia with moderate activity. Runners will frequently report there is no pain during the early stages of a run, but pain returns toward the end or after the workout. Similarly, it is not uncommon to hear that the pain, after the morning aggravation, is alleviated during the day but worsens at the end of the day. Plantar pain is usually of insidious onset, but may be seen more acutely after strenuous levels of activity.

By far, the most likely diagnosis of heel pain is plantar fasciitis, especially if it follows the predictable patterns of aggravation covered above. However, there are several other possible causes of heel pain the practitioner should not overlook. Achilles tendonitis and achilles bursitis sometimes refer pain to the heel region. Trigger points in the soleus muscle of the calf may also refer pain distally to the calcaneous. Dr. Janet Travell, in her text on trigger points, refers to referred pain from the soleus muscle as "jogger's heel".[4] In addition, entrapment of the medial plantar nerve in the foot is a bit more difficult to diagnose, and while uncommon, can present with some similar symptoms to plantar fasciitis. And sometimes the pain is simply calcaneal bruising or periostitis, from mechanical injury to the heel bone. While none of these conditions place the patient in a compromised state if undiagnosed, further orthopedic evaluation may be necessary for those cases that fail to respond to treatment.

As for examination, start with palpation at the center of the plantar surface of the heel. This is the extraordinary point *Shimian*.[5] Also palpate over the medial tubercle of the calcaneous, as the pain often is found on this surface of the heel. Pain with modest pressure from the finger or thumb strongly suggests plantar fasciitis, but you should compare sensitivity with the unaffected side. You may be able to palpate a heel spur.

The calf muscles (the gastrocnemius and soleus group) should be palpated from the popliteal fossa at Bl 40 inferiorly to Bl 57. This area of the muscle may present with *ahshi* points that are often incorporated into the treatment protocol. You might also palpate the achilles tendon to assure that it is not radiating pain to the heel. I recently saw a patient who had been treated for a month for heel pain due to plantar fasciitis. She was not getting results. While examining the patient, pain was elicited by the "pinch" test on the achilles tendon just superior to the calcaneous. Adding points for the inflammed tendon brought about significant improvement in one treatment. If you find that the tendon is inflamed, read the achilles chapter on page 53, and add some of these simple techniques.

Make sure you question the patient about the onset of the condition. Plantar fasciitis is frequently associated with a change in training, such as increased mileage, hills, or speed. A change in running shoe or running surface may also contribute to the condition. As with most lower-extremity injuries, consider having the patient evaluated for foot biomechanical imbalances. Some texts suggest that up to 80 percent of these injuries are due to excessive foot pronation.[6] Anatomical problems, like decreased fat pad thickness, leg length discrepancy, or high or low arches may also increase the chance of developing plantar fasciitis.

SUMMARY OF THE INJURY

Clinical Features
- Repetitive stress causes inflammation of the fascia
- Pain usually starts after change in activity level, such as runners increasing mileage, hills, or speed
- Foot biomechanics, such as excessive pronation, leg length discrepancy, or high or low arches may increase chances of developing plantar fasciitis
- Pain reproduced with pressure over the medial tubercle of the calcaneous or near the center of the plantar surface of the heel

Common Patient Complaints
- Pain on the plantar aspect of the heel
- Heel pain may extend down the arch towards the base of the toes (Kid 1)
- May be accompanied by stiffness in the plantar aspect of the foot
- Symptoms often experienced upon taking first steps in the morning or after prolonged sitting or rest
- Symptoms alleviated as the heel "warms up" with moderate activity, but pain returns again during or after exercise

Differentiation from Similar Injuries and Conditions
- Presence of a calcaneal heel spur
- Achilles tendonitis or achilles bursitis
- Tear or rupture of the plantar fascia
- Calcaneal bruising or periostitis, "fat pad" syndrome
- Entrapment of the medial plantar nerve
- Referred pain from the calf muscles

Typical Medical Recommendations
- Ice is typically applied when acute.
- Anti-inflammatory medications
- Modify activity
  Decrease activities that aggravate the condition, especially during treatment. Cross-train, including cycling, swimming, running in water.
- Stretching
  Stretching of the gastrocnemius and soleus muscles of the calf is usually part of rehabilitation. Some patients get relief from a night dorsiflexion splint.
- Biomechanics
  Correct pronation or supination with shoes and/or orthotics. Other lower-extremity biomechanical imbalances may need to be assessed. Some podiatrists recommend a heel lift.
- Physical therapy
  Ultrasound, deep-friction massage, and other physical therapy modalities.
- Orthopedic procedures
  Cortisone injection is sometimes used in the inflamed tissues; however, it is associated with an increased risk of plantar fascia rupture.[7]

66 • Heel Pain *Plantar Fasciitis*

TREATMENT & TECHNIQUES

Overview: Plantar fasciitis is most commonly diagnosed under the category of accident/trauma. This is usually a repetitive stress disorder due to the accumulation of micro-trauma. However, it may occasionally occur as an acute strain. The plantar fascia includes the region of Kid 1, and may be related to Kidney meridian pathology. Because many patients with this type of heel pain have tight calf muscles, the Bladder meridian may also be involved. Inflammation is at the level of the tendons, ligaments, and bones. There is qi and blood stagnation in the channels and collaterals. Internal organ imbalances possibly contribute.

Prognosis: Treat twice a week for three weeks, then re-evaluate. Most cases without complications may have improvement within six treatments. With chronic cases, continue treatment at least once weekly after the first three-week period.

STEP ONE: INITIAL TREATMENT

Choose among these four techniques, carefully determining if there is an immediate decrease in pain or an increase in range of motion.

Technique #1: **The Tendino-Muscle Meridians**

Kid 1 (alternate location)   Bleeding technique
The alternate location of Kid 1 is on the medial aspect of fifth digit (the little toe), about .1 cun proximal to the corner of the nail. While it does not have a high degree of effectiveness, it is certainly worth a try.

Technique #2: **Opposite Side (contra-lateral)**

Corresponding points on the opposite (unaffected) side may be considered; however, treatment to the affected side is usually preferred.

Technique #3: **Opposite Extremity (upper/lower)**

★ H 8   Shao Yin corresponding point
P 7.5   Corresponding point on the palmar surface of the hand, halfway between P 7 and P 8
P 8   Correspondence of the "heel of palm" with heel of the foot

In general, treat upper/lower corresponding points on the opposite (unaffected) side when acute, and the affected side when chronic. Use palpation to assist in this choice.

67 • Heel Pain *Plantar Fasciitis*

Technique #4: **Empirical Points**

Mu guan* + *Gu guan
Empirical point combination for heel pain from the Master Tong system. This may also be viewed as a correspondence of treating the "heel of the palm" with the heel of the foot. *Mu guan* is located on the ulnar eminence of the palm, level with *Gu guan*, about .5 cun distal to the prominence of the pisiform bone. *Gu guan* is located on the thenar eminence of the palm, level with *Mu guan*, about .5 cun distal the the prominence of the scaphoid bone.[8]

STEP TWO: MERIDIANS & MICROSYSTEMS

Choose among these four techniques, selecting points that are appropriate for the signs and symptoms of the patient.

Technique #5: **The Shu-Stream Point Combination**

Bl 65 affected side + SI 3 opposite side
For treatment of the Bladder (Tai yang) region of the calf muscles.

Technique #6 **Traditional Point Categories**

★ **Kid 7 + Kid 8**   Jing-river point + xi-cleft point of the Yang Qiao mai

Kid 4 + Kid 5   Luo-connecting point + xi-cleft point
One of these two paired-point combinations may be helpful to activate the Kidney meridian and treat heel pain symptoms. Use on the affected side only, and consider electrical stimulation between the two points.
★ Palpation may assist in your choice of points; however, if one fails, try the other set.

Sp 6	Crossing point of three leg yin
Bl 57	Releases the gastrocnemius muscle
Bl 58	Luo-connecting point
Bl 40	He-sea point
GB 34	Hui-influential point of tendons

Technique #7: **The Extraordinary Meridians**

GB 41 + SJ 5   Activate the Dai mai
Compensating for dysfunction of the foot sometimes results in secondary hip and gluteal imbalances, which may be considered Dai mai pathology.

Bl 62 + SI 3   Activate the Yang Qiao mai
Sometimes lower-extremity biomechanical imbalances are involved in plantar fasciitis, which may be considered Yang Qiao mai pathology.

Technique #8: **Microsystems**

Auricular Therapy
Local: Heel (French), heel (Chinese), lumbar spine
Zang-fu points: Kidney, Liver
Systemic points for pain: Shen men, Thalamus, Adrenal, Endocrine

STEP THREE: INTERNAL ORGAN IMBALANCES

Choose appropriate points to treat internal organ imbalances that may contribute to the injury or pain syndrome.

Technique #9: **Qi, Blood, and the Zang-fu Organs**

Plantar fasciitis is a repetitive stress injury, and therefore, internal organ imbalances are usually not causative. However, there are several zang-fu syndromes that may contribute to the condition:

Liver imbalances Liver qi stagnation, Liver yin deficiency, and Liver blood deficiency
Liver imbalances may be observed in the patient with plantar fasciitis. These imbalances result in susceptibility to inflammation and repetitive stress injury to the tendons. Consider the following:

Liv 3	Yuan-source point; supports the Liver in its function of controlling the muscles and tendons
GB 34	Hui-influential point of tendons

Treat GB 34 on the affected side and Liv 3 on the opposite side.

Kidney imbalances Kidney deficiency
Kidney deficiency may result in deficiency in the Kidney and Bladder meridians, increasing the susceptibility of the plantar fascia to repetitive stress injury.

Points should be determined by the practitioner from both palpation and analysis of the signs and symptoms of the patient.

STEP FOUR: THE SITE OF INJURY

Choose among the local and adjacent points at the site of injury. Points may be determined by palpation, orthopedic testing, and analysis of the signs and symptoms of the patient.

Technique #10: **Local and Adjacent Points**

The plantar fascia **The extraordinary point *Shimian***

The extraordinary point *Shimian* is the "target" zone of the plantar fascia and its attachment to the calcaneus. This point is located in the center of the plantar surface of the heel.[9] All local needling is in relationship to *Shimian*. Predictably, palpation will help determine the precise site of needle insertion.

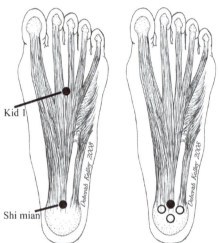

● – Acupuncture points
○ – Point variations

Variations on Shimian The following is a summary of the variations on this local point:

 1. Two paired points at *Shimian*
Two needles are inserted perpendicularly into the most sensitive *ahshi* points. The depth is about .5 inch, which varies with each patient. Some patients have a very thin "fat pad" on the heel, making insertion depth less than .5 inch. Consider electrical stimulation.

 2. "Medial" *Shimian*
Palpation often reveals point tenderness near the medial tubercle of the calcaneous. This is about one-third of the distance between *Shimian* and the point Kid 6. I call this "medial" *Shimian*. Needling into the medial aspect of the heel can be less painful than *Shimian*, so this point should always be considered. Insert the needle at "medial" *Shimian*, directed toward the center of the heel. The depth is about 1 inch. I frequently use two paired points from this zone, determined by palpation. Consider electrical stimulation.

3. *Shimian* + "medial" *Shimian*
"Medial" *Shimian* may be paired with a perpendicular needle at *Shimian* in the center of the heel. Again, consider electrical stimulation. In some cases, palpation reveals pain in both of these points in a zone from 1 to 2 centimeters in length. This allows the practitioner to place two needles in both *Shimian* and "medial" *Shimian*.

4. "Lateral" *Shimian*
Palpation occasionally reveals point tenderness on the lateral side of the calcaneous. This is about one-third of the distance between *Shimian* and the point Bl 62. I call this "lateral" *Shimian*. Insert the needle at "lateral" *Shimian*, directed toward the center of the heel. The depth is about 1 inch. I frequently pair this point with either *Shimian* or "medial" *Shimian*. Consider electrical stimulation.

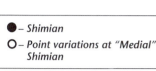
● – *Shimian*
○ – *Point variations at "Medial" Shimian*

Comments on needle technique — With each of these variations above, needling is directly into the plantar fascia at or near its attachment to the calcaneus. In TCM language, this is the site of qi stagnation and blood stasis. In theory, we are increasing micro-circulation through these tissues. However, with all direct needling comes the possibility of aggravation. I have seen many patients limp out of the office after this treatment, their confidence wavering, only to call the next day reporting significant improvement. If you explain this to your patients, they can be prepared for the aggravation. The risk of flaring up these tissues often has great reward.

Three depths of insertion — This technique may be more comfortable to the patient and reduce the possibility of aggravation. Use three depths of needle insertion during a 30-minute treatment session. For the first 10 minutes, the needles are inserted to a superficial depth. For the second 10 minutes, the needles are inserted deeper, to an intermediate depth. For the final 10 minutes, the needles are inserted to the deepest position. With this final depth, the needle approaches the plantar surface of the periosteum and the bone. If the needle hits the calcaneus, retract it slightly. Electrical stimulation may be used between paired points in each of the three depths.

Moxa — Moxa may also be considered in this treatment. Some practitioners avoid needling directly into the heel, and use only thread moxa. They report good results with this technique. I, however, am too stubborn, and will always try to find a way to needle the heel while keeping the patient comfortable. However, sometimes I follow the needle treatment with thread moxa over the site of insertion. Consider five small, rice grain-size threads on each point needled.

Adjacent points ★ **Liv 3 + Kid 1** Yuan-source point + jing-well point
Liv 3 benefits the controls tendons and ligaments. Kid 1 is an adjacent point located directly in the plantar fascia where it separates into bands attaching toward the digits. I frequently use electrical stimulation between Liv 3 and Kid 1.

Kid 3 Yuan-source point
Bl 60 "Fire" point

The belly of the calf muscles **The region of Bl 56, Bl 57**
Needling acupuncture and *ahshi* points in the calf may release the gastrocnemius and soleus muscle group, and assist as secondary points in the treatment of plantar fasciitis.

| X – Trigger points |
| ▲ – Motor points |

COMPLEMENTARY PROCEDURES

- When acute, ice massage along the plantar fascia may alleviate pain and reduce inflammation.

- Alternating ice and heat after the acute stage, when the condition is "neither hot (re) nor cold (han)", may enhance recovery.

- Topical applications (herbal liniments, plasters, etc.) may benefit.

- A heel lift with a central hole cut out (sometimes called a "donut") may allow for walking and other activities without direct irritation to the region of calcaneous at the attachment of the plantar fascia. This is also where a heel spur, if present, is located.

- Self-massage to the plantar region of the foot with a golf ball or other similar devices may be beneficial.

- A night-time dorsiflexion splint is recommended by many medical practitioners. This device maintains the foot in dorsiflexion, providing a prolonged stretch to the plantar fascia.

★ While all techniques listed above have shown clinical relevance, the starred items are predictably effective for this specific injury. Consider them first in a treatment plan.

REFERENCES

[1] Garrick, J: *Orthopaedic Knowledge Update, Sports Medicine 3.* North American Academy of Orthopaedic Surgeons, Illinois, 2004 (page 250).

[2] Dutton, M: *Orthopeadic Examination, Evaluation, and Intervention,* Second Edition. McGraw-Hill, USA, 2008 (page 1139).

[3] Dutton, M: *Orthopeadic Examination, Evaluation, and Intervention,* Second Edition. McGraw-Hill, USA, 2008 (page 1139).

[4] Travell & Simons: *Myofascial Pain and Dysfunction: The Trigger Point Manual, Volume 2 (The Lower Extremities).* Williams & Wilkins, Philadelphia, 1992 (pages 427-429).

[5] Shanghai College of Traditional Medicine: *Acupuncture, A Comprehensive Text.* Eastland Press, Chicago, 1981 (page 387).

[6] Dutton, M: *Orthopeadic Examination, Evaluation, and Intervention,* Second Edition. McGraw-Hill, USA, 2008 (page 1139).

[7] Garrick, J: *Orthopaedic Knowledge Update, Sports Medicine 3.* North American Academy of Orthopaedic Surgeons, Illinois, 2004 (page 249).

[8] Tan & Rush: *Twelve and Twelve in Acupuncture*, San Diego, 1994 (pages 25-26).

[9] Shanghai College of Traditional Medicine: *Acupuncture, A Comprehensive Text.* Eastland Press, Chicago, 1981 (page 387).

Notes

3
Foot Pain

Lateral (Inversion) Ankle Sprain

Pain, swelling, and bruising of the lateral ankle and foot

This common sports injury results in ligament sprain and joint inflammation from inverting or inward rolling of the ankle.

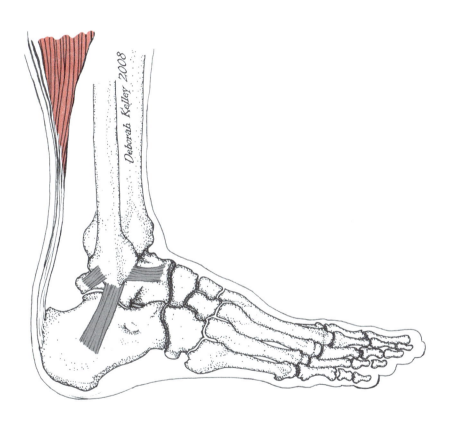

DIAGNOSIS & ASSESSMENT

One of the most common of all sports injuries is the sprained ankle. It is an acute injury that most acupuncturists treat at one time or another. Studies show that 38 to 45 percent of all sports injuries are ankle sprains, and there are 25,000 ankle injuries sustained per day.[1] Inversion injuries involving the lateral ligaments account for 85 percent of all ankle sprains, and it is this specific type that is discussed in this chapter.[2]

Lateral ankle sprains occur while running or jumping on an uneven surface or during quick lateral movements, often seen in sports such as soccer or basketball. It may even occur to the unfortunate hiker who happens to roll the ankle from a rock or uneven surface. With this inversion trauma, the ligaments are stretched or torn. This involves one or more of the three lateral ligaments – the anterior talo-fibular, the calcaneo-fibular, and the posterior talo-fibular. This is in the region of the points GB 40 and Bl 62. Occasionally a loud "snap" or "pop" is heard at the time of the sprain. This is usually followed by pain, swelling, and bruising. Muscle spasms may result, as well as stiffness and decreased range of motion. Pain may radiate up the lateral leg towards the point GB 34. Or it may radiate in the direction of the anterior ankle crease in the region of St 41.

Ankle sprains, like all ligament injuries, are classified by the degree of severity. Grade I sprains are the most common, and require the least amount of treatment and rehabilitation. The ligament may be stretched and micro-tears may occur without any significant instability developing. With a grade II injury, the ligaments are partially torn with the possibility of minor ankle instability. Both grade I and moderate grade II sprains can be easily treated with acupuncture and complementary modalities. However, severe grade II and grade III sprains sustain significant ligamentous damage, and evaluation by an orthopedic physician may be necessary. Fracture, tendon injury, and other pathology might require medical procedures beyond acupuncture treatment. It is important to get a correct diagnosis because 40 percent of those who are untreated or misdiagnosed may develop chronic ankle problems.[3]

After assessment, there are three general ways to proceed with acupuncture treatment. In the acute stage, pain, swelling, and bruising are pronounced. Heat signs from inflammation may also be present. Treatment to the local tissues may have to be avoided. In the subacute and chronic stages, pain, swelling, and bruising are less pronounced. In these cases, the techniques in Step Four at the site of injury are usually both necessary and beneficial. In the chronic stage, after all inflammation and swelling has subsided, there may be joint instability and weakness due to ligamentous laxity. Treatment is directed towards strengthening the ligaments and stabilizing the ankle joint.

A note should be added here about the "high" ankle sprain. Most texts indicate that 10 percent of all ankle sprains are injuries to the syndesmotic ligament.[4] It attaches between the fibula and the tibia, above the ankle joint, thus the name "high" ankle sprain. It is difficult to access with the acupuncture needle, and there are no traditional points that directly treat this ligament. However, GB 39 and St 41 are adjacent points to this site of injury. We will not discuss the treatment of high ankle sprain, although many of the techniques discussed below could be adapted to this injury. The reader should be aware that it is often stubborn to treat, and full recovery takes some time.

SUMMARY OF THE INJURY

Clinical Features
- The majority of all ankle sprains are inversion sprains on the lateral side
- Inversion sprains involve the anterior talo-fibular ligament, the calcaneo-fibular ligament, and sometimes posterior talo-fibular ligament
- Trauma to the ligament may range from a mild grade I sprain to a serious grade III injury

Common Patient Complaints
- Pain in the lateral ankle and foot
- Pain may radiate up the lateral leg or toward the anterior ankle crease
- Swelling and bruising around ankle joint may accompany pain
- Muscle spasms may result, as well as stiffness and decreased range of motion
- Pain may be experienced during weight bearing activities

Differentiation from Similar Injuries and Conditions
- Fracture of the malleolus, tibia, fibula, or one of the tarsal bones
- Loose body within the ankle joint
- Tendon tear, tendon rupture
- Subluxation of peroneal tendon
- High ankle sprain (syndemotic injury)
- Talar joint dysfunction

Typical Medical Recommendations
- R.I.C.E. (Rest, Ice, Compression, and Elevation) when acute
- Anti-inflammatory medication
- Modify activity
  Crutches may be considered if walking is painful. Cross-train, including cycling, swimming, and running in water.
- Biomechanics
  After the acute phase, correct pronation or supination with shoes and/or orthotics, which may assist in long-term stability of the joint.
- Physical therapy
  Ultrasound, manual therapy, and other physical therapy modalities. Taping may be used to provide ankle stability. Strengthening exercises are often included for the lateral peroneal muscles during rehabilitation.
- Orthopedic evaluation and procedures
  If you suspect a serious injury, such as a grade III sprain or a possible fracture, refer to an orthopedic physician. Prolotherapy is often successful for strengthening the ligaments by sclerosing injection. Reconstructive surgery is a consideration for significant ankle instability after a severe sprain if rehabilitation fails.

77 • Foot Pain *Lateral (Inversion) Ankle Sprain*

TREATMENT & TECHNIQUES

Overview: Ankle sprains are most commonly diagnosed under the category of accident/trauma. The injury is at the level of the tendons, ligaments, and the joint. There is qi and blood stagnation in the channels and collaterals. The Gall Bladder is usually the primary meridian involved, although the Bladder and Stomach channels may also be affected. Internal organ imbalances usually do not contribute. Local needling may aggravate and is often avoided during the early stages of acute symptoms.

Prognosis: Treat twice a week for three weeks, then re-evaluate. However, acute ankle sprain may respond very well to three times a week for the first week. Most acute cases have good results within six treatments. In the chronic stage, treating once weekly is usually sufficient.

STEP ONE: INITIAL TREATMENT

Choose among these four techniques, carefully determining if there is an immediate decrease in pain or an increase in range of motion.

Technique #1: **The Tendino-Muscle Meridians**

GB 44	Bleeding technique
Bl 67	Bleeding technique
St 45	Bleeding technique

Bleeding the jing-well point of the Gall Bladder (Shao yang) meridian is usually effective for pain and swelling, and is the first technique to consider. It may be repeated three to six times during the first two weeks. The Bladder (Tai yang) and the Stomach (Yang ming) meridians may also be affected.

Technique #2: **Opposite Side (contra-lateral)**

Ahshi point(s)   On the opposite (unaffected) side
Palpate for sensitive points on the lateral aspect of the ankle.

GB 40   Corresponding point on the opposite (unaffected) side

GB 40, the yuan-source point, is usually the most effective contra-lateral point. Use deep insertion if possible.

Bl 60, Bl 62, Bl 63   Corresponding points on the opposite (unaffected) side

St 41   Corresponding point on the opposite (unaffected) side

Technique #3:	**Opposite Extremity (upper/lower)**	
	SJ 4	Shao yang corresponding point on the opposite extremity

This is the perfect mirror of GB 40; however, strong needle technique is not easily accomplished at this point.

	SI 4, SI 5	Tai yang corresponding points on the opposite extremity

These Tai yang points may benefit lateral ankle symptoms of swelling and bruising.

	LI 5	Yang ming corresponding point on the opposite extremity

Beneficial when the pain is on the anterior side of the ankle around the region of St 41.

In general, treat upper/lower corresponding points on the opposite (unaffected) side when acute, and the affected side when chronic. Use palpation to assist in this choice.

Technique #4: **Empirical Points**

No well-known empirical points for ankle sprain.

STEP TWO: MERIDIANS & MICROSYSTEMS

Choose among these four techniques, selecting points that are appropriate for the signs and symptoms of the patient.

Technique #5: **The Shu-Stream Point Combination**

★ **GB 41 (or GB 42) affected side + SJ 3 opposite side**
GB 42 is often more sensitive than GB 41, and should be considered as an alternative shu-stream point.

Bl 65 affected side + SI 3 opposite side
Pain, swelling, and contusion on the Tai yang channel

St 43 affected side + LI 3 opposite side
Pain, swelling, and contusion on the Yang ming channel

Technique #6: **Traditional Point Categories**

★ Palpation may assist in your choice of Gall Bladder, Bladder, and Stomach meridian points. Other important local points are discussed in Step Four.

GB 43	"Water" point
St 44	"Water" point

Technique #7: **The Extraordinary Meridians**

GB 41 + SJ 5	Activate the Dai mai

Compensating for an ankle sprain sometimes results in secondary hip and gluteal imbalances, which may be considered Dai mai pathology.

79 • Foot Pain *Lateral (Inversion) Ankle Sprain*

Bl 62 + SI 3   Activate the Yang Qiao mai
Inversion ankle sprain produces symptoms on the lateral aspect of the leg, which may be considered Yang Qiao mai pathology.

Technique #8: **Microsystems**

Auricular Therapy
Local: Ankle (French), ankle (Chinese)
Zang-fu points: Liver, Gall Bladder
Systemic points for pain: Shen men, Thalamus, Adrenal, Endocrine

---

STEP THREE: INTERNAL ORGAN IMBALANCES

Choose appropriate points to treat internal organ imbalances that may contribute to the injury or pain syndrome.

Technique #9: **Qi, Blood, and the Zang-fu Organs**

Ankle sprains are acute traumatic injuries and therefore internal organ imbalances are usually not causative. However, there are several zang-fu syndromes which may contribute to the condition.

Liver imbalances   Liver qi stagnation, Liver yin deficiency, and Liver blood deficiency
Liver imbalances may be observed in the patient with recurring ankle sprain and chronic ankle pain. While it is often said that the Kidney controls the knees, some texts suggest the Liver controls the ankle. This could relate to the lateral compartment muscle group of the legs. This includes the peroneus longus and brevis, which aid in lateral stability of the ankle joint. The Gall Bladder meridian precisely follows this muscle group. Consider the following:

Liv 3   Yuan-source point; supports the Liver in its function of controlling the muscles and tendons

GB 34   Hui-influential point of tendons
Treat GB 34 on the affected side and Liv 3 on the opposite side.

Kidney imbalances   Kidney deficiency
Some modern clinicians suggest that the ligaments, which attach on bone and stabilize the joints, are controlled by the Kidney.[5] Therefore, Kidney imbalances may result in ligamentous laxity and increased susceptibility to sprain and joint injury. This should be considered only with chronic and recurring ankle sprains.

Points should be determined by the practitioner from both palpation and analysis of the signs and symptoms of the patient.

80 • Foot Pain *Lateral (Inversion) Ankle Sprain*

STEP FOUR: THE SITE OF INJURY

Choose among the local and adjacent points at the site of injury. Points may be determined by palpation, orthopedic testing, and analysis of the signs and symptoms of the patient.

Technique #10: **Local and Adjacent Points**

The lateral ligaments **Local *ahshi* points**

The most important decision the practitioner must make with acute ankle sprain is whether to treat locally at the site of injury. Within the first week after injury, if symptoms include significant pain, swelling, bruising, and inflammation, you may choose to avoid local needles. The techniques of Step One and Step Two above are often sufficient to treat the acute ankle and have virtually no chance of aggravation.

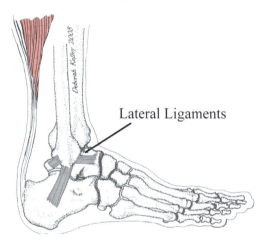

The anterior talo-fibular ligament
The calcaneo-fibular ligament
The posterior talo-fibular ligament

 If you choose to treat locally, palpate for tenderness in the region of GB 40 and Bl 62. Deep to these points lies the anterior talofibular ligament, which is involved in 60 to 70 percent of all ankle sprains.[6] The calcaneofibular ligament may also be involved in the injury. Electrical stimulation may be considered between two paired *ahshi* points.

Local and adjacent points		
	GB 40	Yuan-source point
	Bl 60	"Fire" point
	Bl 62	Master point of Yang Qiao mai
	Bl 63	Xi-cleft point
	St 41	"Fire" point

 When there are numerous *ahshi* points with widespread pain in the lateral ankle and foot, coupling two yang meridian acupuncture points often suffices. GB 40 + Bl 60 is often effective, but the practitioner may need to experiment. Consider electrical stimulation between the two paired points.

81 • Foot Pain *Lateral (Inversion) Ankle Sprain*

Cupping, bleeding — Other techniques may be considered. Some practitioners insist on blood letting to dispel blood stasis. You should not rule out using a small cup; however, maintaining suction may not be always possible. I use a bleeding cup from time to time with success. Remember that some lotion or lubricant on the skin may help keep the cup in place.

The talus sinus ("opening" to the talar joint) ★ **GB 40**

The area of GB 40 anatomically is the talus sinus, an opening that accesses the talus region of the ankle joint. Sub-acute and chronic pain following a lateral sprain are often due to swelling and inflammation in this region of the joint capsule. Rotate the foot while palpating the point to find a position where the depression is most pronounced. Deep needling into the point is quite effective. It is often required at some point in the treatment of all patients recovering from ankle sprain.

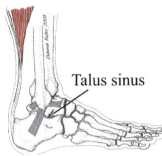

Lingering pain, decreased range of motion and stiffness respond well to this treatment. But don't do it too soon; wait until the acute stage has long passed! Use one or two needles, inserted perpendicularly to a depth of .5 to 1.5 inches, if possible.

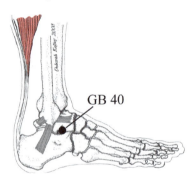

Needle technique ★ Electrical stimulation on the paired points at GB 40 is my preferred technique. However, in chronic cases with no signs of heat and swelling, needle-top moxa may be considered. Indirect as well as direct moxa should be used in the chronic stage to assist in joint stability, as it can strengthen the lateral ligaments.

Adjacent points **GB 39** — Located adjacent to the peroneus longus tendon

★ Frequently sensitive with ankle sprain. Needle obliquely in an inferior direction, pointing towards the painful area of the lateral ankle.

★ **GB 34** — Hui-influential point of tendons

Frequently sensitive with inversion ankle sprain. Located near the origin of the peroneus longus, this muscle distally "wraps around" the lateral malleolus.

COMPLEMENTARY PROCEDURES

- When acute, ice massage in the region of the lateral ankle may alleviate pain and reduce inflammation.

- Alternating ice and heat after the acute stage, when the condition is "neither hot (re) nor cold (han)", may enhance recovery.

- Applications of heat often benefit when there is chronic pain and inflammation of the ankle joint.

- Topical applications (herbal liniments, plasters, etc.) may benefit.

- Consider strength exercises for the peroneus longus and brevis to assist in lateral ankle stability.

- A supplement with glucosamine and chondroitin may be considered for nutritional support of the joint. While usually not dramatic, it may contribute to recovery.

- Homeopathic remedies are sometimes effective for pain and inflammation in chronic arthritis. Hyland's Arthritis Pain Formula (Standard Homeopathic Company) is one product to consider for ankle sprains that are slow to fully recover.

★ While all techniques listed above have shown clinical relevance, the starred items are predictably effective for this specific injury. Consider them first in a treatment plan.

REFERENCES

[1] Rimando, M: *Physical medicine and rehabilitation.* www.emedicine.com. June 2008.

[2] O'Donoghue, DH: *Treatment of Injuries to Athletes, Third Edition.* W. B. Saunders Co, Philadelphia, 1976 (page 707).

[3] Rimando, M: *Physical medicine and rehabilitation.* www.emedicine.com. June 2008.

[4] Rimando, M: *Physical medicine and rehabilitation.* www.emedicine.com. June 2008.

[5] Callison, M: *Sports Medicine Acupuncture.* AcuSport Seminar Series LLC, San Diego, In Printing.

[6] Dutton, M: *Orthopeadic Examination, Evaluation, and Intervention,* Second Edition. McGraw-Hill, USA, 2008 (page 1129).

Notes

4
Foot Pain
Pain of the First MTP Joint (The Big Toe)

Pain, stiffness, and decreased range of motion of the first metatarsal-phalanges joint of the big toe

Osteoarthritis and degeneration of the articular surface of the first MTP joint associated with repetitive stress or prior injury.

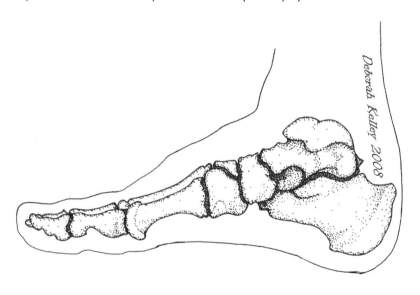

DIAGNOSIS & ASSESSMENT

Many of the injuries discussed in this book involve treatment to broad tissues such as the gluteal muscles, the ilio-tibial band, and the rotator cuff. The first metatarsal-phalanges joint focuses our attention to a relatively small and fixed location. Yet it is included in this handbook because anyone with this pain knows that exercise and daily activities are significantly affected by first MTP joint dysfunction. It is commonly seen in clinical practice, and I am usually treating at least one patient with this annoying pain syndrome at any given time.

Osteoarthritis is the general diagnostic viewpoint to start this discussion. Pain, stiffness, and decreased range of motion predominate, and similar to other cases of chronic arthritis, the onset of symptoms is gradual. The big toe may appear swollen, and there is obvious inflammation. This condition is a degeneration of the articular surface of the first MTP joint, characterized by progressive "wear-and-tear." It is often chronic and commonly affects patients over 50 years old. There may be an association with prior traumatic injury to the cartilage or other tissues of the joint. Like many arthritic conditions, pain is usually worse from walking, hiking and other weight-bearing activities. Symptoms are often relieved with rest; the patient may walk with a limp.

While osteoarthritis is the most likely diagnosis, occasionally the practitioner will see an acute traumatic injury to the first MTP joint. Causes can be simply "stubbing" the toe while walking, as well as a variety of injuries involving hyper-flexion or hyper-extension during sports activity. The result of pain and inflammation to the joint is the same, and these acute cases are generally treated similar to a chronic arthritic case.

Literature includes various structural issues – often called "deformities" – that relate to this condition.[1] Hallux valgus is the lateral deviation of the big toe as it points towards the outside of the foot. This includes the bunion on the medial side of the joint in the region of the point Sp 3. Women are significantly more likely to have this condition.[2] Pain may originate from the arthritic joint or be due to swelling and inflammation of the subcutaneous tissues of the bunion itself. As this condition progresses, the bunion becomes thickened and symptoms often escalate. Hallux rigidus describes the stiffness and decreased range of motion of the big toe. It is a "frozen joint" syndrome, where toe flexion and extension become compromised, with progression forcing the patient into abnormal foot biomechanics that further add to pain and dysfunction. These two deformities often contribute to the arthritic condition of the first MTP joint.

The examination of the first MTP joint may show pain on both active and passive range of motion. You might also compress and mildly distract ("pull apart") the joint of the big toe to see if it reproduces pain. Palpate for pain, also feeling for signs of heat and inflammation. Observe for the presence of a structural deformity, which will be obvious to the practitioner. An X-ray will reveal if there is arthritis and joint space narrowing, which will be quite helpful for your prognosis.

The patient may need a variety of modalities. The acupuncture techniques discussed below often provide relief of pain and increase the level of activity that can be tolerated. In fact, most of my patients with this arthritis never need a reminder to reschedule. They experience the benefit and generally want to schedule regular treatments. The entire protocol usually includes physical therapy to assist in range of motion and orthotics to correct the biomechanical imbalances of the foot. The patient will be pleasantly surprised by how effective this can be, especially if they have been told by an orthopedist that they have to live with the pain.

SUMMARY OF THE INJURY

Clinical Features	• Repetitive stress may cause inflammation and irritation of the joint • Overuse and "wear and tear" or prior injury may cause degenerative changes to the joint • Hallux valgus and hallux rigidus are "deformities" often present and contribute to the arthritic condition of the first MTP joint • Other lower-extremity biomechanical imbalances may be contributing factors • Often seen as a chronic condition in patients over 50 years old
Common Patient Complaints	• Pain in the first MTP joint (big toe) • Pain may be accompanied by stiffness and decrease range of motion • Swelling, inflammation, and signs of heat may be present • Pain is aggravated during exercise and weight-bearing activities • Symptoms often relieved with rest and inactivity • Patient may walk with a limp
Differentiation from Similar Injuries and Conditions	• Metatarsalgia, where pain is localized under the metatarsal head on the plantar surface • Metatarsal stress fracture • Inflammation of the numerous tendons in the region of the big toe • Rule out systemic inflammatory conditions such as gout and rheumatoid arthritis • Disorders of the sesamoid bone of the big toe
Typical Medical Recommendations	• R.I.C.E. (Rest, Ice, Compression, and Elevation) when acute • Anti-inflammatory medications • Modify activity *Cross-train, including, swimming and running in water.* • Biomechanics *Orthotics are often customized to the patient's foot structure and factor in deformities such as hallux valgus. Custom-made shoes, stiff-soled footwear, and shoes with wider toe boxes or rocker soles often help. Other lower-extremity biomechanical imbalances may need to be assessed.* • Physical therapy *Ultrasound, and other physical therapy modalities.* • Orthopedic procedures *Cortisone injection is sometimes used in the inflamed region. Weight loss or control is helpful to reduce stress to the big toe joint. Surgery may benecessary for the patient with chronic untreatable symptoms.*

87 • Foot Pain *Pain of the First MTP Joint*

TREATMENT & TECHNIQUES

Overview: First MTP joint pain is most commonly diagnosed under the category of accident/trauma. This is usually a repetitive stress disorder due to the accumulation of micro-trauma. However, occasionally it may occur as an acute traumatic injury. The injury is at the level of the tendons, bone, and the joint. There is qi and blood stagnation in the channels and collaterals. The Liver and Spleen meridians are most commonly affected. Internal organ imbalances vary.

As a form of arthritis, this condition could be diagnosed as a *Bi* syndrome. Care should be taken to assess hot (re), cold (han), damp (shi), and wind (feng) contributions. This will assist in the choice of points, needle technique, and herbal prescription.

Prognosis: Treat twice a week for three weeks, then re-evaluate. With many patients, there may be some degree of improvement within six treatments. With chronic cases and progressed joint degeneration, continue treatments at least once weekly after the first three-week period. I will often see the patient every three to four weeks for maintenance.

STEP ONE: INITIAL TREATMENT

Choose among these four techniques, carefully determining if there is an immediate decrease in pain or an increase in range of motion.

Technique #1: **The Tendino-Muscle Meridians**

Liv 1, Sp 1   Bleeding technique
The Liver and Spleen tendino-muscle meridians do not get to the deepest levels of the joint, but bleeding the jing-well point may be effective for stiffness and swelling. There may be contraindications for these points.

Technique #2: **Opposite Side (contra-lateral)**

 Sp 3, Liv 2, Liv 3   Corresponding points on the opposite (unaffected) side
This technique is often a good way to begin treatment. Needle one or two of the point-sensitive corresponding points on the opposite side. For two minutes, move the affected toe through passive movements. It is also a good way to end treatment after the local points (if used) are removed.

Technique #3: **Opposite Extremity (upper/lower)**

Corresponding points on the opposite extremity may be considered; however, treatment to the affected extremity is usually preferred.

Technique #4: **Empirical Points**

No well-known empirical points for this condition.

STEP TWO: MERIDIANS & MICROSYSTEMS

Choose among these four techniques, selecting points that are appropriate for the signs and symptoms of the patient.

Technique #5: **The Shu-Stream Point Combination**

Sp 3 affected side + Lu 9 opposite side
Liv 3 affected side + P 7 opposite side
These paired shu-stream points are not clinically reliable.

Technique #6: **Traditional Point Categories**

★ Palpation may assist in your choice of lower-extremity meridian points.

Liv 4	Jing-river point
Sp 4	Luo-connecting point
Sp 6	Crossing point
Sp 9	He-sea point
St 36	He-sea point
GB 34	Hui-influential point of tendons

Technique #7: **The Extraordinary Meridians**

GB 41 + SJ 5   Activate the Dai mai
Compensating for dysfunction of the first MTP joint sometimes results in secondary hip and gluteal imbalances, which may be considered Dai mai pathology.

Technique #8: **Microsystems**

Auricular Therapy
Local: Toe (French), toe (Chinese)
Zang-fu points: Liver, Spleen, Kidney
Systemic points for pain: Shen men, Thalamus, Adrenal, Endocrine

STEP THREE: INTERNAL ORGAN IMBALANCES

Choose appropriate points to treat internal organ imbalances that may contribute to the injury or pain syndrome.

Technique #9: **Qi, Blood, and the Zang-fu Organs**

There are various internal imbalances seen in the patient with chronic pain in the first MTP joint. Consider the following:

Spleen and Liver imbalances Spleen qi deficiency, Liver qi stagnation
Spleen and Liver imbalances are most common, as could be predicted from the course of the two meridians. This should be fairly straightforward for the practitioner to assess.

Kidney imbalances Kidney deficiency
Syndromes of the Kidney are considered by some practitioners as an internal organ imbalance present in all patients with chronic arthritis and joint degeneration. However, treatment to the Kidney alone rarely is sufficient for this arthritic condition.

Bi syndrome Pain of the first MTP joint due to osteoarthritis is commonly diagnosed as a *Bi* syndrome. Care should be taken to assess the hot (re), cold (han), damp (shi) and wind (feng) contributions. This will assist in the choice of points, needle technique, and herbal prescription.

Points should be determined by the practitioner from both palpation and analysis of the signs and symptoms of the patient.

STEP FOUR: THE SITE OF INJURY

Choose among the local and adjacent points at the site of injury. Points may be determined by palpation, orthopedic testing, and analysis of the signs and symptoms of the patient.

Technique #10: **Local and Adjacent Points**

The first MTP joint Local treatment to the first MTP joint is simple and direct, and for the most part can be accomplished with known acupuncture points. There are, however, several variations of these points to consider.

Point combinations **Sp 3 + Liv 3**
★ Combining these two shu-stream points is the most frequent protocol and should be considered as the first place to start when treating locally. Liv 3 is on the lateral aspect of the joint, with Sp 3 on the medial side. Unless contra-indicated, use electrical stimulation between these paired points.

★ **Sp 3 + Liv 2**
Combining the shu-stream point of the Spleen with the sedation point of the Liver should be considered as the second protocol to consider. Like Sp 3 + Liv 3, use electrical stimulation unless contraindicated.

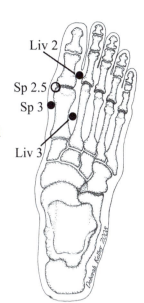

★ **Sp 3 + Liv 2.5**
This combines Sp 3 with a point halfway between Liv 2 and Liv 3, which can be named Liv 2.5. Again, consider electrical stimulation between these two points.

Liv 2.5 on the plantar surface of the foot
Though not an easy point to needle without discomfort, this point sometimes works wonders! On the plantar surface of the foot, find the depression between the first and the second metatarsals. This is the "ball of the foot", in the interspace just distal (anterior) to the metatarsal heads. This is a plantar surface mirror of Liv 2.5, and may be needled perpendicularly about .5 inch. Combine it with one of the other points described above, using electrical stimulation.

The medial joint space **Sp 2.5**
of the big toe The medial joint space of the big toe can be threaded
★ with a needle. I call this point Sp 2.5, which is halfway between Sp 2 and Sp 3. You should be able to palpate the obvious but small line of the joint that runs perpendicular to the Spleen meridian. Use a small-diameter 1 inch needle, and thread superficially along the line of the joint. It can be combined with other points such as Liv 2, Liv 2.5, or Liv 3, using electrical stimulation.

91 • Foot Pain *Pain of the First MTP Joint*

Clinical comments ★ I will frequently use electrical stimulation between the paired points Sp 3 + Liv 3 for the first half of the treatment, followed by one of the other point combinations discussed above. However, I rarely treat more than four of these local points – two paired point combinations – on any given treatment. Any more needles could be too strong and possibly aggravate symptoms.

COMPLEMENTARY PROCEDURES

- Topical applications (herbal liniments, plasters, etc.) may benefit.

- Applications of heat often benefit with chronic pain and inflammation of the first MTP joint.

- Mild distraction and compression of the joint can be self-performed by the patient. Along with gentle range of motion, these exercises may increase blood flow to the first MTP joint and enhance recovery.

- A supplement with glucosamine and chondroitin may be considered for nutritional support of the joint. While usually not dramatic, it may contribute to recovery.

- Homeopathic remedies are sometimes effective for pain and inflammation in chronic arthritis. Hyland's Arthritis Pain Formula (Standard Homeopathic Company) is one product to consider.

- A Chinese herbal formula specific to the signs and symptoms of the condition complements the acupuncture treatment of chronic arthritis.

★ While all techniques listed above have shown clinical relevance, the starred items are predictably effective for this specific injury. Consider them first in a treatment plan.

REFERENCES

[1] Corrigan & Maitland: *Practical Orthopaedic Medicine*. Butterworths & Co, United Kingdom, 1989 (pages 206-208).

[2] Dutton, M: *Orthopeadic Examination, Evaluation, and Intervention,* Second Edition. McGraw-Hill, USA, 2008 (page 1127).

5
Foot Pain

Metatarsal neuroma (Morton's neuroma)

Pain in the metatarsal region of the foot, on either the dorsal or plantar surfaces

A repetitive stress injury characterized by inflammation and irritation of the inter-digital nerves between the metatarsal bones.

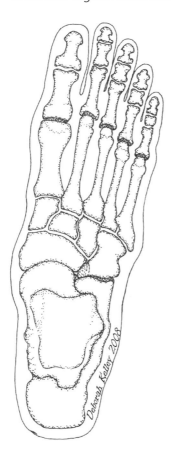

DIAGNOSIS & ASSESSMENT

Metatarsal neuroma, also known as Morton's neuroma, is a source of nagging and annoying foot pain. It may be seen in runners, hikers, and jumpers. Yet this condition is not confined to the athletic community. Like arthritis of the first metatarsal-phalanges joint, the lesion is relatively small and fixed in location, yet it impacts most lower-extremity activities. Some patients may report pain significant enough to be called "disabling." While my experience is that acupuncture is effective only 50 percent of the time, the ones who are helped are usually quite grateful.

Metatarsal neuroma is often described as swelling and inflammation of the inter-digital nerve located between the second and third, third and fourth, and occasionally the fourth and fifth metatarsals of the foot. Some sources suggest the inflammation leads to a thickening of the tissues around the nerve and its sheath, thus the term "neuroma" is a misnomer.[1] The more correct medical term would call this a perineural fibrosis. In any case, repetitive compression of nerves between the metatarsal spaces of the foot results in irritation and inflammation. And acupuncture treatment can certainly get precisely to the site, so it is worth a try.

Metatarsal neuroma usually presents with insidious onset, as this is a repetitive stress injury. The patient reports pain ranging from a dull ache to sharp and shooting. Sometimes it is burning and radiating, and may be accompanied by numbness and tingling. The location of the symptoms are experienced on the dorsal surface of the foot, but sometimes patients report the pain deep in the inter-metatarsal space, and also on the plantar region of the ball of the foot. The pain is clearly related to the amount of time spent in lower-extremity activities. It is also associated with tight and restrictive shoes. The practitioner should always refer the patient to a podiatrist or other practitioner for the necessary corrections. While pronation of the foot is considered the most likely cause, other biomechanical imbalances may contribute.

You may be able to diagnose metatarsal neuroma simply from the signs and symptoms. Palpation in the interspaces of the metatarsals on either the dorsal or plantar surfaces of the foot usually confirms the condition. You might also compress the metatarsals by squeezing the foot from the medial and lateral sides. This causes compression of the bone onto the inflamed nerve bundle and may reproduce the pain. However, you must rule out metatarsalgia, which presents with similar symptoms. Palpate for tenderness on (instead of between) the second, third, and occasionally the fourth metatarsal heads on the plantar surface of the foot. Metatarsalgia is an inflammatory condition of the metatarsal head or the joint capsule, and pain is reproduced with pressure on the bone. The pain of a Morton's neuroma is found in the metatarsal interspace between the bones.

One important last comment on foot pain: you must rule out a stress fracture. This is usually a hairline fracture on the shaft of one of the metatarsals. With this injury, the pain is palpable on the shaft of the bone from pressure on the dorsal side of the foot. The patient with a suspected stress fracture should immediately be referred to a podiatrist or an orthopedic physician. They require further assessment, and will need rest and immediate cessation of weight-bearing activities to avoid complications.

SUMMARY OF THE INJURY

Clinical Features
- Repetitive stress causes swelling and inflammation of the inter-digital nerve
- The 2nd/3rd and the 3rd/4th spaces are the two most common sites
- Pain may result from compression of the nerve bundle by the bony metatarsal heads.
- Excessive pronation and other lower-extremity biomechanical imbalances may be precipitating factors

Common Patient Complaints
- Pain in the metatarsal region of the foot, on either the dorsal or plantar surfaces
- Pain ranges from dull ache to sharp and shooting
- Pain may be accompanied by numbness and tingling
- Pain is aggravated during exercise and weight-bearing activities
- Symptoms relieved with rest, but pain returns again during or after exercise
- Pain is worsened by tight and restrictive shoes

Differentiation from Similar Injuries and Conditions
- Metatarsalgia, where pain is localized under the metatarsal head on the plantar surface
- Metatarsal stress fracture
- Inflammation of the numerous tendons in the region
- Rule out osteoarthritis as well as systemic inflammatory conditions such as gout and rheumatoid arthritis

Typical Medical Recommendations
- Some patients report that ice alleviates, others prefer heat.
- Anti-inflammatory medications
- Modify activity
  Decrease activities that aggravate the condition, especially during treatment. Cross train, including cycling, swimming, running in water.
- Biomechanics
  Correct pronation or supination with shoes and/or orthotics. Orthotics, padding, and taping are used to "open" the metatarsal spaces and to disperse weight away from the neuroma. Wearing shoes with wide toe boxes and avoiding high heels are sometimes necessary.
- Physical therapy
  Ultrasound, manual therapy, other physical therapy modalities.
- Orthopedic procedures
  Cortisone injection is sometimes used in the inflamed region, but must be limited because of possible atrophy to the plantar fat pad. Surgery is considered for the patient with chronic untreatable symptoms.

TREATMENT & TECHNIQUES

Overview: Metatarsal neuroma is most commonly diagnosed under the category of accident/trauma. It is usually a repetitive stress disorder due to the accumulation of micro-trauma. The injury is at the level of the nerves, the tendons, and the bone. There is qi and blood stagnation in the channels and collaterals. The Stomach meridian follows the 2nd/3rd metatarsal interspace. The Gall Bladder meridian follows the 4th/5th interspace. There is no primary meridian in the 3rd/4th interspace. Internal organ imbalances are not clear.

Prognosis: Treat twice a week for three weeks, then re-evaluate. Not all patients with metatarsal neuroma respond to acupuncture. If there are not beneficial results after six treatments, I usually refer the patient for other modalities.

STEP ONE: INITIAL TREATMENT

Choose among these four techniques, carefully determining if there is an immediate decrease in pain or an increase in range of motion.

Technique #1: **The Tendino-Muscle Meridians**

St 45, GB 44   Bleeding technique
St 45 is used for pain in the 2nd/3rd metatarsal interspace. GB 44 is used for pain in the 4th/5th interspace. The jing-well points should be tried, but they rarely provide lasting relief.

Technique #2: **Opposite Side (contra-lateral)**

Corresponding points on the opposite (unaffected) side may be considered; however, treatment to the affected side is usually preferred.

Technique #3: **Opposite Extremity (upper/lower)**

Corresponding points on the opposite extremity may be considered; however, treatment to the affected extremity is usually preferred.

Technique #4: **Empirical Points**

No well known empirical points for metatarsal neuroma.

96 • Foot Pain *Metatarsal Neuroma*

STEP TWO: MERIDIANS & MICROSYSTEMS

Choose among these four techniques, selecting points that are appropriate for the signs and symptoms of the patient.

Technique #5: **The Shu-Stream Point Combination**

St 43 affected side + LI 3 opposite side
GB 41 (or GB 42) affected side + SJ 3 opposite side
GB 42 is often more sensitive than GB 41, and should be considered as an alternative shu-stream point.

Technique #6: **Traditional Point Categories**

★ Consider the following he-sea points:

In the 2nd/3rd interspace	St 36
In the 3rd/4th interspace	*Ahshi* point between St 36 and GB 34
In the 4th/5th interspace	GB 34

There may be other points on the affected meridians proximal to the foot. Palpate for point sensitivity.

Technique #7: **The Extraordinary Meridians**

GB 41 + SJ 5   Activate the Dai mai
Compensating for foot pain sometimes results in secondary hip and gluteal imbalances, which may be considered Dai mai pathology.

Technique #8: **Microsystems**

Auricular Therapy
Local: Foot (French), foot (Chinese)
Systemic points for pain: Shen men, Thalamus, Adrenal, Endocrine

STEP THREE: INTERNAL ORGAN IMBALANCES

Choose appropriate points to treat internal organ imbalances that may contribute to the injury or pain syndrome.

Technique #9: **Qi, Blood, and the Zang-fu Organs**

Metatarsal neuroma is a repetitive stress injury and internal organ imbalances are usually not a factor in treatment.

STEP FOUR: THE SITE OF INJURY

Choose among the local and adjacent points at the site of injury. Points may be determined by palpation, orthopedic testing, and analysis of the signs and symptoms of the patient.

Technique #10:
The metatarsal interspaces

Local and Adjacent Points

Local treatment in the metatarsal interspaces is simple and direct. Once you have determined which metatarsal space is involved, treatment can be directed in the zone distal to the junction of the two metatarsals. It extends as far distally as the Ba feng points in the webs of the toes. In addition, both the dorsal and the plantar surfaces of the foot can be needled. Consider the following variations:

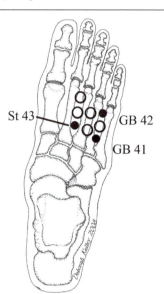

● – *Acupuncture points*
○ – *Point variations*

Point combinations

★ **1. Proximal and distal to the site of the neuroma**
The proximal point is just distal to the junction of the metatarsals. The distal point is .5 cun proximal to the margin of the web.
In the 2nd/3rd interspace   St 43 + St 44
In the 3rd/4th interspace   *Ahshi* points
In the 4th/5th interspace   GB 41 + GB 43
Electrical stimulation between these two points, which are essentially slightly "above" and "below" the inflamed nerve, often benefits.

★ **2. Direct needling into the neuroma**
It is not really possible to know precisely where the focal point of nerve inflammation exists. Palpation may reveal the most sensitive zone, which is usually about the midpoint of the metatarsal interspace. I usually use two paired points, with electrical stimulation.
In the 2nd/3rd interspace   St 43.5
In the 3rd/4th interspace   Midpoint of the interspace
In the 4th/5th interspace   GB 42

★ **3. Direct needling into the neuroma from the dorsal and plantar surfaces**
With this technique, the *ahshi* point in the metatarsal space on the dorsum of the foot is coupled with the *ahshi* point from the plantar surface. As such, this is a variation of the "through and through" technique.

Electrical stimulation between these points should be considered. However, needling the plantar surface of the foot is no easy task!

Three depths of insertion Consider three depths of needle insertion during a typical 30-minute treatment. For the first 10 minutes, the needles are in a superficial depth of about .3 inches. For the second 10 minutes, the needles are inserted deeper, to an intermediate depth of about .6 inches. For the final 10 minutes, the needles are inserted to the deepest position, approaching 1 inch. Use electrical stimulation between the two paired needles for each of the three depths. Keep in mind that these depths are relative to patient size, and slow needle insertion to the intermediate and deep levels should be used to avoid irritation to the nerve bundle.

COMPLEMENTARY PROCEDURES

- Alternate ice and heat, as this condition is "neither hot (re) nor cold (han)".
- Nutritional supplementation with Vitamin B6 (50 mg, two times daily) may benefit.
- As stated earlier, the importance of orthotics must be emphasized. They are designed to "open" the metatarsal interspaces, thereby reducing the mechanical irritation to the nerve bundle.

★ While all techniques listed above have shown clinical relevance, the starred items are predictably effective for this specific injury. Consider them first in a treatment plan.

REFERENCES

[1] Dutton, M: *Orthopeadic Examination, Evaluation, and Intervention,* Second Edition. McGraw-Hill, USA, 2008 (page 1145).

Notes

6
Leg Pain

Shin Splints (Anterior Tibial Stress Syndrome)

Pain and tenderness along the anterior lateral aspect of the leg just lateral to the tibia

A repetitive stress injury characterized by strain or inflammation of the anterior tibialis or other anterior compartment muscles of the leg. The site of injury may be the muscle, the tendon, or at the attachment to the periosteum and bone.

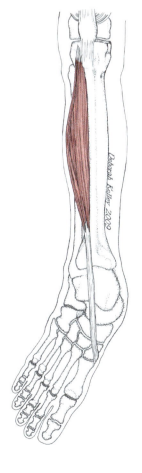

DIAGNOSIS & ASSESSMENT

Shin splints is the common term for anterior tibial stress syndrome. It is a frequent sports injury, as it comprises approximately 60 percent of all leg pain injuries.[1] In this chapter, we will cover anterior shin splints, with a separate discussion of the medial compartment injury in the chapter that follows on page 111.

Shin splints are generally considered a strain to one or more of the anterior compartment muscles. This includes the anterior tibialis, the extensor digitorum longus, and the extensor hallucis longus. The injury is characterized by pain and tenderness along the anterior lateral aspect of the leg. The pain ranges from a dull ache to sharp, depending on the extent of the injury. The pain pattern follows precisely the pathway of the Stomach meridian on the leg. It is frequently aggravated from running, with increased speed and hills often associated with the onset, but other lower-extremity activities can also strain these muscles. I once experienced anterior shin splints from 10 days of walking on cobblestone streets in Europe, and it followed the predictable pattern of being relieved with rest, with the pain returning upon activity.

The anterior tibialis is the muscle most likely involved in this repetitive stress injury. It is interesting that the precise etiology of this condition is debated, with sources varying as to where the primary site of injury exists.

Regardless of the eliology, shin splints usually produces numerous *ahshi* points lateral to the anterior border of the tibia in the upper half of the leg. This would be from the level of St 36 as far inferior as St 38 or St 39.

The differing causes of anterior tibial stress syndrome can be summarized as follows:

1. Strain of the anterior tibialis muscle. This may occur anywhere along the course of the muscle, the muscle-tendon junction, and the tendon.
2. Strain of one of the other anterior compartment muscles.
3. Irritation and inflammation of the tendon at its attachment to the medial tibia, resulting in periostitis. Actual tearing of the muscle or tendon along its attachment to the bone is also possible.[2] It is not uncommon to use the term "tendo-periostitis" which may include both of these causes.

You can test the anterior compartment muscles by placing your hand on the dorsal surface of the foot. The patient dorsiflexes the ankle (flexes toes and foot upwards) while you resist the motion. Pain with resisted dorsiflexion is common with anterior shin splints. You might even try passive stretching of the muscle by placing the patient's foot into plantar-flexion (toe pointing). This stretches the anterior compartment muscles and may be uncomfortable, helping to confirm the diagnosis.

Anterior tibialis tendonitis is often grouped into shin splints, but with this condition, the pain is in the lower (distal) third of the lateral leg. This is from the muscle-tendon junction to the foot where the tendon attaches. The pain is generally along the Stomach meridian, starting at the area of St 39 and continuing distally to and beyond the ankle at St 41 and Liv 4. Some cases of this tendonitis will have such pronounced inflammation that the patient has crepitus – a "squeaky" feeling in the lower anterior leg with foot movements. Place your palm above the ankle and have the patient dorsiflex and plantar-flex the ankle. Crepitus due to inflammation will be pronounced and quite apparent with palpation. Anterior tibial tendonitis will also be painful on resisted dorsiflexion.

I received a phone call last year from an acupuncture colleague who was in the emergency room with her son, a soccer star in the state of Colorado. He had injured his ankle during a tournament earlier in the day. I went to the ER and found them waiting in a treatment room for the physician. So I had a quick opportunity to examine the ankle and could not find anything pointing to a sprain or other foot injury. It was the inquiry about the onset of the event that was revealing. The patient was about to kick the ball, only to be abruptly stopped by a player's foot from the opposing team. And you have to understand this kid kicks the ball very hard! With his ankle in dorsiflexion, stopping that movement caused significant strain on the muscle. Simply testing resisted dorsiflexion confirmed the anterior compartment was affected. Even though the injury had occurred just several hours before, crepitus could be felt in the tendinous area above the ankle, even with mild active dorsiflexion.

I was confident with the diagnosis, and when the physician finally came to the room and examined, he concurred. All that was left was an X-ray to assure there was no injury to the bone from the trauma. Five or six days of acupuncture, rest, ice, and some topical Chinese herbal liniments, our young star was back on the soccer field.

But that's not all! Before leaving the hospital, the emergency room physician gave a warning about anterior compartment syndrome, a condition that the acupuncture practitioner must not overlook. It has similar pain along the Stomach meridian of the lateral leg, but definitely needs to be differentiated from simple shin splints. The pain is usually more severe, inflammation is pronounced and the leg may feel very "full" and distended. As this condition progresses, neurologic symptoms may arise from pressure on the deep peroneal nerve, which runs in this muscle compartment. If severe pain, numbness and tingling, and loss of sensation or movement develop, immediate medical attention is necessary. A surgical compartment release may be performed in order to prevent permanent tissue damage to the lower extremity. If there is any doubt, send the patient to the emergency room for assessment, as this is not a wait-and-see medical condition.

Tibial stress fracture is the other complication that should be mentioned. The symptoms may resemble shin splints, but there is point tenderness on the boney aspect of the tibia. It is sometimes difficult to differentiate in the clinic, and only a bone scan is reliable. Failure to assess this condition, however, is problematic. With tibial stress fracture, modifying activity is not good enough. The patient must cease running or other weight-bearing activities until the fracture is healed. If in doubt, refer your patient to an orthopedic physician.

As a final note, correction of pronation and other lower-extremity biomechanical imbalances need to be assessed. This should not be ignored, and will complement the acupuncture treatments by reducing the repetitive stress on the tissues.

SUMMARY OF THE INJURY

Clinical Features	• Repetitive stress causes inflammation of the anterior tibialis or one of the other anterior group muscles, tendons, or their attachments to the periosteum • Overuse injury is usually from increased intensity of walking or running • Sudden increases in speed and hill running are associated with onset • May have pain with resisted dorsiflexion of the ankle • Pain upon palpation along the lateral border of the tibia, and possibly along the anterior compartment muscle group • May be caused by excessive pronation and other lower-extremity biomechanical imbalances
Common Patient Complaints	• Pain and tenderness along the anterior lateral aspect of the leg • Pain may radiate toward the ankle • Patient reports pain is aggravated during exercise, and relieved with rest
Differentiation from Similar Injuries and Conditions	• Anterior compartment syndrome • Tibial stress fracture
Typical Medical Recommendations	• Ice is typically used when acute. • Anti-inflammatory medications • Modify activity *Decrease activities that aggravate the condition, especially during treatment. Cross-train, including cycling, swimming and running in water. For runners, a decrease in mileage and intensity, especially hills, is essential.* • Stretching *Stretching of the anterior compartment muscles* • Biomechanics *Correct pronation or supination with shoes and/or orthotics. Other lower-extremity biomechanical imbalances may need to be assessed.* • Physical therapy *Ultrasound, deep-friction massage, and other physical therapy modalities.* • Orthopedic evaluation *Rule out anterior compartment syndrome, where surgery is necessary to release compartmental pressure and prevent tissue damage to the lower extremity.*

TREATMENT & TECHNIQUES

Overview: Anterior shin splints is most commonly diagnosed under the category of accident/trauma. This is usually a repetitive stress disorder due to the accumulation of micro-trauma. However, shin splints may occur as an acute strain. The injury is at the level of the muscles, tendons, and bones. There is qi and blood stagnation in the channels and collaterals. This case is clearly Stomach meridian pathology. Internal organ imbalances of the Stomach and Spleen sometimes contribute.

Prognosis: Treat twice a week for three weeks, then re-evaluate. Most cases without complications have good results within six treatments. With chronic cases, continue treatment at least once weekly after the first three-week period.

STEP ONE: INITIAL TREATMENT

Choose among these four techniques, carefully determining if there is an immediate decrease in pain or an increase in range of motion.

Technique #1: **The Tendino-Muscle Meridians**

 St 45   Bleeding technique
The Stomach tendino-muscle meridian definitely treats anterior tibialis symptoms. I start all treatments of anterior shin splints by bleeding St 45.

Technique #2: **Opposite Side (contra-lateral)**

Ahshi point(s)   On the opposite (unaffected) side
Palpate for point sensitivity along the lateral border of the tibia.

St 36 to St 39   Corresponding points on the opposite (unaffected) side

Liv 5, Liv 6   Corresponding points on the opposite (unaffected) side

Technique #3: **Opposite Extremity (upper/lower)**

 LI 8 to LI 11   Yang ming corresponding points on the opposite extremity

In general, treat upper/lower corresponding points on the opposite (unaffected) side when acute, and the affected side when chronic. Use palpation to assist in this choice.

Technique #4: **Empirical Points**

No well known clinically effective empirical points for shin splints.

STEP TWO: MERIDIANS & MICROSYSTEMS

Choose among these four techniques, selecting points that are appropriate for the signs and symptoms of the patient.

Technique #5: **The Shu-Stream Point Combination**

★ St 43 affected side + LI 3 opposite side
One or both of these are often point sensitive.

Technique #6: **Traditional Point Categories**

★ Other Stomach meridian points should be palpated, although the jing-well and the shu-stream points are frequently the most clinically effective. Consider the following:

St 41	Jing-river point, "fire" point
St 44	Ying-spring point, "water" point
GB 34	Hui-influential point of tendons

Technique #7: **The Extraordinary Meridians**

GB 41 + SJ 5   Activate the Dai mai
Shin splints could possibly originate from hip and gluteal imbalances, which may be considered Dai mai pathology.

Technique #8: **Microsystems**

Auricular Therapy
Local: Between the knee to the ankle (French and Chinese), lumbar spine
Zang-fu points: Stomach, Liver
Systemic points for pain: Shen men, Thalamus, Adrenal, Endocrine

STEP THREE: INTERNAL ORGAN IMBALANCES

Choose appropriate points to treat internal organ imbalances that may contribute to the injury or pain syndrome.

Technique #9: **Qi, Blood, and the Zang-fu Organs**

Shin splints are a repetitive stress injury, and therefore, internal organ imbalances are not necessarily causative. However, there are several zang-fu syndromes that may contribute to the condition:

Spleen and Stomach imbalances Spleen and Stomach qi deficiency

Spleen and Stomach imbalances are surprisingly common in patients with acute as well as chronic and recurring anterior shin splints. This is not surprising considering the course of the Stomach meridian. Assessment should be fairly straightforward for the practitioner.

Note: Consider St 41 (the tonification point) as an alternative to the more traditionally used point St 36. A more detailed explanation can be found on page 354.

Liver imbalances Liver qi stagnation, Liver yin deficiency, and Liver blood deficiency

Liver imbalances may result in the susceptibility of the tendons to inflammation and repetitive stress injury. Consider the following:

Liv 3	Yuan-source point; supports the Liver in its function of controlling the tendons and muscles
GB 34	Hui-influential point of tendons

Consider GB 34 on the affected side and Liv 3 on the opposite side.

Points should be determined by the practitioner from both palpation and analysis of the signs and symptoms of the patient.

STEP FOUR: THE SITE OF INJURY

Choose among the local and adjacent points at the site of injury. Points may be determined by palpation, orthopedic testing, and analysis of the signs and symptoms of the patient.

Technique #10: **Local and Adjacent Points**

The anterior tibialis muscle The origin of the anterior tibialis muscle is at the lateral condyle of the tibia and along a broad zone of the upper half of the lateral tibia.[3] Palpation of the upper half of the anterior lateral leg should produce numerous *ahshi* points lateral to the anterior border of the tibia. This would be from the level of St 36 as far inferior as St 38 or St 39. Choose one or two sets of paired points based solely upon palpation. Thread these points with 1.5 inch needles at a 45-degree angle in an inferior (distal) direction. These needles are placed just lateral to the anterior crest of the tibia, and about .5 cun medial to the Stomach meridian. Deep needles approach the region of the tendinous origin of the anterior tibialis. With deep insertion, inflammation at the level of the periosteum may be treated. I always use electrical stimulation between these paired points.

● – St 36
○ – Ahshi points lateral to the anterior border of the tibia

107 • Leg Pain *Anterior Shin Splints*

The belly of the anterior tibialis **St 36 and the extraordinary point Lanweixue**

St 36 is in the muscle belly of the tibialis anterior, distal to the portion of the muscle that attaches to the lateral condyle of the tibia. *Lanweixue*, located 2 cun inferior to St 36, is the motor point of the muscle.[4] These two points may help release the anterior tibialis and assist in healing strain and tendonitis.

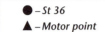

● – St 36
▲ – Motor point

Threading the tendon of the anterior tibialis

If the point tenderness is more pronounced in the lower (distal) third of the leg, anterior tibialis tendonitis should be suspected. This is the zone of the muscle-tendon junction and the tendon as it courses distally to its attachment. Choose a set of paired points based solely upon palpation. Thread these points with 1.5 inch needles at an oblique to transverse angle in an inferior (distal) direction. This angle should be close to 30 degrees. These needles are placed just lateral to the anterior crest of the tibia, and are threaded alongside the palpable tendon. Needling too far laterally, directly into the tendon, may aggravate the existing inflammation.

The attachment of the anterior tibialis

Liv 4 is located anterior to the medial malleolus on the medial side of the the anterior tibialis tendon. A perpendicular or slightly lateral insertion will allow the needle to reach the under surface of the tendon.

St 41 is located between the other two anterior compartment muscles: the extensor hallicus longus and the extensor digitorum longus. Needle St 41 at a 45-degree angle toward the toes, which allows the needle to glide between the two tendons. For this case, you could choose an alternate location of St 41, which would be slightly medial to the text location. That places it between the tendons of the anterior tibialis and the extensor hallicus longus.

Adjacent points **Sp 4, Kid 2**

These two points are adjacent to the attachment of the anterior tibialis on the medial aspect of the foot. While this muscle so clearly follows the Yang ming pathway along the leg, the attachment on the yin side of the foot is a bit tricky!

COMPLEMENTARY PROCEDURES

- When acute, ice massage along the anterior border of the tibia may alleviate pain and reduce inflammation.
- Topical applications (herbal liniments, plasters, etc.) may benefit.
- Massage of the entire anterior compartment muscle group may benefit.
- Small Japanese-style retainer needles in *ahshi* points along the anterior compartment may be considered.

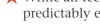 While all techniques listed above have shown clinical relevance, the starred items are predictably effective for this specific injury. Consider them first in a treatment plan.

REFERENCES

[1] Dutton, M: *Orthopeadic Examination, Evaluation, and Intervention,* Second Edition. McGraw-Hill, USA, 2008 (page 1144).

[2] O'Donoghue, DH: *Treatment of Injuries to Athletes,* Third Edition. W. B. Saunders Co, Philadelphia, 1976 (pages 686-687).

[3] Hollinshead, WH: *Textbook of Anatomy,* Third Edition. Harper & Row, Maryland, 1974 (pages 443-445).

[4] Callison, M: *Motor Point Index*. AcuSport Seminar Series LLC, San Diego, 2007 (page 130).

Notes

7
Leg Pain

Shin Splints (Medial Tibial Stress Syndrome)

Pain and tenderness along the medial aspect of the leg at the medial border of the tibia

A repetitive stress injury characterized by strain or inflammation of the posterior tibialis or other medial compartment muscles of the leg. The site of injury may be the muscle, the tendon, or at the attachment to the periosteum and bone.

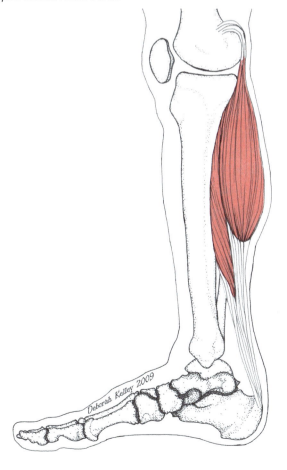

DIAGNOSIS & ASSESSMENT

Shin splints is the common term for both anterior and medial tibial stress syndrome. In this chapter, we will cover medial shin splints, with a separate discussion of the anterior compartment injury on page 101. Shin splints is a frequent sports injury, as it comprises approximately 60 percent of all leg pain injuries.[1] The practitioner needs to be well-versed in its assessment and treatment.

Medial shin splints is considered a strain to one or more of the medial compartment muscles. Most sources consider the posterior tibialis muscle as the most probable site. The injury is characterized by pain and tenderness along the medial border of the tibia. The pain ranges from a dull ache to sharp, depending on the extent of the injury. This follows the pathways of both the Spleen and the Liver meridians. It is frequently aggravated from running, with increased speed and hills often associated with the onset, but other lower-extremity activities can also strain these muscles.

It is interesting that the precise etiology of this condition is debated, with sources varying as to where the primary site of injury exists. The differing causes of medial tibial stress syndrome can be summarized as follows:

1. Strain of the posterior tibialis muscle. This may occur anywhere along the course of the muscle, the muscle-tendon junction, and the tendon.

2. Strain of one of the other medial compartment muscles

3. Irritation and inflammation of the tendon at its attachment to the medial tibia, resulting in periostitis. Actual tearing of the muscle or tendon along its attachment to the bone is also possible.[2] It is not uncommon to use the term "tendo-periostitis" which may include both of these causes.

4. Recent information has identified the fascial insertion of the medial soleus of the posterior group as a possible source of pain.[3]

Medial shin splints usually produce numerous *ahshi* points at or slightly posterior to the medial border of the tibia. This would be from the level of Sp 9 as far inferior as Sp 6, and would also include the zone of Liv 5 and Liv 6. There may be palpable "lumps and bumps" from the inflammatory process if the case is chronic.

Like the anterior tibialis muscle, the posterior tibialis assists with dorsiflexion. You can test this action by placing your hand on the dorsal surface of the foot. The patient dorsiflexes the ankle (flexes toes and the foot upwards) while you resist the motion.Pain with resisted dorsiflexion may be found with medial shin splints. However, inversion of the foot is probably more important. To test this, the patient inverts their foot, best described by turning the plantar surface of the foot inward. The practitioner holds the whole foot to resist the motion. Pain with resisted inversion indicates involvement of the posterior tibialis.

Posterior tibialis tendonitis is often grouped into shin splints, but with this condition, the pain is closer to the ankle. The site of inflammation is the distal aspect of the tendon as it wraps around the medial malleolus. Or it may present in the region of its attachment in the medial and plantar surface of the foot. Pain can be found near the points Kid 7, Kid 6, and Kid 2. Sometimes this injury is described as a tenosynovitis, which can be easily palpated inferior to the medial malleolus. Some cases will have such pronounced inflammation that crepitus – a "squeaky" feeling – may also be felt.

112 • Leg Pain *Medial Shin Splints*

Although much less common than anterior compartment syndrome, you need to rule out medial compartment syndrome. If there are neurologic symptoms and pronouned pain, refer the patient for immediate assessment. Tibial stress fracture is a complication that should also be mentioned. The symptoms may resemble shin splints, but there is point tenderness on the bony aspect of the tibia. It is sometimes difficult to differentiate in the clinic, and only a bone scan is reliable. Failure to assess this condition, however, is problematic. With tibial stress fracture, modifying activity is not good enough. The patient must cease running or other weight-bearing activities until the fracture is healed. If in doubt, refer your patient to an orthopedic physician.

As a final note, correction of pronation and other lower-extremity biomechanical imbalances need to be assessed. This should not be ignored, and will complement the acupuncture treatments by reducing the repetitive stress on the tissues.

SUMMARY OF THE INJURY

Clinical Features
- Repetitive stress causes inflammation of the one of the medial group muscles, tendons or their attachments to the periosteum
- Some studies suggest the medial head of the gastrocnemius as a possible source
- Overuse injury is usually from increased intensity of walking or running
- Onset often associated with increased speed and hills
- May have pain with resisted plantar-flexion
- Pain upon palpation along the medial border of the tibia, and possibly along the medial compartment muscle group
- Excessive pronation and other lower-extremity biomechanical imbalances may be precipitating factors

Common Patient Complaints
- Pain, tenderness and a feeling of tightness along the medial border of the tibia
- Pain may radiate toward the inside of the ankle
- Patient reports pain is aggravated during exercise, and relieved with rest
- After rest, pain returns again during or after exercise

Differentiation from Similar Injuries and Conditions
- Tibial stress fracture
- Tarsal tunnel syndrome
- Complete rupture of the posterior tibialis tendon
- Medial compartment syndrome

Typical Medical Recommendations
- Ice is typically used when acute.
- Anti-inflammatory medications
- Modify activity
  Cross-train, including cycling, swimming and running in water. For runners, a decrease in mileage and intensity, especially hills, is essential.
- Stretching
  Stretching of the medial compartment muscles
- Biomechanics
  Correct pronation or supination with shoes and/or orthotics. Other lower-extremity biomechanical imbalances may need to be assessed.
- Physical therapy
  Ultrasound, deep-friction massage, and other physical therapy modalities.
- Orthopedic evaluation
  Although much less common than anterior compartment syndrome, rule out medial compartment syndrome. A small percentage of patients have an accessory navicular bone (two navicular bones!), which contributes to the condition as it affects foot pronation as well as the attachment of the posterior tibialis tendon.

TREATMENT & TECHNIQUES

Overview: Medial shin splints are most commonly diagnosed under the category of accident/trauma. This is usually a repetitive stress disorder due to the accumulation of micro-trauma. However, occasionally it may occur as an acute strain. The injury is at the level of the muscles, tendons, and bones. There is qi and blood stagnation in the channels and collaterals. This case is usually Spleen and Liver meridian pathology. Internal organ imbalances of the Spleen and Liver sometimes contribute.

Prognosis: Treat twice a week for three weeks, then re-evaluate. Most cases without complications have good results within six treatments. With chronic cases, continue treatment at least once weekly after the first three-week period.

STEP ONE: INITIAL TREATMENT

Choose among these four techniques, carefully determining if there is an immediate decrease in pain or an increase in range of motion.

Technique #1: **The Tendino-Muscle Meridians**

 Sp 1, Liv 1   Bleeding technique
Bleeding Liv 1 and Sp 1 may benefit pain along the medial border of the tibia. There may be contra-indications for these yin meridian points.

Technique #2: **Opposite Side (contra-lateral)**

Ahshi **point(s)**   On the opposite (unaffected) side
Palpate for point sensitivity along the medial border of the tibia.

Sp 6 to Sp 9   Corresponding points on the opposite (unaffected) side

Liv 5, Liv 6   Corresponding points on the opposite (unaffected) side

Technique #3: **Opposite Extremity (upper/lower)**

Lu 6   Tai yin corresponding point on the opposite extremity.

In general, treat upper/lower corresponding points on the opposite (unaffected) side when acute, and the affected side when chronic. Use palpation to assist in this choice.

Technique #4: **Empirical Points**

No well known clinically effective empirical points for shin splints.

STEP TWO: MERIDIANS & MICROSYSTEMS

Choose among these four techniques, selecting points that are appropriate for the signs and symptoms of the patient.

Technique #5: **The Shu-Stream Point Combination**

Liv 3 affected side + P 6 opposite side
Sp 3 affected side + Lu 9 opposite side
There may be contra-indications for these yin meridian points.

Technique #6: **Traditional Point Categories**

★ Palpation may assist in your choice of Spleen and Liver meridian points.

Sp 4	Luo-connecting point
Sp 5	Sedation point
Liv 2	Sedation point
GB 34	Hui-influential point of tendons

Technique #7: **The Extraordinary Meridians**

GB 41 + SJ 5   Activate the Dai mai
Shin splints could possibly originate from hip and gluteal imbalances, which may be considered Dai mai pathology.

Technique #8: **Microsystems**

Auricular Therapy
Local: Between the knee to the ankle (French and Chinese), lumbar spine
Zang-fu points: Spleen, Liver
Systemic points for pain: Shen men, Thalamus, Adrenal, Endocrine

Wrist-ankle Acupuncture
Wrist-ankle acupuncture may be considered, as the site of injury often covers multiple meridians. Use the zones on the medial surface of the leg.[4]
Lower #1   The medial surface of the leg
Located 3 cun proximal to the medial malleolus, on the anterior border of the achilles tendon. This zone approximates the Kidney meridian.
Lower #2   The medial surface of the leg
Located 3 cun proximal to the medial malleolus, on the posterior border of the tibia. This zone approximates the Spleen meridian, and includes the point Sp 6.
Lower #3   The medial surface of the leg
Located 3 cun proximal to the medial malleolus, along the tibia, posterior to its anterior border.

STEP THREE: INTERNAL ORGAN IMBALANCES

Choose appropriate points to treat internal organ imbalances that may contribute to the injury or pain syndrome.

Technique #9: **Qi, Blood, and the Zang-fu Organs**

Shin splints are a repetitive stress injury, and therefore, internal organ imbalances are not necessarily causative. However, there are several zang-fu syndromes that may contribute to the condition:

Spleen and Stomach Spleen and Stomach qi deficiency
imbalances Spleen and Stomach imbalances are surprisingly common
★ in patients with acute as well as chronic and recurring medial shin splints. This is not surprising considering the course of the Spleen meridian. This should be fairly straightforward for the practitioner to assess.

Note: Consider St 41 (the tonification point) as an alternative to the more traditionally used point St 36. A more detailed explanation can be found on page 354.

Liver imbalances Liver qi stagnation, Liver yin deficiency, and Liver blood deficiency
Liver imbalances may result in the susceptibility of the tendons to inflammation and repetitive stress injury. Consider the following:

Liv 3	Yuan-source point; supports the Liver in its function of controlling the tendons and muscles
GB 34	Hui-influential point of tendons

Consider GB 34 on the affected side and Liv 3 on the opposite side.

Points should be determined by the practitioner from both palpation and analysis of the signs and symptoms of the patient.

117 • Leg Pain *Medial Shin Splints*

STEP FOUR: THE SITE OF INJURY

Choose among the local and adjacent points at the site of injury. Points may be determined by palpation, orthopedic testing, and analysis of the signs and symptoms of the patient.

Technique #10: **Local and Adjacent Points**

The posterior tibialis muscle

The origin of the posterior tibialis muscle is along a broad zone of the upper half of the medial tibia. It also attaches on the fibula and the interrosseus membrane that spans the fibula and tibia. Thus, deep needling may be necessary to get to the site of stagnation. Palpation of the medial border of the tibia should produce numerous *ahshi* points, and as stated above, there could be "lumps and bumps" from the inflammatory process. This would be from the level of Sp 9 as far inferior as Sp 6. It could also include the zone of Liv 5 and Liv 6 on the flat surface of the tibia itself. If recent research proves correct, and the medial border periostitis is from the soleus muscle, these points will still suffice.

● – Sp 9 (superior)
Sp 6 (inferior)
○ – Ahshi points posterior to the medial border of the tibia

Needle technique

Choose one or two sets of paired points based solely upon palpation. Treat these points with 1.5 inch needles, starting from a perpendicular orientation. The needles are placed just posterior to the medial border of the tibia. You may need to vary from the perpendicular starting-point, depending on the specific anatomy of the patient. With deep insertion, the needles approach the region of the tendinous origin of the posterior tibialis. Deep insertion also treats inflammation at the level of the periosteum. I always use electrical stimulation between these paired points.

Ahshi points in the muscle

The muscle belly of the posterior tibialis may be more difficult to locate because of the other muscles of the medial group and those of the more superficial calf. However, palpation along the medial aspect of the leg may reveal *ahshi* points, as well as taut bands. These points are located about one inch posterior to the medial border of the tibia, from the level of Sp 6 up to about Sp 8. Needle with perpendicular insertion from .5 to 1 inch.

Generally, I recommend treatment to both the muscle attachment (with deep insertion) and the *ahshi* points in the muscle (more superficial insertion) outlined above.

The soleus muscle The role of the soleus muscle may be an important adjacent treatment in medial tibial stress syndrome. *Ahshi* points in the calf may be needled to release the gastrocnemius and soleus muscle groups. Look for these inferior to the popliteal fossa at Bl 40 and superior to Bl 57. The motor point of the soleus is halfway between Bl 56 and Bl 57.[5] This is also the approximate location of an important trigger point of the muscle.[6]

X – Trigger points
▲ – Motor points

Tendonitis of the posterior tibialis

Threading the tendon of the posterior tibialis
If swelling and tenderness is pronounced along the posterior tibialis as it wraps around the medial malleoulus, tendonitis should be suspected. This is the region of Kid 6. A pair of transverse needles threaded along the sides of the tendon and its sheath may help with inflammation. Palpation and the local anatomy will dictate location and technique. Consider electrical stimulation between these points, and be careful to avoid needling into the tendon and sheath.

The attachment of the posterior tibialis

Sp 4, Kid 2
These two points are adjacent to the attachment of the posterior tibialis on the medial aspect of the foot. Its attachment is to the navicular bone, several tarsals, and two metatarsals on the plantar surface of the foot. So, Sp 4 and Kid 2 are close, but not perfect.

Adjacent points

Sp 6 + Sp 9
Often, medial shin splints present with pain inferior to Sp 9 and superior to Sp 6. Electrical stimulation between Sp 6 and Sp 9 is a possible point combination, using the technique of "above and below".

COMPLEMENTARY PROCEDURES

- When acute, ice massage along the medial border of the tibia may alleviate pain and reduce inflammation.

- Topical applications (herbal liniments, plasters, etc.) may benefit.

- Massage of the entire medial compartment muscle group may benefit.

- Small Japanese-style retainer needles in *ahshi* points along the medial border of the tibia may be considered.

★ While all techniques listed above have shown clinical relevance, the starred items are predictably effective for this specific injury. Consider them first in a treatment plan.

REFERENCES

[1] Dutton, M: *Orthopeadic Examination, Evaluation, and Intervention,* Second Edition. McGraw-Hill, USA, 2008 (page 1144).

[2] O'Donoghue, DH: *Treatment of Injuries to Athletes,* Third Edition. W. B. Saunders Co, Philadelphia, 1976 (pages 686-687).

[3] Dutton, M: *Orthopeadic Examination, Evaluation, and Intervention,* Second Edition. McGraw-Hill, USA, 2008 (page 1144).

[4] Matsumoto & Birch: *Extraordinary Vessels.* Paradigm Publishers, Massachusetts, 1986 (pages 182-188). *Note: Dr. Zhang Xin Shu's* Wrist Ankle Acupuncture (Wan Ke Zhen) *is the source quoted in the above text.*

[5] Callison, M: *Motor Point Index.* AcuSport Seminar Series LLC, San Diego, 2007 (page 131).

[6] Travell & Simons: *Myofascial Pain and Dysfunction: The Trigger Point Manual, Volume 2 (The Lower Extremities).* Williams & Wilkins, Philadelphia, 1992 (page 429).

8
Anterior Knee Pain
Patello-femoral Joint Dysfunction

Pain in the anterior knee in the region of the patella and the patello-femoral groove

A repetitive stress injury characterized by inflammation and irritation of the undersurface of the patella. This may progress to chondromalacia or anterior compartment arthritis.

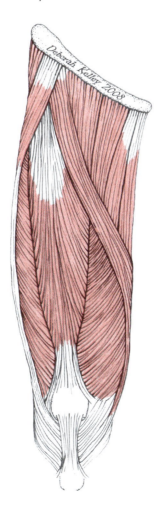

DIAGNOSIS & ASSESSMENT

Knee pain from patello-femoral joint dysfunction is the most common knee disorder encountered by the orthopedic physician.[1] Over the next 10 years, I am convinced that the aging population will seek acupuncture in record numbers to relieve this chronic pain syndrome and to stay active and avoid surgery. Some sources simply call this condition osteoarthritis, and suggest that 33 percent of the population between the ages of 63 and 94 years are affected by it in one of the three compartments of the knee.[2] Runners, jumpers, and cyclists are typical patients. However, patellar pain can be seen in all ages and with all levels of activity, even with moderate levels of walking and hiking. Understanding the complexity of the causes and the available western treatments is important knowledge to add to the relatively simple and straightforward treatments of acupuncture.

The patient usually complains of anterior knee pain in the region of the patella. The patellar tendon may be involved, which is fairly easy for the practitioner to spot. This common type of tendonitis is discussed separately on page 133. For patello-femoral joint syndrome, pain may be reported in the central area of the patella. The patient often describes it as "under the knee cap". It may also be felt along both the medial and lateral borders of the patella. Pain walking up or down stairs is one of the most likely confirming symptoms, so make sure you inquire. It may also occur with squatting and kneeling. Aggravation upon rising from a seated position, sometimes referred to as the "movie theater sign", occurs after prolonged sitting. There may be crepitus or a "grating" sensation reported by the patient, and the feeling of the knee giving out is not uncommon. Pain is typically aggravated by activity and relieved by rest. In some cases the pain radiates to the posterior or popliteal region of the knee. Stiffness and mild swelling may also accompany pain.

Patello-femoral stress syndrome or patellar joint dysfunction are two of the common generic names for this anterior knee pain. The patella glides in the articular groove of the patello-femoral joint during extension and flexion of the knee. When there are biomechanical imbalances, repetitive stress results in inflammation, irritation, and pain. Dysfunction of the foot, the ankle, or the hip, and abnormalities such as leg length discrepancy may all contribute. The common medical viewpoint describes a muscle imbalance between the vastus medialis on the medial side and the vastus lateralis, and possibly the ilio-tibial tract, on the lateral side. These biomechanical factors must be assessed and corrected. I never treat patello-femoral joint pain without the patient also under the care of a physical therapist or other practitioner to address these structural issues.

The orthopedic examination of the knee is complicated, and takes considerable skill to correctly diagnose the cause of knee pain. You may need to refer the patient for a comprehensive exam by an orthopedic physician. X-ray and/or MRI may be required to determine the precise tissues that are involved. However, there are some simple tests that can be performed by the practitioner. With your hand on the patella, the patient slightly flexes and extends the knee as you feel for crepitus ("creaking" or "grinding"). Crepitus can give a general "feel" about the level of inflammation and dysfunction in the patello-femoral joint. Compression of the patella against the femoral groove may also reveal an arthritic joint if painful. Also, test the quadriceps muscle group with resisted knee extension. With the patient seated on the treatment table and the knee flexed, simply have them extend the leg forward while you resist the movement with your hand on their ankle. Consulting a text on these and other orthopedic exams is recommended.

Chondromalacia is another condition related to patello-femoral pain. Medically, it is described as a premature degeneration or a "softening" of the articular cartilage of the undersurface of the patella. The articular surface becomes roughened, and the smooth glide of the knee cap over the knee joint is compromised. Care should be taken with the diagnostic language, as patello-femoral joint syndrome is technically not the same as chondromalacia, even though sometimes these two names may be used interchangeably. Some texts point out that chondromalacia – the actual softening of the cartilage on the posterior aspect of the patella – is estimated to occur in only 20 percent of persons who present with anterior knee pain.[3] So if your patient comes in with the diagnosis of chondromalacia, don't assume that to be fact.

In summary, anterior knee pain may be due to patello-femoral joint dysfunction, and when more severe, chondromalacia. Patellar tendonitis may also be associated with this condition. Many patients benefit from acupuncture, and treating this condition is among my favorites. The local sub-patellar needle techniques discussed in Step Four get to the site of injury with more precision than most other therapeutic modalities. The acupuncturist who can perfect this treatment will do well with this injury. But make sure you include physical therapy in the overall treatment protocol, as correction of the biomechanical and muscle imbalances is essential. Muscle weakness is suggested to be the best established correlate of functional limitations in osteoarthritis of the knee.[4] This will complement the acupuncture treatments and provide more lasting benefit for the patient.

123 • Anterior Knee Pain *Patello-femoral Joint Dysfunction*

SUMMARY OF THE INJURY

Clinical Features
- Patello-femoral joint syndrome is pain caused by dysfunctional tracking of the patella.
- Chondromalacia is a softening of the cartilage on the posterior aspect of the patella. It is often used as a catch all term for anterior knee pain. However, it is estimated to occur in less than 20 percent of patients with anterior knee pain.[5]
- Repetitive stress causes inflammation and irritation of the undersurface of the patella.
- Overuse injury is usually from running or cycling where there is knee flexion and extension with resistance.
- Excessive pronation and other lower-extremity biomechanical imbalances may be precipitating factors.

Common Patient Complaints
- Anterior knee pain, reported in the region of the patella and patellar tendon
- Pain aggravated with exercise, going up and down stairs, and various positions like squatting
- Pain may radiate to the posterior knee in the region of the popliteal fossa
- Creaking (crepitus) under the knee cap
- May have a feeling of the knee giving out

Differentiation from Similar Injuries and Conditions
- Medial or lateral ligament or meniscus injury may radiate pain anteriorly
- Medial or lateral compartment osteoarthritis may radiate pain anteriorly
- Patellar bursitis, patellar tendonitis
- Direct trauma to the patella
- Plica irritation and inflammation
- ACL or PCL sprain or injury

Typical Medical Recommendations
- R.I.C.E. (Rest, Ice, Compression, and Elevation) when acute. Compression may not be indicated.
- Anti-inflammatory medications
- Modify activity
  Decrease running mileage and intensity, jumping, and other aggravating activities. Cross-train, including cycling, swimming, and running in water.
- Biomechanics
  Correct pronation or supination with shoes and/or orthotics. For chronic and recurring cases, other lower-extremity biomechanical imbalances may need to be assessed. Structural issues such as "small" patella or shallow patellar groove makes the patient more prone to this type of anterior knee pain.

Typical Medical
Recommendations (cont'd)

- Physical therapy
  Ultrasound, manual therapy, other physical therapy modalities. The common medical viewpoint describes a muscle imbalance between the vastus medialis and the vastus lateralis, along with the ilio-tibial tract on the lateral side. Studies show that patients with patello-femoral pain have decreased vastus medialis function.[6] Refer to a physical therapist for assessment and recommendations on the proper therapeutic exercises, stretching, and strengthening.

- Orthopedic procedures
  Patello-femoral joint dysfunction may respond to a series of hyalgan (Synvisc) injections. In more advanced cases of chondromalacia, surgery may be considered. Surgical debridement may be performed to smooth the rough undersurface of the patella. A sheath release of the vastus lateralis is a possible procedure, although its effectiveness is debated. As the condition worsens, knee replacement surgery is becoming commonplace in the older patient.

TREATMENT & TECHNIQUES

Overview: Anterior knee pain is most commonly diagnosed under the category of accident/trauma. This is usually a repetitive stress disorder due to the accumulation of micro-trauma. However, occasionally it may occur as an acute inflammatory condition. The injury is at the level of the tendons, ligaments, and bone. There is qi and blood stagnation in the channels and collaterals. The meridians affected are the Stomach and Spleen. However, the patella lies between these two channels, and therefore choosing points according to jing-luo theory is not always reliable. Internal organ imbalances of the Stomach and Spleen often contribute.

Prognosis: Treat twice a week for three weeks, then re-evaluate. Most cases without complications have noticeable improvement within six treatments. With chronic cases, continue treatment at least once weekly after the first three-week period. As mentioned earlier, a series of hyalgan (Synvisc) injections may benefit. It is not uncommon that after a course of injections, acupuncture treatments have greater effect.

STEP ONE: INITIAL TREATMENT

Choose among these four techniques, carefully determining if there is an immediate decrease in pain or an increase in range of motion.

Technique #1: **The Tendino-Muscle Meridians**

St 45, Sp 1   Bleeding technique

Jing-well points to activate the tendino-muscle meridians of the Stomach and Spleen are not always reliable.

Technique #2: **Opposite Side (contra-lateral)**

 St 36, St 35   Corresponding points on the opposite (unaffected) side

Technique #3: **Opposite Extremity (upper/lower)**

 LI 11, LI 10   Yang ming corresponding points on the opposite extremity

I avoid LI 11 on the Spleen and Stomach deficiency patients, which is described in the Appendices on page 354.

In general, treat upper/lower corresponding points on the opposite (unaffected) side when acute, and the affected side when chronic. Use palpation to assist in this choice.

Technique #4: **Empirical Points**

Liv 3 affected side + P 6 opposite side
This technique is documented in the work of Master Tong's empirical points.[7] Many practitioners report that this point combination is of benefit in patellar pain syndromes.

STEP TWO: MERIDIANS & MICROSYSTEMS

Choose among these four techniques, selecting points that are appropriate for the signs and symptoms of the patient.

Technique #5: **The Shu-Stream Point Combination**

St 43 affected side + LI 3 opposite side
Sp 3 affected side + Lu 9 opposite side
Shu-stream points to activate the meridians of the Stomach and Spleen are not always reliable.

Technique #6: **Traditional Point Categories**

Distal points to activate the meridians of the Stomach and Spleen are not always reliable. Palpation may assist in your choice of lower-extremity meridian points.

Technique #7: **The Extraordinary Meridians**

GB 41 + SJ 5   Activate the Dai mai
Patello-femoral joint dysfunction sometimes originates from hip and gluteal imbalances, which may be considered Dai mai pathology. Furthermore, compensation during exercise and activity from knee pain can affect the Dai mai.

Technique #8: **Microsystems**

Auricular Therapy
Local: Knee (French), knee (Chinese), lumbar spine
Zang-fu points: Spleen, Stomach, Liver
Systemic points for pain: Shen men, Thalamus, Adrenal, Endocrine

Wrist-ankle Acupuncture
Wrist-ankle acupuncture may be considered, as the site of injury is not precisely along either the Stomach or the Spleen meridians. Use three zones on the leg.[8]
Lower #2   The medial surface of the leg
Located 3 cun proximal to the medial malleolus, on the posterior border of the tibia. This zone approximates the Spleen meridian, and includes the point Sp 6.

Lower #3   The medial surface of the leg
Located 3 cun proximal to the medial malleolus, along
the tibia, posterior to its anterior border.
Lower #4   The lateral surface of the leg
Located 3 cun proximal to the lateral malleolus, halfway
between the anterior border of the tibia and the anterior
border of the fibula. This zone approximates the Stomach
meridian.

STEP THREE: INTERNAL ORGAN IMBALANCES

*Choose appropriate points to treat internal organ imbalances that
may contribute to the injury or pain syndrome.*

Technique #9: **Qi, Blood, and the Zang-fu Organs**

Patello-femoral joint pain is a repetitive stress injury and
therefore internal organ imbalances are not necessarily
causative. However, there are several zang-fu syndromes
which may contribute to the condition.

Liver imbalances Liver qi stagnation, Liver yin deficiency, and
Liver blood deficiency
Liver imbalances may result in the susceptibility of the
patellar tendon to inflammation and repetitive stress
injury. Consider the following:

Liv 3   Yuan-source point; supports the Liver
in its function of controlling the
muscles and tendons

GB 34   Hui-influential point of tendons
Treat GB 34 on the affected side and Liv 3 on the
opposite side.

Spleen and Stomach Spleen and Stomach qi deficiency
imbalances Spleen and Stomach imbalances are common in patients
with chronic and recurring patellar pain. This is not
surprising considering the course of the two meridians.
Assessment should be fairly straightforward for the
practitioner.

*Note: Consider St 41 (the tonification point) as an alternative to the
more traditionally used point St 36. A more detailed explanation can
be found on page 354.*

*Points should be determined by the practitioner from both palpation
and analysis of the signs and symptoms of the patient.*

128 • **Anterior Knee Pain** *Patello-femoral Joint Dysfunction*

STEP FOUR: THE SITE OF INJURY

Choose among the local and adjacent points at the site of injury. Points may be determined by palpation, orthopedic testing, and analysis of the signs and symptoms of the patient.

Technique #10:	**Local and Adjacent Points**
The sub-patellar region ★	**The extraordinary point *Xiyan* ("eyes of the knees")** Oblique to transverse insertion under the patella, to a depth of 1 inch.

Acupuncturists are quite familiar with the points *Xiyan* ("eyes of the knees") in the treatment of knee pain. For patello-femoral joint dysfunction, this is usually an effective local treatment. I have high regard for the relatively simple techniques below. However, it is important to mention correct position. Start with the patient supine, using a bolster under the knees to get about a 30-degree angle of knee flexion. If insertion is difficult, increase or decrease the angle of flexion with a different sized bolster.

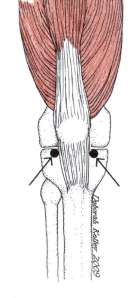

● – Xiyan
↗ – Sub–patellar needling

Needle technique ★

The needles at *Xiyan* are inserted deep to the patella and superficial to the patello-femoral groove, right in the region of inflammation and irritation.

"Lateral" *Xiyan* (St 35) should be needled toward the superior medial aspect of the patella (in the direction of Sp 10). "Medial" *Xiyan* is needled toward the superior lateral aspect of the patella (in the direction of St 34). Both are inserted at an oblique to transverse angle.

Clinical comments

I recommend 1.5 inch needles, using as thin of a gauge as possible while still maintaining some control and precision with your technique. It may take several attempts to find the proper angle of the needle to reach the desired depth. I always am looking for little or no resistance, and any discomfort or sharp pain means the needle is not perfectly inserted. Care should be taken that the needles are not actually inserted against the bone, as this may further irritate and inflame the tissues. It should be noted that on some patients, a perfect pair of needles is not possible. This may occur with the chronic patient when there is the diagnosis of "bone on bone".

Electrical stimulation Electrical stimulation between the medial and lateral needles usually increases the effectiveness of the treatment, as it undoubtedly relieves some of the sub-patellar inflammatory response. Needle-top moxa may also be considered in cold (han) cases.

Variations of patellar needle technique There are several possible variations on needle placement and choice of points, expanding beyond the two needles at *Xiyan*:

 1. Two paired points at *Xiyan*
The first set of points at *Xiyan* are chosen at the inferior-most depression of the palpable zone medial and lateral to the patellar tendon. The second set of points is approximately 1 centimeter superior to the first, at the superior portion of the zone of *Xiyan*. When inserted deeply, this second set of points penetrate further superior under the patella and into the patello-femoral groove. These two sets of points should cover a wider area of the sub-patellar region. Electrical stimulation and needle-top moxa may be considered.

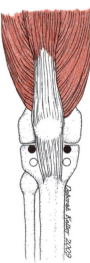

● – *Xiyan*
○ – *"Inferior" Xiyan*

 2. Two paired points at "lateral" *Xiyan* (St 35)
Frequently "medial" *Xiyan* is more difficult to needle deeply than the lateral point. If this is the case, use two paired points at "lateral" *Xiyan* (St 35), considering electrical stimulation or needle-top moxa.

3. Threading the patellar borders

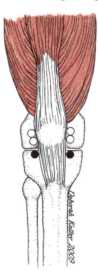

The medial and lateral borders of the patella are sometimes found to be painful during examination. This technique uses threaded needles along the medial and lateral borders of the kneecap. Insertion is transverse. I think of this as "knocking on the door" of the patello-femoral groove from the medial and lateral sides. We don't actually get into the joint, but close to it. Palpate to determine if needles should be threaded inferiorly or superiorly. Electrical stimulation may be used between these two points, or with the *Xiyan* points.

● – *Xiyan*
○ – *Point variations along the medial and lateral borders of the patella*

Motor points of the rectus femoris

Inflammation of the sub-patellar region may be treated with points on the centerline of the anterior thigh. This includes two motor points of the rectus femoris, which is the central muscle of the quadriceps group.⁹ The first is the acupuncture point St 31. It is located inferior to the anterior superior iliac spine, on the lateral side of the sartorius muscle. The second is at the midpoint of the line joining St 31 with the superior border of the patella. Insertion is perpendicular, from 1 to 1.5 inches.

● – Acupuncture points
▲ – Motor points

The quadriceps muscle group

★ St 34, St 33, St 32
These three Yang ming points are along the vastus lateralis, and may be helpful in the case. Releasing tension in this muscle may assist the patella in tracking properly through the joint.

★ **Sp 10 and the extraordinary point *Baichongwo***
These two points are along the vastus medialis, often considered the weak muscle group in patellar dysfunction. *Baichongwo* is the motor point of the muscle.¹⁰ It is located 1 cun proximal to Sp 10, in the vastus medialis muscle. Treatment to this muscle may assist the patella in tracking properly through the joint.

The extraordinary point *Heding*
The point *Heding* should be mentioned, as it is a commonly referenced extraordinary point. It is located in the depression at the midpoint of the superior border of the patella.¹¹ While anatomically interesting for patellar dysfunction, I rarely use *Heding* due to the difficulty of needling into this dense tendinous tissue. If the practitioner is so inclined, consider the point.

The IT band

★ GB 31, GB 32
Shao yang points follow the iliotibial band, and may also assist patellar pain. Releasing tension in the IT band may assist the tracking of the patella.

Adjacent points

★ GB 34 + Sp 10
GB 34 is the hui-influential point of tendons. Sp 10 is the "sea of blood". This combination moves the blood and nourishes the blood at the level of the tendons and ligaments.

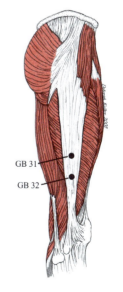

COMPLEMENTARY PROCEDURES

- When acute, ice massage along the patellar tendon may alleviate pain and reduce inflammation.

- Alternating ice and heat after the acute stage, when the condition is "neither hot (re) nor cold (han)", may enhance recovery.

- Topical applications (herbal liniments, plasters, etc.) may benefit.

★ While all techniques listed above have shown clinical relevance, the starred items are predictably effective for this specific injury. Consider them first in a treatment plan.

REFERENCES

[1] Dutton, M: *Orthopeadic Examination, Evaluation, and Intervention,* Second Edition. McGraw-Hill, USA, 2008 (page 961).

[2] Dutton, M, (page 1010).

[3] Dutton, M, (page 1011).

[4] Dutton, M, (page 1010).

[5] Dutton, M, (page 1011).

[6] Dutton, M, (page 945).

[7] Tan & Rush: *Twelve and Twelve in Acupuncture.* San Diego, 1994 (page 33).

[8] Matsumoto & Birch: *Extraordinary Vessels.* Paradigm Publishers, Massachusetts, 1986 (pages 182-188). *Note: Dr. Zhang Xin Shu's* Wrist Ankle Acupuncture (Wan Ke Zhen) *is the source quoted in the above text.*

[9] Callison, M: *Motor Point Index.* AcuSport Seminar Series LLC, San Diego, 2007 (page 122).

[10] Callison, M: *Motor Point Index.* AcuSport Seminar Series LLC, San Diego, 2007 (page 123).

[11] Deadman, Al-Khafaji, & Baker: *A Manual of Acupuncture.* Journal of Chinese Medicine Publications, East Sussex, 2001 (page 583).

9
Anterior Knee Pain
Patellar tendonitis

Pain in the anterior knee anywhere along the tendon, from the inferior border of the patella to its attachment at the tuberocity of the tibia

Called "jumper's knee," patellar tendonitis is usually a repetitive stress injury characterized by inflammation and irritation of the patellar tendon. It may occur as acute trauma.

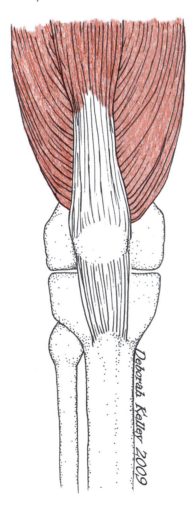

DIAGNOSIS & ASSESSMENT

Patellar tendonitis is a lower-extremity repetitive stress injury commonly called "jumper's knee". Volleyball, basketball, and track-and-field athletes are prone to the injury, but it is also seen in runners, walkers and weight lifters. The patellar tendon is the attachment of the quadriceps muscle group, and many sports involving forceful knee extension are associated with this condition. This is especially true with intense "de-celeration" activities, like repeated jumping and landing and downhill running. The cause is usually repetitive stress, resulting in inflammation and irritation of the patellar tendon. It is closely related to patello-femoral joint syndrome, which is discussed in detail on page 121. It might be helpful for the reader to review this material.

Pain is usually experienced directly on or over the patellar tendon from the lower border of the patella to its attachment at the tuberocity of the tibia. The patient may report sharp pain during exercise and persistent dull pain during rest and inactivity. The tendon itself may be swollen and inflamed, as well as the site of its attachment at the tibia. The patient reports that pain is worse with exercise, especially jumping, running and going up or down stairs. As with all repetitive stress injuries, make sure you inquire about the patient's training and activities. Increased mileage and intensity are frequently associated. And excessive pronation and other lower-extremity biomechanical imbalances may also be precipitating factors.

Start the examination by observing the patellar tendon for swelling and signs of heat. Then, palpate the tendon by pinching along its length from the patella to the tibia. You are essentially at *Xiyan* ("eyes of the knees") to do this pinch test, and pain is positive for inflammation. Press on the tuberosity of the tibia; if this is tender, the patient likely has jumper's knee. You might even test the quadriceps muscle group with resisted knee extension. With the patient seated on the treatment table and knees flexed, simply have them extend the leg forward while you resist the movement with your hand on their ankle. Again, pain suggests patellar tendonitis, but it could also point to patello-femoral joint dysfunction.

Osgood-Schlatter's disease is one condition not to overlook. This is a type of patellar tendonitis that occurs during a growth spurt in adolescent boys and girls somewhere between 10 and 14 years old. This period of rapid growth causes the tendon to become inflamed and avulsion ("pulling away") from the bone at the tuberosity may occur. I remember many afternoons in our home with a gang of early teenage friends of my son complaining of knee pain after shooting baskets or riding skateboards. They all outgrew the condition, but most will have a bony "knot" at the attachment of the tendon as a reminder. It is treated like other cases of patellar tendonitis, but you might want to review this condition to help reassure the parents who accompany their teenager. See Complementary Procedures for some effective nutritional advice.

My son is a professional slalom skateboard racer. In his sport, speeds of 30 miles per hour are reached while carving turns through a course much like downhill ski or snowboard racing. Several years ago he had a fall while skating to the bus stop at about five miles per hour. What resulted was an avulsion fracture of the patellar tendon, which completely ruptured from the tuberocity of the tibia, along with a sizable fragment of the bone with it. He had experienced chronic patellar tendonitis from Osgood-Schlatter's syndrome, so the injury was not a total surprise. Surgery was obviously required. During post-surgical rehabilitation, we used acupuncture along with physical therapy and other complementary therapies. Two years later, he went on to win the North American Slalom Championships. As a proud father, I just had to mention this. But of equal importance is that acupuncture and electrical stimulation played an important role in his recovery.

SUMMARY OF THE INJURY

Clinical Features
- Called "jumper's knee", it is commonly seen in volleyball and basketball players
- Repetitive stress causes inflammation and irritation of the patellar tendon
- Inflammation may be anywhere along the tendon from the patella to the attachment at the tuberocity of the tibia
- Often seen with patello-femoral joint dysfunction
- In adolescents during a growth spurt, Osgood-Schlatter's disease is the common diagnosis
- Excessive pronation and other lower-extremity biomechanical imbalances may be precipitating factors

Common Patient Complaints
- Pain directly on or over the patellar tendon
- Pain aggravated with exercise, especially jumping and going up or down stairs
- Sharp pain is reported during exercise, while dull pain is present even during rest

Differentiation from Similar Injuries and Conditions
- Patello-femoral joint dysfunction
- Chondromalacia
- Osgood-Schlatter's disease
- Patellar bursitis
- Medial or lateral ligament or meniscus injury may radiate pain anteriorly
- ACL or PCL sprain or injury
- Anterior compartment osteoarthritis
- Direct trauma to the patella, tibial stress fracture

Typical Medical Recommendations
- R.I.C.E. (Rest, Ice, Compression, and Elevation) when acute
- Anti-inflammatory medications
- Modify activity
  Decrease running mileage and intensity, jumping, and other aggravating activities. Cross-train, including cycling, swimming, and running in water.
- Biomechanics
  Correct pronation or supination with shoes and/or orthotics. For chronic and recurring cases, other lower-extremity biomechanical imbalances may need to be assessed.
- Physical therapy
  Ultrasound, manual therapy, other physical therapy modalities. In athletic populations, quadriceps and hamstring muscle dysfunction has been found to be a significant factor in the development of patellar tendonitis.[1] One common viewpoint describes a muscle imbalance between the vastus medialis and the vastus lateralis, along with the ilio-tibial tract on the lateral side. Refer to a physical therapist for assessment and recommendations on the proper therapeutic exercises, stretching, and strengthening.

135 • Anterior Knee Pain *Patellar Tendonitis*

TREATMENT & TECHNIQUES

Overview: Patellar tendonitis is most commonly diagnosed under the category of accident/trauma. This is usually a repetitive stress disorder due to the accumulation of micro-trauma. However, it may occur as an acute inflammatory condition. The injury is at the level of the tendons and bone, with qi and blood stagnation in the channels and collaterals. The meridians affected are the Stomach and Spleen. However, the patella lies between these two channels, and therefore choosing points according to jing-luo theory is not always reliable. Internal organ imbalances of the Stomach and Spleen often contribute.

Prognosis: Treat twice a week for three weeks, then re-evaluate. With chronic cases, continue treatment at least once weekly after the first three-week period.

STEP ONE: INITIAL TREATMENT

Choose among these four techniques, carefully determining if there is an immediate decrease in pain or an increase in range of motion.

Technique #1: **The Tendino-Muscle Meridians**

St 45, Sp 1   Bleeding technique
Jing-well points to activate the tendino-muscle meridians of the Stomach and Spleen are not always reliable.

Technique #2: **Opposite Side (contra-lateral)**

 St 36, St 35   Corresponding points on the opposite (unaffected) side

Technique #3: **Opposite Extremity (upper/lower)**

LI 11, LI 10   Yang ming corresponding points on the opposite extremity

In general, treat upper/lower corresponding points on the opposite (unaffected) side when acute, and the affected side when chronic. Use palpation to assist in this choice.

Technique #4: **Empirical Points**

Liv 3 affected side + P 6 opposite side
This technique is documented in the work of Master Tong's empirical points.[2] Many practitioners report this point combination benefits patellar pain syndromes.

STEP TWO: MERIDIANS & MICROSYSTEMS

Choose among these four techniques, selecting points that are appropriate for the signs and symptoms of the patient.

Technique #5: **The Shu-Stream Point Combination**

St 43 affected side + LI 3 opposite side
Sp 3 affected side + Lu 9 opposite side
Shu-stream points to activate the meridians of the Stomach and Spleen are not always reliable.

Technique #6: **Traditional Point Categories**

Palpation may assist in your choice of other points. Distal points used to activate the meridians of the Stomach and Spleen are not always reliable.

St 36	He-sea point
St 40	Luo-connecting point
Sp 9	He-sea point
Sp 6	Crossing point of three leg yin
GB 34	He-sea point, hui-influential point of tendons

Technique #7: **The Extraordinary Meridians**

GB 41 + SJ 5   Activate the Dai mai
Patellar tendonitis sometimes originates from hip and gluteal imbalances, which may be considered Dai mai pathology. Furthermore, compensation during exercise and activity from knee pain can affect the Dai mai.

Technique #8: **Microsystems**

Auricular Therapy
Local: Knee (French), knee (Chinese), lumbar spine
Zang-fu points: Spleen, Stomach, Liver
Systemic points for pain: Shen men, Thalamus, Adrenal, Endocrine

Wrist-ankle Acupuncture
Wrist-ankle acupuncture may be considered, as the site of injury is not precisely along either the Stomach or the Spleen meridians. Use three zones on the leg.[3]
Lower #2   The medial surface of the leg
Located 3 cun proximal to the medial malleolus, on the posterior border of the tibia. This zone approximates the Spleen meridian, and includes the point Sp 6.
Lower #3   The medial surface of the leg
Located 3 cun proximal to the medial malleolus, along the tibia, posterior to its anterior border.

Lower #4   The lateral surface of the leg
Located 3 cun proximal to the lateral malleolus, halfway
between the anterior border of the tibia and the anterior
border of the fibula. This zone approximates the Stomach
meridian.

STEP THREE: INTERNAL ORGAN IMBALANCES

*Choose appropriate points to treat internal organ imbalances that
may contribute to the injury or pain syndrome.*

Technique #9: **Qi, Blood, and the Zang-fu Organs**

Patellar tendonitis is a repetitive stress injury and
therefore internal organ imbalances are not necessarily
causative. However, there are several zang-fu syndromes
which may contribute to the condition.

Liver imbalances Liver qi stagnation, Liver yin deficiency, and
Liver blood deficiency
Liver imbalances may result in the susceptibility of the
patellar tendon to inflammation and repetitive stress
injury. Consider the following:

Liv 3   Yuan-source point; supports the Liver
in its function of controlling the
muscles and tendons

GB 34   Hui-influential point of tendons
Treat GB 34 on the affected side and Liv 3 on the
opposite side.

Spleen and Stomach Spleen and Stomach qi deficiency
imbalances Spleen and Stomach imbalances are common in patients
with chronic and recurring patellar tendonitis. This is not
surprising considering the course of the two meridians.
Assessment should be fairly straightforward for the
practitioner.

*Note: Consider St 41 (the tonification point) as an alternative to the
more traditionally used point St 36. A more detailed explanation can
be found on page 354.*

*Points should be determined by the practitioner from both palpation
and analysis of the signs and symptoms of the patient.*

138 • Anterior Knee Pain *Patellar Tendonitis*

STEP FOUR: THE SITE OF INJURY

Choose among the local and adjacent points at the site of injury. Points may be determined by palpation, orthopedic testing, and analysis of the signs and symptoms of the patient.

Technique #10: **Local and Adjacent Points**

The sub-patellar region ★ **The extraordinary point *Xiyan* ("eyes of the knees")**
Oblique to transverse insertion under the patella, to a depth of 1 inch.

The extraordinary point *Xiyan* is useful in the treatment of patello-femoral joint dysfunction. This protocol is also effective with patellar tendonitis. The needles at *Xiyan* are inserted deep to the patella and superficial to the patello-femoral groove. Start with the patient supine, using a bolster under the knees to get about a 30-degree angle of knee flexion. If insertion is difficult, increase or decrease the angle of flexion with a different sized bolster. "Lateral" *Xiyan* (St 35) should be needled obliquely toward the superior medial aspect of the patella (in the direction of Sp 10). "Medial" *Xiyan* is needled obliquely toward the superior lateral aspect of the patella (in the direction of St 34). I recommend 1.5 inch needles, using as thin of a gauge as possible while still maintaining some control and precision with your technique. Consider electrical stimulation between these paired points.

● – *Xiyan*
↗ – Sub–patellar needling

The patellar tendon ★ **The region of *Xiyan***
Perpendicular insertion, up to a depth of 1 inch.

The paired points *Xiyan* are located at the medial and lateral sides of the patellar tendon, just below its attachment to the inferior border of the patella. Treating the tendon starts at these points. Needle insertion is perpendicular, with a depth of up to 1 inch. Two sets of paired needles may be considered, as the patellar tendon is several inches in length from the lower border of the patella to the tuberocity of the tibia. Consider electrical stimulation between the medial and lateral needles.

Threading the tendon

Threading the patellar tendon is also a technique to consider. Start with insertion at the two *Xiyan* points. Thread in an inferior direction along the medial and lateral sides of the tendon. The angle is from oblique to transverse. Consider electrical stimulation.

Clinical comments

From my clinical experience, threading of the patellar tendon is not always reliable. Sometimes the inflamed tendon does not respond well to this local treatment technique, although aggravation is not the problem. A tenuous blood supply is believed to be a factor in the development of patellar tendonitis, as well as its poor healing potential.[4] The practitioner may need to experiment with other techniques for any given patient. Treatment of *Xiyan* into the sub-patellar region is sometimes more beneficial than threading the tendon, even though it is not precisely at the site of inflammation.

● – *Xiyan*
○ – "Inferior" *Xiyan*
↗ – Threading the patellar tendon

Motor points of the rectus femoris

Motor points of the quadriceps

Patellar tendonitis may be treated with points on the centerline of the anterior thigh. This includes two motor points of the rectus femoris, which is the central muscle of the quadriceps group.[5] The first is the acupuncture point St 31. It is located inferior to the anterior superior iliac spine, on the lateral side of the sartorius muscle. The second is at the midpoint of the line joining St 31 with the superior border of the patella. Insertion is perpendicular, from 1 to 1.5 inches.

The quadriceps muscle group

The extraordinary point *Heding*

The point *Heding* should be mentioned, as it is a commonly referenced extraordinary point. It is located in the depression at the midpoint of the superior border of the patella.[6] While interesting for patellar dysfunction, I rarely use *Heding* due to the difficulty of needling into this dense tendinous tissue. If the practitioner is so inclined, consider it.

● – Acupuncture points
▲ – Motor points

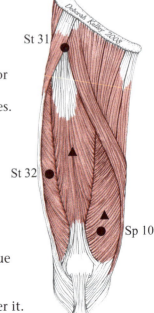

140 • Anterior Knee Pain *Patellar Tendonitis*

- ★ **St 34, St 33, St 32**
  These three Yang ming points are along the vastus lateralis, and may be helpful with patellar tendonitis.

- ★ **Sp 10 and the extraordinary point *Baichongwo***
  These two points are along the vastus medialis, often considered the weak muscle group in patellar dysfunction. *Baichongwo* is the motor point of the muscle.[7] It is located 1 cun proximal to Sp 10, in the vastus medialis.

Adjacent points **GB 34 + Sp 10**
- ★ GB 34 is the hui-influential point for tendons. Sp 10 is the "sea of blood". This combination moves the blood and nourishes the blood at the level of the tendons and ligaments.

COMPLEMENTARY PROCEDURES

- When acute, ice massage along the patellar tendon may alleviate pain and reduce inflammation.
- Alternating ice and heat after the acute stage, when the condition is "neither hot (re) nor cold (han)", may enhance recovery.
- Topical applications (herbal liniments, plasters, etc.) may benefit.
- Vitamin E (400 iu, two times daily) and Selenium (50-100 mcg, two times daily) is a specific nutritional recommendation for Osgood-Schlatter's disease. Some studies indicate these antioxidants are beneficial for inflammation of the tendon.

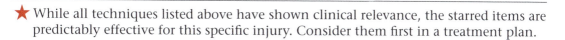

★ While all techniques listed above have shown clinical relevance, the starred items are predictably effective for this specific injury. Consider them first in a treatment plan.

REFERENCES

[1] Garrick, J: *Orthopaedic Knowledge Update, Sports Medicine 3*. North American Academy of Orthopaedic Surgeons, Illinois, 2004 (page 218).

[2] Tan & Rush: *Twelve and Twelve in Acupuncture*. San Diego, 1994 (page 33).

[3] Matsumoto & Birch: *Extraordinary Vessels*. Paradigm Publishers, Massachusetts, 1986 (pages 182-188). *Note: Dr. Zhang Xin Shu's* Wrist Ankle Acupuncture (Wan Ke Zhen) *is the source quoted in the above text.*

[4] Garrick, J: *Orthopaedic Knowledge Update, Sports Medicine 3*. North American Academy of Orthopaedic Surgeons, Illinois, 2004 (page 218).

[5] Callison, M: *Motor Point Index*. AcuSport Seminar Series LLC, San Diego, 2007 (page 122).

[6] Deadman, Al-Khafaji, & Baker: *A Manual of Acupuncture*. Journal of Chinese Medicine Publications, East Sussex, 2001 (page 583).

[7] Callison, M: *Motor Point Index*. AcuSport Seminar Series LLC, San Diego, 2007 (page 123).

Notes

10
Medial Knee Pain – Acute

Injury to the Medial Collateral Ligament or the Medial Meniscus

Acute pain, inflammation, and swelling in the medial knee experienced after injury or trauma

An acute injury of the knee due to sprain of the medial collateral ligament (MCL) or tear to the medial meniscus.

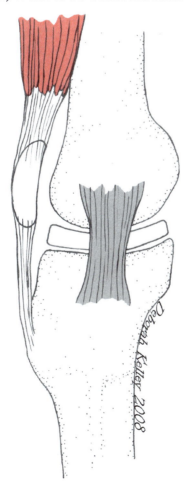

DIAGNOSIS & ASSESSMENT

Acute pain in the medial aspect of the knee is commonly seen in a variety of sports injuries. It usually results from a denfinite traumatic event in a variety of sports and other activities. From a meridian (jing-luo) perspective, we usually think of the three leg yin meridians – the Spleen, the Kidney, and the Liver. However, medial knee pain should be understood in terms of western orthopedic diagnosis. Your treatment plan, rehabilitation and prognosis for the patient all arise from this assessment. But most importantly, prognosis – what you communicate to the patient – is what is unique to each diagnosis.

We start with the medial collateral ligament (MCL), which spans the medial joint space of the knee from the medial femoral condyle at the superior aspect to the medial surface of the tibia inferiorly. The MCL is located in the center of the medial aspect of the knee, precisely on the Liver meridian. The function of the MCL is to stabilize the knee from valgus (lateral) movement by "holding together" the joint space on the medial side. Sprain occurs from twisting movements or direct force from the lateral side during contact sports. I have treated numerous skiers and soccer players over the years who have sprained their medial collateral ligament. And like all ligaments, injury can range from a mild injury at grade I to complete rupture at grade III.

Your patient may have acute sprain, or they could have a more chronic condition from previous injury and are not back to full activity. The patient will report pain on the medial aspect of the knee. Tenderness extends above and below the joint line, as the ligament attaches to both the femur or the tibia. There could be joint laxity, which can be evaluated on valgus challenge. By stabilizing the knee on the lateral side, and forcing the lower leg laterally, you put stress on the MCL. This movement "gaps" the medial joint space. Joint laxity can be felt if the ligament has been stretched or torn. Pain may also be produced by this maneuver. And of course, the more valgus, or lateral, the knee moves, the more significant the injury. If you can't visualize how to do this test, refer to an orthopedic text. It is easy to perform, and may help the acupuncturist in arriving at a proper diagnosis.

You will most likely see a grade I or a mild grade II sprain in the clinic. Instability is so significant with the grade III sprain that most patients go directly to the emergency room. I remember cross-country skiing one day after two feet of fresh spring snow. Some of us skied ahead, and on our return, there was a note on the car windshield. My wife had fallen in the deep snow and injured her knee, and we were asked to meet her group at the emergency room in town. We made it there as the physician began testing her knee. As he was performing the valgus stress test, her knee bent laterally, past 45 degrees, then 60 degrees. I don't remember how far it got, because I nearly passed out. I had never seen a complete rupture of the MCL, and this is what it produced: an injured wife and a pathetic husband. So much for my experience and toughness! It took me a while to get over that one; however, my wife had complete recovery.

The force involved in an injury to the medial collateral ligament may affect other structures in the knee, including the medial meniscus. The meniscus is the cartilage that covers the inferior surface of the knee joint. It distributes force around the knee, and actually bears as much as 40 percent of the load transmitted through the joint.[1] It is like a gasket or cushion between the femur and the tibia, protecting the knee from bone on bone contact. However, the meniscus is relatively avascular; there is not a significant amount of blood flow. Because qi and blood are so interdependent, the avascular nature of the medial menicus makes treating it with acupuncture and Chinese herbs more

144 • Medial Knee Pain – *Acute*

problematic. While we may be able to affect pain and swelling that accompanies a meniscus tear, I do not see a high percentage of cases proceed to a favorable outcome with a course of acupuncture treatments. This is so ingrained in my clinical experience that I rarely treat the condition when a significant tear has been diagnosed.

The medial side is the most common site of injury to the meniscus. Like the medial collateral ligament, it is injured with forceful twisting movements, like those seen in skiing, soccer and basketball. Compression combined with rotation is just too much, and the meniscus becomes torn or frayed. However, in older patients, the onset might not be from a traumatic event, but rather related to a degenerative process. Pain, swelling and stiffness are the usual complaints, along with the feeling that the knee "gives out". Sometimes the patient experiences locking, clicking or catching as a fragment of the meniscus may be interrupting the joint space on extension of the knee.

Examine the patient by palpating the medial joint line. Start near the lower border of the patella on the medial side. Palpate posteriorly towards Liv 8, and continue from Liv 8 towards Kid 10. Most patients have a clearly defined joint line; however, swelling may make this more difficult to palpate. Pain on palpation may indicate inflammation due to the menisus tear, but could also be due to medial compartment arthritis. Both McMurray's and Apley's tests are used most often to assess if the meniscus is damaged. It is beyond the scope of this writing to detail these tests, so refer to an orthopedic text for guidance. However, even these two tests sometimes fail to definitively reveal a meniscus injury. While an MRI is more conclusive, it too may miss a meniscus tear.

Acupuncture treatment of a meniscus tear depends on the temperament of both the practitioner and the patient. It would be reasonable to say that the lack of blood flow to the tissue makes acupuncture and other modalities more difficult to stimulate healing. However, treatments could help with pain, swelling, stiffness, and improve overall function of the joint. If the patient is determined to try acupuncture, I am sometimes willing to start a course of six to ten treatments. If there are aggravations and setbacks as they increase their activity, it is usually a sign that treatment will probably never be lasting. Other modalities, including surgery, may be necessary. It is only the "patient" patient who is willing to wait several years or more before knowing if the injury can heal or not.

In summary, the most likely causes of acute medial knee pain are from the MCL or the medial meniscus. Medial compartment arthritis, sometimes referred to as osteoarthritis, may be the cause of chronic knee pain and is covered on page 153. The practitioner should stay alert to other causes, such as patello-femoral dysfunction that sometimes refers to the medial aspect of the knee. The anterior cruciate ligament within the knee joint may also present with pain on the medial side, as do some soft tissue injuries of the hamstring or adductor tendons. Due to the complexity of the knee, if there are any questions about the cause of the pain, get some diagnostic assistance from an orthopedic physician.

SUMMARY OF THE INJURY

Clinical Feature	*Injury may be a sprain to the medial collateral ligament* • Pain along the medial joint space at the site of the ligament, along the Liver meridian • Knee instability on valgus stress in more serious sprains *Injury may involve damage to the medial meniscus* • Pain on medial aspect of the knee • Possible "giving out", locking, clicking or catching • Very limited blood supply, so healing capability may be limited *Some cases may be more chronic, from previous injury or repetitive stress. The ligament, meniscus, joint or other soft tissues could be affected.*
Common Patient Complaints	• General pain in the medial aspect of the knee • May have the feeling of instability of the knee joint • May be accompanied by swelling and stiffness • Acute injury commonly occurs with a twisting motion when the foot is planted, or from being hit on the lateral side of the knee
Differentiation from Similar Injuries and Conditions	• Patellar dysfunction may radiate pain toward the medial knee • Fold of synovial membrane (plica) mimics a meniscus tear • ACL or PCL sprain or injury may exist with an acute injury to the medial knee • Tendonitis • Rule out rheumatoid arthritis, gout and other systemic causes of inflammation • Medial compartment osteoarthritis
Typical Medical Recommendations	• R.I.C.E. (Rest, Ice, Compression, and Elevation) when acute • Anti-inflammatory medications • Modify activity *There may be some cross-training activities, including cycling, swimming and running in water.* • Biomechanics *Correct pronation or supination with shoes and/or orthotics.* • Physical therapy *Ultrasound, manual therapy, other physical therapy modalities. The common medical viewpoint describes a muscle imbalance between the vastus medialis and the vastus lateralis, along with the ilio-tibial tract on the lateral side. While may be true for patellar dysfunction, it may also apply to the medial knee. Refer to a physical therapist for assessment and recommendations on the proper therapeutic exercises, stretching, and strengthening.*

Typical Medical Recommendations (cont'd)

- Orthopedic procedures
  Medial meniscus injury may respond to a series of hyalgan (Synvisc) injections. Prolotherapy may assist in strengthening the MCL by sclerosing injection. Surgery may be required for some patients with ligament or meniscus damage.
- Orthopedic evaluation
  McMurray's test, Apley's test (distraction for the ligament), and Apley's test (compression for the meniscus) help to differentiate. Don't hesitate to get a complete orthopedic examination and an MRI to reveal the pathology and the causes of pain. Even if surgery is avoided, this assessment may be helpful for both treatment and prognosis.

TREATMENT & TECHNIQUES

Overview: Acute MCL sprain and injury to the medial meniscus is most commonly diagnosed under the category of accident/trauma. The injury is at the level of the ligaments, tendons, and bone. There is qi and blood stagnation in the channels and collaterals. The Liver meridian follows the medial collateral ligament. All of the three leg yin meridians – the Kidney, Liver, and Spleen – encompanss the medial joint space.

Prognosis: Treat twice a week for three weeks, then re-evaluate. A grade I or moderate grade II injury to the MCL usually responds well to acupuncture. The avascular nature of the medial meniscus makes treatment less predictable.

STEP ONE: INITIAL TREATMENT

Choose among these four techniques, carefully determining if there is an immediate decrease in pain or an increase in range of motion.

Technique #1: **The Tendino-Muscle Meridians**

 Liv 1   Bleeding technique
Bleeding Liv 1 may benefit the medial collateral ligament and related inflammation. There may be contra-indications for this yin meridian point.

Technique #2: **Opposite Side (contra-lateral)**

***Ahshi* point(s)**   On the opposite (unaffected) side
Palpate for point sensitivity along the medial joint space.

Liv 8, Kid 10, Sp 9   Corresponding points on the opposite (unaffected) side
He-sea points of the three leg yin meridians often benefit.

Technique #3: **Opposite Extremity (upper/lower)**

P 3, Lu 5, H 3   Corresponding acupuncture points on the opposite extremity

In general, treat upper/lower corresponding points on the opposite (unaffected) side when acute, and the affected side when chronic. Use palpation to assist in this choice.

Technique #4: **Special Empirical Points**

 Liv 3 affected side + P 6 opposite side
This point combination comes from the Master Tong system of empirical points.[2] It can be viewed as a variation on the shu-stream point combination of Liv 3 + P 7 discussed below in Technique #5.

STEP TWO: MERIDIANS & MICROSYSTEMS

Choose among these four techniques, selecting points that are appropriate for the signs and symptoms of the patient.

Technique #5: The Shu-Stream Point Combination

Liv 3 affected side + P 7 opposite side
Sp 3 affected side + Lu 9 opposite side
Kid 3 affected side + H 7 opposite side

Shu-stream point combinations of the yin meridians are not always reliable, and there may be contra-indications for these points.

Technique #6: Traditional Point Categories

★ **Liv 2 + Liv 7 (affected side)**

This point combination is quite effective in treating acute medial knee pain, and is often my first choice. Liv 2 is the sedation point, which reduces excess from the channel. The practitioner may need a reminder that Liv 7 is one cun posterior to Sp 9, with the needle inserting into the fibers of the medial head of the gastrocnemius muscle. Liv 7 is often point-sensitive after medial knee trauma, which will help the practitioner in location and choice for needling. I often use electrical stimulation between these two points.

★ **Sp 6**   Crossing point of three leg yin

Palpation may assist in your choice of other Spleen, Liver, and Kidney meridian points

Technique #7: The Extraordinary Meridians

Kid 6 + Lu 7   Activate the Yin Qiao mai

While not clinically definitive, the Yin Qiao mai may be involved in medial knee disorders.

Technique #8: Microsystems

Auricular Therapy
Local: Knee (French), knee (Chinese), lumbar spine
Zang-fu points: Liver
Systemic points for pain: Shen men, Thalamus, Adrenal, Endocrine

STEP THREE: INTERNAL ORGAN IMBALANCES

Choose appropriate points to treat internal organ imbalances that may contribute to the injury or pain syndrome.

Technique #9: **Qi, Blood, and the Zang-fu Organs**

The cause of disease in most acute injuries to the MCL and the medial meniscus is trauma, and therefore internal organ imbalances are usually not causative. If the case is chronic, you might consider the following:

Liver imbalances Liver qi stagnation, Liver yin deficiency, and Liver blood deficiency
Liver imbalances may result in susceptibility of the tendons and ligaments to inflammation and may increase healing time. Consider the following:

Liv 3	Yuan-source point; supports the Liver in its function of controlling the muscles and tendons
GB 34	Hui-influential point of tendons

Treat GB 34 on the affected side and Liv 3 on the opposite side.

Points should be determined by the practitioner from both palpation and analysis of the signs and symptoms of the patient.

STEP FOUR: THE SITE OF INJURY

Choose among the local and adjacent points at the site of injury. Points may be determined by palpation, orthopedic testing, and analysis of the signs and symptoms of the patient.

Technique #10: **Local and Adjacent Points**

The medial knee **Liv 8**

One or two points, with oblique to transverse insertion, threaded along the medial joint space

While the three leg yin meridians traverse the medial knee, the Liver channel is the most important for treatment. Its pathway is over the medial collateral ligament. The point Liv 8 is the reference point for treatment. The location of Liv 8 varies in different texts, but Deadman's location is probably correct, placing it over the medial joint space.[3] In more simple anatomical terms, Liv 8 may also be described as being located immediately posterior to the medial collateral ligament.

150 • Medial Knee Pain – *Acute*

| *Threading the medial joint space* ★ | It is possible to simply needle the point Liv 8. However, threading this medial joint space may be a more effective treatment for acute injuries to the medial knee. If acupuncture is going to work for the medial meniscus, this is also the treatment. A simple guide to find the joint line is to start approximately level with the lower border of the patella. Palpate in the direction of Liv 8, and further posteriorly towards Kid 10. There is usually a defined joint space, which may be sensitive to palpation. |

★ With the medial joint space located, treatment with two paired points is straightforward, although not always easy. Remember that the medial collateral ligament lies in the center of the medial knee. Needling at Liv 8, which is posterior to the MCL, use an oblique to transverse angle directed anteriorly. The second needle, which I often call "anterior" Liv 8, is located on the anterior side of the ligament. Needle anterior Liv 8 with an oblique to transverse angle in a posterior direction. The two paired needles in effect are threaded along the medial joint space of the knee. They are on the anterior and posterior aspects of the MCL, and if the ligament is injured, this may benefit. And it also may be effective for joint inflammation. Electrical stimulation between the two points can be considered After the acute stage, needle-top moxa may be indicated and effective.

| *Ligament tapping* | With an MCL sprain, you also might want to consider the technique of ligament tapping – that is, if you and your patient are feeling brave. Running perpendicularly to the joint space is the medial collateral ligament. Tapping along the ligament from its superior attachment at the femur to its inferior attachment on the tibia is an aggressive, sometimes uncomfortable, but often effective procedure. This, in effect, irritates and inflames the ligament, but after an aggravation, the increased blood flow to the tissues assists the ligament in healing and "tightening up". If you are not quite up to this technique, a bleeding cup over the medial knee may increase micro-circulation locally and invigorate the blood in these tissues. |

| *The sub-patellar region* ★ | **The extraordinary point *Xiyan* ("eyes of the knees")** The basic viewpoint is that the two paired points *Xiyan* are the most effective for patellar dysfunction. However, "medial" *Xiyan* sometimes benefits the patient experiencing medial knee pain. You may read a more detailed description of these points under patello-femoral joint pain on page 129. |

151 • Medial Knee Pain – *Acute*

● – *Xiyan*
⬏ – *Sub–patellar needling*

I will frequently use two paired points at "medial" *Xiyan* or couple this medial patellar point with Liv 8. Electrical stimulation may be considered, with needle-top moxa when the condition is not in an acute flareup.

Adjacent points

★

GB 34 + Sp 10

GB 34 is the hui-influential point for tendons. Sp 10 is the "sea of blood". This combination moves the blood and nourishes the blood at the level of the tendons and ligaments.

Sp 9 + Sp 10

These two points seem reasonable from a jing-luo perspective, but I do not rely on them clinically for a significant contribution to the treatment of medial knee pain.

Liv 7

Liv 7 is located 1 cun posterior to Sp 9. It is frequently point sensitive with medial knee pain. See Technique #6 for the use of Liv 7 combined with Liv 2.

COMPLEMENTARY PROCEDURES

- When acute, ice massage along the MCL or the medial joint space may alleviate pain and reduce inflammation.

- Alternating ice and heat after the acute stage, when the condition is "neither hot (re) nor cold (han)", may enhance recovery.

- Topical applications (herbal liniments, plasters, etc.) may benefit.

- A supplement with glucosamine and chondroitin may be considered for nutritional support of the joint.

★ While all techniques listed above have shown clinical relevance, the starred items are predictably effective for this specific injury. Consider them first in a treatment plan.

REFERENCES

[1] Dutton, M: *Orthopeadic Examination, Evaluation, and Intervention,* Second Edition. McGraw-Hill, USA, 2008 (page 942).

[2] Tan & Rush: *Twelve and Twelve in Acupuncture.* San Diego, 1994 (page 33).

[3] Deadman, Al-Khafaji, & Baker: *A Manual of Acupuncture.* Journal of Chinese Medicine Publications, East Sussex, 2001 (page 485).

11
Medial Knee Pain – Chronic
Degenerative Arthritis of the Medial Compartment

Chronic pain, inflammation, swelling, and stiffness of the medial knee

Chronic knee pain due to medial compartment osteoarthritis. May be associated with prior injury or from chronic degeneration of the articular surface.

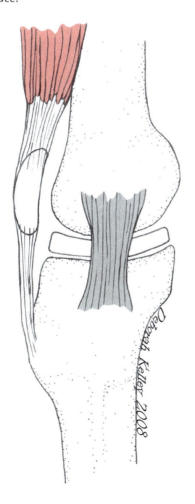

DIAGNOSIS & ASSESSMENT

Chronic medial knee pain is often due to degenerative arthritis, sometimes referred to as osteoarthritis. Sources suggest that 33 percent of individuals between the ages of 63 and 94 are affected by this condition in one of the three compartments of the knee.[1] That percentage will likely increase over the next decade, and therefore its inclusion in this handbook. While all three compartments of the knee may be affected with arthritis, we will cover the medial aspect of the joint in this chapter.

Considered a repetitive stress injury, the pain and limitations of medial compartment arthritis is usually due to prolonged "abuse" of the knee. Like other chronic arthritic conditions, its onset is insidious and is more likely seen in individuals over 50 years old. In TCM terms, this is considered a *Bi* syndrome. This type of degenerative joint disease is the degradation of the articular cartilage and the joint capsule. Associated with these changes is the inflammation of the synovial membrane, the lining that surrounds the knee joint.

Pain is experienced on the medial side of the knee and is chronic and fairly diffuse. The patient may report a deep aching sensation in the joint, and it is often accompanied by stiffness, particularly in the morning. Osteoarthritis of the knee is typically worse with prolonged activity as well as weight-bearing activities, and is alleviated with rest. Sometimes swelling may be noted. There may be a history of acute injury to the medial knee, such as a ligament sprain or meniscal tear.

Examine the patient by palpating the medial joint line. Start near the lower border of the patella on the medial side. Palpate posteriorly towards Liv 8, and continue from Liv 8 towards Kid 10. Most patients have a clearly defined joint line; however, swelling may make this more difficult to palpate. Pain on palpation may indicate inflammation due to medial compartment arthritis. However, injury to the MCL and the medial meniscus may also produce this pain. While X-ray and MRI will reveal degeneration of the knee joint, part of the diagnosis is clinically based upon the signs and symptoms of the patient. If there are any questions about the cause of pain, get some diagnostic assistance from an orthopedic physician.

In summary, chronic medial knee pain may be due to the degenerative condition of osteoarthritis. While prior trauma and injury may be associated, the condition may simply be "wear and tear" of the joint. Make sure you include physical therapy in the overall treatment protocol, as correction of the biomechanical and muscle imbalances is essential. Inclusion of complementary modalities enhances the effectiveness of acupuncture treatments and provide more lasting benefit for the patient.

SUMMARY OF THE INJURY

Clinical Features
- Chronic degenerative arthritis, medial compartment arthritis, or osteoarthritis are common descriptions of the condition
- Pain on medial aspect of the knee
- Pain and inflammation along the medial joint
- Aggravated by movement and weight-bearing activities
- Relieved with rest
- May be an overuse injury, or the patient may have a prior history of trauma or injury

Common Patient Complaints
- General pain in the medial aspect of the knee
- May be accompanied by swelling and stiffness
- May have other symptoms characteristic of chronic arthritis, such as aggravation from cold weather and relief from warmth

Differentiation from Similar Injuries and Conditions
- Chronic pain from prior MCL or meniscus injury
- Patellar dysfunction may radiate painmedially
- Chronic tendonitis
- Rule out rheumatoid arthritis, gout, and other systemic causes of inflammation

Typical Medical Recommendations
- Ice may be considered with acute flare-ups of a chronic condition. Applications of heat often benefit chronic inflammation.
- Anti-inflammatory medications
- Biomechanics
  Correct pronation or supination with shoes and/or orthotics. Other lower-extremity biomechanical imbalances may need to be assessed.
- Physical therapy
  Ultrasound, manual therapy, and other physical therapy modalities. The common medical viewpoint describes a muscle imbalance between the vastus medialis on the medial side and the vastus lateralis, and possibly the ilio-tibial tract, on the lateral side. While this is true for patellar dysfunction, it may also apply to the medial knee. Refer to a physical therapist for assessment and recommendations.
- Orthopedic procedures
  Arthritis may respond to a series of hyalgan (Synvisc) injections. Surgery may be an option for some patients with damage to the joint. Severe arthritic degeneration may require knee replacement surgery.
- Orthopedic evaluation
  Don't hesitate to get a complete orthopedic examination and an MRI to reveal the pathology and the causes of pain. This assessment may be helpful for both treatment and prognosis.

TREATMENT & TECHNIQUES

Overview: Medial knee pain due to arthritis is commonly diagnosed as a *Bi* syndrome. Care should be taken to assess the heat (re), cold (han), damp (shi), and wind (feng) contributions. This will assist in the choice of points, needle technique, and herbal prescription. The injury is at the level of the tendons, ligaments, and bone. There is qi and blood stagnation in the channels and collaterals. The three leg yin meridians – the Kidney, Liver, and Spleen – encompass the medial joint space. Internal organ imbalances of the Liver and the Kidney frequently contribute.

Prognosis: Treat once or twice a week for six weeks, then re-evaluate. The entire treatment protocol should include other complementary therapies, such as Chinese herbal medicine, dietary supplements, and physical therapy. Chronic cases will obviously need on-going treatment.

STEP ONE: INITIAL TREATMENT

Choose among these four techniques, carefully determining if there is an immediate decrease in pain or an increase in range of motion.

Technique #1: **The Tendino-Muscle Meridians**

Sp 1, Liv 1   Bleeding technique

The tendino-muscle meridians of these two yin pathways probably do not get to the knee joint. There may be contraindications for these points.

Technique #2: **Opposite Side (contra-lateral)**

 Ahshi **point(s)**   On the opposite (unaffected) side
Palpate for point sensitivity along the medial joint space.

Liv 8, Kid 10, Sp 9 Corresponding points on the opposite (unaffected) side

He-sea points of the three leg yin meridians often benefit.

Technique #3: **Opposite Extremity (upper/lower)**

P 3, Lu 5, H 3   Corresponding acupuncture points on the opposite extremity

In general, treat upper/lower corresponding points on the opposite (unaffected) side when acute, and the affected side when chronic. Use palpation to assist in this choice.

156 • Medial Knee Pain – *Chronic*

Technique #4: **Empirical Points**

 Liv 3 affected side + P 6 opposite side
This point combination comes from the Master Tong system of empirical points.[2] It can be viewed as a variation on the shu-stream point combination of Liv 3 + P 7 mentioned below in Technique #5.

STEP TWO: MERIDIANS & MICROSYSTEMS

Choose among these four techniques, selecting points that are appropriate for the signs and symptoms of the patient.

Technique #5: **The Shu-Stream Point Combination**

Liv 3 affected side + P 7 opposite side
Sp 3 affected side + Lu 9 opposite side
Kid 3 affected side + H 7 opposite side

Shu-stream point combinations of the yin meridians are not always reliable, and there may be contra-indications for these points.

Technique #6: **Traditional Point Categories**

Sp 6	Crossing point of three leg yin
Sp 9	He-sea point
Kid 10	He-sea point

Kid 7 + Kid 9
These two paired points are a less-common point combination that benefits the Kidney and are helpful in treating arthritic knee pain.

Palpation may assist in your choice of Spleen, Liver and Kidney meridian points.

Technique #7: **The Extraordinary Meridians**

GB 41 + SJ 5   Activate the Dai mai
Compensating for dysfunction of the knee sometimes results in secondary hip and gluteal imbalances, which may be considered Dai mai pathology.

Technique #8: **Microsystems**

Auricular Therapy
Local: Knee (French), knee (Chinese), lumbar spine
Zang-fu points: Kidney, Liver
Systemic points for pain: Shen men, Thalamus, Adrenal, Endocrine

Wrist-ankle Acupuncture
Wrist-ankle acupuncture may be considered, as the site of injury may cover multiple meridians. Use three zones on the medial leg.[3]

Lower #1   The medial surface of the leg
Located 3 cun proximal to the medial malleolus, on the anterior border of the achilles tendon. This zone approximates the Kidney meridian.

Lower #2   The medial surface of the leg
Located 3 cun proximal to the medial malleolus, on the posterior border of the tibia. This zone approximates the Spleen meridian, and includes the point Sp 6.

Lower #3   The medial surface of the leg
Located 3 cun proximal to the medial malleolus, along the tibia, posterior to its anterior border.

STEP THREE: INTERNAL ORGAN IMBALANCES

Choose appropriate points to treat internal organ imbalances that may contribute to the injury or pain syndrome.

Technique #9:   **Qi, Blood, and the Zang-fu Organs**

There are various internal imbalances seen in the patient with chronic pain due to osteoarthritis of the knee. Internal imbalances of the Spleen, Liver, and Kidney are probably the most common, as could be predicted from the course of these three leg yin meridians. Consider the following:

Kidney imbalances   Kidney deficiency
Syndromes of the Kidney are considered by some practitioners as an internal organ imbalance present in all patients with chronic arthritis and joint degeneration. However, treatment to the Kidney alone rarely is sufficient for this arthritic condition.

Liver imbalances   Liver qi stagnation, Liver yin deficiency, and Liver blood deficiency
Liver imbalances may result in Gall Bladder meridian dysfunction, increasing the susceptibility of the knee to inflammation and degeneration. Consider the following:

Liv 3   Yuan-source point; supports the Liver in its function of controlling the muscles and tendons

GB 34   Hui-influential point of tendons
Treat GB 34 on the affected side and Liv 3 on the opposite side.

Bi syndrome   Medial knee pain due to osteoarthritis is commonly ★ diagnosed as a *Bi* syndrome. Care should be taken to assess the heat (re), cold (han), damp (shi), and wind (feng) contributions. This will assist in the choice of points, needle technique and herbal prescription.

Points should be determined by the practitioner from both palpation and analysis of the signs and symptoms of the patient.

158 • **Medial Knee Pain – *Chronic***

STEP FOUR: THE SITE OF INJURY

Choose among the local and adjacent points at the site of injury. Points may be determined by palpation, orthopedic testing, and analysis of the signs and symptoms of the patient.

Technique #10: **Local and Adjacent Points**

The medial knee **Liv 8**

One or two points, with oblique to transverse insertion, threaded along the medial joint space.

While the three leg yin meridians traverse the medial knee, the Liver channel is the most important for treatment. Its pathway is over the medial collateral ligament. The point Liv 8 is the reference point for treatment. The location of Liv 8 varies in different texts, but Deadman's location is probably correct, placing it over the medial joint space.[4] In more simple anatomical terms, Liv 8 may also be described as being located immediately posterior to the medial collateral ligament.

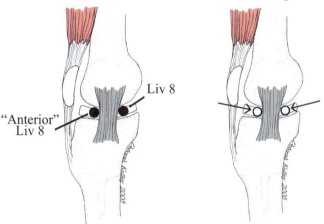

Threading the medial joint space It is possible to needle the point Liv 8. However, threading this medial joint space may be a more effective treatment for medial knee arthritis. If acupuncture is going to work for the medial meniscus, this is also the treatment. A simple guide to find the joint line is to start approximately level with the lower border of the patella. Palpate in the direction of Liv 8, and further posteriorly towards Kid 10. There is usually a defined joint space, which may be sensitive to palpation.

With the medial joint space located, treatment with two paired points is straightforward, although not always easy. Remember that the medial collateral ligament lies in the center of the medial knee. Needling at Liv 8, which is posterior to the MCL, use an oblique to transverse angle directed anteriorly. The second needle, which I often call "anterior" Liv 8, is located on the anterior side of the

159 • Medial Knee Pain – *Chronic*

ligament. Needle anterior Liv 8 with an oblique to transverse angle in a posterior direction. The two paired needles in effect are threaded along the medial joint space of the knee. They are on the anterior and posterior aspects of the MCL, and may be effective for chronic joint inflammation. Electrical stimulation between them can be considered, and with chronic arthritis, needle-top moxa may be the technique of choice.

The sub-patellar region

★ **The extraordinary point *Xiyan* ("eyes of the knees")**
The two paired points at *Xiyan* are most commonly used for patellar pain and dysfunction. However, for chronic medial knee joint pain, you might consider their use, as these extraordinary points benefit the entire joint space of the knee. Sometimes treatment using two paired points at "medial" *Xiyan* is effective. Electrical stimulation, or in cold (han) cases of arthritis, needle-top moxa may benefit.

● – Xiyan
↗ – Sub-patellar needling

Adjacent points

★ **GB 34 + Sp 10**
GB 34 is the hui-influential point for tendons. Sp 10 is the "sea of blood". This combination moves the blood and nourishes the blood at the level of the tendons and ligaments.

Sp 9 + Sp 10
These two points seem reasonable from a jing-luo perspective, but do not rely on them for a significant contribution to the arthritic knee.

Liv 7
Liv 7 is located 1 cun posterior to Sp 9. It is frequently point sensitive with medial knee pain. Consider it a secondary point.

COMPLEMENTARY PROCEDURES

- Applications of heat often benefit chronic inflammation of an arthritic joint.

- A supplement with glucosamine and chondroitin may be considered for nutritional support of the joint. While usually not dramatic, it may contribute to recovery.

- Homeopathic remedies are sometimes effective for pain and inflammation in chronic arthritis. Hyland's Arthritis Pain Formula (Standard Homeopathic Company) is one product to consider.

- A Chinese herbal formula specific to the signs and symptoms of the condition complements the acupuncture treatment of chronic arthritis.

★ While all techniques listed above have shown clinical relevance, the starred items are predictably effective for this specific injury. Consider them first in a treatment plan.

REFERENCES

[1] Dutton, M: *Orthopeadic Examination, Evaluation, and Intervention,* Second Edition. McGraw-Hill, USA, 2008 (page 1010).

[2] Tan & Rush: *Twelve and Twelve in Acupuncture.* San Diego, 1994 (page 33).

[3] Matsumoto & Birch: *Extraordinary Vessels.* Paradigm Publishers, Massachusetts, 1986 (pages 182-188). *Note: Dr. Zhang Xin Shu's* Wrist Ankle Acupuncture (Wan Ke Zhen) *is the source quoted in this text.*

[4] Deadman, Al-Khafaji, & Baker: *A Manual of Acupuncture.* Journal of Chinese Medicine Publications, East Sussex, 2001 (page 485).

Notes

12
Lateral Knee Pain
Ilio-tibial Band Syndrome

Pain in the lateral knee and thigh

A repetitive stress injury characterized by inflammation and irritation of the ilio-tibial (IT) band just proximal to the lateral knee. Sometimes referred to as "runner's knee".

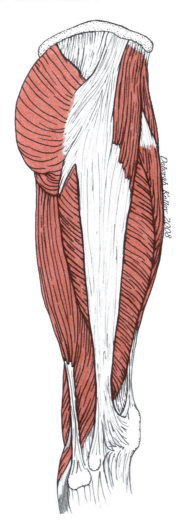

DIAGNOSIS & ASSESSMENT

Ilio-tibial band syndrome is the most common cause of lateral knee pain, and is a sports injury that every acupuncturist should become proficient in treating. It is estimated that up to eight percent of long-distance runners are affected by IT band syndrome.[1] Some studies suggest that up to 12 percent of all running-related injures are from the ilio-tibial band.[2] The patient usually reports lateral knee pain that is worse with prolonged exercise, especially running, and thus it is frequently called "runner's knee".

Its characteristic sharp lateral knee pain during activity is the result of the ilio-tibial tendon sliding over the lateral aspect of the knee during flexion and extension. This occurs at the lateral femoral condyle, usually about 2 to 4 cm proximal to the lateral joint space of the knee. Recurrent friction causes inflammation and irritation on the undersurface of the IT band. Sometimes there may even be "popping" or "snapping" as the band slides over this boney structure of the lateral knee. It is frequently worse on stairs, and when walking or running hills. Pain from IT band syndrome often resolves with rest, although a dull ache may persist. Stiffness and tightness can be felt up the ilio-tibial band to the greater trochanter and the gluteal area.

The patient's description of the pain and its onset are often enough to diagnose ilio-tibial band syndrome with some degree of confidence. I have successfully treated this injury for years, and consider acupuncture to be perhaps the most effective modality available to the patient. In fact, during the last 10 years in my clinic, there are very few patients with this injury who have not experienced significant relief with acupuncture treatment.

You do need to confirm the diagnosis with further examination. Start with palpating directly on the IT band just proximal to the lateral joint space. Also look for point tenderness at the anterior and posterior margins of the tendon, in the region of GB 33 and an anterior version of GB 33. You will probably elicit pain with palpation. Compression of the band against the lateral knee with firm pressure may reproduce the pain. You may also want to compress the band with the patient flexing and extending the knee slightly. Pain will assist in confirming that there is irritation and inflammation on the undersurface of the ilio-tibial tract.

The ilio-tibial band is a continuation of the tensor fascia lata muscle, and indirectly, the other gluteal muscles. You should always check for sensitive points in this gluteal area, as IT band syndrome frequently presents with these *ahshi* points. This is covered in detail in Step Four.

Take the time to question the patient about the onset of the injury. It is usually associated with a change in training, such as increased mileage, hills, or speed. A change in running shoe or running surface may also be the problem. As with most lower-extremity injuries, consider having the patient evaluated for foot biomechanics. Both excessive pronation or supination as well as other lower-extremity biomechanical imbalances may need to be corrected.

As for internal organ imbalances, the Liver and Gall Bladder are frequently associated with this injury. I remember a several month period in the early years of my practice when a half-dozen of my runners with ilio-tibial band syndrome were all attorneys. Each of them had significant stress due to excessive "planning and strategizing" and "executing plans and strategies". Of course, we recognize this from the Chinese classics as traditional functions of the Liver and Gall Bladder. One IT band patient was caught by surprise during the first visit when I asked, "What kind of law do you practice?" He replied that he was indeed a lawyer, but was presently working 60 hours

164 • Lateral Knee Pain *Ilio-tibial Band Syndrome*

a week developing a strategic plan for a start-up company about to issue stock and go public. While you might try to counsel these patients toward a different lifestyle, they are unlikely to quit their jobs! However, acupuncture and herbal medicine may be incorporated into the treatment plan to correct internal organ imbalances of the Liver and Gall Bladder. This may assist in maintaining a healthy flow of qi and blood in their respective meridians, contributing to the healing of the ilio-tibial band and the gluteal soft tissues.

SUMMARY OF THE INJURY

Clinical Features	• Repetitive stress causes inflammation and irritation of the undersurface of the ilio-tibial tract • Often called "runner's knee" • Pain from recurrent friction is usually 2 to 4 centimeters proximal to the lateral joint space of the knee • Overuse injury is usually from running or other activities involving repetitive knee flexion and extension • Excessive foot pronation and other biomechanical imbalances may be precipitating factors
Common Patient Complaints	• Pain in the lateral knee, ranging from dull to sharp ache • Pain and stiffness may radiate up ilio-tibial band to the greater trochanter • Symptoms aggravated during exercise • Symptoms relieved with rest, but pain returns again during or after exercise • May have "popping" or "snapping" during activities involving knee flexion and extension
Differentiation from Similar Injuries and Conditions	• Inflammation of the bursa deep to the IT band • Bone spur that irritates the tendon • Lateral collateral ligament sprain and lateral meniscus injury • Arthritis of the lateral compartment of the knee • Differentiate from sciatic pain referred from the lumbar spine or the sacral-iliac joint
Typical Medical Recommendations	• R.I.C.E. (Rest, Ice, Compression, and Elevation) when acute. Compression may not be indicated. • Anti-inflammatory medications • Modify activity *Decrease mileage and intensity, especially hill running. Cross-train, including cycling, swimming, and running in water.* • Stretching *Consult a good text on stretching of the IT band, which should be included in the overall protocol for the patient.* • Biomechanics *Correct pronation or supination with shoes and/or orthotics. Gait analysis for runners may correct some repetitive stress. For chronic and recurring cases, other lower-extremity biomechanical imbalances may need to be assessed.* • Physical therapy *Ultrasound, deep-friction massage, and other physical therapy modalities.* • Orthopedic procedures *Cortisone injection is sometimes used in the inflamed region of the tendon or the bursa.*

TREATMENT & TECHNIQUES

Overview: Ilio-tibial band syndrome is most commonly diagnosed in the category of accident/trauma. This is usually a repetitive stress disorder due to the accumulation of micro-trauma. However, occasionally it may be seen as an acute trauma. The injury is at the level of the muscles and tendons, with qi and blood stagnation in the channels and collaterals. This case is clearly Gall Bladder meridian pathology. Sometimes the diagnosis of wind (feng) may be used for the "popping" and "snapping" pain at the lateral knee. Internal organ imbalances of the Liver and Gall Bladder frequently contribute.

Prognosis: Treat twice a week for three weeks, then re-evaluate. Most cases without complications have good results within six treatments. I have confidence in the techniques that follow, which I usually communicate to the patient on the first visit. With chronic cases, continue treatment at least once weekly after the first three-week period.

STEP ONE: INITIAL TREATMENT

Choose among these four techniques, carefully determining if there is an immediate decrease in pain or an increase in range of motion.

Technique #1: **The Tendino-Muscle Meridians**

 GB 44　　　　　　Bleeding technique
Treating the Gall Bladder tendino-muscle meridian may be effective for the symptoms of stiffness and tightness of the IT band.

Technique #2: **Opposite Side (contra-lateral)**

GB 33, "anterior" GB 33　　Corresponding points on the opposite (unaffected) side
GB 33 is located proximal to the knee joint, on the posterior side of the ilio-tibial band. "Anterior" GB 33 is located anterior to the ilio-tibial band, on the same level as GB 33. Both may be considered in contra-lateral treatment.

Technique #3: **Opposite Extremity (upper/lower)**

Corresponding points on the opposite extremity may be considered; however, treatment to the affected extremity is usually preferred.

Technique #4: **Empirical Points**

No well-known empirical points for IT band syndrome.

STEP TWO: MERIDIANS & MICROSYSTEMS

Choose among these four techniques, selecting points that are appropriate for the signs and symptoms of the patient.

Technique #5: **The Shu-Stream Point Combination**

 GB 41 (or GB 42) affected side + SJ 3 opposite side
GB 42 is often more sensitive than GB 41, and should be considered as an alternative shu-stream point.

Technique #6: **Traditional Point Categories**

 Palpation may assist in your choice of Gall Bladder meridian points.

GB 40	Yuan-source point
GB 43	"Water" point
GB 34	He-sea point, hui-influential point of tendons

GB 34 is located near the insertion site on the tibia of the IT band.

 GB 31   Dispels wind (feng) from the lower extremity

This point is in the tissue of the ilio-tibial band itself. Its Chinese name, "wind market" (feng shi), implies its use in the treatment of wind symptoms. This includes the sudden onset, sudden disappearance, and the "snapping" of the tendon in the lateral knee. Also, the migrating pain and stiffness that often radiates up the ilio-tibial band to the pelvic region may be considered wind in nature.

I often use the technique of two paired points at the region of GB 31. With perpendicular insertion into the IT band, these points are about 1 inch apart on the Gall Bladder meridian, and can be determined simply by palpation. A variation is GB 31 and GB 32 as the two paired points. Electrical stimulation on these two points may also be considered. The needle should penetrate the ilio-tibial band except for the occasional patient with such tightness that deep needling is uncomfortable.

Technique #7: **The Extraordinary Meridians**

 GB 41 + SJ 5   Activate the Dai mai
Frequently IT band syndrome originates from hip and gluteal imbalances, which may be considered Dai mai pathology.

Bl 62 + SI 3   Activate the Yang Qiao mai
The IT band produces symptoms on the lateral aspect of the thigh, which may be considered Yang Qiao mai pathology.

Technique #8: **Microsystems**

Auricular Therapy
Local: Knee (French), knee (Chinese), hip, lumbar spine
Zang-fu points: Gall Bladder, Liver
Systemic points for pain: Shen men, Thalamus, Adrenal, Endocrine

STEP THREE: INTERNAL ORGAN IMBALANCES

Choose appropriate points to treat internal organ imbalances that may contribute to the injury or pain syndrome.

Technique #9: **Qi, Blood, and the Zang-fu Organs**

Even though ilio-tibial band syndrome is a repetitive stress injury, internal organ imbalances frequently seem to contribute.

Liver imbalances
★
Liver qi stagnation, Liver yin deficiency, and Liver blood deficiency
Liver imbalances may result in the susceptibility of the IT band to inflammation and repetitive stress injury. Consider the following:

Liv 3	Yuan-source point; supports the Liver in its function of controlling the muscles and tendons
GB 34	Hui-influential point of tendons

Treat GB 34 on the affected side and Liv 3 on the opposite side.

Liver and Gall Bladder damp heat
Excess syndromes of the Liver and Gall Bladder are also frequently observed in the patient with IT band sydnrome. These imbalances may result in Gall Bladder meridian dysfunction, increasing the susceptibility of the ilio-tibial band to inflammation.

Points should be determined by the practitioner from both palpation and analysis of the signs and symptoms of the patient.

STEP FOUR: THE SITE OF INJURY

Choose among the local and adjacent points at the site of injury. Points may be determined by palpation, orthopedic testing, and analysis of the signs and symptoms of the patient.

Technique #10: **Local and Adjacent Points**

The ilio-tibial band at the lateral knee

★

Thread needles under the IT band at GB 33 and "anterior" GB 33

Threading the tendon is an effective technique for IT band syndrome, and is the first place to start when treating locally. Needles are inserted under the tendinous band from both the anterior and posterior margins. The location is just proximal to the lateral aspect of the knee. The posterior needle is at or near GB 33, and is inserted under the IT band (in an anterior direction). At an anterior version of GB 33, another needle is inserted under the IT band (in a posterior direction). Both needles are at an oblique to transverse angle.

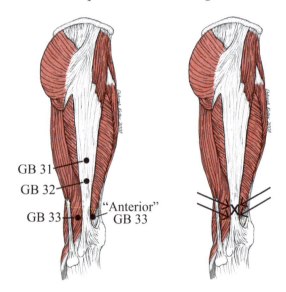

● – Acupuncture points
X – Region of pain
↗ – Needle insertion deep to the IT band

I frequently use a second set of paired needles about 1 to 2 cun proximal to the first set described above. Note that needles are not actually inserted into the ilio-tibial tract, as this may further irritate and inflame the tissues. Electrical stimulation between the anterior and posterior needles is usually effective and fortunately rarely aggravates.

Patient position Properly position the patient in the lateral recumbent position (side-lying) with a pillow between his or her knees. The painful side is up and they are lying on the unaffected side. Some knee flexion is helpful to get the greatest access under the tendinous band. The posterior needle at GB 33 is usually the easiest to insert under the tendon. The anterior needle is often more problematic, as the IT band and its fascia often "merge" with the lateral quadriceps group, and there might not be space for a needle to be inserted posteriorly under the tendon. In this case, don't fret, as perpendicular insertion is acceptable. Electrical stimulation between the two paired needles will help make up the difference!

The extraordinary point Jiankua

★

Jiankua ("posterior" GB 29)
One to two needles, perpendicular insertion, to a depth of 2 to 3 inches, depending on patient size.

The extraordinary point *Jiankua* is located halfway between the greater trochanter and the crest of the ilium.[3] It is approximately 2 to 4 cun posterior to the traditional location of GB 29, and is sensitive in virtually all cases of IT band syndrome. The point is just posterior to the dense muscle tissue of the tensor fascia lata. With deep palpation the gluteus medius and minimus are reached.

Needle technique

★

Jiankua is needled perpendicularly 2 to 3 inches, depending on patient size. Deep needling is necessary, and with care, insertion is generally comfortable for the patient. I frequently use two paired points at *Jiankua*, found with palpation in a zone of pain that is from 1 to 3 centimeters in length. The upper point of this zone may include the motor point of the gluteus minimus. It is located halfway between the superior border of the greater trochanter and the crest of the ilium. Electrical stimulation between these two paired points often provides significant relief.

★ The importance of the point *Jiankua* needs to be emphasized. It is not a traditional acupuncture point, nor is it a commonly known extraordinary point. However, most practitioners have found it a significant *ahshi* point at one time or another while palpating the hip and gluteal area. Hopefully, you will be able to locate this point with precision and use it with confidence, as many patients respond well to its treatment. *Jiankua* is one of the most important local points I use in the treatment of IT band syndrome.

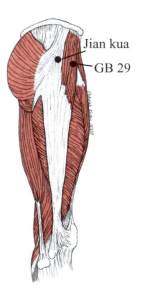

Gluteus medius, gluteus minimus One to four *ahshi* points.
Perpendicular insertion, to a depth of 2 to 3 inches, depending upon patient size.

Treat from one to four sensitive *ahshi* points of the gluteus medius and gluteus minimus muscles. These points are found inferior to the iliac crest over the broad area of the iliac fossa, superior to GB 29 and *Jiankua*. These two muscles are extremely important, as they contribute to many lumbo-sacral, hip, pelvic and lower-extremity pain syndromes. And there are no acupuncture points or well-known extraordinary points that lie in these muscles. Fortunately, palpation serves as an excellent guide in point selection.

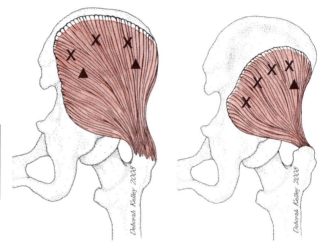

Gluteus medius, superficial (left)
Gluteus minimus, deep (right)
X – Trigger points
▲ – Motor points

Motor points If the practitioner wants more precise point selection, there are two motor points of the gluteus medius.[5] The first is located at the junction of the medial third and the lateral two-thirds of a line joining the posterior superior iliac spine with the superior border of the greater trochanter. The second motor point is 3 cun superior and 1 cun posterior from the superior border of the greater trochanter.

Trigger points Dr. Janet Travell describes numerous trigger points for both of these gluteal muscles that produce hip and gluteal pain syndromes.[6] They don't have defined and precise locations; however, palpation serves as an excellent guide in point selection. Generally, trigger points of the gluteus medius are found about 1 to 2 inches below the iliac crest. Those of the gluteus minimus are found 2 to 4 inches below.

Needle technique Techniques for treating points of the gluteus medius and minimus

1. Needling into *ahshi* points between taut bands of muscle is the most comfortable for the patient. On palpation, these points feel like depressions. There is often a specific needle depth in the fascial planes where mild "de qi" is obtained.

2. Needling directly into the taut bands is effective for releasing the muscle, but obviously less comfortable for the patient. On deeper insertion, the needle will penetrate these bands, which can be felt by the practitioner.

3. Pecking and rotating technique may be used with either of the two needling procedures above. The muscle will grab the needle, which also may facilitate a twitch response. This usually results in a release of tension in the muscle. If the needles are retained for 20 to 30 minutes, consider the pecking and rotating technique every five to 10 minutes, possibly achieving the twitch response multiple times.

4. Electric stimulation may be applied to paired points. This can be done with either needling into depressions or needling taut bands.

Clinical comments It is difficult to predict which needle technique is most effective on any individual patient. However, I choose one or more of these techniques and pay careful attention to needle depth for each point. If the response to treatment is not acceptable, or if there is an aggravation of symptoms without relief, I simply try one of the others. And remember, lateral recumbent (side-lying) offers the best access to these important gluteal points.

Adjacent points **GB 30**   Crossing point of the Gall Bladder and Bladder meridians
Used in many pain syndromes of the lumbar, sacral, and gluteal regions.

Bl 53.5   The piriformis muscle
Halfway between Bl 53 and Bl 54, Bl 53.5 is located just outside the lateral border of the sacrum. It is the motor point of the piriformis muscle.[7]

COMPLEMENTARY PROCEDURES

- As stated earlier, consult a good text on stretching of the IT band, which should be included in the overall protocol for the patient.

- A foam roller or similar device, used along the tense IT band, is a helpful home exercise for the patient.

- Alternate ice and heat after the acute stage at the lateral knee when the condition is "neither hot (re) nor cold (han)".

- Topical applications (herbal liniments, plasters, etc.) may benefit.

- Massage of the gluteus medius and gluteus minimus muscle group may benefit.

★ While all techniques listed above have shown clinical relevance, the starred items are predictably effective for this specific injury. Consider them first in a treatment plan.

REFERENCES

[1] Martinez, J: *Ilio-tibial Band Syndrome*. www.emedicine-sportsmedicine, December, 2006.

[2] Stirling, J: *Ilio-tibial Band Syndrome*. www.emedicine-sportsmedicine, January, 2008.

[3] Shanghai College of Traditional Medicine: *Acupuncture, A Comprehensive Text*. Eastland Press, Chicago, 1981 (page 363).

[4] Callison, M: *Motor Point Index*. AcuSport Seminar Series LLC, San Diego, 2007 (page 113).

[5] Callison, M: *Motor Point Index*. AcuSport Seminar Series LLC, San Diego, 2007 (page 112).

[6] Travell & Simons: *Myofascial Pain and Dysfunction: The Trigger Point Manual, Volume 2 (The Lower Extremities)*. Williams & Wilkins, Philadelphia, 1992 (pages 150-152 and pages 168-169).

[7] Callison, M: *Motor Point Index*. AcuSport Seminar Series LLC, San Diego, 2007 (page 103).

13
Posterior Thigh Pain
The Hamstring Muscle Group

Pain, spasm, and stiffness of the posterior thigh along the course of the hamstring muscle group

An acute injury with strain to one or more of the hamstring muscles, the muscle-tendon junction, or the attachments to the ischial tuberocity. Chronic cases may be due to repetitive stress disorder.

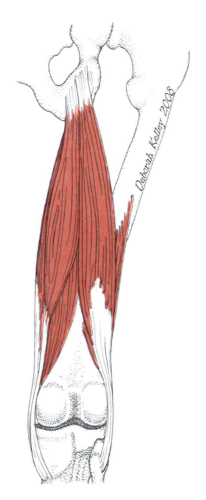

DIAGNOSIS & ASSESSMENT

Hamstring strain is a common injury to all athletes and active individuals, including runners, hikers, and jumpers. Even yoga practitioners can strain this muscle. Often called a "pulled hamstring", it is a tear in one or more of the muscles of the hamstring group. The biceps femoris is on the lateral aspect of the muscle group, and is the most common site of injury.[1] However, strain can also occur to the semimembranosus or the semitendinosus muscles on the medial side. Patients with minor to moderate hamstring strain often turn to acupuncture for treatment, and with proper assessment and the right techniques, the injury responds quite well.

Acute hamstring strain is usually of sudden onset, and pain is felt in the posterior thigh. The patient may report hearing a "popping" noise or feeling a "tearing" sensation. Pain may be experienced anywhere along the hamstring group, from the origin in the pelvis to its insertions at the posterior knee. In addition, spasm and stiffness of the entire muscle group may occur. The patient may even have an abnormal gait with movement. In acute cases, pain may be accompanied by bruising and swelling.

With acute trauma, the patient usually knows immediately that they have been injured. They have probably been doing some activity involving rapid acceleration and deceleration, such as sprinting, running hills, jumping, or sudden bursts of speed in such sports as soccer or basketball. I have seen numerous cases of acute hamstring strain from over-stretching the thigh in a vigorous yoga posture. However, gradual onset is possible. Some patients have mild chronic hamstring strain from repeated overuse, considered a repetitive stress injury. Here, the pain is in the same location of the posterior thigh but less severe, and there may be little to no bruising or swelling.

To confirm the diagnosis, palpate the posterior thigh along the entire course of the hamstring group. Painful points, as well as tightness, will be obvious. The three major muscles of the hamstring group originate at the ischial tuberosity of the pelvis, in the region of Bl 36. The short head of the biceps femoris, however, originates from the lower outer portion of the femur bone itself. All of these muscles cross the knee joint to their inferior attachments. The semimembranosus and the semitendinosus insert into the medial aspect of the tibia near Kid 10. The biceps femoris inserts at the head of the fibula on the lateral side. The points Bl 38 and Bl 39 are adjacent to this attachment. The belly of the muscle in the general region of Bl 37 is commonly point-sensitive, regardless of the site of the actual muscle injury.

Next, test the hamstrings with resisted flexion of the knee. The patient lies prone (face down) on the treatment table. Simply have them flex the knee while you resist the movement with your hand on their heel. If this causes pain, the hamstring group is probably involved. Remember the rules of muscle strain. With a grade I or moderate grade II injury, the muscle fibers are stretched or only moderately torn. These are great cases for the acupuncturist, and you should feel confident with the treatments described below. As you proceed to a grade III injury, the hamstring muscle is severely torn, and may even be completely ruptured. If pain and other symptoms are severe, and you are able to palpate a depression in the muscle, refer the patient for further orthopedic evaluation. While acupuncture might be a reasonable complementary treatment, immobilization or surgery may be required.

Treating the hamstring group is among my favorites. Not only does the patient usually respond quickly, but access to the muscle is easy and needle insertion straightforward. The hamstrings are a common site of injury for athletes, but learning how to effectively treat this muscle has added benefits. Releasing muscular tension in this group benefits many pain patterns of the gluteal, lumbo-sacral, and hip region.

176 • Posterior Thigh Pain *The Hamstring Muscle Group*

SUMMARY OF THE INJURY

Clinical Features
- Acute trauma causes strain to one or more of the hamstring muscles
- Pain may be palpated at the hamstring attachment at the ischial tuberosity in the region of Bl 36
- The muscle-tendon junction, inferior to Bl 36, is also a frequent site of injury
- Pain is often found on palpation in the belly of muscle, in the region of Bl 37
- Pain reproduced with resisted knee flexion
- Injury usually occurs during activities involving fast acceleration or deceleration
- The biceps femoris on the lateral side is the most commonly injured muscle of the hamstring group

Common Patient Complaints
- Sudden onset of pain in the posterior thigh area
- Pain may be accompanied by muscle spasms and stiffness, especially as the injury becomes more chronic
- In acute cases, pain may be accompanied by bruising and swelling
- May have heard a "popping" noise or felt a "tearing" sensation
- Hamstring strain may be from repeated overuse
- Symptoms aggravated during activities such as running, walking or jumping

Differentiation from Similar Injuries and Conditions
- Differentiate from pain referred from the lumbar spine, the sacral-iliac joint, or the gluteal region
- Contusion due to a direct blow or strike to the area
- Ischial bursitis
- Hamstring tendonitis at the attachments in the knee

Typical Medical Recommendations
- The initial care of the hamstring is dependent on the severity of the injury. With bruising and swelling in more severe cases, stop activity and rest immediately. An ice pack and compressive bandage can be applied to control swelling. Crutches may be considered if walking is painful or if spasms are severe.
- Anti-inflammatory medications
- Hot applications
  Heat may be used after the acute stage to relax spasm.
- Stretching
  Gentle stretching benefits mild to moderate strain.
- Physical therapy
  Ultrasound, massage, other physical therapy modalities.
- Orthopedic evaluation
  Refer for further orthopedic evaluation if is there is significant pain not relieved by rest, and/or a palpable depression in the muscle. Rest and immobilization may be required and surgery may be necessary.

177 • Posterior Thigh Pain *The Hamstring Muscle Group*

TREATMENT & TECHNIQUES

Overview: Hamstring strain is most commonly diagnosed under the category of accident/trauma. The injury is at the level of the muscles and tendons, with qi and blood stagnation in the channels and collaterals. Hamstring strain is clearly Bladder meridian pathology, although the Kidney meridian may also be involved. Occasionally, strain and muscle tightness may be a repetitive stress disorder due to the accumulation of micro-trauma. Both cases are treated with similar points and techniques. Internal organ imbalances of the Bladder and Kidney are not necessarily related. It may be more likely to see Liver dysfunction, as it fails to control the muscles and tendons.

Prognosis: Treat twice a week for three weeks, then re-evaluate. Most cases without complications have good results within six treatments. A simple strain may take only several treatments for significant improvement. With chronic cases, continue treatment at least once weekly after the first three-week period.

STEP ONE: MERIDIANS & MICROSYSTEMS

Choose among these four techniques, carefully determining if there is an immediate decrease in pain or an increase in range of motion.

Technique #1: **The Tendino-Muscle Meridians**

 Bl 67   Bleeding technique

Bleeding the jing-well point should always be considered the first place to start, as it is often immediately effective for some of the symptoms.

Technique #2: **Opposite Side (contra-lateral)**

Corresponding points on the opposite (unaffected) side may be considered; however, treatment to the affected side is usually preferred.

Technique #3: **Opposite Extremity (upper/lower)**

Corresponding points on the opposite extremity may be considered; however, treatment to the affected extremity is usually preferred.

Technique #4: **Empirical Points**

No well-known empirical points for hamstring strain.

STEP TWO: MERIDIANS & MICROSYSTEMS

Choose among these four techniques, selecting points that are appropriate for the signs and symptoms of the patient.

Technique #5: **The Shu-Stream Point Combination**

 Bl 65 affected side + SI 3 opposite side
This point combination works wonderfully in most cases of hamstring strain and stiffness.

Technique #6: **Traditional Point Categories**

★ Palpation may assist in your choice of other less-common Bladder meridian points.

Bl 57	Distal point
Bl 58	Luo-connecting point
Bl 59	Xi-cleft point of the Yang Qiao mai
Bl 60	Jing-river point
Bl 63	Xi-cleft point
GB 34	Hui-influential point of tendons

Technique #7: **The Extraordinary Meridians**

GB 41 + SJ 5   Activate the Dai mai
Hamstring injuries often present with hip and gluteal imbalances, which may be considered Dai mai pathology.

Technique #8: **Microsystems**

Auricular Therapy
Local: Between the hip and the knee (Chinese and French locations), lumbar spine
Zang-fu points: Kidney, Bladder, Liver
Systemic points for pain: Shen men, Thalamus, Adrenal, Endocrine

STEP THREE: INTERNAL ORGAN IMBALANCES

Choose appropriate points to treat internal organ imbalances that may contribute to the injury or pain syndrome.

Technique #9: **Qi, Blood, and the Zang-fu Organs**

Strain of the hamstring muscle group is an acute injury and therefore internal organ imbalances are usually not a factor in treatment. However, there are several zang-fu syndromes which may contribute to the condition.

Liver imbalances   Liver qi stagnation, Liver yin deficiency, and
Liver blood deficiency
Liver imbalances may result in susceptibility of the
muscles and tendons to both acute and chronic injury.
Consider the following:

Liv 3   Yuan-source point; supports the Liver
in its function of controlling the
muscles and tendons

GB 34   Hui-influential point of tendons

Treat GB 34 on the affected side and Liv 3 on the
opposite side.

Kidney deficiency   Kidney imbalances may result in deficiency in the Kidney
and Bladder meridians, increasing the susceptibility of
the hamstring group to injury.

*Points should be determined by the practitioner from both palpation
and analysis of the signs and symptoms of the patient.*

STEP FOUR: THE SITE OF INJURY

*Choose among the local and adjacent points at the site of injury.
Points may be determined by palpation, orthopedic testing, and
analysis of the signs and symptoms of the patient.*

Technique #10:   **Local and Adjacent Points**

The belly of the hamstring   **Bl 37**

⭐ One or two needles, with perpendicular insertion,
to a depth 1.5 to 2 inches

Bl 37 is located 6 cun inferior
to Bl 36, and is in the region
of the belly of the hamstring
group. The actual point
is located in a depression
between the biceps femoris
on the lateral side and the
semimembranosus and the
semitendinosus on the medial
side. The sciatic nerve lies deep
to the point. I use Bl 37 for
all cases of hamstring strain
and tightness, and it is the
first local point to consider. I
will use one or two needles in
the tender zone that is easily
found on palpation. On the
average-sized patient, needle
perpendicularly with a 2 to 3
inch needle to a depth of 1.5
to 2 inches.

● – Bl 37
○ – Bl 37 point variations

Bl 37

180 • Posterior Thigh Pain *The Hamstring Muscle Group*

Be sure to insert into the depression between the taut palpable bands of the muscle, which lie both medially and laterally. Whether the pain is in the belly of the muscle or at the attachment at the ischial tuberocity, this point benefits most cases and it rarely aggravates. Consider electrical stimulation between the two paired needles, with the exception of acute patients with significant pain and swelling.

Clinical comments

Over the years, I have observed very good results with the treatment of Bl 37, and have developed great respect for the point. It always seems to be effective in treating hamstring strain from over-vigorous yoga postures or from over-stretching the muscle during running or other athletic activities. Hamstring strain often presents with pain at the ischial tuberocity near Bl 36, and patients often remark that my needles are nowhere near the site of their pain. I attempt to reassure them, only to have it confirmed when they get off the table feeling little or no pain and experiencing increased flexibility.

Hamstring ahshi points

Ahshi points in the taut bands of the muscle. Perpendicular insertion, to a depth of 1 to 1.5 inches.

Consider treatment to *ahshi* points in the belly of the hamstring. They can be found in the biceps femoris on the lateral side as well as in the semimembranosus and the semitendinosus muscles on the medial side. Use the depression at Bl 37 as the reference point as well as the posterior centerline of the hamstring, which is the Bladder meridian. These points are the sites of the hamstring trigger points, as Dr. Janet Travell suggests in her work on myofascial pain syndromes.[2] There are also several motor points in the hamstring group in this region.[3] Most are located both medial and lateral to Bl 37 in the belly of the muscle. Consider two paired points in one or two of the most taut bands of the muscle. Perpendicular insertion from 1 to 1.5 inches usually suffices.

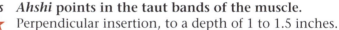

X – *Trigger points*
▲ – *Motor points*

Clinical comments

Many muscles have one or two precisely located trigger points and motor points. However, with the hamstring group they are numerous. Palpating for taut bands and point sensitivity often suffices to locate these points.

181 • Posterior Thigh Pain *The Hamstring Muscle Group*

The ischial attachment	**Bl 36**
of the hamstring	Perpendicular insertion, depth varies.

★ Hamstring strain may affect the tendon at its attachment to the ischial tuberosity in the region of Bl 36. If Bl 36 is chosen for treatment, there are several reasonable techniques. A needle may be inserted at Bl 36, needled deeply towards the tendon. Care should be taken to approach the tendon without actually penetrating it, as this may irritate and further inflame the tissue. You could also consider a set of paired needles inserted deeply on the medial and lateral sides of the tendon. These would be about 1 cun medial and 1 cun lateral to the text location of Bl 36. Electrical stimulation between these two needles may help reduce inflammation of the hamstring tendon.

● – Bl 37 (inferior)
    Bl 36 (superior)
○ – Bl 36 point variations

The muscle-tendon junction   **"Lower" Bl 36**

★ Perpendicular insertion, depth varies.

The muscle-tendon junction is also a frequent injury site for the hamstring group. Some sources suggest that it is the most likely site for strain.[4] This zone is about 1 to 3 cun distal to Bl 36. This "lower" Bl 36 point may be needled deeply into the muscle-tendon junction. It can also be paired with Bl 36, these two needles being in a vertical line along the Bladder meridian. Again, electrical stimulation between these paired-points may be considered.

Hamstring tendonitis at the attachments near the posterior knee may be more problematic, and won't be considered in detail here. However, the general treatment for the hamstring using two paired needles at Bl 37, or other hamstring *ahshi* points, is often effective.

Adjacent and "below" points	GB 30	Crossing point of the Gall Bladder and Bladder meridians
	Bl 40	He-sea point
	Bl 38	Adjacent to the tendon of the biceps femoris
	Bl 39	Adjacent to the tendon of the biceps femoris
	Kid 10	Between the tendons of the semimembranosus and semitendinosus

COMPLEMENTARY PROCEDURES

- Topical applications (herbal liniments, plasters, etc.) may benefit.

- Acute hamstring strain often responds well to topical application of arnicated oil.

- Small Japanese-style retainer needles in *ahshi* points of the hamstring may be considered.

- Massage of the entire hamstring muscle group may benefit.

★ While all techniques listed above have shown clinical relevance, the starred items are predictably effective for this specific injury. Consider them first in a treatment plan.

REFERENCES

[1] Dutton, M: *Orthopeadic Examination, Evaluation, and Intervention,* Second Edition. McGraw-Hill, USA, 2008 (page 900).

[2] Travell & Simons: *Myofascial Pain and Dysfunction: The Trigger Point Manual, Volume 2 (The Lower Extremities).* Williams & Wilkins, Philadelphia, 1992 (pages 315-318).

[3] Callison, M: *Motor Point Index.* AcuSport Seminar Series LLC, San Diego, 2007 (pages 126-127).

[4] Dutton, M: *Orthopeadic Examination, Evaluation, and Intervention,* Second Edition. McGraw-Hill, USA, 2008 (page 900).

Notes

14
Hip Pain

Trochanteric Bursitis of the Hip

Pain in the hip and lateral thigh which may radiate down the ilio-tibial band

A repetitive stress injury characterized by inflammation of the trochanteric bursa of the hip. Sometimes it may occur from acute trauma. Hip bursitis usually involves the gluteal muscles and the ilio-tibial band.

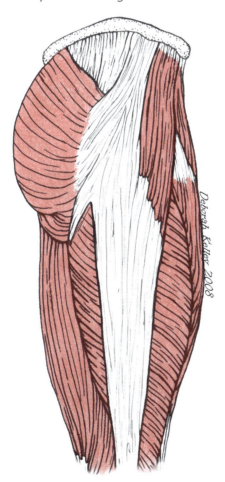

DIAGNOSIS & ASSESSMENT

Trochanteric bursitis is a common cause of pain in the hip and the lateral thigh.[1] While not frequently a sports injury, I have included this pain syndrome because it is often overlooked in the clinic. Many patients with a tight ilio-tibial band or with lateral knee pain due to the IT band often have undiagnosed bursitis at the greater trochanter. The practitioner may miss it, in part because there are no acupuncture points at the site.

I had a patient years ago who came to my clinic with the prior diagnosis of osteoarthritis of the hip. She was a distance runner, and reported pain, as well as "popping" in the hip, all of which was affecting her training. When I found she was running 60 to 70 miles a week, I immediately questioned the diagnosis. It would be quite unusual for an athlete with degenerative hip disease to train and compete at such a high level.

I tested my assumptions as we walked together down the hall with my hand placed over her greater trochanter. Indeed, I could feel the popping, and after other simple exams, suggested it was hip bursitis. The popping was merely the ilio-tibial band snapping over the inflamed trochanteric bursa. Most importantly, the problem was outside of the hip joint capsule, which was a great relief to the patient. Acquainting yourself with this condition will assist in the diagnosis and treatment of many future patients with hip pain.

The trochanteric bursa rests between the bony prominence of the greater trochanter and the tendon that passes over it. Technically, this is the tendon of the tensor fascia lata muscle as it becomes the ilio-tibial tract, running distally down the lateral aspect of the thigh. However, the gluteus maximus, gluteus medius and gluteus minimus are connected to this tendon with their respective fascia. Thus the patient will frequently present with hip pain throughout the gluteal region, and may not necessarily report specific pain at the site of the bursa. Symptoms in the hip and the lateral thigh range from a general dull ache to extreme sharp pain. Some patients report the pain is worse when lying on the affected side, such as during sleep. In addition to the hip and gluteal region, pain may radiate down the ilio-tibial band distally towards the knee.

When the bursa is inflamed, pain may be triggered from lower-extremity activities like running, soccer and football. However, discomfort can come from movements as simple as walking. Some patients, like the runner mentioned above, may present with a "snapping" or "popping" sensation. Make sure you check for it with a hand placed lightly over the greater trochanter during hip flexion and extension.

Trochanteric bursitis is usually chronic, with insidious onset, and may be viewed as a repetitive stress injury. However, it can be seen acutely after an injury, such as a fall on the lateral thigh or a direct blow in football or other contact sports. Fortunately, hip bursitis is usually a clear diagnosis. With the patient in the lateral recumbent (side-lying) position, press directly on the greater trochanter. Try using the palm of your hand first, although if very localized, you may need to use a finger or a thumb. If there is pain with pressure, bursitis is most likely the problem. I have had many patients exclaim, "That's where the pain starts!" when palpating the bursa, even when they don't report this during the interview. You may be able to palpate swelling of the bursa, with perhaps a "spongy" feeling that may implicate dampness from the TCM perspective. However, make sure you compare sensitivity with the unaffected side.

As we stated above, the ilio-tibial band is a continuation of the tensor fascia lata muscle and, indirectly, the other gluteal muscles. You should always check for sensitive points in this gluteal area, as hip bursitis frequently presents with these *ahshi* points. This is covered in detail in Step Four with the treatment of local and adjacent points.

186 • Hip Pain *Trochanteric Bursitis of the Hip*

Take time to question the patient about the onset of the condition. It may be associated with a change in training, such as increased mileage, hills, or speed. A change in running shoe or running surface may also be related. As with most lower-extremity injuries, consider having the patient evaluated for foot biomechanics. Both abnormal or excessive pronation or supination, as well as other lower-extremity biomechanical imbalances, may create additional repetitive strain and need to be corrected. Other structural issues may exist, such as an anatomical short leg and an increased "Q" angle in women (due to a wider pelvis).

As for internal organ imbalances, the Liver and Gall Bladder are frequently associated with non-athletic cases of hip bursitis. I have observed a high correlation of women who also have gall bladder dysfunction, such as damp heat as seen in cholecystitis (gall bladder inflammation). You might try to counsel these patients about a more favorable diet for the syndrome of damp heat in the gall bladder. Acupuncture and herbal medicine may also be incorporated into the treatment plan to correct these internal organ imbalances. This may assist in maintaining healthy flow of qi and blood in their respective meridians, contributing to the healing of the bursa, the ilio-tibial band, and the gluteal soft tissues.

SUMMARY OF THE INJURY

Clinical Features
- Repetitive stress causes inflammation and irritation of the hip bursa
- Pain with pressure directly over the greater trochanter
- Associated with a change in training, such as increased mileage, hills, or speed
- Structural considerations such as wide pelvic "Q" angle and an anatomical short leg increase the stress on the bursa
- Abnormal or excessive pronation or supination, as well as other lower-extremity biomechanical imbalances may contribute
- Liver and Gall Bladder imbalances often contribute

Common Patient Complaints
- Pain in the hip and the lateral thigh
- Symptoms range from a general dull ache to extreme sharp pain
- Pain radiates down the IT band toward the knee
- Pain is usually experienced during lower-extremity activities, such as running and hiking
- Pain lying on the affected side at night
- May have audible popping or snapping with hip flexion and extension

Differentiation from Similar Injuries and Conditions
- Osteoarthritis of the hip
- Tear of the labrum or other joint capsule lesions
- Differentiate from sciatic pain referred from the lumbar spine or the sacral-iliac joint
- Other soft tissue lesions of the hip and pelvis
- Inflammation of the other smaller hip bursa
- IT band syndrome may be associated with hip bursitis

Typical Medical Recommendations
- Ice may be applied when acute.
- Anti-inflammatory medications
- Stretching
  Consult a good text on stretching of the IT band, which should be included in the overall protocol for the patient.
- Biomechanics
  Correct pronation or supination with shoes and/or orthotics. Other lower-extremity biomechanical imbalances may need to be assessed.
- Physical therapy
  Ultrasound, massage, other physical therapy modalities. Western orthopedics frequently prefer the application of heat in cases of bursitis.
- Orthopedic procedures
  Steroid injection into the bursa provides very good results. I have seen a single injection provide relief to a patient when acupuncture failed to give adequate and lasting results.

TREATMENT & TECHNIQUES

Overview: Hip pain due to trochanteric bursitis is most commonly diagnosed under the category of accident/trauma. This is usually a repetitive stress disorder due to the accumulation of micro-trauma. However, occasionally it may occur as acute trauma. The injury is at the level of the tendons (the bursa) and the bone, with qi and blood stagnation in the channels and collaterals. Hip bursitis is clearly a Gall Bladder meridian pathology. Internal organ imbalances of the Liver and Gall Bladder frequently contribute.

Prognosis: Treat twice a week for three weeks, then re-evaluate. Most cases without complications will have good results within six treatments. With chronic cases, continue treatment at least once weekly after the first three-week period. In the rare case where results are not satisfactory, I will refer the patient for steroid injection. However, I suggest to the patient that acupuncture should be continued after the injection to treat the soft tissue components of the condition.

STEP ONE: INITIAL TREATMENT

Choose among these four techniques, carefully determining if there is an immediate decrease in pain or an increase in range of motion.

Technique #1: **The Tendino-Muscle Meridians**

 GB 44   Bleeding technique

The Gall Bladder tendino-muscle meridian probably does not get to the level of the bursa. However, bleeding the jing-well point is sometimes effective for stiffness and tightness of the IT band.

Technique #2: **Opposite Side (contra-lateral)**

Corresponding points on the opposite (unaffected) side may be considered; however, treatment to the affected extremity is usually preferred.

Technique #3: **Opposite Extremity (upper/lower)**

Corresponding points on the opposite extremity may be considered; however, treatment to the affected side is usually preferred.

Technique #4: **Empirical Points**

No well known empirical points for hip bursitis.

STEP TWO: MERIDIANS & MICROSYSTEMS

Choose among these four techniques, selecting points that are appropriate for the signs and symptoms of the patient.

Technique #5: **The Shu-Stream Point Combination**

★ **GB 41 (or GB 42) affected side + SJ 3 opposite side**
GB 42 is often more sensitive than GB 41, and should be considered as an alternative shu-stream point.

Technique #6: **Traditional Point Categories**

★ Palpation may assist in your choice of other Gall Bladder meridian points.

GB 40	Yuan-source point
GB 43	"Water" point
GB 34	He-sea point, hui-influential point of tendons

★ GB 31   Dispels wind (feng) from the lower extremity

This point is located on the ilio-tibial band. Its Chinese name, "wind market" (feng shi), implies its use in the treatment of wind symptoms. This includes the sudden onset, sudden disappearance, and the "snapping" of the tendon at the greater trochanter. Also, the migrating pain and stiffness that often radiates down the ilio-tibial band may be considered wind in nature.

I often use the technique of two paired points at the region of GB 31. With perpendicular insertion into the IT band, these points are about 1 inch apart on the Gall Bladder meridian, and can be determined simply by palpation. A variation is GB 31 and GB 32 as the two paired points. Electrical stimulation on these two points may also be considered. The needle should penetrate the ilio-tibial band, except for the occasional patient with such tightness that deep needling is uncomfortable.

Technique #7: **The Extraordinary Meridians**

★ **GB 41 + SJ 5**   Activate the Dai mai
Frequently, trochanteric bursitis originates from hip and gluteal imbalances, which may be considered Dai mai pathology.

Technique #8: **Microsystems**

Auricular Therapy
Local: Hip, lumbar spine
Zang-fu points: Gall Bladder, Liver
Systemic points for pain: Shen men, Thalamus, Adrenal, Endocrine

STEP THREE: INTERNAL ORGAN IMBALANCES

Choose appropriate points to treat internal organ imbalances that may contribute to the injury or pain syndrome.

Technique #9: **Qi, Blood, and the Zang-fu Organs**

Inflammation of the trochanteric bursa may be either an acute or chronic injury, yet internal organ imbalances frequently seem to contribute.

Liver imbalances Liver qi stagnation, Liver yin deficiency, and
★ Liver blood deficiency
Liver imbalances may result in susceptibility of the gluteal tendons to inflammation and repetitive stress injury. Consider the following:

Liv 3	Yuan-source point; supports the Liver in its function of controlling the muscles and tendons
GB 34	Hui-influential point of tendons

Treat GB 34 on the affected side and Liv 3 on the opposite side.

Liver and Gall Bladder damp heat
Excess syndromes of the Liver and Gall Bladder are also frequently observed in the patient with hip bursitis. These imbalances may result in Gall Bladder meridian dysfunction, increasing the susceptibility of the trochanteric bursa to inflammation.

Spleen imbalances Spleen deficiency with dampness
Some female patients with hip bursitis present with Spleen deficiency and dampness. This should be fairly straightforward for the practitioner to assess.

Points should be determined from both palpation and analysis of the signs and symptoms of the patient.

STEP FOUR: THE SITE OF INJURY

Choose among the local and adjacent points at the site of injury. Points may be determined by palpation, orthopedic testing, and analysis of the signs and symptoms of the patient.

Technique #10: **Local and Adjacent Points**

The trochanteric bursa There are various ways to approach treatment to the
★ trochanteric bursa. Obviously, as a painful *ahshi* point, you can needle directly into the bursa, with either perpendicular or oblique insertion. I prefer two paired points over the bursa, which is usually large enough to allow multiple needles. More aggressively, you could use a "surround the dragon" technique with four needles: superior, inferior, anterior and posterior to the bursa.

191 • Hip Pain *Trochanteric Bursitis of the Hip*

○ – Area of pain at the greater trochanter
↗ – "Surrounding the dragon" at the trochanteric bursa

Pay attention to whether you are needling at the margin of the bursa or actually penetrating into the bursal sac. If you fail to get satisfactory results, or if there is aggravation, try the other technique.

Techniques

Electrical stimulation may be considered with needles into or adjacent to the bursa. Cupping over the bursa is also a possible technique. Occasionally I will use a bleeding cup with beneficial results. Western orthopedics suggest the application of heat in cases of bursitis, so the use of indirect or needle-top moxa may be indicated.

The extraordinary point Jiankua

Jiankua ("posterior" GB 29)
One to two needles, perpendicular insertion, to a depth of 2 to 3 inches, depending on patient size.

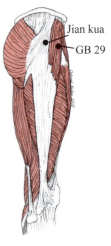

The extraordinary point *Jiankua* is located halfway between the greater trochanter and the crest of the ilium.[2] It is approximately 2 to 4 cun posterior to the traditional location of GB 29, and is sensitive in most cases of hip bursitis. The point is just posterior to the dense muscle tissue of the tensor fascia lata. With deep palpation the gluteus medius and minimus are reached.

Needle technique

Jiankua is needled perpendicularly 2 to 3 inches, depending on patient size. Deep needling is necessary, and with care, insertion is generally comfortable for the patient. I frequently use two paired points at *Jiankua*, found with palpation in a zone of pain that is from 1 to 3 centimeters in length. The upper point of this zone may include the motor point of the gluteus minimus. It is located 3 cun superior to the superior border of the greater trochanter.[3] Electrical stimulation between these two paired points often provides significant relief.

Gluteus medius, gluteus minimus

One to four *ahshi* points.
Perpendicular insertion, to a depth of 2 to 3 inches, depending upon patient size.

Treat from one to four sensitive *ahshi* points of the gluteus medius and gluteus minimus muscles. These points are found inferior to the iliac crest over the broad area of the iliac fossa, superior to GB 29 and *Jiankua*.

These two muscles are extremely important, as they contribute to many lumbo-sacral, hip, pelvic and lower-extremity pain syndromes. And there are no acupuncture points or well-known extraordinary points that lie in these muscles. Fortunately, palpation serves as an excellent guide in point selection. This treatment is discussed in more detail on page 172.

> *Gluteus medius*
> X – *Trigger points*
> ▲ – *Motor points*

The piriformis muscle

Bl 53.5
The gluteal points Bl 53 and Bl 54 are located just outside the lateral border of the sacrum. Bl 53 lies superior to the piriformis muscle, level with the second sacral foramen. Bl 54 is level with the fourth sacral foramen, placing it just inferior to the piriformis. Halfway between them lies "Bl 53.5", which is in the piriformis muscle just lateral to its attachment on the sacrum. This is also considered the motor point of the muscle.[4]

Needle Bl 53.5 with perpendicular insertion to a depth of 1.5 to 2 inches, depending on patient size. When treating directly into this muscle, pay attention for the dense feeling in the needle and possibly some discomfort for the patient. The practitioner may also elect to treat *ahshi* points lateral to Bl 53.5, on the taut muscle as it courses towards its attachment at the greater trochanter. Electrical stimulation sometimes aggravates the piriformis, so caution is advised.

Patient position
The gluteal points as well as the piriformis points just lateral to the sacrum may be needled with the patient in the lateral recumbent (side-lying) or prone (face-down) positions.

Adjacent points

Bl 53, Bl 54
Rather than treatment directly in the piriformis, the practitioner may consider Bl 53 and Bl 54, as they are found in depressions and are generally more comfortable for the patient. Although these two points are above and below the piriformis, they often help to release the muscle. Use perpendicular insertion to a depth of 1.5 to 2 inches, depending on patient size.

GB 30 Crossing point of the Gall Bladder and Bladder meridians
Used in many pain syndromes of the lumbar, sacral, and gluteal regions.

193 • Hip Pain *Trochanteric Bursitis of the Hip*

COMPLEMENTARY PROCEDURES

- Applications of heat often benefit pain and inflammation of the hip bursa.

- A foam roller or similar device, used along the tense IT band, is a helpful home exercise for the patient.

- As stated earlier, consult a good text on stretching of the IT band, which should be included in the overall protocol for the patient.

- Topical applications (herbal liniments, plasters, etc.) may benefit.

★ While all techniques listed above have shown clinical relevance, the starred items are predictably effective for this specific injury. Consider them first in a treatment plan.

REFERENCES

[1] Dutton, M: *Orthopeadic Examination, Evaluation, and Intervention,* Second Edition. McGraw-Hill, USA, 2008 (page 905).

[2] Shanghai College of Traditional Medicine: *Acupuncture, A Comprehensive Text.* Eastland Press, Chicago, 1981 (page 363).

[3] Callison, M: *Motor Point Index.* AcuSport Seminar Series LLC, San Diego, 2007 (page 113).

[4] Callison, M: *Motor Point Index.* AcuSport Seminar Series LLC, San Diego, 2007 (page 103).

15
Hip Pain

Arthritis of the Hip

Pain, stiffness, and limited range of motion of the hip. Pain may radiate to the inguinal and groin region

A repetitive stress injury or osteoarthritis characterized by chronic degeneration of the articular surface of the hip joint.

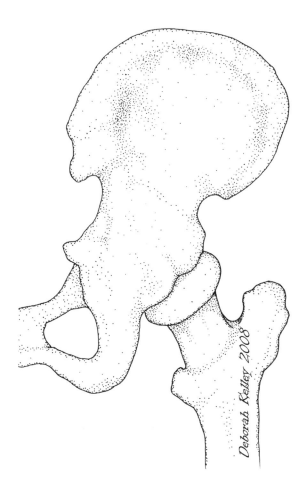

DIAGNOSIS & ASSESSMENT

Hip pain due to osteoarthritis is a common condition seen by the acupuncture practitioner. In all likelihood, this trend will continue with such a large population of active individuals over the age of 50. This chronic condition is a degeneration of the articular surface of the hip joint – a "wear-and-tear" type of injury. The patient presents with gluteal and thigh pain, with considerable variation of signs and symptoms. There is often a referred pain to the anterior aspect of the pelvis in the inguinal and groin region. This is characteristic and predictable in hip joint arthritis. Limited range of motion and stiffness often accompany pain. Like other cases of chronic arthritis, exercise and weight-bearing activities aggravate the patient, and symptoms are relieved by rest. The patient may walk with a limp.

When examining the patient, pain is usually reproduced with passive internal rotation of the thigh. You can easily perform this test with the patient supine or seated at the edge of the table. With the hip and knee flexed, rotate the lower leg laterally, away from the center line of the body. This internally rotates the femur in the hip joint. This test is positive if it produces pain. You might also want to test hip flexion, as this movement may become limited in patients with hip arthritis. As for imaging, a simple hip X-ray may show the degeneration of the joint space, and an MRI helps rule out a tear of the labrum or other capsular lesions within the joint. It is important to examine for trochanteric bursitis, a condition that also causes hip pain. This can be done by palpating the bursa at the high point of the greater trochanter. A complete discussion of hip bursitis is covered on page 185.

An arthritic hip will always present with *ahshi* points in the gluteal region. The practitioner will likely palpate the common points of GB 30, GB 29, and closer to the sacrum at Bl 53 and Bl 54. However, you must not overlook the predictable *ahshi* points found at a posterior version of GB 29 (*Jiankua*), located halfway between the greater trochanter and the crest of the ilium. Also, the quadratus lumborum muscle may contribute, which is one of the most overlooked sources for hip pain.[1] These considereations are covered in detail in Step Four.

I have confidence in the techniques discussed in this chapter, and really enjoy treating hip joint pain. While not as immediate and dramatic as other acute injuries, acupuncture treatment provides significant benefit. My hip pain patients are always ready to reschedule without hesitation, as they experience good results. However, the entire treatment protocol usually includes other complementary therapies, including Chinese herbal medicine and dietary supplements. Physical therapy modalities also complement acupuncture quite well for patients with hip joint disease.

SUMMARY OF THE INJURY

Clinical Features
- Osteoarthritis, manifesting as a degeneration of the articular surface of the hip joint
- Sometimes considered a repetitive stress injury; some patients have previous acute trauma involving the hip
- Often seen as a chronic condition in patients over 50
- Pain with passive internal rotation of hip, and frequently, limited hip flexion
- Osteoarthritis may be diagnosed as a *Bi* syndrome

Common Patient Complaints
- Gluteal and thigh area pain, with limited range of motion and stiffness
- Pain often radiates to inguinal and groin region
- Symptoms are aggravated during exercise and weight-bearing activities
- Pain usually relieved with rest
- Patient may walk with a limp

Differentiation from Similar Injuries and Conditions
- Trochanteric bursitis
- "Hip pointer" and direct trauma to the ilium
- Rule out tear of the labrum or other capsular lesions
- Rule out rheumatoid arthritis and other systemic inflammatory conditions
- Differentiate from sciatic pain referred from the lumbar spine or the sacral-iliac joint. Higher vertebral levels of the lumbar spine may refer to the inguinal region.
- With the elderly patient, rule out hip fracture.

Typical Medical Recommendations
- Anti-inflammatory medications
- Modify activity
  With many patients, certain activities need to be reduced or altogether avoided in order to control pain.
- Biomechanics
  Correction of all lower-extremity biomechanical imbalances are essential for the overall protocol.
- Physical therapy
  Ultrasound, massage, other physical therapy modalities. Application of heat may relieve the pain of chronic hip arthritis.
- Orthopedic procedures
  Western procedures used to manage arthritic hip pain vary and need to be evaluated for each individual patient. Surgical hip replacement is considered when other treatments fail.

197 • Hip Pain *Arthritis of the Hip*

TREATMENT & TECHNIQUES

Overview: Hip pain due to arthritis is commonly diagnosed as a *Bi* syndrome. Care should be taken to assess the heat (re), cold (han), damp (shi), and wind (feng) contributions. This will assist in the choice of points, needle technique and herbal prescription. Some practitioners may diagnose hip joint pathology under the category of accident/ trauma. This is seen in long-term athletic and active individuals with accumulated micro-trauma. The injury is at the level of the tendons, ligaments, and bone. There is qi and blood stagnation in the channels and collaterals. The Gall Bladder and possibly the Bladder meridians are involved. Internal organ imbalances of the Liver and the Kidney frequently contribute.

Prognosis: Treat once or twice a week for three to six weeks, then re-evaluate. Ongoing acupuncture treatment is usually necessary. The patient frequently experiences improvement, so they are usually willing.

STEP ONE: INITIAL TREATMENT

Choose among these four techniques, carefully determining if there is an immediate decrease in pain or an increase in range of motion.

Technique #1: **The Tendino-Muscle Meridians**

GB 44   Bleeding technique
The Gall Bladder tendino-muscle meridian does not get deep enough to affect the hip joint. However, bleeding the jing-well point may be effective for some of the soft-tissue symptoms.

Technique #2: **Opposite Side (contra-lateral)**

Corresponding points on the opposite (unaffected) side may be considered; however, treatment to the affected side is usually preferred.

Technique #3: **Opposite Extremity (upper/lower)**

Corresponding points on the opposite extremity may be considered; however, treatment to the affected extremity is usually preferred.

Technique #4: **Empirical Points**

No well known empirical points for hip arthritis.

STEP TWO: MERIDIANS & MICROSYSTEMS

Choose among these four techniques, selecting points that are appropriate for the signs and symptoms of the patient.

Technique #5: **The Shu-Stream Point Combination**

★ **GB 41 (or GB 42) affected side + SJ 3 opposite side**
GB 42 is often more sensitive than GB 41, and should be considered as an alternative shu-stream point for this meridian.

Technique #6: **Traditional Point Categories**

★ Palpation may assist in your choice of Gall Bladder meridian points.

GB 40	Yuan-source point
GB 43	"Water" point
GB 37	Luo-connecting point
GB 34	Hui-influential point of tendons
GB 31	Dispels wind (feng) from the lower extremity

Technique #7: **The Extraordinary Meridians**

★ **GB 41 + SJ 5**   Activate the Dai mai
Arthritis in the hip presents with gluteal imbalances, which may be considered Dai mai pathology.

Technique #8: **Microsystems**

Auricular Therapy
Local: Hip (French), hip (Chinese), lumbar spine
Zang-fu points: Gall Bladder, Liver, Kidney
Systemic points for pain: Shen men, Thalamus, Adrenal, Endocrine

STEP THREE: INTERNAL ORGAN IMBALANCES

Choose appropriate points to treat internal organ imbalances that may contribute to the injury or pain syndrome.

Technique #9: **Qi, Blood, and the Zang-fu Organs**

There are various internal imbalances seen in the patient with chronic pain due to osteoarthritis of the hip. The following imbalances may be considered:

Kidney imbalances   Kidney deficiency
Syndromes of the Kidney are considered by some practitioners as an internal organ imbalance present in all patients with chronic arthritis and joint degeneration. However, treatment to the Kidney alone rarely is sufficient for this arthritic condition.

Liver imbalances	Liver qi stagnation, Liver yin deficiency, and Liver blood deficiency

Liver imbalances may result in Gall Bladder meridian dysfunction, increasing the susceptibility of the hip to inflammation and degeneration. Consider the following:

Liv 3	Yuan-source point; supports the Liver in its function of controlling the muscles and tendons
GB 34	Hui-influential point of tendons

Treat GB 34 on the affected side and Liv 3 on the opposite side.

Bi syndrome ★ Hip pain due to osteoarthritis is commonly diagnosed as a *Bi* syndrome. Care should be taken to assess the heat (re), cold (han), damp (shi), and wind (feng) contributions. This will assist in the choice of points, needle technique and herbal prescription.

Points should be determined by the practitioner from both palpation and analysis of the signs and symptoms of the patient.

STEP FOUR: THE SITE OF INJURY

Choose among the local and adjacent points at the site of injury. Points may be determined by palpation, orthopedic testing, and analysis of the signs and symptoms of the patient.

Technique #10: **Local and Adjacent Points**

The extraordinary point Jiankua ★ **Jiankua ("posterior" GB 29)**
One to two needles, perpendicular insertion, to a depth of 2 to 3 inches, depending on patient size.

The extraordinary point *Jiankua* is located halfway between the greater trochanter and the crest of the ilium.[2] It is approximately 2 to 4 cun posterior to the traditional location of GB 29, and is sensitive in virtually all cases of hip joint disease. The point is just posterior to the dense muscle tissue of the tensor fascia lata. With deep palpation the gluteus medius and minimus are reached. And deep to these tissues lies the hip joint.

Needle technique ★ *Jiankua* is needled perpendicularly 2 to 3 inches, depending on patient size.
Deep needling is necessary, and with care, insertion is generally comfortable for the patient.

200 • Hip Pain *Arthritis of the Hip*

I frequently use two paired points at *Jiankua*, found with palpation in a zone of pain that is from 1 to 3 centimeters in length. The upper point of this zone may include the motor point of the gluteus minimus. It is located halfway between the superior border of the greater trochanter and the crest of the ilium.[3] Electrical stimulation between these two paired points often provides significant relief. Also, consider needle-top moxa in the case of *Bi* syndrome with cold (han).

★ The importance of the point *Jiankua* needs to be emphasized. It is not a traditional acupuncture point, nor is it a commonly known extraordinary point. However, most practitioners have found it a significant *ahshi* point at one time or another while palpating the hip and gluteal area. Hopefully, you will be able to locate this point with precision and use it with confidence, as many patients respond well to its treatment. *Jiankua* is usually the most important local point I use in the treatment of hip joint pain.

Patient position — Properly position the patient in the lateral recumbent position (side-lying) with a pillow between his or her knees. The painful side is up and they are lying on the unaffected side. Some hip flexion is helpful to get the best access to the joint from the point *Jiankua*.

Point combination — **GB 29 + *Jiankua***

 The texts describe GB 29 as halfway between the greater trochanter and the anterior superior iliac spine. This paired point combination uses the point GB 29 with *Jiankua*. If you look at an anatomy text, you will find that both of these points approach the hip joint on deep insertion. Consider electrical stimulation between these two paired points, as well as needle-top moxa in cases of *Bi* syndrome with cold (han).

The quadratus lumborum — **Bl 52 and *Pigen***

 Consider two paired points in the region of the extraordinary point *Pigen* to release the quadratus lumborum muscle. Treatment of the QL is discussed on pages 213-214.

Gluteus medius, gluteus minimus — **One to four *ahshi* points.**
Perpendicular insertion, to a depth of 2 to 3 inches, depending upon patient size.

Treat from one to four sensitive *ahshi* points of the gluteus medius and gluteus minimus muscles. These points are found inferior to the iliac crest over the broad area of the iliac fossa, superior to GB 29 and *Jiankua*.

These two muscles are extremely important, as they contribute to many lumbo-sacral, hip, pelvic and lower-extremity pain syndromes. And there are no acupuncture points or well-known extraordinary points that lie in these muscles. Fortunately, palpation serves as an excellent guide in point selection. This treatment is discussed in more detail on pages 171-173.

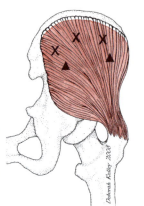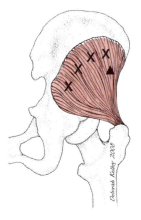

Gluteus medius, superficial (left)
Gluteus minimus, deep (right)
X – *Trigger points*
▲ – *Motor points*

Adjacent points **Bl 37**   The hamstring muscle
★ Consider two paired points at Bl 37 to release the hamstring. Treatment of hamstring strain is discussed on pages 180-182.

GB 30   Crossing point of the Gall Bladder and Bladder meridians
Used in many pain syndromes of the lumbar, sacral, and gluteal regions.

Bl 53.5   The piriformis muscle
Halfway between Bl 53 and Bl 54, Bl 53.5 is located just outside the lateral border of the sacrum. It is the motor point of the piriformis muscle.[4]

COMPLEMENTARY PROCEDURES

- Applications of heat often benefit with chronic pain and inflammation of the hip joint.

- A supplement with glucosamine and chondroitin may be considered for nutritional support of the joint. While usually not dramatic, it may contribute to recovery.

- Homeopathic remedies are sometimes effective for pain and inflammation in chronic arthritis. Hyland's Arthritis Pain Formula (Standard Homeopathic Company) is one product to consider.

- A Chinese herbal formula specific to the signs and symptoms of the condition complements the acupuncture treatment of chronic arthritis.

★ While all techniques listed above have shown clinical relevance, the starred items are predictably effective for this specific injury. Consider them first in a treatment plan.

REFERENCES

[1] Dutton, M: *Orthopeadic Examination, Evaluation, and Intervention,* Second Edition. McGraw-Hill, USA, 2008 (page 909).

[2] Shanghai College of Traditional Medicine: *Acupuncture, A Comprehensive Text.* Eastland Press, Chicago, 1981 (page 363).

[3] Callison, M: *Motor Point Index.* AcuSport Seminar Series LLC, San Diego, 2007 (page 113).

[4] Callison, M: *Motor Point Index.* AcuSport Seminar Series LLC, San Diego, 2007 (page 103).

Notes

16
Low Back Pain
The Quadratus Lumborum Muscle

Acute or chronic low back pain and spasm due to the quadratus lumborum (QL), which may radiate to the gluteal region. Pain is often one-sided.

Acutely is seen in acute sprain/strain of the low back, but may be a source of chronic or lingering lumbo-sacral pain. The QL is involved as a secondary lesion in many cases of back pain from other causes.

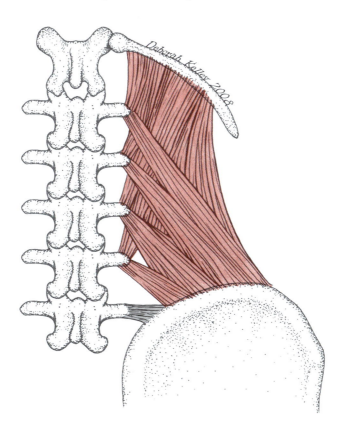

DIAGNOSIS & ASSESSMENT

After years of experience, I have come to believe there is nothing more complex to differentiate, diagnose, and treat than neck and low back pain. After countless reviews of the medical literature on the subject, I am astounded by how many astute and experienced physicians actually admit to not understanding the causes and treatments for back pain. Western orthopedic evaluation does a great job when there is a disc herniation with a protrusion or fragment lodged on a spinal nerve root. Anything else, in my opinion, is either art or guesswork. I see many patients who have been to numerous physicians, each diagnosing a different cause of pain. Unfortunately, TCM diagnosis is no better. I gave up on treatment based upon the meridian perspective years ago when Bladder meridian points such as Bl 23, Bl 25, Bl 40 and Bl 60 gave my patients inadequate results. And from an internal organ viewpoint, I have never found treating the Kidney, which controls the lower back, to be clinically reliable.

The anatomy of the spine is complex, and it seems to be both a strong structural pillar of the body as well as a fragile functional mechanism. The vertebral bodies are stabilized by complex ligaments, muscles and fascia. The intervertebral discs provide cushion to the spine, yet as we know, are quite susceptible to trauma and postural imbalances. Inter-discal pressure in the lumbar vertebrae rises precipitously with the mere act of sitting, so it is no wonder discs bulge, protrude and herniate. Then, the spinal nerves must exit from the small recesses of the lateral foramen, delivering qi via the peripheral nervous system to the extremities as well as the abdominal organs. Considering the tendency of the muscles of the lower back to tighten and guard this complex structure, the potential for pain and dysfunction is enormous.

So, with the complexity of this in mind, and knowing my own limitations as a practitioner, I have chosen not to include back pain as a comprehensive treatment topic in this handbook of sport injuries. However, I do have a contribution on the treatment of the quadratus lumborum muscle, which in its stealth sort of way benefits many patients with lumbo-sacral and gluteal pain. While QL dysfunction might not be the entire cause of pain – other points, treatments, and techniques may be necessary – the simple techniques that follow benefit many patients and may serve as an important protocol for acupuncture treatment.

Dr. Janet Travell calls the quadratus lumborum the "joker of low back pain".[1] Most of us have seen the Batman movies, and know how pervasive and annoying The Joker can be. When the QL has active trigger points or is in spasm, a wide range of pain patterns present. However, the quadratus is often overlooked because of the resultant muscle guarding in the lumbar, sacral and gluteal regions. It is also one of the most overlooked sources of hip pain.[2] Strain to the quadratus may be seen acutely, caused by movements involving lifting and twisting. Motor vehicle accidents, trauma and falls may also injure the QL. I have seen golfers, tennis players, and cyclists during hill-climbing strain the muscle due to the peculiar twisting mechanics of their sport. However, chronic dysfunction may occur from poor posture and position during sleep and sitting.

The origin of the quadratus lumborum is along the posterior iliac crest, in the region of the extraordinary point *Yaoyan*. It inserts superiorly on the 12th rib near the extraordinary point *Pigen*, as well as at the transverse processes of L1, L2, L3 and L4. It is important to note that the QL is deep to the para-spinal muscles, where the inner and outer Bladder meridians are located. No major acupuncture points access this important lumbar muscle. From a meridian perspective, most of the QL is too far lateral to be considered purely a Bladder meridian dysfunction. Yet, it is not on the Shao yang surface of the lateral body, and thus Gall Bladder meridian pathology is not definitive.

206 • Low Back Pain *The Quadratus Lumborum Muscle*

Palpation usually reveals a tender *ahshi* point below the 12th rib, approximately 3.5 inches lateral to the first lumbar vertebrae, in the region of the point *Pigen*. Press toward the spine, rather than performing the common perpendicular palpation on the Bladder channel. The patient will often exclaim "that's the spot!" The practitioner should continue to palpate down the lateral edge of the muscle. There is often an *ahshi* point at the inferior attachment at the extraordinary point *Yaoyan*, just superior to the iliac crest.

Two characteristic patterns stand out when the quadratus lumborum is involved. First, the symptoms of pain and muscle guarding are one-sided. There may be central back pain, as well as bilateral tension along the para-spinal muscles. But when the patient reports the addition of pain, whether sharp or a dull ache, that is shifted off to one side, you should suspect the QL. It may radiate inferiorly towards the hip, predictable because of the attachment of the muscle at the iliac crest. The second characteristic pattern is the patient in the "antalgic" position – they are laterally flexed or inclined to the side of pain with the hip elevated on the same side. This is obvious because the primary actions of the QL are lateral flexion and elevation of the pelvis. This is more clearly seen in the patient with acute strain, but the practitioner may observe a less pronounced scenario in the chronic patient.

While the quadratus lumborum is often the primary cause of pain due to acute strain of the low back, it should be considered in other lumbar, sacral and gluteal conditions. The QL is frequently taut and guarded with lumbar disc lesions, as it functions to stabilize the lumbar spine and pelvis. The techniques discussed below may be added to the treatment protocol of the lumbar disc patient. Even with sacral-iliac joint inflammation, hip pain and sciatica, its treatment may benefit the patient. While other points and techniques may be necessary for many low back pain patients, the QL should always be considered part of the treatment plan.

SUMMARY OF THE INJURY

Clinical Features	• Pain upon palpation at the superior attachment of the quadratus lumborum in the region of the extraordinary point *Pigen* about 3.5 cun lateral to the first lumbar vertebrae. • Elevated pelvis on the side of pain • Lumbar region may be slightly flexed laterally to the side of pain • Acute injury often accompanied by lifting and twisting movements • The quadratus lumborum is involved in many cases of acute and chronic back sprain and strain, degenerative spine disorders, and disc disease
Common Patient Complaints	• Acute back pain and spasm • Patient may report the spine feels "locked up" • Pain is often one-sided • Pain may radiate towards the gluteal region • Additional symptoms may be reported when other etiologies of back pain also contribute.
Differentiation from Similar Injuries and Conditions	• Referral pain from lumbar nerve root • Lumbar disc syndrome • Lumbar facet joint dysfunction • Sprain/strain of other lumbar soft tissues

Typical Medical Recommendations	• Ice may be considered with acute cases. Applications of heat often benefit tension and contraction of the muscle.
	• Anti-inflammatory medications
	• Stretching
	  Stretching the quadratus lumborum and other lumbar muscles may benefit
	• Biomechanics
	  Avoid lifting and twisting movements. Position at work and computer stations and other postural imbalances should be assessed.
	• Physical therapy
	  Ultrasound, manual therapy, and other physical therapy modalities.
	• Orthopedic evaluation
	  The most important diagnostic issue is to determine if the pain is due to a lumbar disc protrusion. Secondarily, to assess which tissues besides the quadratus lumborum muscle are involved. Be aware of the patient with an anatomical short leg, which affects the biomechanics of the hip and places extra stress on the QL.

208 • Low Back Pain *The Quadratus Lumborum Muscle*

TREATMENT & TECHNIQUES

Overview: Acute low back pain involving the quadratus lumborum muscle may be diagnosed under the category of accident/trauma. However, trauma may not be apparent when the onset is associated with poor posture or positioning. The injury is at the level of the muscles and tendons, with qi and blood stagnation in the channels and collaterals. The Bladder and the Gall Bladder meridians are usually affected. Internal organ imbalances vary; the Kidney should not be assumed.

Treatment to the QL may be specific in acute low back sprain/strain. It may be combined with treatments for other causes of low back pain, including degenerative changes to the lumbar spine, disc disease, and lumbar nerve root involvement.

Prognosis: Treat twice a week for three weeks, then re-evaluate. More treatment will be needed in chronic cases due to degenerative spine disorders and disc lesions.

STEP ONE: INITIAL TREATMENT

Choose among these four techniques, carefully determining if there is an immediate decrease in pain or an increase in range of motion.

Technique #1: **The Tendino-Muscle Meridians**

 Bl 67, GB 44   Bleeding technique
Bleeding the Jing-well points of the Bladder and Gall Bladder meridians may be effective for the symptoms of pain and spasm of the quadratus lumborum.

Technique #2: **Opposite Side (contra-lateral)**

Corresponding points on the opposite side may be considered; however, treatment to the affected side is usually preferred. Furthermore, treating bilaterally when the QL dysfunction is one-sided may diminish the effectiveness of treatment.

Technique #3: **Opposite Extremity (upper/lower)**

SI 11 to SI 14   Tai yang corresponding points on the opposite extremity
These points mirror the Bladder (Tai yang) meridian. Located in the levator muscle, SI 14 may be the most clinically effective of the group.

In general, treat upper/lower corresponding points on the opposite (unaffected) side when acute, and the affected side when chronic. Use palpation to assist in this choice.

209 • Low Back Pain *The Quadratus Lumborum Muscle*

Technique #4: **Empirical Points**

 Yao tong xue
This set of paired points is used for acute lumbar strain/sprain. These two points are located just distal to the junction of the second and third metacarpals and the fourth and fifth metacarpals, on the dorsal surface of the hand. While Chinese texts frequently mention *Yao tong xue*, I do not find this point combination works on a high percentage of patients with acute lumbar pain. However, it is certainly worth a try!

Ling gu + Da bai
From the Master Tong system of empirical points, *Ling gu* and *Da bai* has been popularized by the work of Richard Tan, L.Ac.[3] Recommended for sciatica, it may benefit back pain due to QL dysfunction. *Ling gu* is located .5 cun proximal to LI 4, just distal to the junction of the first and second metacarpals. *Da bai* is located .5 cun proximal to LI 3, and is distal to LI 4.

STEP TWO: MERIDIANS & MICROSYSTEMS

Choose among these four techniques, selecting points that are appropriate for the signs and symptoms of the patient.

Technique #5: **The Shu-Stream Point Combination**

 BL 65 affected side + SI 3 opposite side
GB 41 (or GB 42) affected side + SJ 3 opposite side
GB 42 is often more sensitive than GB 41, and should be considered as an alternative shu-stream point for this meridian. Both the Tai yang and Shao yang channel shu-stream points are an important part of the treatment protocol.

Technique #6: **Traditional Point Categories**

 Other Tai yang points on the Small Intestine and Bladder meridians should be palpated. Don't overlook the following:

SI 6	Xi-cleft point
Bl 63	Xi-cleft point
Bl 59	Xi-cleft point of the Yang Qiao mai
Bl 58	Luo-connecting point
Bl 57	No point category
Bl 40	He-sea point

Bl 40 + Bl 60   For low back pain
This classic TCM combination may be effective in some cases, yet fails in others.

★ **GB 34 + Bl 60**   For lumbo-sacral and gluteal pain
This combination includes both Shao yang and Tai yang points, and is generally more effective on the QL patient than the more commonly used formula Bl 40 + Bl 60. I frequently use electrical stimulation between these two points with surprisingly good results.

Technique #7: **The Extraordinary Meridians**

★ **SI 3 + Bl 62**   Activate the Du mai
Activating the Du mai may assist if there is lumbar nerve root pathology.

GB 41 + SJ 5   Activate the Dai mai
The Dai mai frequently contributes to low back pain, and can be considered along with the Du mai treatment above.

For patients with acute low back pain, I frequently use both the Du mai and the Dai mai. The technique that I prefer starts with palpating GB 41, the master point of the Dai mai. The point sensitive side is needled. Then SJ 5, the coupled point, is needled on the opposite side. The Du mai is needled at the master point SI 3, on the same side as GB 41. Its coupled point, Bl 62 is needled on the opposite side. With some patients I will consider electrical stimulation between the master point and the coupled point. Ion pumping chords may also be used between the crossed master point and coupled point.

Technique #8: **Microsystems**

Auricular Therapy
Local: Lumbar spine, sacral spine, hip
Zang-fu points: Liver, Kidney
Systemic points for pain: Shen men, Thalamus, Adrenal, Endocrine, Muscle Relaxation

Wrist-ankle Acupuncture
Wrist-ankle acupuncture may be considered, as the site of injury often covers multiple meridians. Use the zones on the lateral surface of the leg.[4]
Lower #5   The lateral surface of the leg
Located 3 cun proximal to the lateral malleolus, along the posterior border of the fibula. This zone approximates the Gall Bladder meridian.
Lower #6   The lateral surface of the leg
Located 3 cun proximal to the lateral malleolus, along the anterior border of the achilles tendon. This zone approximates the Bladder meridian.

STEP THREE: INTERNAL ORGAN IMBALANCES

Choose appropriate points to treat internal organ imbalances that may contribute to the injury or pain syndrome.

Technique #9: **Qi, Blood, and the Zang-fu Organs**

Acute strain and spasm of the quadratus lumborum muscle is usually not associated with internal organ imbalances. However, with chronic and recurring cases, it would be remiss not to consider the Kidney, which controls the low back. However, the sometimes Shao yang nature of QL dysfunction should keep the practitioner alerted to Liver and Gall Bladder dysfunction. Consider the following:

Liver imbalances Liver qi stagnation, Liver yin deficiency, and Liver blood deficiency
Liver imbalances may be observed in the patient with lumbar pain due to the QL. In fact, it is more common than syndromes of the Kidney. Consider the following obvious and frequently used point combinations:
Liv 4   "Metal" point
This point treats back spasm and muscular tension. Some senior practitioners consider Liv 4 effective for psoas muscle spasm, which is the antagonist muscle to the QL.

Liv 3 + LI 4   "Four gates" combination
This commonly used combination proves reliable in some cases of QL spasm.

Kidney imbalances Kidney deficiency
Kidney deficiency is considered by some practitioners as an internal organ imbalance present in all patients with low back pain. While this may be true in some cases, I seldom observe improvement in the symptoms of pain due to QL dysfunction with treatment only to the Kidney as a root imbalance.

Stress The syndrome of stress is not a TCM term, but clearly this modern diagnosis affects the internal organ systems. The QL seems to react to stressful conditions with spasms, tightness, and active trigger points. It should be considered for treatment, along with the affected organ systems as assessed by the practitioner.

Points should be determined by the practitioner from both palpation and analysis of the signs and symptoms of the patient.

STEP FOUR: THE SITE OF INJURY

Choose among the local and adjacent points at the site of injury. Points may be determined by palpation, orthopedic testing, and analysis of the signs and symptoms of the patient.

Technique #10: **Local and Adjacent Points**

The quadratus lumborum muscle ★

Bl 52 and the extraordinary point *Pigen*
The extraordinary point *Pigen* is at or near one of the important trigger points of the QL. It is often a predictable *ahshi* point.[5] The texts locate *Pigen* 3.5 cun lateral to the spinous process of the first lumbar vertebrae.[6] But don't be concerned if it is located level with L2 or further lateral than 3.5 cun, as there are some variations on this empirical point.

Palpation is the key to both its location and successful needling. With the patient prone (face-down), start palpating about 4 cun lateral to the spine, approximately level with L1, and immediately inferior to the 12th rib. You should be just off the lateral border of the para-spinal muscles and the outer Bladder meridian. Palpate medially towards the vertebral column until the painful point is found, which is deep to the para-spinal muscles. If the patient is in the lateral recumbent position (side-lying), palpate toward the spine in a vector that is approximately perpendicular to the treatment table. Either position is acceptable to needling. However, it is important to needle with the same angle, direction, and vector that produced the pain during palpation.

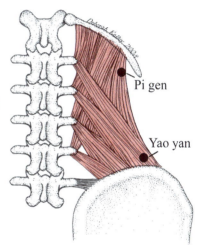

Needling precautions ★

Patient size will determine the length of the needle to be used, which is usually 2 to 3 inches. After insertion, direct the needle obliquely toward the spine, deep to the para-spinal muscles, until the taut and dense tissue of the QL is reached. The practitioner should review the anatomy, as it is important to avoid deeper insertion into the kidney or angling in a superior direction that could reach the rib or the pleural cavity. If you are unsure, get some guidance from an experienced practitioner before needling this point. If your angle is not deep enough, the needle will penetrate the para-spinal muscles, which may be beneficial, but will generally not release the QL muscle.

Motor point, trigger points

I will frequently use two paired points for the quadratus lumborum. After inserting the first needle at *Pigen* as described above, a second point is inserted in the muscle about 1 cun inferior. This is in the region of the motor point of the QL. It is located level with L2, from .5 to 1 cun lateral to Bl 52.[7] This combination of the trigger point and the motor point of the QL is usually most successful in relieving pain and spasm of the muscle. Consider electrical stimulation, although some patients do not tolerate such strong stimulation to these points.

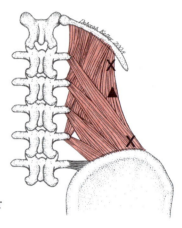

There is often an *ahshi* point at the pelvic attachment of the muscle, which is also considered a trigger point. From *Pigen* and the motor point, continue to palpate down the lateral edge of the muscle until you reach its attachment at the iliac crest. This is the region of the extraordinary point *Yaoyan*, described in the texts as 3.5 cun lateral to the lower border of the spinous process of L4.[8]

X – Trigger points
▲ – Motor points

This point is just superior to the iliac crest, which is not how the point is pictured in Deadman's text.

Needle technique Needle insertion is much less complex, because at this inferior aspect of the muscle, the point is lateral to the para-spinal muscles and avoiding vital organs is less of an issue. Start with perpendicular insertion, needling up to 1.5 inches, and angle in the direction that pain was produced by palpation. And because the QL inserts along a considerable portion of the iliac crest, point location may vary from the text location. *Yaoyan* can be paired with *Pigen* or the motor point, and electrical stimulation considered.

It is not uncommon to complete the needle treatment with cupping. And if the case is relieved with heat, indirect moxa or thread moxa may be applied.

Gluteus medius The gluteus medius muscle is frequently involved with the quadratus lumborum dysfunction. Consider one or two sets of paired points in sensitive *ahshi* points of the gluteus medius. Perpendicular needles are inserted to a depth of 2 to 3 inches, depending upon patient size. This treatment is discussed in detail on pages 172-173.

Gluteus medius
X – Trigger points
▲ – Motor points

Jiankua ("posterior" GB 29)
Treat with one needle or two paired points at the extraordinary point *Jiankua*, a posterior version of GB 29. It is located halfway between the greater trochanter and the crest of the ilium. This treatment is discussed in detail on page 171.

Adjacent points   GB 30   Crossing point
Used in many pain syndromes of the lumbar, sacral and gluteal region.

Bl 23, Bl 52
These two points, level with L2, are adjacent to the lumbar attachments of the quadratus lumborum. While they should not be relied upon to release the QL, they sometimes are beneficial secondary points.

COMPLEMENTARY PROCEDURES

- Applications of heat often benefit tension, contraction, and "guarding" of a muscle group. Heat may also be considered after the needling of trigger points.

- Massage to release tension of the quadratus lumborum can be performed between treatments at home. Self-massage is possible with a tennis ball against a wall, being careful to avoid bruising the 12th rib.

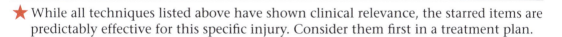

★ While all techniques listed above have shown clinical relevance, the starred items are predictably effective for this specific injury. Consider them first in a treatment plan.

REFERENCES

[1] Travell & Simons: *Myofascial Pain and Dysfunction: The Trigger Point Manual, Volume 2 (The Lower Extremities).* Williams & Wilkins, Philadelphia, 1992 (pages 28-31).

[2] Dutton, M: *Orthopeadic Examination, Evaluation, and Intervention,* Second Edition. McGraw-Hill, USA, 2008 (page 909).

[3] Tan & Rush: *Twelve and Twelve in Acupuncture.* San Diego, 1994 (pages 14-16).

[4] Matsumoto & Birch: *Extraordinary Vessels.* Paradigm Publishers, Massachusetts, 1986 (pages 182-188).
Note: Dr. Zhang Xin Shu's Wrist Ankle Acupuncture (Wan Ke Zhen) *is the source quoted in the above text.*

[5] Travell & Simons: *Myofascial Pain and Dysfunction: The Trigger Point Manual, Volume 2 (The Lower Extremities).* Williams & Wilkins, Philadelphia, 1992 (page 30).

[6] Shanghai College of Traditional Medicine: *Acupuncture, A Comprehensive Text.* Eastland Press, Chicago, 1981 (page 378).

[7] Callison, M: *Motor Point Index.* AcuSport Seminar Series LLC, San Diego, 2007 (page 94).

[8] Deadman, Al-Khafaji, & Baker: *A Manual of Acupuncture.* Journal of Chinese Medicine Publications, East Sussex, 2001 (page 572).

Notes

17
Hand Pain
Carpal Tunnel Syndrome

Pain, tingling, and numbness in the palmar aspect of the hand and wrist

A repetitive stress injury characterized by entrapment, compression or irritation to the median nerve in its narrow passageway of the carpal tunnel at the wrist.

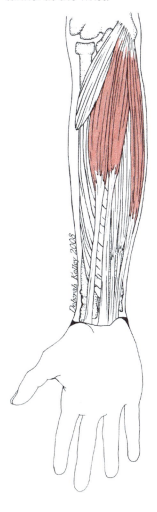

DIAGNOSIS & ASSESSMENT

Carpal tunnel syndrome is a common repetitive stress injury, and patients frequently seek acupuncture for treatment. This condition is a form of entrapment, compression or irritation to the median nerve in its narrow passageway of the carpal tunnel at the wrist. It is the most common type of compressive neuropathy seen in the clinic.[1] This is the region of the point P 7. However, the carpal tunnel patient is never that simple, as there often seems to be additional factors that contribute to the condition.

The causes of carpal tunnel syndrome are varied, and are summarized as follows:

1. Swelling of the median nerve and its sheath.

2. Median nerve compression from inflammation and swelling of the numerous tendons located deep to the median nerve in the wrist. There are actually nine flexor tendons that could contribute.

3. Swelling of the superficial-lying transverse carpal ligament (flexor retinaculum) that irritates the median nerve.

4. Bony lesions or soft-tissue masses that compress or entrap the nerve.

5. Indirect contributions from degenerative changes to the cervical spine and possible nerve root involvement affecting the median nerve.

The patient often presents with paresthesia – the sensation of tingling, numbness and "pins and needles" – in the palmar aspect of the hand and wrist. These symptoms follow the distribution area of the median nerve, which includes the first three digits and the radial side of the fourth digit. Pain may also be reported, ranging from a dull ache to sharp and piercing. It may radiate from the wrist proximally up the forearm, arm, and possibly to the neck and shoulder. Symptoms usually are of gradual onset, and may be continuous or intermittent. Pain is often reported to be worse at night, and the patient may experience morning stiffness in the hand and wrist.

Repetitive stress from hand motions is usually the suspected cause, and is often associated with the onset of symptoms. Construction workers, painters, musicians, and massage therapists commonly experience carpal tunnel syndrome. But this micro-trauma injury occurs in individuals from seemingly less-traumatic activities, like computer keyboarding and mousing. Women are far more likely to experience carpal tunnel syndrome than men.[2] Texts also point to hormonal changes and fluid retention related to pregnancy and menopause as causes, probably due to changes in the strength and function of ligaments.

As the condition worsens, the patient may report weakness, and grasping objects can become difficult. When progressed, you may be able to observe muscle atrophy in the thenar eminence in the region of Lu 10. It is advised that in this progressed state, the patient should be referred to an orthopedic hand specialist. EMG testing is usually performed, testing nerve conduction and velocity to determine the extent of nerve dysfunction. Surgery may be recommended to prevent irreversible damage. Keep in mind that swelling and inflammation due to systemic conditions, such as rheumatoid arthritis, gout and hypothroidism, may contribute. And, a whole host of other internal metabolic conditions, such as collagen disorders, may be associated.

The simple Tinel sign is performed by lightly tapping on the wrist crease over the carpal tunnel at or near the acupuncture point P 7. If this produces tingling and/or numbness, there is inflammation of the median nerve. These symptoms must be felt distal to the

218 • Hand Pain *Carpal Tunnel Syndrome*

wrist in the distribution area of the median nerve for the test to be considered positive. The Phalen's maneuver should be performed for 30 to 60 seconds. The dorsum of the hands are placed together, with the wrists in forced flexion. Increased tingling and/or numbness distally is positive for carpal tunnel syndrome. These tests are easily performed by the practitioner. However, they don't necessarily differentiate the cause of the nerve dysfunction.

The techniques that follow give the practitioner numerous options for treating the carpal tunnel patient. Given the varied causes of the nerve entrapment and irritation, experimenting with the different protocols may be necessary. My experience, from both success and failure in using acupuncture to treat carpal tunnel syndrome, leads to several conclusions. First, include treatment to the cervical spine and the shoulder, which is discussed in Step Four. It is reported that 40 percent of athletes with symptoms of carpal tunnel syndrome also have shoulder pain and upper arm pain.[3] Second, have the patient concurrently see a physical therapist. And if acupuncture fails, the orthopedic hand specialist may be a necessary referral, as it is essential that your patient avoid irreversible nerve damage.

SUMMARY OF THE INJURY

Clinical Features
- Repetitive stress from hand motions is usually the suspected cause
- Causes of the nerve dysfunction vary, and include swelling of the flexor tendons, ligament irritation, and other lesions at the wrist
- Symptoms follow the distribution area of the median nerve, which includes the first three digits and radial side of fourth digit
- Progressed cases may present with muscle atrophy in the thenar eminence in the region of Lu 10. In this case, it is important to refer to a hand specialist to avoid permanent damage.
- Positive Tinel's test and/or positive Phalen's test
- Degenerative changes to the cervical spine may contribute

Common Patient Complaints
- Pain, tingling, numbness, and "pins and needles" in the palmar aspect of the hand and wrist
- Pain ranges from a dull ache to sharp and piercing
- Pain may radiate from the wrist proximally up the forearm, arm, and possibly to the shoulder
- As the condition worsens, the patient may report weakness, and grasping objects can become difficult

Differentiation from Similar Injuries and Condition
- Referred pain from cervical nerve root
- Referred pain from the shoulder or elbow, including thoracic outlet syndrome
- Radial nerve entrapment in the forearm
- Wrist tendonitis
- Pronator teres syndrome or median nerve compression in the forearm
- Inflammation due to systemic conditions, such as rheumatoid arthritis, gout, and hypothyroidism

Typical Medical Recommendations
- Anti-inflammatory medications
- Modify activity
  Decrease or avoid upper extremity activities that aggravate.
- Biomechanics
  Correct ergonomics of work and computer stations. A wrist splint or brace is frequently recommended to reduce repetitive stress.
- Physical therapy
  Ultrasound and other physical therapy modalities.
- Orthopedic procedures
  A cortisone injection will often provide temporary relief. In cases with muscle atrophy, surgery may be recommended to prevent irreversible damage.
- Orthopedic evaluation
  EMG testing is used to assess the degree of nerve damage.

TREATMENT & TECHNIQUES

Overview: Carpal tunnel syndrome is most commonly diagnosed under the category of accident/trauma. It is usually a repetitive stress disorder due to the accumulation of micro-trauma. The injury is at the level of the tendons, ligaments, and possibly the bone. There is qi and blood stagnation in the channels and collaterals. The Pericardium (Jue yin) meridian is affected, which precisely follows the course of the median nerve through the carpal tunnel. Internal organ imbalances include shen disturbances due to the the Heart and Pericardium.

Prognosis: Treat twice a week for three weeks, then re-evaluate. With chronic cases, continue treatment at least once weekly after the first three-week period. Treatment should never be prolonged if the patient is not benefiting or if signs of muscle weakness and thenar atrophy are present.

STEP ONE: INITIAL TREATMENT

Choose among these four techniques, carefully determining if there is an immediate decrease in pain or an increase in range of motion.

Technique #1: **The Tendino-Muscle Meridians**

P 9   Bleeding technique

Use the alternate location of P 9, on the radial side of the third digit (the middle finger), about .1 cun proximal to the corner of the nail.

Technique #2: **Opposite Side (contra-lateral)**

Corresponding points on the opposite (unaffected) side may be considered; however, treatment to the affected side is usually preferred.

Technique #3: **Opposite Extremity (upper/lower)**

Liv 4   Jue yin corresponding point on the opposite extremity

This jing-river point is not a precise anatomical mirror to P 7, but it is on the same Six Division meridian.

In general, treat upper/lower corresponding points on the opposite (unaffected) side when acute, and the affected side when chronic. Use palpation to assist in this choice.

Technique #4: **Empirical Points**

  St 41   Jing-river point
St 41 has been discussed in the work of Richard Tan, L.Ac.[4] Its use for carpal tunnel syndrome is based upon mirroring the middle of the wrist with the middle of the ankle. In this tradition, treatment on the same side is recommended.

STEP TWO: MERIDIANS & MICROSYSTEMS

Choose among these four techniques, selecting points that are appropriate for the signs and symptoms of the patient.

Technique #5: **The Shu-Stream Point Combination**

P 7 affected side + Liv 3 opposite side
These paired shu-stream points are not clinically reliable.

Technique #6: **Traditional Point Categories**

  Other points of the Pericardium meridian proximal to the carpal tunnel should always be considered. Palpation may assist in your choice of points.
P 3   He-sea point
P 4   Xi-cleft point
P 5   Jing-river point
P 6   Luo-connecting point

  Point combinations to consider:
P 3 + P 4
P 4 + P 5
These two paired-point combinations proximal to the carpal tunnel activate the meridian and are anatomically located along the median nerve.

Technique #7: **The Extraordinary Meridians**

SI 3 + Bl 62   Activate the Du mai
Treating the Du mai may assist if there is cervical nerve root pathology contributing to the condition.

Technique #8: **Microsystems**

Auricular Therapy
Local: Wrist (French), wrist (Chinese), shoulder, master shoulder, cervical spine
Zang-fu points: Heart
Systemic points for pain: Shen men, Thalamus, Adrenal, Endocrine

STEP THREE: INTERNAL ORGAN IMBALANCES

Choose appropriate points to treat internal organ imbalances that may contribute to the injury or pain syndrome.

Technique #9: **Qi, Blood, and the Zang-fu Organs**

Carpal tunnel syndrome is a repetitive stress injury and therefore internal organ imbalances are not necessarily causative. However, Heart and Pericardium imbalances may contribute to the condition.

Shen disturbances Some patients present with imbalances of the Heart and Pericardium, reporting insomnia, mental restlessness and other related mental and emotional symptoms. This is not surprising, considering this injury manifests on the Pericardium channel.

Points should be determined by the practitioner from both palpation and analysis of the signs and symptoms of the patient.

STEP FOUR: THE SITE OF INJURY

Choose among the local and adjacent points at the site of injury. Points may be determined by palpation, orthopedic testing, and analysis of the signs and symptoms of the patient.

Technique #10: **Local and Adjacent Points**

The carpal tunnel **The region of P 7**

Local treatment starts at the carpal tunnel, which is the site of the suspected nerve entrapment. The acupuncture point P 7 lies over this zone, where the median nerve passes through the wrist. The practitioner should be reminded that P 7 is at the palmar wrist crease, between the tendons of the palmaris longus and the flexor carpi radialis. Precision is essential, as needling into the median nerve and its sheath should be avoided.

Needle technique Threading a needle through the carpal tunnel starts with insertion about .5 cun proximal to the P 7. Use a 1.5 inch needle with the smallest diameter possible to minimize any trauma to the tissues in this narrow passage. At an oblique angle of 30 to 45 degrees, direct the needle distally toward the palm. Insertion should be slow and deliberate, and the angle may need to be altered in

● – P 6 (proximal)
P 7 (distal)
○ – Point variation for needle insertion

223 • Hand Pain *Carpal Tunnel Syndrome*

order to avoid the nerve, tendons, and bone. While not always achievable, I attempt to needle at least one inch, which means the needle has passed through the wrist and is approaching the palm and P 8 distally. Give yourself three attempts at this technique, and if unsuccessful, try some of the other local and adjacent points.

Patient position   There are several factors that make the needling of P 7 more successful. First is the position of the wrist. Starting in neutral position, slightly flex the wrist from 10 to 30 degrees. Place support under the dorsal side of the hand to keep the wrist flexed and stable. I usually use a small towel or a pillow case. Next is the angle of insertion, which is stated above at 30 to 45 degrees. If the needle does not effortlessly glide through the tunnel, then change the angle. Also, directing the needle more to the radial or the ulnar side may make a difference. Remember to experiment, which must be done without trauma to the tissues. And don't misinterpret hitting the nerve, which would cause sharp, radiating pain, with "de qi". They are two distinctly different sensations. Sharp and painful is not the right one!

Point combinations   P 7 + P 8
P 6 + P 7

With P 7 successfully inserted, it may be combined with other adjacent meridian points. P7 + P 8 or P 6 + P 7 are the two most frequently used paired points for this condition. Consider electrical stimulation between the two paired points, although care should be taken to assure patient comfort. Occasionally, I will use P 7 + Lu 10 when there is thenar muscle atrophy.

Adjacent points   P 6 + P 8
P 6 + Lu 10

If you are not successful in threading the carpal tunnel with the point P 7, then combining P 6 with P 8 is a possibility. P 6 can also be combined with Lu 10, especially if there is thenar muscle atrophy. Consider electrical stimulation.

The flexor muscles of the forearm   The nerve entrapment at the wrist may be influenced by inflammation of the numerous flexor tendons deep to the median nerve. The practitioner may consider the use of *ahshi* points in the taut bands of the flexor group of the forearm. These can be found from 1 to 5 cun distal to the elbow crease, and may be determined by palpation. Multiple points in this region may be needled. Use perpendicular insertion, from .5 to 1 inch.

X – Trigger points

224 • Hand Pain *Carpal Tunnel Syndrome*

The neck and scapula ★ Degenerative changes to the cervical spine and possible nerve root involvement often contribute to upper-extremity pain syndromes. Carpal tunnel syndrome is no exception. In general, treatment of tension in the neck and shoulder may need to be included to obtain lasting results. Choose several neck and/or scapula points in any one treatment session, determined by palpation.

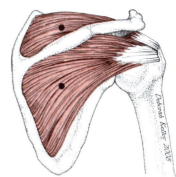

● – *SI 12 – the supraspinatous (superior)*
SI 11 – the infraspinatous (inferior)

GB 20, Bl 10   Upper cervical region

The extraordinary point *Bailao*
This point is 2 cun superior and 1 cun lateral to Du 14, in the region of C4, C5, or C6.

Huatuo jiaji **points (C1 to C7[5])**
The median nerve arises from the cervical nerve roots of C6 to T1. C5 may also contribute.

SI 10, SI 11	The infraspinatous muscle
SI 12	The supraspinatous muscle
SI 14, SI 15	The levator scapulae muscle

The axillary plexus **SI 9**
Deep needling to the point SI 9 is adjacent to the axillary plexus, from which the median nerve arises. Needling 2 to 3 inches into SI 9 may benefit the carpal tunnel patient. Care should be taken to avoid both the nerve plexus and the pleural cavity.

COMPLEMENTARY PROCEDURES

- Nutritional supplementation with Vitamin B6 (pyridoxine) may benefit. While research varies, some studies point to its effectiveness in carpal tunnel syndrome.

- Alternating ice and heat when the condition is "neither hot (re) nor cold (han)", may enhance recovery.

- As stated earlier, a wrist splint or brace is frequently recommended to reduce repetitive stress. This should not be overlooked as a complementary modality.

★ While all techniques listed above have shown clinical relevance, the starred items are predictably effective for this specific injury. Consider them first in a treatment plan.

REFERENCES

[1] Garrick, J: Orthopaedic *Knowledge Update, Sports Medicine 3*. North American Academy of Orthopaedic Surgeons, Illinois, 2004 (page 125).

[2] Corrigan & Maitland: *Practical Orthopaedic Medicine*. Butterworth & Co, United Kingdom, 1989 (page 100).

[3] Garrick, J: *Orthopaedic Knowledge Update, Sports Medicine 3*. North American Academy of Orthopaedic Surgeons, Illinois, 2004 (page 125).

[4] Tan & Rush: *Twenty Four More in Acupuncture*, San Diego, 1994 (page 16).

[5] *The huatuo jiaji points technically do not exist in the cervical region. The classic texts state that they only follow the thoracic and lumbar spine. Some practitioners insist that the cervical spine should be included. If used, the vertebral artery should be avoided.*

18
Elbow Pain

Lateral epicondylitis (Tennis elbow)

Pain in the elbow at the lateral epicondyle and distally along the extensor tendon and muscles of the forearm

A repetitive stress injury characterized by inflammation and irritation of the forearm extensors and possibly the supinators. This injury is often referred to as "tennis elbow".

DIAGNOSIS & ASSESSMENT

There hasn't been a month during the past 25 years of my practice where I have not seen a patient with lateral epicondylitis. From my experience, alleviating tennis elbow with acupuncture treatment is not always successful. Some cases are stubborn and don't respond well. And if the patient experiences improvement, it often vanishes when they return to the activities that caused the problem. Understanding the etiology of this common sports injury is essential in developing an effective treatment plan for the patient.

Tennis elbow, or lateral epicondylitis, is the most common injury in patients seeking treatment for elbow pain. It is reported to be from four to seven times more likely than epicondylitis on the medial side.[1] This is typical of many sports injuries, with the site of injury occurring more frequently on a yang surface (the extensors) than a yin surface (the flexors). While most patients are usually between 30 and 50 years old, tennis elbow can occur in any age group. Like many overuse injuries, its onset is insidious. There is often no specific traumatic event associated with the start of symptoms. However, the patient is predictably involved in recreational activities that require repetitive and vigorous use of the forearm muscles, like tennis and other racquet sports. Occupational stress such as construction work also results in the injury. And don't fail to account for the effects of computer keyboarding and mousing as a stress to the extensor group.[2]

The patient complains of lateral elbow pain which may radiate distally down the forearm. Pain is often dull and intermittent. Acute strain, while quite rare, results in moderate to severe pain. Hand and wrist activities usually aggravate the condition, especially wrist extension, radial deviation, and supination. The patient will often have difficulty lifting or grasping objects or unscrewing a lid to a container. I have had tennis elbow patients refrain from shaking my hand due to pain.

The etiology of lateral epicondylitis can be summarized as follows:

1. Epicondylitis, which implies inflammation of the bony lateral epicondyle without specifically implicating pathology to the tendon. Some sources suggest the presence of degeneration of the bone associated with the condition.

2. Inflammation due to micro-tears of the common extensor tendon at or near its attachment to the lateral epicondyle.

3. Inflammation of the tendon, often called tendinosis. This is described as a degenerative process within the tendon and its sheath without the presence of strain or micro-tears.

4. The contribution from degenerative changes to the cervical spine and possible nerve root involvement. While technically not a pain referral pattern, muscle dysfunction in the forearm may be associated with the cervical spine, resulting in either strain or inflammation.

Examination of the patient is straightforward. First, palpate the bony lateral epicondyle. If there is pain, this is the site of injury and the primary stagnation of qi and blood. Pain slightly distal to the attachment indicates inflammation of the common tendon. And pain two to three cun distal to the epicondyle is often found in taut fascial bands of the extensor muscles. Tennis elbow involves the muscles that control wrist extension, radial deviation, and supination. Each of these movements should be assessed separately with manual muscle testing. These tests are easy to perform, and are described in the Appendices on page 336.

In general, acupuncture is directed to the primary site of qi and blood stagnation. Both palpation and muscle testing helps to locate this site more precisely. The bony epicondyle, the common tendon, and the taut fascial bands of the extensor muscles may all need to be treated. Not to be overlooked is the possible contribution from neck and shoulder tension. And including physical therapy modalities often complements the overall treatment plan.

There will be both successes and failures with treatment. One summer, while teaching my son how to play tennis, I noticed two very accomplished players on the court next to us. I could not help from watching them play, as the sound of their rackets hitting the ball was thunderous. One of the players jogged over to our court, and I recognized that he was a patient of mine. He wanted to thank me for successfully treating his elbow, as he was now playing tennis pain-free. Thinking back, it seemed to be longer and more difficult to treat his injury than I had hoped for. But after watching the vigor of his shots, I could see why. As practitioners who treat sports injuries, it is essential to understand just how much stress and strain an athlete experiences in his or her event.

Then there was the patient I treated several times who had absolutely no change in her elbow pain. My feeling was that acupuncture would not help, and we stopped treatment. She returned to her orthopedist, and within two weeks had surgery. What they found was a tear of almost 50 percent of the common tendon, which had separated from its attachment to the epicondyle by almost an inch. Surgically reattached, she had to endure significant recovery and rehabilitation. But six months later, the patient was back to full activity. Acupuncture could never had addressed this medical condition.

SUMMARY OF THE INJURY

Clinical Features
- Inflammation of the common extensor tendon, with the possibility of micro tears at the site of the attachment
- Usually a repetitive stress disorder, but may be seen as an acute strain
- Sometimes referred to as tendinosis, a degenerative process within the tendon and its sheath without the presence of strain or micro-tears.
- Tenderness with palpation at the lateral epicondyle and distal to the attachment following the extensor tendon
- Pain with resisted wrist extension, radial deviation, and/or hand supination

Common Patient Complaints
- Pain in the lateral elbow
- Pain and stiffness may radiate distally down the forearm
- Onset is often gradual
- Pain may be dull and intermittent
- With acute strain moderate to severe pain results
- Hand and wrist activities usually aggravate the condition
- The patient will often have difficulty lifting or grasping objects or unscrewing a lid to a container

Differentiation from Similar Injuries and Conditions
- Partial tear of one or more of the extensor muscles
- Referral pain from the neck or shoulder
- Radial nerve entrapment
- Rule out elbow fracture if associated with trauma

Typical Medical Recommendations
- Ice is typically used when acute
- Anti-inflammatory medications
- Modify activity
  Decrease upper extremity activities that aggravate.
- Stretching
  Use a stretching program for the extensor group.
- Biomechanics
  Correct ergonomics of work and computer stations. If caused from tennis or racquet sports, modification of swing biomechanics may benefit.
- Physical therapy
  Ultrasound, deep-friction massage, and other physical therapy modalities. A counterforce elbow brace is sometimes recommended. Rehabilitation usually consists of strengthening exercises, including wrist curls.
- Orthopedic procedures
  Cortisone injection is sometimes used in the inflamed region; the patient must evaluate the risks of the procedure. Surgery is considered the treatment of last resort.

230 • Elbow Pain *Lateral Epicondylitis*

TREATMENT & TECHNIQUES

Overview: Tennis elbow is most commonly diagnosed under the category of accident/trauma. This is usually a repetitive stress disorder due to the accumulation of micro-trauma. However, it may occur as an acute strain. The injury is at the level of the tendons and bone, with qi and blood stagnation in the channels and collaterals. The Large Intestine and San Jiao meridians encompass the region of the extensor muscles. However, neither of these two channels precisely encompass the lateral epicondyle. Internal organ imbalances are unclear.

Prognosis: Treat twice a week for three weeks, then re-evaluate. With chronic cases, continue treatment at least once weekly after the first three-week period. If there is not significant improvement within ten treatments, I usually refer the patient for other modalities.

STEP ONE: INITIAL TREATMENT

Choose among these four techniques, carefully determining if there is an immediate decrease in pain or an increase in range of motion.

Technique #1: **The Tendino-Muscle Meridians**

SI 1, LI 1, SJ 1   Bleeding technique

The tendino-muscle meridians of the three arm yang treat general symptoms of the extensor group, but this technique may not get to the bony attachment at the epicondyle.

Technique #2: **Opposite Side (contra-lateral)**

 Ahshi point(s)   On the opposite (unaffected) side
Palpate for sensitive points in the extensor muscle group.

LI 11   Corresponding point on the opposite (unaffected) side

This he-sea point is often a good place to start, even if it is not a precise contra-lateral mirror.

Technique #3: **Opposite Extremity (upper/lower)**

 St 35   Yang ming corresponding point on the opposite extremity

St 35 should be considered when the pain is at the lateral epicondyle

St 36 — Yang ming corresponding point on the opposite extremity

St 36 is considered with pain slightly distal to bone in the extensor muscle group.

St 35 or St 36 often give some relief of pain and may increase range of motion immediately after needle insertion.

In general, treat upper/lower corresponding points on the opposite (unaffected) side when acute, and the affected side when chronic. Use palpation to assist in this choice.

Technique #4: **Empirical Points**

 GB 33, "anterior" GB 33

GB 33 is located proximal to the knee joint, on the posterior side of the ilio-tibial band. "Anterior" GB 33 is located anterior to the ilio-tibial band, on the same level as GB 33. These points are considered empirical points in the work of Richard Tan, L.Ac.[3] The anterior version of GB 33 is between the Yang ming and Shao yang channels, making it an excellent mirror for the lateral epicondyle.

STEP TWO: MERIDIANS & MICROSYSTEMS

Choose among these four techniques, selecting points that are appropriate for the signs and symptoms of the patient.

Technique #5: **The Shu-Stream Point Combination**

LI 3 affected side + St 43 opposite side
SJ 3 affected side + GB 41 (or GB 42) opposite side

GB 42 is often more sensitive than GB 41 in the treatment of pain, and should be considered as an alternative shu-stream point.

Technique #6: **Traditional Point Categories**

★ Palpation may assist in your choice of the three arm yang meridians proximal to the wrist:

LI 4	Yuan-source point
LI 5	Jing-river point
LI 6	Luo-connecting point
SJ 5	Luo-connecting point
SJ 6	Jing-river point
SJ 8	Crossing point of three arm yang

Technique #7: **The Extraordinary Meridians**

SI 3 + Bl 62   Activate the Du mai

Treating the Du mai may assist if there is cervical nerve root pathology contributing to the condition.

Technique #8: **Microsystems**

Auricular Therapy
Local: Elbow, shoulder, master shoulder, cervical spine
Systemic points for pain: Shen men, Thalamus, Endocrine, Adrenal

Wrist-ankle Acupuncture
Wrist-ankle acupuncture may be considered, as the site of injury may cover multiple meridians. Use three zones on the dorsal surface of the forearm.[4]
Upper #4 The dorsal surface of the forearm Located 2 cun proximal to the wrist crease, along the radius. This zone approximates the Large Intestine meridian.
Upper #5 The dorsal surface of the forearm Located 2 cun proximal to the wrist crease, between the radius and the ulna. This zone is the San Jiao meridian, and includes the point SJ 5.
Upper #6 The dorsal surface of the forearm Located 2 cun proximal to the wrist crease, along the ulna. This zone approximates the Small Intestine meridian.

STEP THREE: INTERNAL ORGAN IMBALANCES

Choose appropriate points to treat internal organ imbalances that may contribute to the injury or pain syndrome.

Technique #9: **Qi, Blood, and the Zang-fu Organs**

Tennis elbow is a repetitive stress injury and therefore internal organ imbalances are usually not causative. However, sometimes the Liver may contribute to the condition.

Liver imbalances Liver qi stagnation, Liver yin deficiency, and Liver blood deficiency
Liver imbalances may result in the susceptibility of the tendons to inflammation and repetitive stress injury. Consider the following:
Liv 3 Yuan-source point; supports the Liver in its function of controlling the muscles and tendons
GB 34 Hui-influential point of tendons
Treat GB 34 on the affected side and Liv 3 on the opposite side.

Points should be determined by the practitioner from both palpation and analysis of the signs and symptoms of the patient.

233 • **Elbow Pain** *Lateral Epicondylitis*

STEP FOUR: THE SITE OF INJURY

Choose among the local and adjacent points at the site of injury. Points may be determined by palpation, orthopedic testing, and analysis of the signs and symptoms of the patient.

Technique #10: **Local and Adjacent Points**

It's likely every acupuncturist has successfully treated this common elbow injury. However, most have probably been frustrated by stubborn cases as well. Whether it be a micro-tear at the attachment to the epicondyle or inflammation of the tendon, the primary lesion of lateral epicondylitis is minute in size. The practitioner needs to be precise with needle technique whether at the epicondyle, the tendon, or in the extensor muscles themselves. Experimenting with depth and various needle techniques may be necessary.

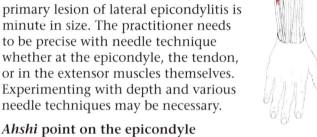

The lateral epicondyle   *Ahshi* **point on the epicondyle**

★ At the lateral epicondyle, insert at an angle from oblique to transverse, threaded distally.

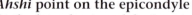

○ – *Point variations at the lateral epicondyle*
↗ – *Oblique to transverse needle insertion*

When there is pain upon palpation at the lateral epicondyle, several techniques may successfully treat this local stagnation. The first choice to consider is needling directly at this painful site. I prefer two needles at the tip or "high point" of the epicondyle. The needles are inserted at an angle from oblique to transverse. They are threaded distally following the extensor group towards the wrist. The depth of insertion is superficial enough to avoid hitting the bone and the common extensor tendon. However, insertion needs to be deeper than the cutaneous zone, as close to the bone and tendon as possible. Use a 1.5 inch needle, inserted at least 1 inch. Electrical stimulation can be used between these two paired points, or coupled with other adjacent or distal points.

If this local treatment aggravates or fails to provide relief, consider thread moxa directly on the high point of the lateral epicondyle. Another possibility is a bleeding cup over epicondyle. Carefully use a lancet superficially at the painful spot at the bony prominence. You then need some luck in retaining a cup, as the sloping surface isn't always easy. Remember that some lotion or lubricant on the skin may help keep the cup in place.

The common extensor tendon

★ **Ahshi points**

About 1 cun distal to the epicondyle, insert at an angle from oblique to transverse, threaded distally along the tendon.

Threading the tendon with insertion just distal to the lateral epicondyle sometimes works well, and is similar to the treatment above. Consider two needles that are inserted about 1 cun distal to the bone, in the tendinous zone of the extensor group. After insertion, thread distally to a depth as close to the tendon as possible. Use a 1.5 inch needle, inserted at least 1 inch in an oblique angle. Electrical stimulation can be used between these two paired points, or coupled with other adjacent or distal points. From one to three sets of paired points can be considered.

Sometimes treatment at the lateral epicondyle or threading the tendon does not benefit. A more aggressive needle technique may be necessary, but you and the patient have to be prepared for the predictable aggravation. Starting distal to the prominence of the bone, the needle is inserted perpendicularly. It will reach the deeper tissues, penetrating the fascia and a superficial zone of the tendon. While this technique causes local irritation and inflammation, it also may increase microcirculation, thus dispelling qi stagnation and blood stasis. Two paired points with electrical stimulation is recommended.

The extensor muscles

★ **Ahshi points**

About 2 to 5 cun distal to the epicondyle, use perpendicular insertion in the most prominent taut bands

X – *Trigger points*

Tennis elbow has predictably painful points in the extensor muscles 2 to 5 cun distal to their attachment at the epicondyle. On the Large Intestine meridian, this would be in the region of LI 10 and LI 9. However, the practitioner should palpate for painful points on both sides of this meridian pathway. I usually use two paired points in the most prominent taut bands, needled perpendicularly to a depth of from .5 to 1 inch. If there are multiple taut bands, I will consider a second set of paired points. Consider electric stimulation between these two points.

235 • Elbow Pain *Lateral Epicondylitis*

Adjacent points **LI 11 + "outer" SI 8**
These two points are on the radial and ulnar sides of the lateral epicondyle. On the radial side, needle LI 11 or consider a variation lateral to LI 11 closer to the bone. "Outer" SI 8 is located in the depression between the lateral epicondyle and the olecranon process of the ulnar. The point is needled obliquely. Consider electrical stimulation between these two points.

LI 12 + LI 10
Use the text location of LI 12, which is 1 cun proximal and posterior to LI 11, in a usually tender depression next to the humerus. Needle either LI 10 or a tender *ahshi* point in the region of the extensor muscles. This is considered "above and below". Electrical stimulation between these two points may be used.

The neck and scapula Degenerative changes to the cervical spine and possible nerve root involvement often contribute to upper-extremity pain syndromes such as tennis elbow. In general, treatment of tension in the neck and shoulder may need to be included to obtain lasting results. Choose several neck and/or scapula points in any one treatment session, determined by palpation.

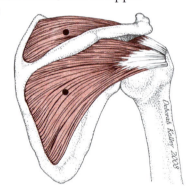

- ● – SI 12 – the supraspinatous (superior)
- SI 11 – the infraspinatous (inferior)

GB 20, Bl 10   Upper cervical region

The extraordinary point *Bailao*
This point is 2 cun superior and 1 cun lateral to Du 14, in the region of C4, C5, or C6.

***Huatuo jiaji* points (C1 to C7, T1[5])**
The extensors and the supinator are innervated by the cervical nerve roots from C5 to T1.

SI 10, SI 11	The infraspinatous muscle
SI 12	The supraspinatous muscle
SI 14, SI 15	The levator scapulae muscle

COMPLEMENTARY PROCEDURES

- When acute, ice massage at the lateral epicondyle and along the common extensor tendon may alleviate pain and reduce inflammation.

- Alternating ice and heat after the acute stage, when the condition is "neither hot (re) nor cold (han)", may enhance recovery.

- Topical applications (herbal liniments, plasters, etc.) may benefit.

- Rock climbers report applications of heat to the area before activity benefits.

- Cross-fiber massage at the tendinous attachment may increase local micro-circulation and enhance recovery. However, it may cause discomfort and temporary aggravation.

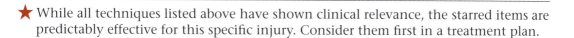 While all techniques listed above have shown clinical relevance, the starred items are predictably effective for this specific injury. Consider them first in a treatment plan.

REFERENCES

[1] Dutton, M: *Orthopeadic Examination, Evaluation, and Intervention,* Second Edition. McGraw-Hill, USA, 2008 (page 700).

[2] *I would not be surprised to see medical texts in the future use the term "computer elbow". "Blackberry thumb" is already showing up in the literature for overuse injuries of the thumb from texting.*

[3] Tan & Rush: *Twenty Four More in Acupuncture,* San Diego, 1994 (page 18).

[4] Matsumoto & Birch: *Extraordinary Vessels.* Paradigm Publishers, Massachusetts, 1986 (pages 182-188).
Note: *Dr. Zhang Xin Shu's* Wrist Ankle Acupuncture (Wan Ke Zhen) *is the source quoted in the above text.*

[5] *The huatuo jiaji points technically do not exist in the cervical region. The classic texts state that they only follow the thoracic and lumbar spine. Some practitioners insist that the cervical spine should be included. If used, the vertebral artery should be avoided.*

Notes

19
Elbow Pain

Medial Epicondylitis (Golfer's Elbow)

Pain in the elbow at the medial epicondyle and distally along the flexor tendon and muscles of the forearm

A repetitive stress injury characterized by inflammation and irritation of the forearm flexors and possibly the pronators. This injury is often referred to as "golfer's elbow" as well as "climber's elbow".

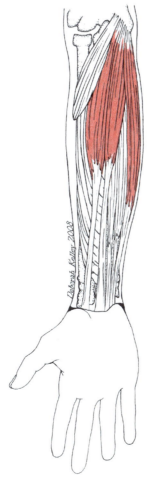

DIAGNOSIS & ASSESSMENT

Medial epicondylitis, often called "golfer's elbow", is an injury to the flexor group of the forearm and a cause of elbow pain. While tendonitis to the lateral side is four to seven times more common than the medial side, the practitioner should still be prepared for this injury.[1] Numerous sport and work-related activities can cause this condition, including the "weekend carpenter" who uses hand tools for a quick project. In my area, at the base of many rock outcroppings on the eastern slope of the Rockies, medial epicondylitis is quite common. "Climber's elbow" results from strain to the flexor tendons from hand holds while rock climbing.

The patient complains of medial elbow pain, which may radiate distally down the forearm. The pain is usually dull and intermittent, but occasionally the patient's symptoms may be more pronounced. Like many overuse injuries, its onset is insidious. There is often no specific traumatic event associated with the start of symptoms. However, the patient is predictably involved in recreational or work activities that require wrist flexion and pronation. The patient will often have difficulty lifting or grasping objects or unscrewing a lid to a container.

The etiology of medial epicondylitis can be summarized as follows:

1. Epicondylitis, which implies inflammation of the bony medial epicondyle without specifically implicating pathology to the tendon. Some sources suggest the presence of degeneration of the bone associated with the condition.

2. Inflammation due to micro-tears of the common flexor tendon at or near its attachment to the medial epicondyle.

3. Inflammation of the tendon, often called tendinosis. This is described as a degenerative process within the tendon and its sheath without the presence of strain or micro-tears.

4. The contribution from degenerative changes to the cervical spine and possible nerve root involvement. While technically not a pain referral pattern, muscle dysfunction in the forearm may be associated with the cervical spine, resulting in either strain or inflammation.

Examination of the patient is straightforward. First, palpate the bony medial epicondyle. If there is pain, this is the site of injury and the primary stagnation of qi and blood. Pain slightly distal to the attachment indicates inflammation of the common tendon. And pain two to three cun distal to the epicondyle is often found in taut fascial bands of the flexor muscles. Golfer's elbow involves the muscles that control wrist flexion and pronation. Each of these movements should be assessed separately with manual muscle testing. These tests are easy to perform, and are described in the Appendices on page 337.

In general, acupuncture is directed to the primary site of qi and blood stagnation. This involves the yin surface of the forearm, which may be a bit more sensitive and tricky than the yang surface. Both palpation and muscle testing helps to locate this site more precisely. The bony epicondyle, the common tendon, and the taut fascial bands of the flexor muscles may all need to be treated. Not to be overlooked is the possible contribution from neck and shoulder tension. And including physical therapy modalities often complements the overall treatment plan.

SUMMARY OF THE INJURY

Clinical Features	• Inflammation of the common flexor tendon, with the possibility of micro-tears at the site of the attachment • Usually a repetitive stress disorder, but may be seen as an acute strain • Sometimes referred to as tendinosis, a degenerative process within the tendon and its sheath without the presence of strain or micro-tears. • Tenderness with palpation at the medial epicondyle and distal to the attachment following the flexor tendon • Pain with resisted wrist flexion and/or hand pronation • The patient will often have difficulty lifting or grasping objects or unscrewing a lid to a container
Common Patient Complaints	• Pain in the medial elbow • Pain and stiffness may radiate distally down the forearm • Onset is often gradual • Pain may be dull and intermittent • Moderate to severe pain with acute strain • Hand and wrist activities usually aggravate the condition
Differentiation from Similar Injuries and Conditions	• Partial tear of one or more of the muscles of the flexor group • Referral pain from cervical nerve root or from the shoulder • Ulnar nerve entrapment, cubital tunnel syndrome • Rule out elbow fracture if associated with trauma
Typical Medical Recommendations	• R.I.C.E. (Rest, Ice, Compression, and Elevation) when acute • Anti-inflammatory medications • Modify activity *Decrease upper-extremity activities that aggravate* • Stretching *Use a stretching program for the flexon group.* • Biomechanics *Correct ergonomics of work and computer stations. If caused from golf, modification of swing biomechanics may benefit. With climbers modification of technique may benefit.* • Physical therapy *Ultrasound, deep-friction massage, and other physical therapy modalities. A counterforce elbow brace is sometimes recommended. Rehabilitation usually consists of strengthening exercises, including wrist curls.* • Orthopedic procedures *Cortisone injection is sometimes used in the inflamed region; the patient must evaluate the risks of the procedure.*

TREATMENT & TECHNIQUES

Overview: Golfer's elbow is most commonly diagnosed under the category of accident/trauma. This is usually a repetitive stress disorder due to the accumulation of micro-trauma. However, it may occur as an acute strain. The injury is at the level of the tendons and bone, with qi and blood stagnation in the channels and collaterals. The Small Intestine and Heart meridians encompass the region of the flexor muscles. However, neither of these two channels precisely encompass the medial epicondyle. Internal organ imbalances are unclear.

Prognosis: Treat twice a week for three weeks, then re-evaluate. With chronic cases, continue treatment at least once weekly after the first three-week period. If there is not significant improvement within ten treatments, I usually refer the patient for other modalities.

STEP ONE: INITIAL TREATMENT

Choose among these four techniques, carefully determining if there is an immediate decrease in pain or an increase in range of motion.

Technique #1: **The Tendino-Muscle Meridians**

SI 1, H 9　　　　　Bleeding technique

The tendino-muscle meridians of the Small Intestine and Heart treat general symptoms of the flexor group, but this technique may not reach the bony attachment at the epicondyle. There may be contraindications for the point H 9.

Technique #2: **Opposite Side (contra-lateral)**

Ahshi **point(s)**　　　On the opposite (unaffected) side

SI 8, H 3　　　　　Corresponding points on the
　　　　　　　　　　　opposite (unaffected) side

These He-sea points are often a good place to start, even if they are not a precise contra-lateral mirror.

Technique #3: **Opposite Extremity (upper/lower)**

★ **Kid 10**　　　　　Shao yin corresponding point on the
　　　　　　　　　　　opposite extremity

In general, treat upper/lower corresponding points on the opposite (unaffected) side when acute, and the affected side when chronic. Use palpation to assist in this choice.

Technique #4: **Special Empirical Points**

No well known clinically effective empirical points for golfer's elbow.

242 • Elbow Pain *Medial Epicondylitis*

STEP TWO: MERIDIANS & MICROSYSTEMS

Choose among these four techniques, selecting points that are appropriate for the signs and symptoms of the patient.

Technique #5: **The Shu-Stream Point Combination**

SI 3 affected side + Bl 65 opposite side
H 7 affected side + Kid 3 opposite side

Technique #6: **Traditional Point Categories**

⭐ Palpation may assist in your choice of points proximal to the wrist:

H 5	Luo-connecting point
SI 4 + H 5	Yuan-source point + luo-connecting point
P 6	Luo-connecting point
P 5	Crossing point of three arm yin

Technique #7: **The Extraordinary Meridians**

SI 3 + Bl 62   Activate the Du mai
Treating the Du Mai may assist if there is cervical nerve root pathology contributing to the condition.

Technique #8: **Microsystems**

Auricular Therapy
Local: Elbow, shoulder, master shoulder, cervical spine
Zang-fu points: Liver
Systemic points for pain: Shen men, Thalamus, Adrenal, Endocrine

Wrist-ankle Acupuncture
Wrist-ankle acupuncture may be considered, as the site of injury may cover multiple meridians. Use three zones on the palmar surface of the forearm.[2]
Upper #1   The palmar surface of the forearm
Located 2 cun proximal to the wrist crease, along the ulna, on the ulnar side of the flexor carpi ulnaris. This zone approximates the Heart meridian.
Upper #2   The palmar surface of the forearm
Located 2 cun proximal to the wrist crease, between the tendons of the palmaris longus and the flexor carpi radialis. This zone is the Pericardium meridian, and includes the point P 6.
Upper #3   The palmar surface of the forearm
Located 2 cun proximal to the wrist crease, on the radial side of the radial artery. This zone approximates the Lung meridian.

STEP THREE: INTERNAL ORGAN IMBALANCES

Choose appropriate points to treat internal organ imbalances that may contribute to the injury or pain syndrome.

Technique #9: **Qi, Blood, and the Zang-fu Organs**

Golfer's elbow is a repetitive stress injury and therefore internal organ imbalances are usually not causative. However, sometimes the Liver may contribute to the condition.

Liver imbalances Liver qi stagnation, Liver yin deficiency, and Liver blood deficiency

Liver imbalances may result in the susceptibility of the tendons to inflammation and repetitive stress injury. Consider the following:

Liv 3	Yuan-source point; supports the Liver in its function of controlling the muscles and tendons
GB 34	Hui-influential point of tendons

Treat GB 34 on the affected side and Liv 3 on the opposite side.

Points should be determined by the practitioner from both palpation and analysis of the signs and symptoms of the patient.

STEP FOUR: THE SITE OF INJURY

Choose among the local and adjacent points at the site of injury. Points may be determined by palpation, orthopedic testing, and analysis of the signs and symptoms of the patient.

Technique #10: **Local and Adjacent Points**

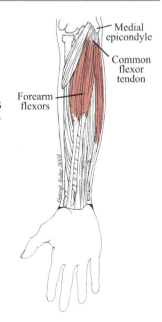

Whether it be a micro-tear at the attachment to the epicondyle or inflammation of the tendon, the primary lesion of medial epicondylitis is minute in size. The practitioner needs to be precise with needle technique whether at the epicondyle, the tendon, or in the extensor muscles themselves. Experimenting with depth and various needle techniques may be necessary. And remember, this is a "yin" surface, which may be more sensitive than the "yang" surface of the extensor group.

The medial epicondyle **Ahshi point on the epicondyle**
At the medial epicondyle, insert at an angle from oblique to transverse, threaded distally.

When there is pain upon palpation at the medial epicondyle, several techniques may successfully treat this local stagnation. The first choice to consider is needling directly at the painful site. I prefer two paired needles at the tip or "high point" of the epicondyle. The needles are inserted at an angle from oblique to transverse. They are threaded distally following the flexor group towards the wrist. The depth of insertion is superficial enough to avoid hitting the bone and the common tendon. However, insertion needs to be deeper than the cutaneous zone as close to the bone and tendon as possible. Electrical stimulation can be considered between these two paired points, or coupled with other adjacent or distal points.

○ – *Point variations at the medial epicondyle*
↗ – *Oblique to transverse needle insertion*

Moxa, cupping If this local treatment aggravates or fails to provide relief, consider thread moxa directly on the high point of the medial epicondyle. Another possibility is a bleeding cup over the epicondyle. Carefully use a lancet superficially at the painful spot at the bony prominence. You then need some luck in retaining a cup, as the sloping surface isn't always easy. Remember that some lotion or lubricant on the skin may help keep the cup in place.

The common flexor tendon **Ahshi points**
About 1 cun distal to the epicondyle, insert at an angle from oblique to transverse, threaded distally along the tendon.

Threading the tendon with insertion just distal to the medial epicondyle sometimes works well, and is similar to the treatment above. Consider two needles that are inserted about 1 cun distal to the bone, in the tendinous zone of the flexor group. After insertion, thread distally to a depth as close to the tendon as possible. Use a 1.5 inch needle, inserted at least 1 inch in an oblique angle. Electrical stimulation can be used between these two paired points, or coupled with other adjacent or distal points. From one to three sets of paired points can be considered.

Sometimes treatment at the medial epicondyle or threading the tendon does not benefit. A more aggressive needle technique may be necessary, but you and the patient have to be prepared for the predictable aggravation. Starting distal to the prominence of the bone, the needle is inserted perpendicularly. It will reach the deeper tissues, penetrating the fascia and a superficial zone of the tendon. While this technique causes local irritation and inflammation, it also may increase micro-circulation, thus dispelling qi stagnation and blood stasis. Two paired points with electrical stimulation is recommended.

The flexor muscles ★ **Ahshi points**

About 2 to 5 cun distal to the epicondyle, use perpendicular insertion in the most prominent taut bands

Golfer's elbow has predictably painful points in the flexor muscles 2 to 5 cun distal to their attachment at the epicondyle. This generally follows the Heart meridian, however, no acupuncture points are located in this zone. However, the practitioner should palpate for painful points on both sides of this meridian pathway. I usually use two paired points in the most prominent taut bands, needled perpendicularly to a depth of from .5 to 1 inch. If there are multiple taut bands, I will consider a second set of paired points. Consider electric stimulation between these two points.

X – Trigger points

Adjacent points ★ **H 3 + SI 8**

These two points are on the ulnar and radial sides of the medial epicondyle. Needle H 3 or consider a variation closer to the bone. SI 8 is located in the depression between the medial epicondyle and the olecranon process of the ulnar. This point should be needled obliquely to avoid penetrating the ulnar nerve. Consider electrical stimulation between these two points.

The neck and scapula ★ Degenerative changes to the cervical spine and possible nerve root involvement often contribute to upper-extremity pain syndromes, and golfer's elbow is no exception. In general, treatment of tension in the neck and shoulder may need to be included to obtain lasting results. Choose several neck and/or scapula points in any one treatment session, determined by palpation.

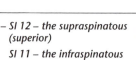
● – SI 12 – the supraspinatous (superior)
SI 11 – the infraspinatous (inferior)

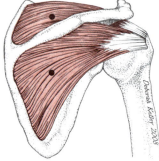

| GB 20, Bl 10 | Upper cervical region |

The extraordinary point *Bailao*
This point is 2 cun superior and 1 cun lateral to Du 14, in the region of C4, C5, or C6.

Huatuo jiaji **points (C1 to C7, T1[3])**
The flexors and the pronator are innervated by the cervical nerve roots from C5 to T1.

SI 10, SI 11	The infraspinatous muscle
SI 12	The supraspinatous muscle
SI 14, SI 15	The levator scapulae muscle

COMPLEMENTARY PROCEDURES

- When acute, ice massage at the medial epicondyle and along the common flexor tendon may alleviate pain and reduce inflammation.

- Alternating ice and heat after the acute stage, when the condition is "neither hot (re) nor cold (han)", may enhance recovery.

- Topical applications (herbal liniments, plasters, etc.) may benefit.

- Cross-fiber massage at the tendinous attachment may increase local micro-circulation and enhance recovery. However, it may cause discomfort and temporary aggravation.

- Rock climbers report applications of heat to the area before activity benefits.

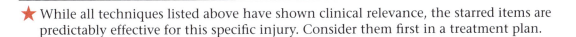

★ While all techniques listed above have shown clinical relevance, the starred items are predictably effective for this specific injury. Consider them first in a treatment plan.

REFERENCES

[1] Dutton, M: *Orthopeadic Examination, Evaluation, and Intervention*, Second Edition. McGraw-Hill, USA, 2008 (page 700).

[2] Matsumoto & Birch: *Extraordinary Vessels*. Paradigm Publishers, Massachusetts, 1986 (pages 182-188).
Note: Dr. Zhang Xin Shu's Wrist Ankle Acupuncture (Wan Ke Zhen) *is the source quoted in the above text.*

[3] The huatuo jiaji points technically do not exist in the cervical region. The classic texts state that they only follow the thoracic and lumbar spine. Some practitioners insist that the cervical spine should be included. If used, the vertebral artery should be avoided.

Notes

20
Shoulder Pain
The Supraspinatous Muscle

Pain in scapular region of the shoulder, with a referral pattern to the area of the deltoid. Possible sudden, sharp pain is due to shoulder impingement syndrome.

An acute or chronic injury characterized by inflammation of the tendon and possible strain or muscle tears at the attachment to the humerus.

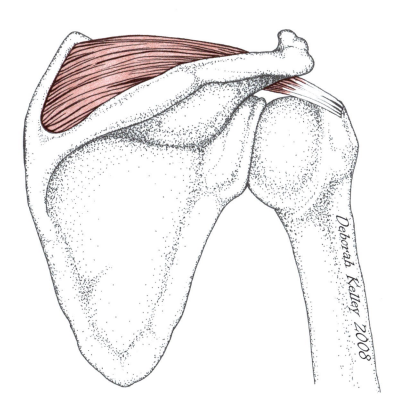

DIAGNOSIS & ASSESSMENT

As a practitioner of acupuncture for more than 25 years, there is no single injury I find more rewarding to treat than shoulder pain due to supraspinatous tendonitis. I was fortunate enough to have studied trigger points with Dr. Janet Travell early in my career. Her work on myofascial pain syndromes changed the way I think about acupuncture and Chinese medicine, and has led to many of the treatments and techniques in this book.

The supraspinatous muscle is one of the four muscles of the rotator cuff, and the most common cause of shoulder tendonitis.[1] I would go further to suggest that the supraspinatous is the most common diagnosis in shoulder pain from all causes. This is probably due to its precarious location beneath the acromion, between the points LI 16 and LI 15.[2] What makes this problematic for the acupuncturist is that the pain often refers to the deltoid region of the shoulder, and occasionally distally down the arm and forearm.[3] This deltoid region pain leads many practitioners to a diagnosis of Large Intestine (Yang ming) and San Jiao (Shao yang) disorders, resulting in treatments that rarely suffice.

The supraspinatous is an abductor, so activities with the arm lifted to the side rely on this muscle. Injury is seen with movements relying on overhead motions, such as those in racquet sports, swimming, and throwing in baseball and football. But you don't need to be involved in sports to have supraspinatous pathology. Hairdressers, painters, and even those using a computer and keyboard whose arms are in a prolonged state of abduction may develop symptoms. With an acute strain, the trauma often occurs with heavy lifting, a fall snowboarding or an outstretched arm in protection from a cycling crash. But don't be limited to these causes – I had a patient with a tear of the supraspinatous from angrily hitting the ground with her golf club after a bad shot!

The patient complains of shoulder pain, usually in the anterior lateral, lateral, and posterior lateral region of the deltoid. It is often dull and diffuse, difficult to locate, and it frequently "comes and goes". There may be pain at night, especially while sleeping on the affected shoulder. Another characteristic symptom is sharp paroxysms of pain with certain movements involving abduction (lifting the arm to the side). It is not uncommon to hear that it hurts to put an arm into the sleeve of a coat or reaching to the back seat of a car. This is due to the impingement of the tendon under the bony acromium.

Supraspinatous dysfunction with its resulting pain syndrome is due to various pathologies within the muscle-tendon unit. Let's look at each separately:

1. The belly of the muscle
   The origin and belly of the supraspinatous are in the suprascapular fossa in the region of the acupuncture point SI 12. This is the site of the trigger point as well as the motor point.[4,5] In the myofascial explanation of pain, Dr. Travell describes active trigger points in the belly of the muscle at SI 12, contributing to the predictable referred pain pattern in the deltoid region. Palpation of the suprascapular fossa may reproduce pain and reveal taut fascial bands of the muscle. This painful zone can extend medially to SI 13, as well as 1 to 3 centimeters lateral to the text location of SI 12. This is the first step in confirming the supraspinatous as the cause of shoulder pain.

250 • Shoulder Pain *The Supraspinatous Muscle*

2. The sub-acromial portion of the tendon
   The muscle-tendon junction is at the lateral aspect of the suprascapular fossa, in the region of the point LI 16. The supraspinatous tendon must pass under the acromion, and this narrow fossa is not particularly forgiving. Many patients with tendonitis in this part of the muscle experience what is termed "impingement" syndrome. With those overhead arm movements and other positions of abduction, the swollen tendon gets impinged under the bony acromion, causing the paroxysms of sudden sharp pain. It should be noted that the pain from impingement is difficult to locate with palpation, as it is deep to the acromion between LI 16 and LI 15.

3. The tendinous attachment
   The supraspinatous tendon attaches at the greater tubercle of the humerus, in the region of LI 15 and sometimes posterior towards SJ 14. It is at this site that both inflammation and possible tears can occur to the tendon. If there is localized pain with palpation in this region, suspect strain of the supraspinatous. The practitioner should also keep in mind that deep to the tendon is the subacromial bursa, which, if inflamed, will probably present with tenderness on palpation. While at the lateral shoulder, you should palpate the deltoid region where the patient reports pain. You probably will not be able to find *ahshi* points that correspond to the symptoms described by the patient. However, be aware that the deltoid, also a muscle of abduction, compensates for the distressed supraspinatous and may present with some tender areas. Be cautious, as these may very well lead you away from the primary problem, which is rarely the deltoid.

Several tests may confirm what you already may suspect after hearing the patient's symptoms and palpating the shoulder. The "empty can" test is easy to perform, using resisted abduction to assess the supraspinatous muscle and its tendon. If there is pain and/or weakness, this muscle is likely involved. Also simple and quick is the "arch of pain" test. If it reveals discomfort around 90 degrees of abduction, tendonitis and impingement are probable. These two tests are described in the Appendices on page 341. They really should be learned by the practitioner, as the supraspinatous is involved in so many cases of neck and shoulder pain.

I must tell a quick story about a unique diagnosis of injury to the supraspinatous muscle. Several years ago, I was treating a rock climber who was returning from a trip in Spain with acute shoulder pain. He called in transit in the Chicago airport, and was convinced that he strained a muscle in his shoulder while scaling a difficult route overhanging the Mediterranean Sea. However, having treated climbers for years with very low incidence of rotator cuff injuries, I thought the cause was likely something else. After some quick internal dialogue, I confidently suggested the following scenario while on the phone with him: "You have an equipment bag that was quite heavy, and it was hand-carried. Changing planes in the Madrid airport, you were running to catch an international flight, carrying this bag at your side. Your pain started several hours after that event while on the plane to Chicago." The patient confirmed all of this was true. What occured is a relatively common injury to the supraspinatous. This muscle had to abduct with the weight of the equipment bag in order to keep it from hitting the sides of his legs. This prolonged abduction with such a heavy load resulted in a strain to the tendon. Several days later, a supraspinatous injury was confirmed in my office after examining the patient. And, fortunately, two weeks of acupuncture treatment was successful!

We are not, however, always successful. Your treatments need to be precise and the belly of the muscle at SI 12, as well as the tendon at LI 16 and LI 15, usually needs to be treated. And, of course, you may need to use one or more of the other non-local points discussed below to complete the protocol. If the patient does not respond, or if their symptoms are aggravated with activity, the injury may be significant. The tendon may have a significant tear that is not able to heal. Or the presence of a sub-acromial bone spur may be constantly irritating the tendon with any abduction or overhead movements. If this is the case, don't hesitate to refer the patient for an orthopedic evaluation, as acupuncture may not be appropriate for these cases.

In summary, shoulder pain due to supraspinatous dysfunction is very common in the clinic. You will see it in the athletic community, as well as in many patients over 50 years old, whether they are athletes or not. Diagnosis is easy when it is an acute injury from a definitive trauma.

Chronic cases due to repetitive stress may seem more difficult to assess, as the causes appear quite benign. However, most patients present with some, if not all, of these signs and symptoms:

1. Dull or diffuse pain in the deltoid region of the shoulder

2. Sudden, sharp pain with certain movements of abduction

3. Pain and taut muscle bands in the belly of the supraspinatous at SI 12

4. Supraspinatous weakness and/or pain with resisted abduction

5. A positive arch of pain

SUMMARY OF THE INJURY

Clinical Features
- Pain from supraspinatous lesions often radiates to the deltoid region of the shoulder, and distally down the arm
- Paroxysms of sharp pain are diagnosed as shoulder impingement syndrome
- Tenderness with palpation in the supraspinatous muscle, in the region of SI 12
- Pain and/or weakness with resisted abduction and a positive "arch of pain"
- Patient may have history of repeated or strenuous overhead motions, or of prior accident involving the shoulder
- Acute cases may involve strain to the tendon
- Chronic cases may be due to repetitive stress causing inflammation of tendon

Common Patient Complaints
- Dull or diffuse pain in the deltoid region of the shoulder
- Sudden sharp pain when lifting arm to the side (abduction) or other overhead movements
- Pain is commonly experienced when putting arm into the sleeve of a coat or reaching to the back seat of a car
- Pain at night, especially while sleeping on the affected shoulder

Differentiation from Similar Injuries and Conditions
- Differentiate from other shoulder injuries, such as those to the infraspinatous and biceps muscles
- Shoulder pain may be referred from intra-thoracic diseases, such as from the diaphragm, heart, and the gall bladder
- Referral pain from cervical nerve root
- Sub-acromial bursitis
- Partial or complete tear of the tendon
- Sub-acromial bone spur or calcification on the inferior aspect of the acromion

Typical Medical Recommendations
- Ice is typically used when acute.
- Anti-inflammatory medications
- Stretching
  Stretching of the supraspinatous may help with tendonitis.
- Biomechanics
  Correct ergonomics of work and computer stations to reduce or eliminate elevation of the scapula and other postural imbalances.
- Modify activity
  Decrease overhead arm activities and other abduction movements that aggravate. If the motion causes pain, the tendon is likely getting impinged, resulting in continued tendon inflammation.

253 • Shoulder Pain *The Supraspinatous Muscle*

Typical Medical Recommendations (cont'd)

- Physical therapy
  Ultrasound, deep-friction massage, and other physical therapy modalities.
- Orthopedic evaluation
  An MRI may be necessary to assess a tear in the supraspinatous or other rotator cuff tendons. A sub-acromial bone spur may be visualized with X-ray.
- Orthopedic procedures
  Cortisone injection into the tendon or bursa may provide relief. If a grade II or grade III tear occurs in the supraspinatous or other rotator cuff tendons, surgery may be required. Chronic cases may be complicated by a sub-acromial bone spur requiring surgical debridement.

TREATMENT & TECHNIQUES

Overview: Shoulder pain due to supraspinatous muscle or tendon pathology is most commonly diagnosed under the category accident/trauma. The acute case usually has a definitive traumatic event. The chronic case is a repetitive stress disorder due to the accumulation of micro-trauma. The injury is at the level of the muscles and tendons, with qi and blood stagnation in the channels and collaterals. The Small Intestine meridian encompasses the belly of the supraspinatous. The Large Intestine meridian covers the muscle-tendon junction. The Large Intestine and San Jiao meridians cover the attachment to the humerus. Sometimes the diagnosis of wind (feng) may be used for the pain of sudden onset and sudden disappearance seen in shoulder impingement syndrome. Internal organ imbalances are unclear.

Prognosis: Treat twice a week for three weeks, then re-evaluate. Many cases without complications of tendon tears or sub-acromial bone spur have good results within six treatments. The more inflamed the tendon due to impingement syndrome, continue treatment at least once weekly after the first three-week period. The patient should be advised to discontinue any overhead and abduction movements of the arm that aggravate the tendon.

STEP ONE: INITIAL TREATMENT

Choose among these four techniques, carefully determining if there is an immediate decrease in pain or an increase in range of motion.

Technique #1: **The Tendino-Muscle Meridians**

 SI 1   Bleeding technique
This jing-well point treats the scapular aspect of the supraspinatous, in the region of the origin and the belly of the muscle.

LI 1   Bleeding technique
This jing-well point treats the area of the tendino-muscle junction, the tendon, and its attachment to the humerus.

Technique #2: **Opposite Side (contra-lateral)**

Corresponding points on the opposite (unaffected) side may be considered; however, treatment to the affected side is usually preferred.

Technique #3: **Opposite Extremity (upper/lower)**

    Bl 53, Bl 54   Tai yang corresponding points on the opposite extremity

These two Bladder meridian points, often overlooked, mirror the Small Intestine (Tai yang) meridian.

    St 31   Yang ming corresponding point on the opposite extremity

St 31 is a mirror for the area of LI 15. While treatment on the affected side is preferred, this point can sometimes provide surprising effectiveness as a secondary point.

In general, treat upper/lower corresponding points on the opposite (unaffected) side when acute, and the affected side when chronic. Use palpation to assist in this choice.

Technique #4: **Empirical Points**

St 38

While its most effective use is for frozen shoulder, St 38 may help with the range-of-motion problems associated with a supraspinatous tendonitis. St 38 is discussed in detail on page 279.

Zongping

An empirical point for frozen shoulder. It is located one cun distal and one cun lateral to St 36, between the Yang ming and Shao yang channels.[6] Like St 38, it may be effective for improving range of motion. See page 279 for more details.

STEP TWO: MERIDIANS & MICROSYSTEMS

Choose among these four techniques, selecting points that are appropriate for the signs and symptoms of the patient.

Technique #5: **The Shu-Stream Point Combination**

 SI 3 affected side + Bl 65 opposite side
Treats the supraspinatous muscle origin and belly (the area of SI 12).

LI 3 affected side + St 43 opposite side
Treats the tendon and the muscle attachment at the humerus (the area from LI 16 to LI 15).

Technique #6: **Traditional Point Categories**

 SI 6   Xi-cleft point
SI 6 is one of the most effective points for the acute case. Palpation may assist in your choice of other meridian points.

SI 4	Yuan-source point
GB 34	Hui-influential point of tendons
St 39	Lower He-sea point for the Small Intestine

St 39 is occasionally effective as a secondary point. It treats the fu organ and, therefore, its exteriorly related meridian.

Technique #7: **The Extraordinary Meridians**

SI 3 + Bl 62	Activate the Du mai

Activating the Du mai may assist if there is cervical nerve root pathology contributing to the condition.

Technique #8: **Microsystems**

Auricular Therapy
Local: Shoulder, master shoulder, cervical spine
Systemic points for pain: Shen men, Thalamus, Adrenal, Endocrine, Muscle Relaxation

---

STEP THREE: INTERNAL ORGAN IMBALANCES

Choose appropriate points to treat internal organ imbalances that may contribute to the injury or pain syndrome.

Technique #9: **Qi, Blood, and the Zang-fu Organs**

Supraspinatous tendonitis is either an acute trauma or a chronic repetitive stress injury and, therefore, internal organ imbalances are usually not a factor in treatment. However, the following should be considered:

Liver imbalances Liver qi stagnation, Liver yin deficiency, and Liver blood deficiency
Liver imbalances may result in the susceptibility of the rotator cuff tendon to inflammation and repetitive stress injury. Consider the following:

Liv 3	Yuan-source point; supports the Liver in its function of controlling the muscles and tendons
GB 34	Hui-influential point of tendons

Points should be determined by the practitioner from both palpation and analysis of the signs and symptoms of the patient.

STEP FOUR: THE SITE OF INJURY

Choose among the local and adjacent points at the site of injury. Points may be determined by palpation, orthopedic testing, and analysis of the signs and symptoms of the patient.

Technique #10: **Local and Adjacent Points**

The supraspinatous muscle **SI 12**

★ One or two needles, perpendicular insertion with a slight oblique inferior angle. Needle depth is .5 to 1 inch.

SI 12 is located in the center of the suprascapular fossa, just superior to the spine of the scapula. As stated above, this is also the precise location of the trigger point and the motor point for the muscle. I usually treat SI 12 with two paired needles, although if there is room in the suprascapular fossa, three or even four needles may be used.

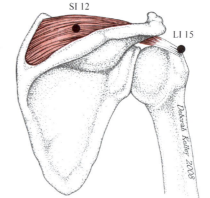

 – SI 12 – the supraspinatous belly
Trigger point and motor point
LI 15 – the attachment of the supraspinatous tendon

★ Insertion is perpendicular, just superior to the spine of the scapula. After insertion, angle slightly inferior through the superficial muscle layers of the trapezius to the deeper and oftentimes taut portion of the supraspinatous. Look for a dense feeling in the needle as it may even "squeak" into this taut muscle tissue. The bony suprascapular fossa provides an end-point to needle depth. Obviously, if you hit the bone, the needle has penetrated the entire depth of the supraspinatous muscle. Withdraw the needle to a more superficial depth, as the best results in needling are achieved in this more superficial portion of the muscle. Keep the needle close to the spine of the scapula – don't be lured into treating the tight bands of the posterior portion of the upper trapezius muscle. Depth is from .5 to 1 inch, and if more than one needle is used, they may be spaced about 1 centimeter apart.

Patient position ★ Patient position is very important to get the best access to the point, which clearly improves the clinical results. A seated patient, with arms adducted and shoulder depressed, works well. But, of course, this increases risk for fainting and needle shock. The lateral recumbant (side-lying) position works equally well. Place the patient on his or her side, so the affected shoulder is up and accessible. After depressing the shoulder and adducting the arm, use a "hugging" pillow to help stabilize the upper extremity in that position. I never treat this condition with the patient prone, as the shoulder tends to elevate and point access is compromised.

Electrical stimulation Electrical stimulation is very effective for this condition, but it also runs the risk of aggravating, so prepare your patient. There are several possible ways to orient the leads. First, with two needles inserted in the area of SI 12, use electrical stimulation between them. Second, e-stim may be used between SI 12 in the belly of the muscle and LI 15 at its insertion. And, finally, SI 12 could be paired with a distal Tai yang point, such as SI 3.

One may take the point of view that wind (feng) exists in the shoulder with shoulder impingement syndrome. This pain has the quality of sudden onset and sudden disappearance; thus, treatment to dispel wind would logically follow. Note that the Chinese name of SI 12, the primary local point, is "grasping the wind" (bing feng). It has the action to dispel wind.

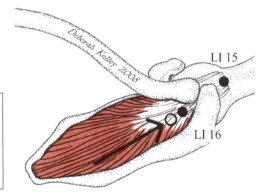

Overhead view of the shoulder
● – LI 16 – the supraspinatous muscle-tendon junction
LI 15 – the attachment of the supraspinatous tendon
↗ – Subacromial needle insertion

The sub-acromial portion of the tendon ★ **LI 16 + LI 15**
This is treating "above and below" (in anatomical terms medial and lateral to) the supraspinatous tendon that lies deep to the acromion. They are the most important two points for both tendonitis and impingement syndrome.

259 • Shoulder Pain *The Supraspinatous Muscle*

Needle technique My needle technique is to insert LI 16 about .5 cun medial to its text location, and thread towards LI 15. The angle is from oblique to transverse. It may take several attempts and changes in angle to avoid hitting the bony clavicle or the spine of the scapula. Try to insert the needle from 1 to 1.5 inches, placed just superficial to the supraspinatous muscle. And, make sure to avoid penetrating the pleural cavity. Use electrical stimulation between LI 16 and LI 15, preparing the patient for possible aggravation.

After treating the muscle at SI 12 and the tendon at LI 16 and LI 15, I retest the supraspinatous for strength. A muscle that had been weak prior to treatment often gets "turned on" by these points. If the muscle remains weak, it is possible the treatment was not precise, and you should consider re-needling the patient. If the muscle continues to test weak with resisted abduction, this could indicate there is more complicated pathology, such as a significant tear of the tendon. In either case, the post-treatment feedback can be useful to the practitioner.

The supraspinatous tendon attachment **LI 15, SJ 14**
While LI 15 is usually at the insertion of the supraspinatous, both LI 15 and SJ 14 cover the broader area of the rotator cuff attachment.

Adjacent points **LI 14**
An adjacent point at the insertion of the deltoid. It may be point-sensitive, as the deltoid muscle also assists in abduction and may be compensating, due to the distressed and weak supraspinatous. Consider LI 14 as a secondary point.

 SI 11 The infraspinatous muscle
The infraspinatous is often involved with supraspinatous dysfunction. The tendon of the supraspinatous has "extensions" which join the infraspinatous, and thus both muscles are often involved in strain injuries.[7] Consider SI 11 as a secondary point.

COMPLEMENTARY PROCEDURES

- Applications of heat often benefit tension, contraction, and "guarding" of a muscle group. Heat may also be considered after the needling of trigger points.

- Massage to release tension of the supraspinatous can be performed between treatments at home. The "theracane" device is quite useful, as it can "hook" around to the spine of the scapula to massage the belly of the muscle.

- As stated earlier, stretching of the supraspinatous may help with tendonitis.

- Careful of overhead movements. Anything that hurts (impingment syndrome) probably will work against the treatment by irritating and inflaming the tendon.

- This is one injury where strengthening exercises for the muscle too early in the treatment process may aggravate the condition.

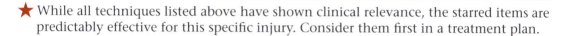 While all techniques listed above have shown clinical relevance, the starred items are predictably effective for this specific injury. Consider them first in a treatment plan.

REFERENCES

[1] Corrigan & Maitland: *Practical Orthopaedic Medicine*. Butterworths & Co, United Kingdom, 1989 (page 41).

[2] Dutton, M: *Orthopeadic Examination, Evaluation, and Intervention,* Second Edition. McGraw-Hill, USA, 2008 (page 601).

[3] Travell & Simons: *Myofascial Pain and Dysfunction: The Trigger Point Manual, Volume 1 (The Upper Extremities)*. Williams & Wilkins, Philadelphia, 1983 (pages 368-369).

[4] Travell & Simons: *Myofascial Pain and Dysfunction: The Trigger Point Manual, Volume 1 (The Upper Extremities)*. Williams & Wilkins, Philadelphia, 1983 (page 368-369).

[5] Callison, M: *Motor Point Index*. AcuSport Seminar Series LLC, San Diego, 2007 (page 46).

[6] The point Zongping has been referred to in various clinical articles on frozen shoulder. It is not included in most text references for extraordinary points.

[7] Dutton, M: *Orthopeadic Examination, Evaluation, and Intervention,* Second Edition. McGraw-Hill, USA, 2008 (page 601).

Notes

21
Shoulder Pain

The Infraspinatous Muscle

Pain in scapular region of the shoulder, with a referral pattern to the area of the deltoid and the shoulder joint

An acute or chronic injury characterized by inflammation of the tendon and possible strain or muscle tears at the attachment to the humerus.

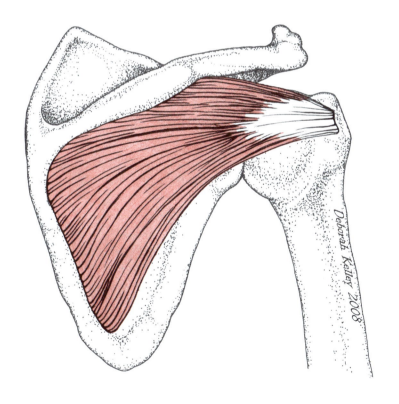

DIAGNOSIS & ASSESSMENT

The infraspinatous muscle is one of the four muscles of the rotator cuff, and is often involved in shoulder pain. However, it is not nearly as frequent as lesions to the supraspinatous. The infraspinatous has a characterisic pain referral pattern to the deltoid region, and occasionally distally down the arm and forearm. Like its adjacent muscle, the supraspinatous, this leads many practitioners to a diagnosis of Large Intestine (Yang ming) and San Jiao (Shao yang) disorders, overlooking this scapular-region muscle. The treatment discussion that follows assumes the clinician has ruled out injuries from supraspinatous dysfunction and other causes of shoulder pain.

The origin of the infraspinatous is the infrascapular fossa in the region of SI 11. As the muscle runs laterally, its muscle-tendon junction is located inferior to the spine of the scapula near the point SI 10. It inserts with the other three rotator cuff tendons at the humerus, in the region of SJ 14. This attachment may extend anteriorly towards LI 15, where it joins the supraspinatous tendon. Its action is that of external rotation; thus, many activities using the upper extremity rely on the infraspinatous. Lesions are found in the belly of the muscle, at the muscle-tendon junction, and at its tendinous attachment to bone.

The patient may complain of pain in the scapular region of the shoulder. It could be reported in the belly of the muscle in the region of SI 11, or at the muscle-tendon junction in the region of SI 10. However, more likely is the referral pain pattern in the lateral, the posterior lateral, and the anterior aspect of the deltoid. Unless there is a significant tendinous tear, the pain is commonly reported as a dull ache. Dr. Janet Travell, in her work on myofascial pain syndromes, suggests that the referral pattern from infraspinatous trigger points resembles "shoulder joint pain".[1] The tendon does not traverse under the acromion, thus the sharp pain of impingement syndrome characteristic to the supraspinatous is uncommon.

Injury to the muscle and tendon is seen in numerous types of athletes and active individuals. If acute, the trauma often occurs with throwing or a fall from skiing or snowboarding. If chronic, the injury may be due to micro-trauma from repetitive arm movements such as swimming or weight lifting. Here, the onset is insidious and the cause may appear quite benign. The patient may report that certain movements of the arm feel weak.

Examining the patient is straightforward. Palpate the muscle in the infrascapular fossa in the area of SI 11. You are looking for painful points, and the possibility that pressure from palpation reproduces the shoulder referral pattern. This area is where both the trigger points and the motor points of the infraspinatous are located. Although you start in the center of the infrascapular fossa, *ahshi* points and taut fascial bands may encompass a wider diameter than the text location of SI 11. Make sure you compare painful points to the unaffected side, as many North American patients have *ahshi* points in this region. Then, check the muscle-tendon junction around SI 10. If there is tendonitis at this site, *ahshi* points will be obvious. Complete your palpation in the region of SJ 14 where the tendon attaches. Most cases of chronic infraspinatous tendonitis will not present with tenderness at this region of the attachment.

After palpating the muscle, there is really only one important test to perform. Described in the Appendices on page 340, use resisted external rotation to assess the infraspinatous. If there is weakness and/or pain, this muscle is almost certainly involved. Once, I had to diagnose and treat a student of mine with shoulder pain in only several minutes. When I found there was pain and weakness with external rotation, I quickly placed four needles in the region of SI 11. She took them out one hour later, and the next week reported there had been no pain for five days. So, this test can be quite helpful in your diagnosis.

In summary, infraspinatous lesions may be the cause of shoulder pain. However, it is more likely that the supraspinatous or other structures are primary. Careful examination, practice, and precise treatments will help differentiate each of these conditions. I treat the infraspinatous frequently with supraspinatous injuries, as well as many other neck and shoulder complaints. And fortunately for the acupuncturist, all of these tissues, from origin to insertion, are easily accessible for both palpation and treatment with needles.

Recently, I had a patient who wanted acupuncture to assist in the rehabilitation of a separated shoulder from a snowboarding accident. I found that the infraspinatous was weak and painful with resisted external rotation. There was significant pain at the attachment of the tendon near SJ 14. Suspecting a possible tear in the infraspinatous, I referred him to an orthopedist. A simple X-ray revealed an avulsion fracture, where the tendon and a fragment of the bone had pulled away from the humerus during the fall. He was put in a sling for immediate immobilization for three weeks. Had the patient started active movements to strengthen and rehabilitate the shoulder, it undoubtedly would have aggravated the problem by separating the fragment further from the humerus. Surgery and other complications were avoided by getting a correct diagnosis early on. The patient was treated with acupuncture and physical therapy. Seven weeks after his injury, he was part of a climbing team that essentially reached the summit of Mount Denali in Alaska, turning back due to weather several hundred feet from the 20,000-foot top.

SUMMARY OF THE INJURY

Clinical Features
- Pain from infraspinatous lesions often radiates to the deltoid region of the shoulder, and distally down the arm
- Tenderness with palpation in the infraspinatous muscle, in the region of SI 11, or at the muscle-tendon junction at SI 10
- Pain and/or weakness with resisted external rotation
- Patient may have history of repeated or strenuous arm motions, or of accidents involving the shoulder
- The infraspinatous often accompanies other rotator cuff injuries
- Acute cases may involve strain to the tendon
- Chronic cases may be due to repetitive stress causing inflammation of tendon

Common Patient Complaints
- Pain in scapular region of the shoulder
- Referral pattern of pain to the area of the deltoid, and distally down the arm
- Sometimes radiation pattern is specific to the anterior aspect of the shoulder
- Patient may report the feeling of pain "in the shoulder joint"

Differentiation from Similar Injuries and Conditions
- Differentiate from other shoulder injuries, such as those to the supraspinatous and biceps muscles
- Shoulder pain may be caused by intra-thoracic disease, such as from the diaphragm, the heart, and the gall bladder
- Referral pain from cervical nerve root
- Partial or complete tear of tendon

Typical Medical Recommendations
- Ice is typically used when acute.
- Anti-inflammatory medications
- Modify activity
  Decrease or avoid overhead arm movements that aggravate.
- Stretching
  Stretching of the infraspinatous may help with tendonitis.
- Biomechanics
  Correct ergonomics of work and computer stations.
- Physical therapy
  Ultrasound, deep-friction massage, and other physical therapy modalities.
- Orthopedic evaluation
  If a grade II or grade III tear occurs in the infraspinatous or other rotator cuff tendons, surgery may be required. Cortisone injection into the tendon or muscle-tendon junction may provide relief.

266 • Shoulder Pain *The Infraspinatous Muscle*

TREATMENT & TECHNIQUES

Overview: Shoulder pain due to infraspinatous muscle or tendon pathology is most commonly diagnosed under the category of accident/trauma. The acute case usually has a definitive traumatic event. The chronic case is a repetitive stress disorder due to the accumulation of micro-trauma. The injury is at the level of the muscles and tendons, with qi and blood stagnation in the channels and collaterals. The Small Intestine meridian encompasses the belly of the infraspinatous and its muscle-tendon junction. The Large Intestine and San Jiao meridians cover its attachment at the humerus. Internal organ imbalances are unclear.

Prognosis: Treat twice a week for three weeks, then re-evaluate. Many cases without significant tendon tear may have good results within six treatments. With chronic cases, continue treatment at least once weekly after the first three-week period.

STEP ONE: INITIAL TREATMENT

Choose among these four techniques, carefully determining if there is an immediate decrease in pain or an increase in range of motion.

Technique #1: **The Tendino-Muscle Meridians**

 SI 1 — Bleeding technique

This jing-well point treats the scapular aspect of the infraspinatous muscle, both the belly and the muscle-tendon junction.

SJ 1 — Bleeding technique

This jing-well point treats the area of attachment to the humerus.

Technique #2: **Opposite Side (contra-lateral)**

Corresponding points on the opposite (unaffected) side may be considered; however, treatment to the affected side is usually preferred.

Technique #3: **Opposite Extremity (upper/lower)**

Bl 53, Bl 54 — Tai yang corresponding points on the opposite extremity

These two Bladder meridian points, often overlooked, mirror the Small Intestine (Tai yang) meridian.

In general, treat upper/lower corresponding points on the opposite (unaffected) side when acute, and the affected side when chronic. Use palpation to assist in this choice.

267 • Shoulder Pain *The Infraspinatous Muscle*

Technique #4: **Empirical Points**

St 38
While its most effective use is for frozen shoulder, St 38 may help with the range-of-motion problems associated with infraspinatous tendonitis. St 38 is discussed in detail on page 279.

Zongping
An empirical point for frozen shoulder. It is located one cun distal and one cun lateral to St 36, between the Yang ming and Shao yang channels.[2] Like St 38, it may be effective for improving range of motion. See page 279 for more details.

STEP TWO: MERIDIANS & MICROSYSTEMS

Choose among these four techniques, selecting points that are appropriate for the signs and symptoms of the patient.

Technique #5: **The Shu-Stream Point Combination**

SI 3 affected side + Bl 65 opposite side
Treats the infraspinatous muscle belly (the area of SI 11) and the muscle-tendon junction (the area of SI 10).

SJ 3 affected side + GB 41 (or GB 42) opposite side
GB 42 is often more sensitive than GB 41, and should be considered as an alternative shu-stream point. This shu-stream point combination treats the tendinous attachment at the humerus (the area SJ 14).

Technique #6: **Traditional Point Categories**

SI 6   Xi-cleft point
SI 6 is one of the most effective points for the acute case. Palpation may assist in your choice of other meridian points.

SI 4	Yuan-source point
SJ 5	Luo-connecting point
GB 34	Hui-influential point of tendons
St 39	Lower He-sea point for the Small Intestine

St 39 is occasionally effective as a secondary point. It treats the fu organ and, therefore, its exteriorly related meridian.

Technique #7: **The Extraordinary Meridians**

SI 3 + Bl 62   Activate the Du mai
Activating the Du mai may assist if there is cervical nerve root pathology contributing to the condition.

Technique #8: **Microsystems**

Auricular Therapy
Local: Shoulder, master shoulder, cervical spine
Systemic points for pain: Shen men, Thalamus, Adrenal, Endocrine

STEP THREE: INTERNAL ORGAN IMBALANCES

Choose appropriate points to treat internal organ imbalances that may contribute to the injury or pain syndrome.

Technique #9: **Qi, Blood, and the Zang-fu Organs**

Infraspinatous tendonitis is either an acute trauma or a chronic repetitive stress injury and, therefore, internal organ imbalances are usually not a factor in treatment. However, the following should be considered:

Liver imbalances Liver qi stagnation, Liver yin deficiency, and Liver blood deficiency
Liver imbalances may result in the susceptibility of the rotator cuff tendon to inflammation and repetitive stress injury. Consider the following:

Liv 3	Yuan-source point; supports the Liver in its function of controlling the muscles and tendons
GB 34	Hui-influential point of tendons

Stress The syndrome of stress is not a TCM term, but this modern "diagnosis" clearly affects the internal organ systems. The infraspinatous muscle seems to react to stress with spasm, tightness, and active trigger points. The practitioner may want to consider all lifestyle factors contributing to stress with chronic pain due to the infraspinatous.

Points should be determined by the practitioner from both palpation and analysis of the signs and symptoms of the patient.

269 • **Shoulder Pain** *The Infraspinatous Muscle*

STEP FOUR: THE SITE OF INJURY

Choose among the local and adjacent points at the site of injury. Points may be determined by palpation, orthopedic testing, and analysis of the signs and symptoms of the patient.

Technique #10: **Local and Adjacent Points**

The infraspinatous muscle

SI 11

From one to four needles, perpendicular insertion, in the trigger points, motor points, and *ahshi* points of the muscle. Needle depth is .5 to 1 inch.

SI 11 is located in the center of the infrascapular fossa, and serves as the reference point for treatment of the infraspinatous muscle. *Ahshi* points can be found in the taut fascial bands of the muscle; they are usually quite apparent. The simple approach is to treat from one to four points, based upon palpation. Use perpendicular insertion, to a depth of .5 to 1 inch. Unlike treating the supraspinatous, patient position is not critical. Seated, lateral recumbent (side-lying), or prone may all be considered.

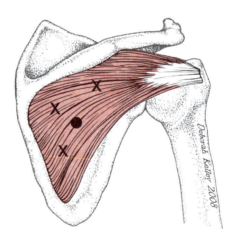

● – SI 11
✕ – Trigger points

Trigger points, motor points

Sometimes more precision is needed in treating shoulder pain due to the infraspinatous. There are several trigger points for the muscle located within 1 cun of SI 11.[3] Sometimes pressure on them will reproduce pain into the deltoid region of the shoulder. There are also two motor points.[4] The first is located 1 cun superior and lateral to the reference point SI 11. The second is 1 to 1.5 cun inferior and medial to SI 11. When treating, the bony infrascapular fossa provides an end-point to needle depth. Obviously, if you hit the scapula, the needle has penetrated the entire depth of the infraspinatous muscle. Withdraw the needle, as best results are achieved in the intermediate layers of the muscle.

Clinical comments Needling the infraspinatous can often illicit a twitch response in the muscle. This is usually beneficial, as it assists in the release of tension in the muscle. It can be accomplished by perpendicular insertion, using pecking and rotating. However, some practitioners use oblique insertion, choosing cross-fiber needling of the muscle.

Electrical stimulation Electrical stimulation may also be effective, and there are several possible ways to orient the leads. First, use stimulation between two paired-points in the muscle. If there is a second set of paired-points, they too may receive e-stim. If the treatment time is 30 minutes, I will usually use 15 minutes on the first set followed by 15 minutes on the second set. Another possibility is that electrical stimulation may be used between SI 11 in the belly of the muscle and at SI 10 at the muscle-tendon junction, or at SJ 14 at its insertion. And finally, SI 11 could be paired with a distal point such as SI 3.

SI 11 is a frequently used point in my clinic. As discussed above, it is not always the primary cause of shoulder pain. But this point is a useful secondary point for many shoulder injuries, as the relatively large infraspinatous muscle will often "tighten" in response to trauma. In addition, treatments for neck pain from the levator and other para-spinal neck muscles may benefit from the addition to SI 11. And finally, it is used by some practitioners for stress, anxiety, and shen disturbances. Perhaps its Chinese name "heavenly ancestor" (tian zhong) gives some clues to these uses.

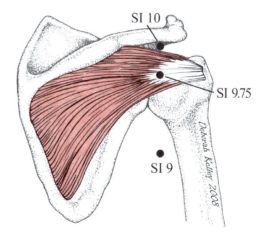

The muscle-tendon junction **The region of SI 10**

★ One or two needles, perpendicular insertion, to a depth of 1 inch.

Some patients report symptoms in the area of SI 10, which is adjacent to the muscle-tendon junction. The point SI 10 is located below the acromial end of the spine of the scapula, directly above SI 9 and the posterior axillary fold.[5] Found in the depression, this places SI 10 slightly superior to the infraspinatous muscle-tendon junction. However, you should also consider needling directly into the muscle, slightly inferior to the text location of SI 10. I call this point SI 9.75, between SI 9 and SI 10. Pay attention to whether you are needling into the depression at SI 10, or actually into *ahshi* point of the denser tissues of the infraspinatous. Both may work, but frequently SI 9.75 is the better choice. Consider using one needle or a set of paired needles at this point, and possibly including electrical stimulation.

The infraspinatous tendon attachment
★

SJ 14 + LI 15
While SJ 14 is usually at the insertion of the infraspinatous, the broader area of the rotator cuff attachment is covered with LI 15 and SJ 14. Electrical stimulation between these two points sometimes is effective for tendonitis.

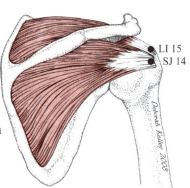

The supraspinatous
★

SI 12
The supraspinatous is often involved when the infraspinatous is strained or injured. The tendon of the supraspinatous has "extensions" which join the infraspinatous, and thus both muscles are often involved in strain injuries.[6] Consider SI 12 as a secondary point.

COMPLEMENTARY PROCEDURES

- Applications of heat often benefit tension, contraction, and "guarding" of a muscle group. Heat may also be considered after the needling of trigger points.

- Massage to release tension of the infraspinatous can be performed between treatments at home. Self-massage with a tennis ball against a wall can be self performed.

- As stated earlier, stretching of the infraspinatous may help with tendonitis.

★ While all techniques listed above have shown clinical relevance, the starred items are predictably effective for this specific injury. Consider them first in a treatment plan.

REFERENCES

[1] Travell & Simons: *Myofascial Pain and Dysfunction: The Trigger Point Manual, Volume 1 (The Upper Extremities)*. Williams & Wilkins, Philadelphia, 1983 (pages 377-381).

[2] *The point Zongping has been referred to in various clinical articles on frozen shoulder. It is not included in most text references for extraordinary points.*

[3] Travell & Simons: *Myofascial Pain and Dysfunction: The Trigger Point Manual, Volume 1 (The Upper Extremities)*. Williams & Wilkins, Philadelphia, 1983 (page 382).

[4] Callison, M: *Motor Point Index*. AcuSport Seminar Series LLC, San Diego, 2007 (page 47).

[5] Deadman, Al-Khafaji, & Baker: *A Manual of Acupuncture*. Journal of Chinese Medicine Publications, East Sussex, 2001 (pages 240-241).

[6] Dutton, M: *Orthopeadic Examination, Evaluation, and Intervention,* Second Edition. McGraw-Hill, USA, 2008 (page 601).

Notes

22
Shoulder Pain

Frozen Shoulder

Decreased range of motion of the shoulder, often accompanied by pain and stiffness

Frozen shoulder may be associated with known etiology, such as capsular lesions, rotator cuff injury, or other trauma. It may also occur post-surgically, however it sometimes has no defined cause.

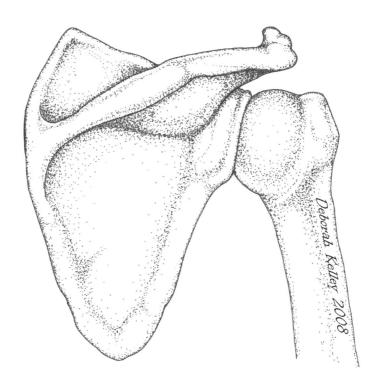

DIAGNOSIS & ASSESSMENT

Frozen shoulder is a condition that acupuncturists are taught may be cured with miraculous one-needle treatment. In the first month of my private practice in 1981, I saw an elderly patient who had suffered from frozen shoulder for more than 20 years. I treated her with St 38, and in one visit, restored almost complete normal range of motion to her shoulder. As a new practitioner, it was exciting, and it generated a high degree of confidence in my new profession. What I did not know then was that it would take another five years before such dramatic results would be achieved again with this condition. Within the last year, I had one of those rewarding cases where a single needle in St 38 immediately restored a majority of function to a patient's shoulder. While I will hope for such an outcome with my next patient, I'll probably use some of the other techniques discussed in this section if the "once in five years" rule continues to be the norm!

Frozen shoulder is not necessarily a precise medical diagnosis. In fact, the causes of frozen shoulder are not fully understood and texts differ in their description of the pathology. The process may involve a thickening and contracture of the capsule surrounding the shoulder joint. Some sources call the condition "adhesive capsulitis", where adhesions within the joint are responsible for decreased mobility. Others suggest that both synovial inflammation and capsular fibrosis are causative. The work of Dr. Janet Travell looks at myofascial causes of frozen shoulder that result from trigger points and dysfunction of the subscapularis muscle.[1] With all these different causes of dysfunction, it is no wonder that no single technique of acupuncture works a majority of the time.

Simply stated, frozen shoulder is characterized by dull, diffuse or aching pain. Decreased or restricted range of motion is often accompanied by stiffness. This loss of normal function occurs with both active and passive movements. This condition is most commonly seen between the ages of 45 and 60, and some practitioners are reporting it with increasing frequency in menopausal women. Some sources suggested that up to 70 percent of all patients with frozen shoulder are female.[2] Frequently, the onset is without known cause, either acute or with gradual onset. It can develop after trauma to the shoulder, usually to one of the rotator cuff tendons or the joint capsule. And, it may be seen after the shoulder has been immobilized for a period of time due to injury or after surgery. For whatever reason, frozen shoulder is reported to frequently improve on its own with little or no treatment – that is, if you are willing to wait one to three years!

It is a good idea to observe the range of motion of the patient's shoulder. You can go back to these simple tests to determine if treatment is in fact beneficial. External rotation is probably the most important movement to assess.[3] To test, place the arm in full adduction with the elbow flexed to 90 degrees. Stabilize the elbow next to the body with your hand. Ask the patient to swing the forearm out like a gate while you observe the movement. This can also be done passively. One hand holds the forearm while the other stabilizes the elbow next to the body. You swing the patient's forearm laterally like a gate. Frozen shoulder usually presents with limitations to this movement. Abduction should also be observed. Ask the patient to raise their arm laterally. Observe the shoulder and scapula, as they may try to achieve this movement by "cheating" with shoulder movements. Again, limitations in abduction is common with the frozen shoulder patient.

In this discussion, we will not attempt to diagnose or differentiate all the causes of frozen shoulder. The practitioner should not hesitate to refer the patient for an orthopedic evaluation if indicated. Rather, we will emphasize the treatment of frozen shoulder, which can be quite remarkable at times.

SUMMARY OF THE INJURY

Clinical Features
- Loss of normal function occurs with both active and passive movements
- Pathology varies, and may include capsular adhesions, synovial inflammation or tendonitis
- More commonly seen in female patients
- May develop after trauma to the shoulder, after immobilization, and post-surgery

Common Patient Complaints
- Decreased or restricted range of motion
- Dull, diffuse or aching pain in the shoulder
- Stiffness often accompanies pain and restricted motion

Differentiation from Similar Injuries and Conditions
- Shoulder pain may be referred from intrathoracic disease, such as the diaphragm, the heart, and the gall bladder
- Referral pain from cervical nerve root
- Partial or complete tear of a rotator cuff tendon
- Other shoulder joint capsular lesions
- Diabetes and other systemic conditions are often associated

Typical Medical Recommendations
- Anti-inflammatory medications.
- Physical therapy
  Physical therapy modalities are used to restore motion. Therapy includes stretching and range-of-motion exercises. Sometimes, heat is used to help decrease pain.
- Orthopedic evaluation
  X-ray or MRI studies are sometimes used to rule out other causes, such as a rotator cuff tear. When there is no improvement in pain or shoulder motion, the two most common procedures are manipulation under anesthesia and shoulder surgery.

277 • Shoulder Pain *Frozen Shoulder*

TREATMENT & TECHNIQUES

Overview: Frozen shoulder due to previous injury or as seen post-surgically may be diagnosed under the category of accident/trauma. As a chronic condition, it is considered a *Bi* syndrome. Care should be taken to assess the heat (re), cold (han), damp (shi), and wind (feng) contributions. This will assist in the choice of points, needle technique and herbal prescription. With frozen shoulder, the affected meridians vary from patient to patient. Internal organ imbalances are unclear, although yin deficiency and blood deficiency are common in older patients and menopausal women with this condition.

Prognosis: Treat twice a week for three weeks, then re-evaluate. You may need to continue treatments at least once weekly after the first three-week period. Unless, of course, you and the patient are fortunate and great results are obtained early in treatment!

STEP ONE: INITIAL TREATMENT

Choose among these four techniques, carefully determining if there is an immediate decrease in pain or an increase in range of motion.

Technique #1: **The Tendino-Muscle Meridians**

SI 1, LI 1, SJ 1   Bleeding technique

The tendino-muscle meridians of the three arm yang meridians probably do not get to the shoulder joint. However, bleeding the jing-well point can be considered, and is sometimes effective for some of the symptoms.

Technique #2: **Opposite Side (contra-lateral)**

Corresponding points on the opposite (unaffected) side may be considered; however, treatment to the affected side is usually preferred.

Technique #3: **Opposite Extremity (upper/lower)**

Corresponding points on the opposite extremity may be considered; however, treatment to the affected extremity is usually preferred.

Technique #4: **Empirical Points**

 St 38

This is the most common empirical point for frozen shoulder. Texts locate St 38 eight cun below St 35, on the Yang ming line. However, it should be noted that in the Master Tong system of empirical points, a point that is

.5 cun superior to St 38 is recommended.[4] Determine the precise location by point sensitivity, but also palpate for a definite depression in the anterior compartment muscles. Chinese texts suggest deep insertion towards Bl 57. That could mean as long as a 3 inch needle for larger patients. Active shoulder movement by the patient is usually used while stimulating the point to determine if there is improvement in range of motion.

Needle technique My experience is that St 38 is most effective with deeper levels of insertion. There is frequently a precise depth, as the needle pierces through muscle and fascial layers of the anterior compartment group. Rather than the more painful pecking and rotating technique, I use a gentler technique of gradually deepening the insertion of the needle. Sometimes you can find this correct needle depth, and the hoped-for improvement in range of motion, without discomfort to the patient.

Clinical comments on St 38 During the 1984 Olympics, I was treating a rather famous patient suffering from frozen shoulder with a student observer at my side. I remember so vividly the precise fascial plane – about 3 inches of insertion in the deep tissues of the muscle group. Every time the needle would penetrate that level, the shoulder would release and normal function be restored. I demonstrated to the student that needle technique several centimeters deeper or more superficial would not have the same effect on range of motion. We used no other point than St 38, and continued stimulating the needle with active movement of the arm every three minutes. The patient left quite satisfied after 25 minutes of treatment. I then felt inclined to explain the needle technique to the student, only to see a glazed-over face as she exclaimed, "He was my childhood hero!" The student was overjoyed, but missed the entire teaching event, and hopefully didn't have to wait five years to see it again!

Same side, opposite side So, back to the technique. The general rule for St 38 is to use the opposite side for acute symptoms, and the same side for chronic symptoms. However, rules never are foolproof. You could palpate for sensitivity, or simply try one side, and if results are not obtained, try the other side.

★ *Zongping*

Zongping is an empirical point for frozen shoulder, but certainly lesser-known than St 38. It is located 1 cun distal and 1 cun lateral to St 36, between the Yang ming and Shao yang channels.[5] Like St 38, it may be effective for improving range of motion. While depth may be important for this point too, it is not necessary to needle as deeply as St 38. The general rule applies for *Zongping*. Use the opposite side for acute symptoms, and the same side for chronic symptoms. If results are not obtained, try the other side.

279 • **Shoulder Pain** *Frozen Shoulder*

STEP TWO: MERIDIANS & MICROSYSTEMS

Choose among these four techniques, selecting points that are appropriate for the signs and symptoms of the patient.

Technique #5: **The Shu-Stream Point Combination**

SI 3 affected side + Bl 65 opposite side
LI 3 affected side + St 43 opposite side
SJ 3 affected side + GB 41 (or GB 42) opposite side
GB 42 is often more sensitive than GB 41, and should be considered as an alternative shu-stream point for this meridian. Use one or more paired shu-stream points of the three arm yang meridians.

Technique #6: **Traditional Point Categories**

 SI 6   Xi-cleft point
Sometimes needling this Tai yang meridian point, with active movement, can improve shoulder abduction. Be careful that the patient does not supinate or pronate the forearm, as the needle may cause pain due to the styloid process or tendons located so close to the shaft of the needle. I recommend you read my comments on needle technique for SI 6 on page 354.

Palpation may assist in your choice of other meridian points. Distal points vary greatly for this condition, and will not be specifically mentioned.

Technique #7: **The Extraordinary Meridians**

SI 3 + Bl 62   Activate the Du mai
Activating the Du mai may assist if there is cervical nerve root pathology contributing to shoulder dysfunction. However, this treatment rarely affects frozen shoulder, at least not immediately.

Technique #8: **Microsystems**

Auricular Therapy
Local: Shoulder, master shoulder, cervical spine
Zang fu points: Kidney, Liver (with yin deficiency)
Systemic points for pain: Shen men, Thalamus, Adrenal, Endocrine

STEP THREE: INTERNAL ORGAN IMBALANCES

Choose appropriate points to treat internal organ imbalances that may contribute to the injury or pain syndrome.

Technique #9: **Qi, Blood, and the Zang-fu Organs**

There are various internal imbalances seen with patients who experience frozen shoulder. It must be remembered that the condition may be a result of injury or a post-surgery complication, and therefore, internal organ imbalances may not be causative. However, chronic cases and with patients over 50 years old, consider the following:

Kidney imbalances Kidney deficiency
Syndromes of the Kidney are considered by some practitioners as an internal organ imbalance present in all patients with chronic joint disease. However, treatment to the Kidney alone rarely is sufficient for frozen shoulder.

Liver imbalances Liver qi stagnation, Liver yin deficiency, and Liver blood deficiency
Liver imbalances may result in dysfunction of the muscles and tendons, increasing the susceptibility of the shoulder to this injury.

Sp 6 + Liv 3 Crossing point + yuan-source point
A useful point combination when Liver and Kidney deficiency contributes to joint inflammation. Treat on the opposite side of the shoulder symptoms.

Bi syndrome Chronic frozen shoulder could be diagnosed as a *Bi* syndrome. Care should be taken to assess the heat (re), cold (han), damp (shi), and wind (feng) contributions. This will assist in the choice of points, needle technique and herbal prescription.

Points should be determined by the practitioner from both palpation and analysis of the signs and symptoms of the patient.

STEP FOUR: THE SITE OF INJURY

Choose among the local and adjacent points at the site of injury. Points may be determined by palpation, orthopedic testing, and analysis of the signs and symptoms of the patient.

Technique #10: **Local and Adjacent Points**

The shoulder joint **SI 9**

★ Perpendicular insertion, to a depth of up to 2 inches

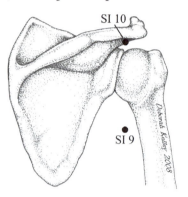

The point SI 9 may be used to treat the shoulder joint capsule. It is located 1 cun superior to the posterior axillary fold when the arm is fully adducted. Use a 3 inch needle with deep insertion, directed toward the anterior axillary fold. Avoiding the nerves, artery, and vein of the axillary plexus is accomplished by maintaining perpendicular insertion, and not allowing the needle to angle superiorly. The pleural cavity and the ribs are avoided by assuring that the needle does not angle medially. A perfect, yet deep, insertion on this point should be virtually painless. The best position for this is either lateral recumbent (side-lying) or seated.

Anterior shoulder **The extraordinary point *Jianqian***

★ I will usually add an anterior point to combine with SI 9. The extraordinary point *Jianqian* may be considered. It is located halfway between the anterior axillary fold and LI 15.[6] In his point text, Deadman cites that *Jianqian* activates the qi and blood and benefits the shoulder joint. I have found this point over the years to be very clinically useful for frozen shoulder as well as other lesions of the shoulder joint.

Posterior shoulder **SI 10**

★ The point SI 10 may also be used to treat the shoulder joint capsule. It is located below the acromial extremity of the spine of the scapula, directly above SI 9. Needle with perpendicular insertion to a depth of 1 to 1.5 inches. The scapula

282 • **Shoulder Pain** *Frozen Shoulder*

lies deep to this point, so the lung is easy to avoid. SI 10 also combines well with the extraordinary point *Jianqian*. Electrical stimulation may be used.

Shoulder point combinations SI 9 + *Jianqian*
SI 10 + *Jianqian*
SI 9 + SI 10

The subscapularis muscle The subscapularis is often involved in cases of frozen shoulder. Some practitioners needle at the medial border of the scapulae, inserting laterally. Others start needle insertion in the region of the axilla and direct towards the lateral border of the scapulae. I will not attempt to describe these two needle techniques, due to the obvious anatomical complications. However, it should be emphasized that the subscapularis is often essential to treat. Manual therapy by physical therapists or other health care practitioners is usually very effective in releasing tension in this muscle. I regularly refer my shoulder patients for this treatment.

Adjacent points LI 16 + LI 15
LI 15 + LI 14
One of these two paired-point combinations may be indicated in treating frozen shoulder. Consider electrical stimulation.

 SI 12 The supraspinatous muscle
The supraspinatous is often involved in cases of frozen shoulder. Consider two paired points determined by palpation. SI 12 should be viewed as as a secondary point.

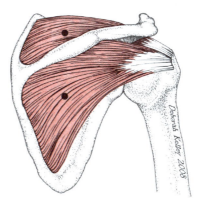

● – *SI 12 – the supraspinatous (superior)*
SI 11 – the infraspinatous (inferior)

 SI 11 The infraspinatous muscle
The infraspinatous is often involved in cases of frozen shoulder. Consider two paired points determined by palpation. SI 11 should be viewed as as a secondary point. It is also the antagonist muscle of the subscapularis.

COMPLEMENTARY PROCEDURES

- Applications of heat often benefit with chronic pain and inflammation of the shoulder joint.

- Range of motion exercises are essential, and the patient should be under the care of a physical therapist. At the least, "slow finger walking" up the side of the wall is often a simple exercise that the patient can perform at home.

- Massage and manual therapy for the subscapularis muscle is often required with the frozen shoulder patient. This is especially true if the practitioner elects not to treat this muscle with acupuncture.

★ While all techniques listed above have shown clinical relevance, the starred items are predictably effective for this specific injury. Consider them first in a treatment plan.

REFERENCES

[1] Travell & Simons: *Myofascial Pain and Dysfunction: The Trigger Point Manual, Volume 1 (The Upper Extremities)*. Williams & Wilkins, Philadelphia, 1983 (pages 410-412).

[2] Dutton, M: *Orthopeadic Examination, Evaluation, and Intervention*, Second Edition. McGraw-Hill, USA, 2008 (page 585).

[3] Dutton, M: *Orthopeadic Examination, Evaluation, and Intervention*, Second Edition. McGraw-Hill, USA, 2008 (page 585).

[4] *Lecture notes from Young Wei-Chieh, Ph.D. 2007. Point #77.09 (Sihuazhong).*
Dr. Young Wei-Chieh is one of Master Tong's senior disciples, and teaches this empirical point tradition.

[5] *The point Zongping has been referred to in various clinical articles on frozen shoulder. It is not included in any of the major acupuncture texts.*

[6] Shanghai College of Traditional Medicine: *Acupuncture, A Comprehensive Text*. Eastland Press, Chicago, 1981 (page 581).

23
Shoulder Pain
The Biceps Muscle Group

Pain in the anterior and the anterior-lateral aspect of the shoulder, which may radiate down the biceps muscle

A repetitive stress injury characterized by inflammation and irritation of the biceps tendon as it passes through the bicepital groove of the anterior shoulder. Injury to the biceps may occur acutely, with strain or tears to the muscle or tendon.

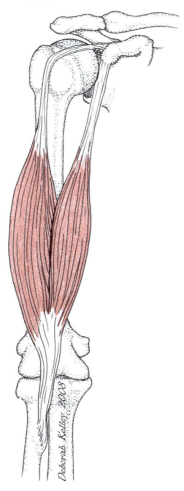

DIAGNOSIS & ASSESSMENT

For the acupuncture practitioner, anterior shoulder pain due to tendonitis of the biceps muscle is an important injury with which to be acquainted. While not as common as rotator cuff injuries, bicepital lesions need to be understood. Diagnosis and assessment is not always definitive, and acupuncture treatment is sometimes complicated. And it does not help that there are no acupuncture points located at the site of the injury.

The tendon of the long head of the biceps is usually the site of injury. The tendon and its sheath lie in the bicipital groove of the humerus, and are held into the groove by the transverse ligament. This is in the anterior-lateral shoulder, between the Lung and the Large Intestine meridians. Here lies part of the problem, as some patients respond to treatment of Lung meridian points, while others to those of the Large Intestine. Perhaps the complication is intensified from the anatomy, where the qi and blood can easily stagnate in these tightly bound tissues of the bicepital groove. This area is uninviting to the acupuncture needle, as the transverse ligament covers the inflamed tendon.

Tendonitis of the long head of the biceps usually occurs as a repetitive stress injury. The onset is insidious, and is often associated with overhead activities such as tennis movements and throwing. Pain is reported in the anterior and the anterior-lateral shoulder. This is anterior and inferior to the point LI 15. Pain often radiates distally down the biceps muscle toward the elbow. Superior to the bicipital groove, the tendon passes beneath the anterior edge of the acromion, where impingement sometimes occurs. Patients with previous rotator cuff injury often end up with biceps tendonitis as a secondary condition. From an assessment viewpoint, the difficulty for the practitioner is that there are signs and symptoms of both rotator cuff injury and biceps pathology.

Another possibility is the subluxation of the biceps tendon in the groove. The tendon slides from one side of the groove to the other during internal and external rotation of the humerus. A shallow groove where the tendon slips out or a tear to the transverse humeral ligament in the process contributes to the subluxing of the biceps tendon.[1] The patient may report "popping" or "snapping" in the anterior shoulder.

I usually use palpation with internal and external rotation of the shoulder, which is often helpful in finding the bicipital groove. With the elbow flexed at 90 degrees, simply swing the forearm medially and laterally while you palpate. Remember, the groove is inferior and medial to the point LI 15. This movement may also reveal subluxation of the tendon, which you will feel as a "pop" or "snap" under your finger, just as the patient reported.

The Yergason's and the Speed's test are commonly used to determine bicipital tendonitis. It is beyond the scope of this handbook to describe these tests, so refer to an orthopedic text for guidance. You would think that simple resisted elbow flexion, the action of the biceps, would produce pain, but this is not consistent. However, resisted flexion of the elbow combined with hand supination (moving the palm upward) is more reliable, so try that. The patient is usually able to perform full range of motion, but pain at the end range of shoulder extension and abduction may be found. Passive stretch of the biceps may also confirm this injury. Holding the elbow, gently pull the arm and forearm behind the patient; pain may be produced if the bicipital tendon is inflamed.

Superior to the bicipital groove, the tendon attaches to the glenoid cavity of the scapula and the labrum. This is where a partial or complete tear of the tendon may occur with an acute injury. The trauma is usually clear, such as with a fall, and the patient may hear a "snap". Pain may last for a couple weeks followed by the restoration of apparent

286 • **Shoulder Pain** *The Biceps Muscle Group*

normal function, because the short head of the biceps is still intact. However, there is typically a bulge in the distal belly of the biceps, called a "Popeye" sign. The muscle rolls down over the distal humerus due to the absence of the superior attachment. I had an elderly patient who reported weakness in his forearm for almost 20 years, which he said followed a traumatic injury from lifting. He felt a snap, but because the pain lasted only a few weeks, he never sought medical care. After starting a new weightlifting program, he complained that biceps exercises were difficult due to weakness. He displayed the "Popeye" sign, and I explained what had probably occurred. Surgery may be considered for such a case to reattach the tendon, but most orthopedists recommend this procedure must be performed immediately after the injury. Another patient had a complete rupture from a single tennis serve, and chose to have surgery for cosmetic reasons, not wanting that bulge in his arm.

The complete rupture is a clear case, and fairly easy to diagnose. Treatment – that is, surgery – is not necessary for most normal functions. John Elway, former quarterback for the Denver Broncos, played in the National Football League without the long head of the biceps attached to the shoulder. However, when there is a partial tear, the options are more complex. Reattaching the tendon through surgery is not always successful, and the patient needs to be informed on this fact. Some patients choose the path of least resistance, which is to surgically cut the tendon rather than reattach it at the anatomically sensitive zone of the glenoid and the labrum.

To summarize, there are several etiologies with the biceps. The first is a complete rupture, which unlike other traumatic injuries, the acupuncture practitioner may be the first professional the patient seeks for treatment, and thus the first to suggest the diagnosis. The second is a subluxing biceps tendon, where the pathology is usually easy to assess. The other cases of tendonitis may not be as clear, and other pathologies, such as injury to the rotator cuff, may be involved. These treatments are discussed in detail in Step Four below.

SUMMARY OF THE INJURY

Clinical Features
- Repetitive stress causes inflammation of the tendon of the long head of the biceps
- Tendonitis is usually found at the bicepital groove of the humerus
- Tenderness with palpation is noted directly over the bicepital groove
- Partial or complete tear may occur more superiorly at the attachment to the glenoid aspect of the joint
- The transverse ligament may be torn, resulting in subluxation of the biceps tendon in the bicepital groove
- Overuse injury is usually from overhead arm activities, such as tennis and throwing
- May occur as an acute traumatic injury

Common Patient Complaints
- Pain in the anterior and the anterior-lateral shoulder
- Pain may radiate distally down the biceps muscle toward the elbow
- Symptoms aggravated during exercise
- Symptoms relieved with rest
- May have "popping" or "snapping" in the anterior shoulder

Differentiation from Similar Injuries and Conditions
- Rotator cuff injuries often affect shoulder stability, resulting in secondary tendonitis of the biceps
- Rotator cuff injuries may radiate pain to the anterior shoulder
- Pectoralis muscle involvement
- Tear of the transverse ligament resulting in subluxation of the tendon
- Tear of the labrum and other lesions to the gleno-humeral joint
- Differentiate pain referred from the cervical spine

Typical Medical Recommendations
- Ice is typically used when acute.
- Anti-inflammatory medications
- Modify activity
  Decrease overhead activities that aggravate symptoms and increase pain.
- Physical therapy
  Ultrasound, deep-friction massage, and other physical therapy modalities.
- Orthopedic procedures
  Cortisone injection is sometimes used in the inflamed region of the tendon. Surgery may be required for partial or complete tear of the biceps tendons.

TREATMENT & TECHNIQUES

Overview: Biceps tendonitis is most commonly diagnosed in the category of accident/trauma. This is usually a repetitive stress disorder due to the accumulation of micro-trauma. However, it may occasionally occur as an acute strain. The injury is at the level of the muscles and tendons, with qi and blood stagnation in the channels and collaterals. Bicepital tendonitis may present as Lung or Large Intestine meridian pathology. Internal organ imbalances of the Lung and Large Intestine may also contribute.

Prognosis: Treat twice a week for three weeks, then re-evaluate. With chronic cases, continue treatment at least once weekly after the first three-week period. Due to the difficulty of treating the site of injury, if acupuncture does not provide significant relief, physical therapy modalities may benefit.

STEP ONE: INITIAL TREATMENT

Choose among these four techniques, carefully determining if there is an immediate decrease in pain or an increase in range of motion.

Technique #1: **The Tendino-Muscle Meridians**

★ **Lu 11, LI 1**   Bleeding technique
Both the Lung and the Large Intestine tendino-muscle meridians may benefit inflammation in the bicepital groove.

Technique #2: **Opposite Side (contra-lateral)**

Ahshi **point(s)**   On the opposite (unaffected) side

Technique #3: **Opposite Extremity (upper/lower)**

St 31, "medial" St 31 Yang ming corresponding point
                           on the opposite extremity
St 31 is located on the lateral side of the sartorius muscle. An alternate location – "medial" St 31 – is located just medial to the sartorius. These two points mirror the Yang ming shoulder area.

★ **Sp 9, "lower" Sp 9** Tai yin corresponding point on
                          the opposite extremity

Sp 9 often benefits shoulder pain on the Lung meridian due to this Tai yin correspondence. However, this upper/lower correspondence breaks some of the rules, as the knee is not the anatomical mirror of the shoulder. "Lower"

Sp 9, called Sp 9a in the work of Richard Tan, L.Ac. is an empirical point for shoulder pain.[2] It is located 1 to 2 cun inferior to Sp 9. The Master Tong system suggests its use for deltoid pain; however, it also benefits biceps tendonitis.

In general, treat upper/lower corresponding points on the opposite (unaffected) side when acute, and the affected side when chronic. Use palpation to assist in this choice.

Technique #4: **Empirical Points**

No well-known clinically effective empirical points for bicepital tendonitis.

STEP TWO: MERIDIANS & MICROSYSTEMS

Choose among these four techniques, selecting points that are appropriate for the signs and symptoms of the patient.

Technique #5: **The Shu-Stream Point Combination**

Lu 9 affected side + Sp 3 opposite side
LI 3 affected side + St 43 opposite side
Use of the shu-stream points of the yin meridians may be less reliable than those of yang meridians.

Technique #6: **Traditional Point Categories**

 Lu 5   He-sea point, "sedation" point
Lu 5, located adjacent to the attachment of the biceps in the elbow, is frequently sensitive.

Palpation may assist in your choice of other Lung and Large Intestine meridian points.

Technique #7: **The Extraordinary Meridians**

No clear extraordinary meridian treatment for bicepital tendonitis.

Technique #8: **Microsystems**

Auricular Therapy
Local: Shoulder, master shoulder, cervical spine
Zang-fu points: Lung, Large Intestine
Systemic points for pain: Shen men, Thalamus, Adrenal, Endocrine

Wrist-ankle Acupuncture
Wrist-ankle acupuncture may be considered, as the site of injury is not precisely along either the Lung or Large Intestine meridians. Use the two zones on the radial surface of the forearm.[3]

Upper #3 The palmar surface of the forearm Located 2 cun proximal to the wrist crease, on the radial side of the radial artery. This zone approximates the Lung meridian.

Upper #4 The dorsal surface of the forearm Located 2 cun proximal to the wrist crease, along the radius. This zone approximates the Large Intestine meridian.

STEP THREE: INTERNAL ORGAN IMBALANCES

Choose appropriate points to treat internal organ imbalances that may contribute to the injury or pain syndrome.

Technique #9: **Qi, Blood, and the Zang-fu Organs**

Tendonitis of the biceps is usually a repetitive stress injury and therefore internal organ imbalances are usually not causative. However, consider the following:

Liver imbalances Liver qi stagnation, Liver yin deficiency, and Liver blood deficiency
Liver imbalances may result in susceptibility of the muscles and tendons to both acute and chronic injury. Consider the following:

Liv 3 Yuan-source point; supports the Liver in its function of controlling the muscles and tendons

GB 34 Hui-influential point of tendons
Treat GB 34 on the affected side and Liv 3 on the opposite side.

Lung and Large Intestine imbalances Sometimes imbalances to these two organs of the metal element may result in deficiency in their respective meridians, increasing the susceptibility of the biceps to injury. I have observed Lung qi deficiency and related syndromes numerous times in clinical practice.

Points should be determined by the practitioner from both palpation and analysis of the signs and symptoms of the patient.

291 • Shoulder Pain *The Biceps Muscle Group*

STEP FOUR: THE SITE OF INJURY

Choose among the local and adjacent points at the site of injury. Points may be determined by palpation, orthopedic testing, and analysis of the signs and symptoms of the patient.

Technique #10: **Local and Adjacent Points**

The tendon at the bicepital groove ★ The bicepital groove usually lies between the Lung and the Large Intestine meridians. This zone lies several inches distal and slightly medial to LI 15. It may also be located several inches superior and slightly lateral to Lu 3. The extraordinary point *Jianqian*, located halfway between the anterior axillary fold and LI 15, is the closest acupuncture point to this injury site.[4]

Palpation will usually reveal a tender zone about 1 to 2 inches long and about a half-inch wide. This is where the stagnation of qi and blood occurs, and where local treatment begins.

Needle technique It is a difficult site to be precise. The deltoid muscle is superficial, and the transverse humeral ligament covers the tendon. I usually use one or two sets of paired points, inserted deeply without piercing the ligament or the tendon and its sheath. Electrical stimulation between these paired points is the desired technique. The use of multiple needles with electrical stimulation serves to accommodate for the lack of precision. The practitioner should pay attention to needle depth. If intermediate depth needles do not affect the pain and stagnation, consider in subsequent treatments approaching the ligament, tendon, and bone more closely.

Bicepital groove

Transverse humeral ligament

Cupping ★ A sliding or a bleeding cup over the groove may also be used, and often benefits when needling and electrical stimulation fail. The case for blood stagnation is so great that when a bleeding cup is used, attempt to get a "generous" amount of blood drawn into the cup. And of course, all procedures need to strictly conform to sterile protocol.

Adjacent points **Lu 1, Lu 2**   The pectoralis muscle
★ These two points should be considered as secondary points.

Lu 4, Lu 3   In the belly of the biceps
Lu 3 and Lu 4 are in the belly of the biceps, are often point sensitive, and may help release the muscle. Lu 3, or slightly on the ulnar side, is a motor point for the muscle. About .5 cun inferior and slightly to the ulnar side of Lu 4 is the second motor point.[5]

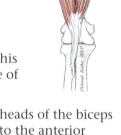

The extraordinary point *Jianqian*
This point is located in the anterior deltoid, adjacent to the bicipital groove. The traditional location of this extraordinary point is not at the site of the bicipital groove.

P 2   Between the two heads of the biceps
This point is located two cun distal to the anterior axillary fold, and lies between the two heads of the biceps.

LI 15, LI 14
These two points are located in the deltoid muscle, adjacent to the bicipital groove.

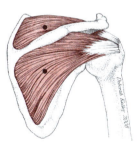

● – SI 12 – the supraspinatous (superior)
SI 11 – the infraspinatous (inferior)

★ The rotator cuff is often involved in tendonitis and other lesions of the biceps muscle. Consider the following:

SI 10, SI 11   The infraspinatous muscle
SI 12   The supraspinatous muscle

COMPLEMENTARY PROCEDURES

- When acute, ice massage along the bicepital groove may alleviate pain and reduce inflammation.

- Alternating ice and heat after the acute stage, when the condition is "neither hot (re) nor cold (han)", may enhance recovery.

- Topical applications (herbal liniments, plasters, etc.) may benefit.

★ While all techniques listed above have shown clinical relevance, the starred items are predictably effective for this specific injury. Consider them first in a treatment plan.

REFERENCES

[1] Dutton, M: *Orthopeadic Examination, Evaluation, and Intervention*, Second Edition. McGraw-Hill, USA, 2008 (page 613).

[2] Tan & Rush: *Twenty Four More in Acupuncture*. San Diego, 1994 (page 14).

[3] Matsumoto & Birch: *Extraordinary Vessels*. Paradigm Publishers, Massachusetts, 1986 (pages 182-188).
Note: Dr. Zhang Xin Shu's Wrist Ankle Acupuncture (Wan Ke Zhen) *is the source quoted in the above text.*

[4] Deadman, Al-Khafaji, & Baker: *A Manual of Acupuncture*. Journal of Chinese Medicine Publications, East Sussex, 2001 (page 581).
This point is sometimes referred to as Jian nei ling.

[5] Callison, M: *Motor Point Index*. AcuSport Seminar Series LLC, San Diego, 2007 (page 63).

24
Shoulder Pain
The Acromial-Clavicular Joint

Pain and inflammation on the top of the shoulder at the acromial-clavicular (AC) joint, often called shoulder separation

An injury due to separation of the AC joint and/or sprain to the acromial-clavicular ligament, characterized by pain, inflammation, and swelling. Joint laxity is possible in moderate to severe injuries.

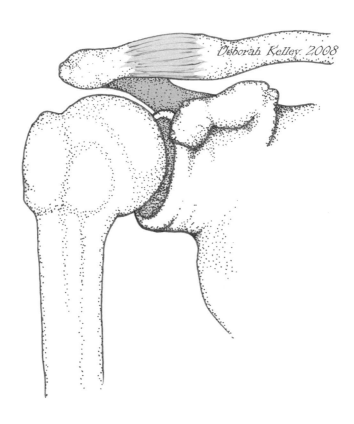

DIAGNOSIS & ASSESSMENT

Shoulder pain from injury to the acromial-clavicular joint is common to many types of activities. I have seen this sports injury with skiers, snowboarders, and hockey players, yet it can occur from a simple fall from a skateboard or a ladder. Injury to the AC joint can also result from a direct blow to the shoulder experienced in contact sports like football or hockey. When the injury is acute and the damage not significant, acupuncture provides immediate relief and quickens the healing time. But sometimes the situation can be more complicated, so let's review the anatomy and the mechanisms of this injury.

The AC joint is the articulation between the lateral end of the clavicle and the acromial end of the scapula. This lies between LI 16 on the medial aspect and LI 15 more laterally. When the AC joint is disrupted from trauma, it is called an acromio-clavicular joint separation, or AC separation. That means the AC ligament is affected, so this may also be considered a sprain. You must clearly differentiate an AC separation from a shoulder dislocation. With dislocation, the humerus is displaced from the shoulder joint. While the AC joint may also be affected, a dislocation is different in treatment, recovery and rehabilitation. In this chapter, only an AC separation is being considered.

Injury to the AC joint is almost always the result of a sudden, traumatic event that can be attributed to a specific incident or action. The trauma may vary in its severity. In a grade I sprain, there is pain, point tenderness, slight swelling and perhaps some loss of arm motion. The AC ligament is probably only slightly stretched. You and your patient hope this is the extent of the injury! In a grade II injury, the point tenderness is more significant, and some joint laxity may present, as injury to the AC ligament is more pronounced. Pain with arm movements will also be increased. A grade III sprain is a continued worsening of these signs and symptoms. Here, shoulder laxity may be pronounced to the degree that the acromion is "tenting" as the shoulder drops inferiorly. In addition to the AC ligament, the conoid or the trapezoid ligaments may be injured.

Your patient will obviously complain of shoulder pain, and will confirm the onset by acute trauma. Inspect for swelling and bruising; some joint laxity may be seen. Palpating the joint space and the ligament between LI 16 and LI 15 should reveal local tenderness. Test the patient's range of motion as he or she stands with the arm adducted to their side. Then, slowly abduct the arm by raising it laterally. An injured AC joint usually produces pain that starts above 90 degrees.[1] Pain may continue past 120 degrees as the arm moves from the horizontal to the vertical position. Of course, if the injury is acute with significant damage, movement may not be tolerated. You should not hesitate to get a more complete orthopedic evaluation to rule out fracture and dislocation. And a grade III injury with complete rupture of all three ligaments may require surgery. You and your patient need to know these details; however, pain has probably already sent them to the emergency room or the orthopedic clinic if the injury is severe.

While an AC separation is a type of ligament sprain, remember that we are dealing with a joint, which can become inflamed from trauma. This occurs acutely but may also be seen as a chronic case of arthritis to the AC joint. Although not considered common, I have seen this arthritic condition over the years and acupuncture has been effective in most if not all cases.

We should also note that muscles play a significant role in shoulder stability. The supraspinatous and infraspinatous of the rotator cuff are often involved with both acute and chronic patients. The deltoid and pectoralis may also contribute after shoulder trauma. So, in addition to treatment of the ligament and the joint space, treatment to the soft tissue is essential.

296 • **Shoulder Pain** *The Acromial-Clavicular Joint*

SUMMARY OF THE INJURY

Clinical Features
- Called a shoulder separation, injury is almost always the result of a sudden, traumatic event
- Tenderness with palpation at the AC joint between LI 16 and LI 15
- AC joint injury usually produces pain with lateral abduction of the arm that may continue past 120 degrees
- The more significant the injury, the greater the joint laxity
- AC separation needs to be differentiated from a shoulder dislocation
- Some patients may report chronic arthritic pain in the AC joint

Common Patient Complaints
- Pain on the superior shoulder at the AC joint
- Pain may be more widespread, and accompanied by swelling and bruising
- Arm movements may be painful and not tolerated

Differentiation from Similar Injuries and Conditions
- Partial or complete tear of rotator cuff or other shoulder muscles
- Fracture of clavicle or humerus must be ruled out
- Shoulder dislocation must be differentiated from AC separation
- Shoulder pain may be referred from intrathoracic disease, such as the diaphragm, the heart, and the gall bladder
- Referral pain from cervical nerve root

Typical Medical Recommendations
- R.I.C.E. (Rest, Ice, Compression, and Elevation) when acute
- Anti-inflammatory medications
- Physical therapy
  Ultrasound and other physical therapy modalities. Strength exercises for the adjacent muscles are necessary to provide shoulder stability. A shoulder sling is often used to maintain shoulder stability.
- Orthopedic evaluation
  Evaluation of the injury (grade I, grade II or grade III) is important to determine treatment, prognosis, and rehabilitation. Shoulder dislocation must be differentiated from AC separation. Surgery may be required to reattach any or all of the three stabilizing ligaments.

TREATMENT & TECHNIQUES

Overview: Shoulder pain due to AC separation is most commonly diagnosed under the category of accident/trauma. It is usually an acute traumatic injury at the level of the ligaments, tendons, and the joint capsule. There is qi and blood stagnation in the channels and collaterals. The Large Intestine is the primary meridian affected. However, the accompanying soft tissue trauma affects the scapular muscles of the rotator cuff, the deltoid, and the pectoralis. Thus, other meridians are involved in this injury. Chronic arthritis and inflammation may develop in the AC joint, which may be considered a *Bi* syndrome. Internal organ imbalances are probably not relevant.

Prognosis: Treat twice a week for three weeks, then re-evaluate. Many cases without significant ligament injury or tendon strain may have good results within six treatments. The patient should be advised to be cautious with any abduction movements of the upper extremity, as the shoulder may be susceptible to re-injury from separation.

STEP ONE: INITIAL TREATMENT

Choose among these four techniques, carefully determining if there is an immediate decrease in pain or an increase in range of motion.

Technique #1: **The Tendino-Muscle Meridians**

 LI 1   Bleeding technique
This jing-well point treats the area of the AC joint.

Technique #2: **Opposite Side (contra-lateral)**

LI 16, LI 15   Corresponding points on the opposite (unaffected) side

Technique #3: **Opposite Extremity (upper/lower)**

Corresponding points on the opposite extremity may be considered; however, treatment to the affected extremity is usually preferred.

In general, treat upper/lower corresponding points on the opposite (unaffected) side when acute, and the affected side when chronic. Use palpation to assist in this choice.

Technique #4: **Empirical Points**

No well known empirical points for AC joint trauma.

STEP TWO: MERIDIANS & MICROSYSTEMS

Choose among these four techniques, selecting points that are appropriate for the signs and symptoms of the patient.

Technique #5: **The Shu-Stream Point Combination**

★ **LI 3 affected side + St 43 opposite side**

Technique #6: **Traditional Point Categories**

★ Palpation may assist in your choice of other meridian points.

LI 11	He-sea point
LI 10	Not a major point category
LI 4	Yuan-source point
GB 34	Hui-influential point of tendons
St 37	Lower he-sea point for the Large Intestine

St 37 can occasionally work wonders as secondary point. It should be considered affecting the fu organ, and therefore its exteriorly related meridian.

Technique #7: **The Extraordinary Meridians**

No clear extraordinary meridian treatment for the acromial-clavicular joint.

Technique #8: **Microsystems**

Auricular Therapy
Local: Shoulder, master shoulder, cervical spine
Systemic points for pain: Shen men, Thalamus, Adrenal, Endocrine

STEP THREE: INTERNAL ORGAN IMBALANCES

Choose appropriate points to treat internal organ imbalances that may contribute to the injury or pain syndrome.

Technique #9: **Qi, Blood, and the Zang-fu Organs**

Shoulder separation is an acute traumatic injury and therefore internal organ imbalances are usually not a factor in treatment.

STEP FOUR: THE SITE OF INJURY

Choose among the local and adjacent points at the site of injury. Points may be determined by palpation, orthopedic testing, and analysis of the signs and symptoms of the patient.

Technique #10: **Local and Adjacent Points**

The acromial-clavicular joint

LI 16 + LI 15
Consider this treatment as "above and below" (or in correct anatomical terms, medial and lateral) to the AC joint. These are the most important two points for treating shoulder separation, and usually relieve pain and inflammation without aggravation. Locate LI 16 as lateral as possible, so that the needle is just medial to the acromion. LI 15 is usually needled obliquely inferior towards LI 11, but with this point, many techniques of insertion probably suffice. Use electrical stimulation between these LI 16 and LI 15.

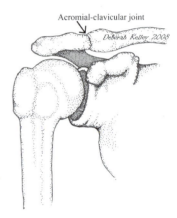
Acromial-clavicular joint

The acromial-clavicular joint space

The AC joint space is approximately halfway between LI 16 and LI 15, which can be called LI 15.5. Threading this joint space and the region of the AC ligament is sometimes useful. One needle starts on the anterior side of the acromion and the joint space, and is inserted in a posterior direction. The second needle starts on the posterior side, and is inserted in an anterior direction. Both needles are at an oblique to transverse angle. Electrical stimulation between both points may be useful, but should be avoided when the condition is acute, painful, and swollen.

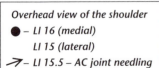

Overhead view of the shoulder
● – LI 16 (medial)
   LI 15 (lateral)
↗ – LI 15.5 – AC joint needling

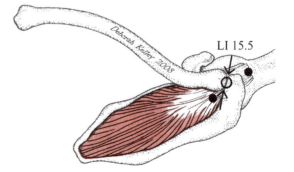
LI 15.5

300 • Shoulder Pain *The Acromial-Clavicular Joint*

Moxa   In the rare chronic case of AC joint arthritis, consider needle-top moxa on LI 16 and LI 15. Needle-top moxa on the two paired points of LI 15.5 may be difficult due to their oblique insertion, which increases the possibility of burning the skin. However, with protection, this technique can be accomplished. Thread moxa or indirect moxa is also a possibility. These heat treatments often benefit the patient with chronic arthritis.

Adjacent points   **SI 12**   The supraspinatous muscle
★ The supraspinatous is often involved in cases of shoulder trauma. Consider two paired points determined by palpation. SI 12 should be viewed as as a secondary point.

One may take the point-of-view that wind (feng) "enters" the shoulder from the trauma of separation. The pain is of sudden onset and sudden disappearance, with radiating qualities. Thus treatment to dispel wind would logically follow. The Chinese name of SI 12, "grasping the wind" (bing feng), implies its use in the treatment of wind symptoms.

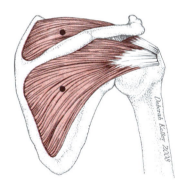

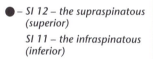
● – SI 12 – the supraspinatous (superior)
SI 11 – the infraspinatous (inferior)

★ **SI 11**   The infraspinatous muscle
The infraspinatous is often involved in cases of shoulder trauma. Consider two paired points determined by palpation. SI 11 should be viewed as a secondary point.

LI 14   Located at the insertion of the deltoid
LI 14 may be point sensitive, as the deltoid muscle is affected by AC joint separation. LI 14 should be viewed as a secondary point.

★ **SI 14, SI 15**   The levator scapulae muscle
The levator is often involved in cases of shoulder trauma. Consider two paired points determined by palpation. SI 14 should be viewed as a secondary point.

★ **Lu 1, Lu 2**   The pectoralis muscle
The pectoralis is often involved in cases of shoulder trauma. Consider two paired points determined by palpation. Lu 1 and/or Lu 2 should be viewed as secondary points.

COMPLEMENTARY PROCEDURES

- When acute, ice massage along the acromial-clavicular ligament and the joint space may alleviate pain and reduce inflammation.

- Alternating ice and heat after the acute stage, when the condition is "neither hot (re) nor cold (han)", may enhance recovery.

- Topical applications (herbal liniments, plasters, etc.) may benefit.

- A shoulder sling is often useful to maintain shoulder stability immediately after the injury.

★ While all techniques listed above have shown clinical relevance, the starred items are predictably effective for this specific injury. Consider them first in a treatment plan.

REFERENCES

[1] Dutton, M: *Orthopeadic Examination, Evaluation, and Intervention,* Second Edition. McGraw-Hill, USA, 2008 (page 526).

25
Neck Pain
The Levator Scapulae Muscle
Pain in the neck and the scapular region of the shoulder

Acutely is seen as torticollis ("stiff neck"), but may be a source of chronic or lingering neck and shoulder pain. The levator is involved as a secondary lesion in many cases of neck pain from other causes.

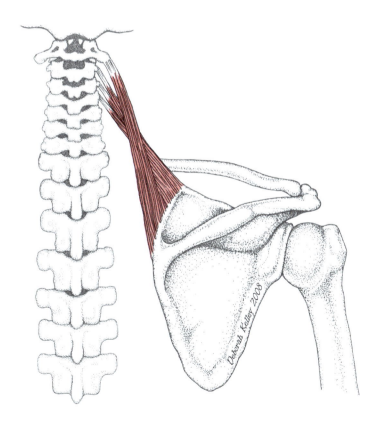

DIAGNOSIS & ASSESSMENT

I have chosen not to include the numerous causes of neck pain as a treatment topic in this handbook of sports injuries. However, it would be remiss of me to not include some discussion on treating neck pain. I have therefore included acupuncture treatment of the levator scapulae muscle as my contribution to this topic. The levator is the cause of neck and shoulder pain for a significant number of patients, and is often overlooked by the acupuncture practitioner. While levator dysfunction might not be the entire cause of pain – other points, treatments, and techniques may be necessary – the simple techniques that follow benefit many patients. And levator dysfunction is often a component of treatment to other injuries, such as strain to the supraspinatous and infraspinatous of the shoulder.

Let's start with the anatomy of the muscle. The origin of the levator scapulae is by tendinous "slips" from the transverse processes of C1, C2, C3 and C4. It inserts along a broad portion of the superior angle of the scapula. While the Bladder meridian follows the para-spinal muscles lateral to the vertebral column, the Small Intestine meridian's pathway is along the levator muscle. In the region of the inferior attachments are the points SI 14 and SI 15. Just inferior to its attachment on the scapula lies SI 13, which is an adjacent point. GB 20 and Bl 10 are in the region of the attachments at C1 and C2. The extraordinary point *Bailao* is adjacent to the portion of the muscle that attaches to C4.

The action of the levator provides insight into the signs and symptoms frequently reported by patients. When the neck is "fixed", the levator elevates the scapula. With the scapula "fixed", it laterally flexes and rotates the neck. Noted as the "stiff neck" muscle by Dr. Janet Travell, the levator is responsible for torticollis when in spasm.[1] The patient presents with the neck laterally flexed or inclined to the side of pain, and the shoulder elevated. Many practitioners find *ahshi* points and muscle tension in the upper trapezius around GB 21 and SJ 15, concluding that treatment to the Shao yang meridians is indicated. While these points may benefit, the primary stagnation is in the levator muscle along the Small Intestine (Tai yang) channel.

For acute cervical sprain and strain, including torticollis with its stiff neck symptoms, treating the levator is the treatment of choice. However, chronic one-sided neck pain may also benefit from this treatment. The patient presents with an elevated scapula on the side of pain, as well as discomfort when laterally flexing or rotating to the side of pain. For lateral flexion, ask the patient to move their ear toward the shoulder on the same side of pain. For rotation, they should look to the shoulder on the painful side. Either or both of these movements may be painful and restricted if the levator is involved. But palpation tells all! It usually reveals obvious point tenderness at SI 14 and SI 15, just above the superior angle of the scapula. Often painful and taut bands will be palpable. While the patient may report and experience pain further up the neck and in the upper trapezius area, when you find these *ahshi* points, they often exclaim, "That's it!"

Several comments need to be added on the treatment of the levator. Because of its attachments at C1, C2, C3 and C4, releasing this muscle often works well for subluxations of the upper cervical vertebrae. Many patients have chiropractic or osteopathic adjustments to the neck that don't "hold". Treatment to a taut and contracted levator muscle may help. As mentioned above, an elevated scapula is often responsible for tension and discomfort in the upper trapezius muscles. I rarely treat the common points GB 21 and SJ 15 without also needling the levator at SI 14 and SI 15. And finally, while other muscles, such as the sterno-cleido-mastoid (SCM), may be involved in whiplash injury, the levator is essential in post-traumatic treatment for neck pain.

In summary, the levator scapulae is the primary muscle involved in acute torticollis and symptoms of stiff neck. However, it may benefit chronic neck pain as well as patients with vertebral subluxation and whiplash. You may need to use other local and adjacent points of the para-spinal, the trapezius, and the SCM muscles. However, the levator should be included as part of the treatment protocol for most acute and chronic neck pain patients.

SUMMARY OF THE INJURY

Clinical Features
- Pain upon palpation at the attachment just above the superior angle of the scapula at SI 14 and SI 15
- Taut fascial bands at SI 14 and SI 15
- Elevated scapula on the side of pain
- Neck may be slightly flexed laterally to the side of pain
- Discomfort when laterally flexing or rotating to the side of pain

Common Patient complaints
- Acute stiff neck, known also as torticollis
- May be chronic neck and shoulder pain
- Stiffness often accompanies pain
- Pain is often one-sided
- Feeling of the upper cervical region being "out of adjustment"

Differentiation from Similar Injuries and Conditions
- Referral pain from cervical nerve root
- Cervical disc syndrome
- Cervical facet joint dysfunction
- Sprain/strain of other cervical soft tissues
- Trigger points of the upper trapezius and other neck and shoulder muscles

Typical Medical Recommendations
- Ice may be considered with acute cases. Applications of heat often benefit tension and contraction of the muscle.
- Anti-inflammatory medications
- Stretching
  Stretching of the levator and other cervical muscles may benefit.
- Biomechanics
  Correct ergonomics of work and computer stations to reduce or eliminate elevation of the scapula and other postural imbalances.
- Physical therapy
  Ultrasound, massage, other physical therapy modalities.
- Orthopedic evaluation
  The most important diagnostic issue is to determine if the pain is due to a cervical disc protrusion. Secondarily, to assess which tissues besides the levator scapulae muscle are involved.

306 • Neck Pain *The Levator Scapulae Muscle*

TREATMENT & TECHNIQUES

Overview: Acute neck pain involving the levator scapula muscle may be diagnosed under the category of accident/trauma. However, trauma may not be apparent when the onset is associated with poor positioning during sleep or from postural imbalances. With acute onset as seen in stiff neck (torticollis), wind (feng) and cold (han) are often considered the pathogens. Chronic neck pain may also involve the levator; its diagnosis in TCM terms is not as definitive. The injury is at the level of the muscles and tendons, with qi and blood stagnation in the channels and collaterals. The Small Intestine meridian is the primary meridian involved. It should be differentiated from the Bladder meridian (the para-spinal muscles) and the Gall Bladder meridian (the upper trapezius). Internal organ imbalances vary.

Treatment to the levator may be specific in acute stiff neck and may be combined with treatments for other causes of neck pain, including degenerative changes to the cervical spine, disc disease, and cervical nerve root involvement.

Prognosis: For chronic cases, treat twice a week for three weeks, then re-evaluate. For torticollis and acute stiff neck, expect good results within one or two treatments.

STEP ONE: INITIAL TREATMENT

Choose among these four techniques, carefully determining if there is an immediate decrease in pain or an increase in range of motion.

Technique #1: **The Tendino-Muscle Meridians**

 SI 1   Bleeding technique
Bleeding the Jing-well point may be effective for the symptoms of pain and stiffness of the levator.

Technique #2: **Opposite Side (contra-lateral)**

Corresponding points on the opposite side may be considered; however, treatment to the affected side is usually preferred.

Technique #3: **Opposite Extremity (upper/lower)**

Bl 53, Bl 54   Tai yang corresponding points on the opposite extremity
These two Bladder meridian points, often overlooked, mirror the Small Intestine (Tai Yang) meridian.

| GB 30 | Shao yang corresponding points on the opposite extremity |

GB 30 is a mirror for the region of GB 21, however sometimes it benefits levator dysfunction. It should be considered a secondary point.

In general, treat upper/lower corresponding points on the opposite (unaffected) side when acute, and the affected side when chronic. Use palpation to assist in this choice.

Technique #4: **Special Empirical Points**

Luozhen
While the Chinese texts frequently mention *Luozhen*, I do not find this point works for a high percentage of patients with stiff neck. But it is worth a try!

STEP TWO: MERIDIANS & MICROSYSTEMS

Choose among these four techniques, selecting points that are appropriate for the signs and symptoms of the patient.

Technique #5: **The Shu-Stream Point Combination**

★ **SI 3 affected side + Bl 65 opposite side**
This shu-stream point treatment often produces significant and immediate relief.

Technique #6: **Traditional Point Categories**

★ | **SI 6** | Xi-cleft point |

SI 6 is one of the most effective points for the acute case.

★ | **Bl 60** | Jing-river point |

An effective point for neck pain, it should be considered if SI 3 or SI 6 do not provide relief.

Palpation may assist in your choice of other less-common Small Intestine and Bladder meridian points, such as:

SI 4	Yuan-source point
Bl 59	Xi-cleft point of the Yang Qiao mai
Bl 63	Xi-cleft point

Technique #7: **The Extraordinary Meridians**

★ | **SI 3 + Bl 62** | Activate the Du mai |

Treating the Du Mai may assist if there is cervical nerve root pathology contributing to the condition.

| **GB 41 + SJ 5** | Activate the Dai mai |

Treatment to the Dai mai often benefits neck pain.
For patients with acute neck pain, whiplash and other trauma to the cervical spine, I frequently use both the Du mai and the Dai mai.

The technique that I prefer starts with palpating GB 41, the master point of the Dai mai. The point sensitive side is needled. Then SJ 5, the coupled point, is needled on the opposite side. The Du mai is needled at the master point SI 3, on the same side as GB 41. Its coupled point, Bl 62 is needled on the opposite side. With some patients I will consider electrical stimulation between the master point and the coupled point. Ion pumping chords may also be used between the crossed master point and coupled point.

Technique #8: **Microsystems**

Auricular Therapy
Local: Neck, shoulder, master shoulder, cervical spine
Zang-fu points: Liver
Systemic points for pain: Shen men, Thalamus, Adrenal, Endocrine, Muscle relaxation

STEP THREE: INTERNAL ORGAN IMBALANCES

Choose appropriate points to treat internal organ imbalances that may contribute to the injury or pain syndrome.

Technique #9: **Qi, Blood, and the Zang-fu Organs**

Spasm and levator muscle dysfunction are usually not associated with internal organ imbalances. However, the following should be considered:

Stress The syndrome of stress is not a TCM term, but clearly this modern diagnosis affects the internal organ systems. The levator muscle seems to react to stressful conditions with spasm and active trigger points. This also produces generalized tension in the upper trapezius muscle group. The practitioner may want to consider all lifestyle factors contributing to stress with chronic neck pain.

Liver imbalances Liver qi stagnation, Liver yin deficiency, and Liver blood deficiency
Liver imbalances may result in the susceptibility of the muscles and tendons to spasm. Consider the following:

Liv 3	Yuan-source point; supports the Liver in its function of controlling the muscles and tendons
GB 34	Hui-influential point of tendons

Points should be determined by the practitioner from both palpation and analysis of the signs and symptoms of the patient.

309 • Neck Pain *The Levator Scapulae Muscle*

STEP FOUR: THE SITE OF INJURY

Choose among the local and adjacent points at the site of injury. Points may be determined by palpation, orthopedic testing, and analysis of the signs and symptoms of the patient.

Technique #10: **Local and Adjacent Points**

The levator scapulae muscle **SI 14, SI 15**

One or two needles, perpendicular insertion, up to a depth of 1 inch.

The region of SI 14 and SI 15, just above the superior angle of the scapula, will frequently be painful to palpation; taut bands are often present. SI 14 is the trigger point for the levator in Dr. Janet Travell's work on myofascial pain, which she calls the "stiff neck" muscle.[2] And sometimes there is even crepitus with cross-fiber palpation and massage.

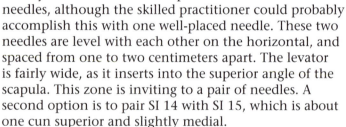

Needle technique I always treat SI 14 with two paired

needles, although the skilled practitioner could probably accomplish this with one well-placed needle. These two needles are level with each other on the horizontal, and spaced from one to two centimeters apart. The levator is fairly wide, as it inserts into the superior angle of the scapula. This zone is inviting to a pair of needles. A second option is to pair SI 14 with SI 15, which is about one cun superior and slightly medial.

My preferred insertion is perpendicular, paying attention for a dense or "squeaky" feel to the needle as it penetrates into this taut muscle tissue. Carefully palpate the superior angle of the scapula, keeping the needles close to the bone so that you are not tempted to treat the tight bands of the posterior portion of the upper trapezius muscle. Depth is from .5 to 1 inch, and of course, carefully avoid the lung and the pleural cavity! Correct needle technique works wonders, but don't hesitate to add electrical stimulation. I have had many patients over the years who respond well to needling with electrical stimulation. Use it between the two paired points, although some practitioners prefer coupling with a distal point.

Cupping In chronic cases of neck tension, I often turn to the technique of the bleeding cup. The presence of taut fascial bands along with crepitus, mentioned above, is suggestive of both qi and blood stagnation. This is a perfect case for a bleeding cup. With a lancet, pierce up to 30 times in the region of SI 14 and SI 15. A large-sized cup should fit over this entire zone, and should be retained for at least 10 minutes. Drawing from a few drops to one teaspoon of blood into the cup assures micro-circulation has been invigorated through this area of the muscle and its tendinous attachment. Of course, follow all the rules of clean and sterile technique, using gloves and proper cleaning and disposal of the equipment.

Patient position Patient position is very important in order to get the best access to the point. A seated patient, with arms adducted and shoulder depressed, is unquestionably the best position. But of course, this increases risk for fainting and needle shock. The lateral recumbent position (side-lying) works equally well. Place the patient on their side, with the affected shoulder up and accessible. After depressing the shoulder and adducting the arm, use a "hugging" pillow to help stabilize the upper extremity in that position.

As the humorist writer Dave Barry often says, "I am not making this up." And truely, I am not making this next sentence up. To ensure that the shoulder stays depressed, I have used duct tape to affix the arm or forearm to the patient's body. This keeps the levator from elevating the scapula, and thus assures proper position. I never treat this condition with the patient prone, as the shoulder tends to elevate and access is compromised; that is, I never treat the patient prone unless I have my duct tape!

The levator at its midsection **SI 16**
SI 16 is an access point to the levator for the skilled and confident practitioner. It is located on the posterior border of the sterno-cleido mastoid (SCM) muscle, level with the laryngeal prominence. It should be noted that the motor point for the levator is located 1 cun posterior and .5 cun superior to SI 16.[3] Perpendicular insertion up to 1 inch should be deep enough to reach the muscle. Due to the complexity of the anatomy at this point, caution and precision is essential.

Cervical points **GB 20**
One may take the point of view that "wind" exists with stiff neck or torticollis. The pain is of sudden onset with radiating qualities. Thus, treatment to expel wind with GB 20 ("wind pond") would logically follow. In addition, GB 20 is an adjacent point to the cervical attachments of the levator.

Bl 10
Like GB 20, Bl 10 is an adjacent point to the cervical attachments of the levator. In addition, it is the motor point of the semispinalis capitis, an important para-spinal muscle in the cervical region.[4]

Scapular points ★ **SI 12**   The supraspinatous
The supraspinatous is often involved with levator spasm and dysfunction. In addition, SI 12 ("facing the wind") has the action of dispelling wind. Consider SI 12 as a secondary point.

★ **SI 11**   The infraspinatous
The infraspinatous is often involved with levator spasm and dysfunction. Consider SI 11 as a secondary point.

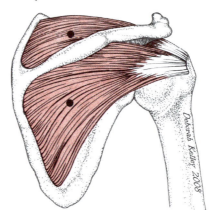

● – SI 12 – the supraspinatous (superior)
SI 11 – the infraspinatous (inferior)

★ **SI 13**
This adjacent point is a secondary point not located on the levator muscle, but in the medial portion of the suprascapular fossa just inferior to its attachment. Consider it as a secondary point only when sensitive.

COMPLEMENTARY PROCEDURES

- Applications of heat often benefit tension, contraction, and "guarding" of a muscle group. Heat may also be considered after the needling of trigger points.

- Slow shoulder rolls and shoulder "circles" may help to release the levator. The patient should be advised that this practice is not a strength exercise, but rather slow, deliberate movements to "reprogram" the muscle from its constant state of contraction.

- Massage or acupressure to release tension of the levator can be performed between treatments at home. The "theracane" device is quite useful, as it can "hook" around to the spine of the scapula to massage the muscle at its attachment near SI 14.

- As stated earlier, stretching of the levator may help with a tense and contracted muscle. Consult a good text on stretching, as it is a bit tricky.

★ While all techniques listed above have shown clinical relevance, the starred items are predictably effective for this specific injury. Consider them first in a treatment plan.

REFERENCES

[1] Travell & Simons: *Myofascial Pain and Dysfunction: The Trigger Point Manual, Volume 1 (The Upper Extremities)*. Williams & Wilkins, Philadelphia, 1983 (page 334).

[2] Travell & Simons: *Myofascial Pain and Dysfunction: The Trigger Point Manual, Volume 1 (The Upper Extremities)*. Williams & Wilkins, Philadelphia, 1983 (pages 334-336).

[3] Callison, M: *Motor Point Index*. AcuSport Seminar Series LLC, San Diego, 2007 (page 39).

[4] Callison, M: *Motor Point Index*. AcuSport Seminar Series LLC, San Diego, 2007 (page 29).

SECTION 3
The Appendices

Appendix A
References

ORTHOPEDIC TEXTS

Corrigan & Maitland: *Practical Orthopaedic Medicine.* Butterworth & Co, United Kingdom, 1989 (pages 206-208).

Cyriax & Cyriax: *Illustrated Manual of Orthopaedic Medicine.* Butterworths, London, 1983. *Comment: This is an older and partially outdated reference with some interesting treatment modalities for inury and pain.*

Dutton, M: *Orthopeadic Examination, Evaluation, and Intervention,* Second Edition. McGraw-Hill, USA, 2008. *Comment: This is one of the primary orthopedic texts used as a reference for this handbook.*

Garrick, J: *Orthopaedic Knowledge Update, Sports Medicine 3.* North American Academy of Orthopaedic Surgeons, Illinois, 2004.

Kendall & McCreary: *Muscles, Testing and Function with Posture and Pain,* Fifth Edition. Lippincott Williams & Wilkins, Philadelphia, 2005.

Kendall & McCreary: *Muscles, Testing and Function,* Third Edition. Williams & Wilkins, Baltimore, 1983. *Comment: The Third Edition does not contain the detailed information on orthopedic diagnosis and assessment found in the Fifth Edition. However, if used for muscle testing, it suffices as an easy-to-use reference.*

O'Donoghue, DH: *Treatment of Injuries to Athletes,* Third Edition. W. B. Saunders Co, Philadelphia, 1976.

REFERENCES ON TRIGGER POINTS AND MOTOR POINTS

Callison, M: *Motor Point Index.* AcuSport Seminar Series LLC, San Diego, 2007. *Comment: This is an excellent reference with clear and concise locations of the motor points.*

Finando & Finando: *Trigger Point Therapy for Myofascial Pain.* Healing Arts Press, Vermont, 2005. *Comment: This reference is similar to Dr. Travell's two volumes on trigger points, however it is considerably less comprehensive.*

Gunn, C: *Treating Myofascial Pain: Intramuscular Stimulation (IMS) for Myofascial Pain Syndromes of Neuropathic Origin*. University of Washington, 1989.
Comment: This text by Dr. Gunn contains useful information, and his work serves as the foundation for the "dry needle technique" used by physical therapists and physicians.

Travell & Simons: *Myofascial Pain and Dysfunction: The Trigger Point Manual, Volume 1 (The Upper Extremities)*. Williams & Wilkins, Philadelphia, 1983.

Travell & Simons: *Myofascial Pain and Dysfunction: The Trigger Point Manual, Volume 2 (The Lower Extremities)*. Williams & Wilkins, Philadelphia, 1992.
Comment: Both Volume I and II are among the most important texts on physical medicine that I personally own. In addition to the detailed descriptions and illustrations of trigger points, both volumes are quite useful as a reference for the origin, insertion, action, and innervation of the muscles. The anatomical illustrations of Barbara Cummings are both precise and viewer-friendly, and her work serves as a model for Deborah Kelley's illustrations in this handbook.

TEXTS ON ACUPUNCTURE AND TRADITIONAL CHINESE MEDICINE

Cheng Xinnong: *Chinese Acupuncture and Moxibustion,* Third Printing. Foreign Language Press, Beijing, 1993 (Fifth Printing, 2004).
Comment: This reference, commonly called "CAM", is considered one of the primary texts for point location.

Deadman, Al-Khafaji, & Baker: *A Manual of Acupuncture*. Journal of Chinese Medicine Publications, East Sussex, 2001.
Comment: This comprehensive reference is considered one of the primary texts for point location.

Fratkin, J: *Chinese Herbal Patent Medicine: The Clinical Desk Reference*. Shya Publications, Boulder, 2001.

Kendall, D: *Dao of Chinese Medicine*. Oxford University Press, United Kingdom, 2002.
Comment: This text contains interesting commentary on the integration of western anatomy and physiology with acupuncture and traditional Chinese medicine.

Shanghai College of Traditional Medicine: *Acupuncture, A Comprehensive Text*. Eastland Press, Chicago, 1981.
Comment: While this text is less commonly used than other point location references, its section on the extraordinary points is comprehensive.

ACUPUNCTURE REFERENCES FOR SPORTS INJURIES AND PAIN

Callison, M: *Sports Medicine Acupuncture*. AcuSport Seminar Series LLC, San Diego, In Printing.
Comment: Unfortunately, this orthopedic text for acupuncturists is not yet published. It will be a complete reference on sports medicine acupuncture, covering more injuries and wider topics than this handbook.

Lee, M: *Master Tong's Acupuncture,* Second Edition. Blue Poppy Press, Colorado, 1998.
Comment: This book details the points of the Master Tong system, but unfortunately lacks precision in their locations and clinical uses.

Legge, D: *Close to the Bone,* Second Edition. Sydney College Press, Australia, 1997.
Comment: David Legge is a highly proficient practitioner and international lecturer. This text was one of the first to integrate acupuncture with sports medicine. However, it is a bit outdated and lacks articulate treatment plans for some of the injuries covered in the book.

Tan & Rush: *Twelve and Twelve in Acupuncture.* San Diego, 1994.

Tan & Rush: *Twenty Four More in Acupuncture,* San Diego. 1994.
Comment: Richard Tan's work includes many points and techniques from the Master Tong system of empirical points. These two simple books are far from comprehensive, but have valuable information for the treatment of pain.

REFERENCES ON ANATOMY

Hollinshead, WH: *Textbook of Anatomy,* Third Edition. Harper & Row, Maryland, 1974.
Comment: I highly recommend a textbook of anatomy to accompany an illustrated atlas. The practitioner may find it helpful to read a precise description of the anatomy at the site of injury when an illustration is unclear. Hollinshead's reference is one of the most comprehensive, and is very reader-friendly.

Netter, F: *Atlas of Human Anatomy,* Fourth Edition. Saunders Elsevier, Philadelphia, 2006.
Comment: No practitioner should be without Frank Netter's anatomical illustrations.

Appendix B
R.I.C.E.
Application of Ice
Application of Heat

R.I.C.E. (REST, ICE, COMPRESSION, AND ELEVATION)

R.I.C.E. is an acronym for rest, ice, compression, and elevation. These four steps are commonly prescribed by physical therapists, physicians, and athletic trainers to help their patients in the initial stages of an acute injury. After trauma, the body initiates the inflammatory process in an attempt to protect the body from further damage. Secondary tissue injury may be caused by excessive swelling and inflammation, as well as from injured tissue "debris" and other metabolites in the affected area. R.I.C.E. is the western protocol used to prevent this secondary tissue injury caused by the inflammatory response.

R.I.C.E. is usually recommended during the acute stage of the injury, usually the first 24 to 48 hours after the traumatic event. Inflammation should decrease naturally after the body no longer responds to protect the site of injury from secondary tissue trauma. At this point the R.I.C.E method is usually discontinued in favor of other modalities of treatment.

Rest

Rest prevents any further trauma to the site of injury. If pain is significant, it tends to remind the patient not to use the affected area. Some patients, however, need definitive instruction to refrain from activities that involve the injured tissues. And rest is essential prior to orthopedic assessment, which may be necessary to rule out serious conditions such as bone fractures or tendon ruptures.

Ice

The main role of ice is to induce vasoconstriction. Cold applications reduce the amount of fluid being released into the tissues at the site of injury. Ice also benefits venous drainage, which decreases some of the local swelling. Additionally, the application of ice simply helps to decrease pain.

With acute trauma, many western texts recommend ice in a cycle of 20 minutes on and 20 minutes off. This helps avoid damage to the superficial tissues from the application of cold as well as to allow fresh blood flow to the area. The application times, however, will

320 • Appendix B *R.I.C.E.*

vary from source to source. It is generally agreed that within the first 72 hours, ice is indicated. After that point, its benefits diminish.

The benefits of the applications of cold will be forever debated within the acupuncture profession. Ice is not mentioned in the classic writing, and thus many TCM practitioners frown upon its use. However, we must remember that when many of the texts were written in China, there was no refrigeration. Thus, during the summer months when most injuries occur, there was no ice. This could obviously have affected the recommended use of this modality.

I am not a traditionalist, and in my treatment of sports injuries, ice plays an important role. I follow the guidelines of its use up to 72 hours after a traumatic event. After 72 hours, more caution must be used, and the practitioner may need to advise the patient about the over-use of ice. However, application of cold can still be effective after the 72-hour window following the acute stage of injury. In these cases, I consider ice massage or alternating ice and heat, both of which are discussed below.

We found an interesting study on cryotherapy (ice) that should silence some of the skeptics. It demonstrated that the application of ice started within 36 hours after injury was statistically better than the use of heat. Those who used cold simply had a more complete and rapid recovery. Patients using ice within 36 hours of injury reached full activity in an average of 13.2 days, compared with 30.4 days for those initiating cryotherapy more than 36 hours after injury. Individuals using heat required 33.3 days for a return to full activity.[1]

Compression

Compression is usually accomplished with an elastic bandage, ace bandage, or wrapping tape. Sometimes a splint or support brace may be added. Compression is another method that decreases local inflammation by reducing blood flow to the site of injury.

Elevation

Elevation is accomplished by raising the injured area to a level above the heart. This simply uses gravity to decrease blood flow to the site of injury. It also increases venous drainage. This is another important method of decreasing inflammation to the injured area and thus reduces the risk of secondary tissue damage.

ICE MASSAGE

Ice massage is simply using an ice cube for the local application of cold. With this technique, the benefits of ice are directed to the specific site of injury. The other local and adjacent tissues are minimally affected by the application of cold. For example, with a hamstring strain, a tear occurs in a fixed site in the belly of the muscle. While this site of injury may benefit from cold applications, the muscle itself may respond better to heat, as it often goes into a spasm or contraction for protective purposes. Thus the application of cold can be localized with ice massage. Another example is with an acute inflammation of the bicepital tendon. Ice massaged along the bicepital groove may alleviate pain and reduce inflammation without "cooling" the entire muscle group.

ALTERNATING ICE AND HEAT

Alternating ice and heat after the acute stage of an injury may enhance recovery. This method may be used with injuries that are neither hot (re) nor cold (han). The application of cold reduces inflammation and alleviates pain. The application of heat relaxes tension in the muscles and tendons. In TCM language, heat moves the qi in the affected tissues.

I use alternating ice and heat frequently with my patients after the acute stage of an injury. I recommend five minutes as the time interval of each application, in a cycle of 20 total minutes. For most patients, start with ice, and end with heat. To state it clearly, the cycle is five minutes of ice, five minutes of heat, five minutes of ice, and ending with five minutes of heat.

APPLICATION OF HEAT

There are various ways of applying heat. Heating pads are the easiest, but this form of "dry" heat may not be optimal. Many patients prefer moist heat, which can be accomplished with a hot pan of water, which is used to heat up a thick wash cloth or hand towel. Caution must be used with this method to avoid burning the skin. Sometimes, moist heat can be included with an herbal soak or decoction. For those well-equipped practitioners, the hydroculator and hot wax devices work wonderfully.

REFERENCES

[1] Hocutt, J: *Cryotherapy in ankle sprains*. The American Journal of Sports Medicine, Sept, 1982, Vol. 10, No. 5 (pages 316-319).

Appendix C
Anti-inflammatory Medications

Anti-inflammatory medications are mentioned under "Typical Medical Recommendations" in each injury of Section II. While it is beyond the scope of this handbook to include recommendations or suggested use of anti-inflammatories, I felt it would be helpful to provide a brief overview of the medications most likely being used by the injured patient, whether over-the-counter or prescribed by their physician.

Aspirin – the salicylates

This is the prototypical non-steroidal anti-inflammatory (NSAID), commonly used for pain and inflammation. Aspirin has anti-pyretic properties, and is often taken to reduce fever. It also slows clotting of the blood; some patients may be on a small dose to prevent cardiovascular disease. Although aspirin is called an anti-inflammatory, its effectiveness as such is questionable, and there may be better and safer methods to achieve this desired effect. Its adverse effects on the gastro-intestinal tract are well documented.

The non-salicylates

There are numerous NSAIDs that do not contain salicylatic acid. This category includes Ibuprofen (Motrin, Advil), Naproxen, Indocin, and Voltaren. These NSAIDs are considered "non-selective" COX inhibitors. Their mode of action is not completely understood, but may be related to prostaglandin inhibition. Their adverse effects on the gastro-intestinal tract are well documented.

Selective COX-2 inhibitors

Celebrex is the most widely prescribed COX-2 inhibitor on the market. The higher risk for cardiovascular side effects has lead to the removal of some of the drugs in this category from the market. COX-2 inhibitors are prescribed for both pain and inflammation, used for such conditions as osteoarthritis and rheumatoid arthritis. Their adverse effects on the gastro-intestinal tract are limited.

Tylenol (Acetaminophen)

This is a non-salicylate pain reliever. While it also has anti-pyretic (fever-reducing) properties, it is not thought to have any significant anti-inflammatory effect. Acetaminophen is metabolized in the liver, and higher doses over a prolonged period of time may result in hepatic dysfunction.

The corticosteroids

Synthetic cortisone (dexamethasone, prednisone) is based on the natural anti-inflammatory hormones produced by the adrenal gland. They may be taken orally, or may be injected at or near the site of inflammation. Both oral and injected steroids have side effects and well-documented risks; the practitioner should be well acquainted with these side effects.

Chinese herbs with anti-inflammatory properties

Many patients choose not to take western anti-inflammatory medications. Chinese herbal medicine has numerous individual herbs and formulas that may be used as a substitute for these western medications. *Chinese Medical Herbology and Pharmacology,* by Chen and Chen, is a good reference on the subject.[1] While "anti-inflammatory" is not a traditional term in Chinese medicine, the general category of herbs that clear heat, promote blood circulation, and dispel blood stasis is a starting point to treat inflammation.

Western and naturopathic anti-inflammatory supplements

The practitioner may prescribe western herbs and supplements that have documented anti-inflammatory properties. Bromelain (from pineapple) and papain (from papaya) are proteolytic enzymes, and are commonly used for inflammation. Turmeric (curcumin) and arnica are other typical recommendations. Nutritional supplements, including the antioxidants and the omega-3-fatty acids are also used by practitioners to treat post-traumatic inflammation.

Conclusion

There are no clinically obvious choices for pain and inflammation, whether the patient is considering western pharmaceuticals or the botanical and nutritional alternatives. Effectiveness is highly variable, depending upon the patient and the specific nature of their injury. I do not have a preferred anti-inflammatory medication or a "go-to" supplement that is clearly beneficial for the majority of patients. Clinical experimentation is the only way that I know to find the right medicine. However, it is also important for the practitioner to check for any interactions when prescribing herbs to patients who are taking other western medications. Chen and Chen's text is a good resource for these herb-drug interactions.

REFERENCES

[1] Chen & Chen: *Chinese Medical Herbology and Pharmacology*. Art of Medicine Press, California, 2004.

Appendix D
Biomechanical Imbalances

Many of the injuries covered in Section II are considered repetitive stress disorders. In TCM terms, they are commonly diagnosed under the category of "accident/trauma". The onset is insidious (gradual), and generally not related to a single traumatic event. The accumulation of micro-trauma over a prolonged time period is the cause of the injury. This is where biomechanical imbalances come into the picture. These abnormalities of structure and function "magnify" the effects of exercise and activity. Thus, micro-trauma more easily manifests as an injury or pain syndrome.

Traditional Chinese medicine does not articulate the role of biomechanical imbalances in treating injuries and pain. The practitioner must therefore integrate the practices of western sports medicine with the TCM model. This will significantly improve the clinical success of acupuncture with your patients.

The foot

The first and most obvious site to analyze is the structure and function of the foot. Foot pronation ("inward" rolling of the ankle) and supination ("outward" rolling of the ankle) are the two most common imbalances of the foot. Pronation is often associated with "flat feet" or "collapsed" arches. With supination, the foot abnormally moves into inversion. With excessive pronation or supination, the foot looses its ability to absorb shock from heel strike to toe-off. This may affect the local tissues, and is commonly seen in plantar fasciitis and achilles tendonitis. However, the effects may occur proximal to the foot, as seen in repetitive stress injuries of the knee, the hip, and the lower back.

With excessive foot pronation or supination, the recommendation may be simple: wear shoes that are designed to correct the abnormality. Running shoes, for example, are made with varying densities on the heel in order to correct for functional abnormalities of the foot. Orthotics are foot-wear "inserts", which also correct the biomechanics during activity. They can be purchased over-the-counter or may be custom fitted. The podiatrist or physical therapist are usually set up to make custom orthotics specific for the abnormality of the patient's foot.

Anatomical short leg

Leg length discrepancy, also known as the anatomical short leg, can be a biomechanical cause of some repetitive stress injuries. Many practitioners attempt to assess leg length discrepancy by visual observation alone. However, this may result in an improper diagnosis, as pelvic tilt may give the "appearance" of a short leg. With a true anatomical short leg, the total length of the femur plus the tibia differs from side to side. The only accurate way to determine this is with a full lower-extremity X-ray. Measurements are made on the film image, and are accurate to the millimeter. While there are varying points of view as to how much of a difference is considered significant, five millimeters may be enough to cause concern. A heel lift in the shoe of the short leg is usually the treatment of choice.

Imbalances in the quadriceps muscle group

For the patient with anterior knee pain, including patello-femoral joint syndrome, it is important to assess the quadriceps muscle group. The common western medical viewpoint describes a muscle imbalance between the vastus medialis and the vastus lateralis, often associated with anterior knee dysfunction. The ilio-tibial tract, on the lateral side of the thigh, may also contribute to these knee injuries. Generally, the vastus medialis is weaker than the muscles on the lateral side, which negatively affects the tracking of the patella through the femoral groove.

Muscle imbalances of the quadriceps are best diagnosed by a physical therapist, a physiatrist, or an orthopedic physician. Stretching and releasing the lateral muscles (the vastus lateralis and the ilio-tibial band) while strengthening the vastus medialis is usually the recommendation. The entire protocol is fairly simple, and is easy for the patient to perform at home.

The pelvis

Pelvic tilt (sometimes called lateral pelvic tilt) is a superior elevation of the ilium on one side, resulting in the opposite side of the ilium "dropping" inferiorly. This imbalance is assessed by observing the crest of the ilium at the mid-axillary line. Looking at both sides, simply compare to see if one ilium is elevated. Pelvic tilt is seen in many injuries, including quadratus lumborum spasm, hip pain, and ilio-tibial band syndrome.

Anterior and posterior rotation of the pelvis is also a common biomechanical imbalance. This can be visualized as the position of the sacrum and the rest of the pelvis in relationship to the lower lumbar spine. With posterior rotation of the pelvis, the sacrum is functionally moved posteriorly, increasing lordosis. Anterior rotation drops the sacrum, and the lumbar spine becomes more "flattened".

Pelvic tilt and pelvic rotation may be caused by a number of factors, including muscular or structural abnormalities. The result is that biomechanical stress is placed on the rest of the structures, including the neck and shoulder, the thoracic and lumbar spine, and the entire lower extremity. There are numerous modalities to correct tilt and rotation of the pelvis; they will not be included in the discussion of this appendix.

Posture

Many pain syndromes are caused by postural abnormalities, as seemingly benign as sitting, standing, or sleeping in incorrect positions. For example, torticollis ("stiff neck") results from poor position during sleep. Acute lumbar spasm may occur after a prolonged period in a seated position. Also, numerous repetitive stress injuries are caused by poor ergonomics of the work station. Incorrect keyboard height and hand position during mousing often contribute to repetitive stress injuries such as lateral epicondylitis and carpal tunnel syndrome.

Correction of posture and ergonomics of the work station are not necessarily straightforward. However, if these postural factors are contributing to the injury or pain syndrome, the practitioner must assist the patient in correcting these issues.

Analysis of athletic activity and movement

Athletes may need to correct how they are performing their specific activity or event. For the runner, gait analysis of stride, cadence, and foot plant may reduce the impact of micro-trauma. This is a very complicated task, and should be assessed by a well-trained professional using video feedback. Cyclists often need to have an individualized bike fit, addressing such issues as seat height, handle bar width, and body position. With tennis and other racquet sports, swing and serve mechanics often need to be altered. Again, the use of video feedback is often helpful for this assessment.

REFERENCES

Hall, S: *Basic Biomechanics*, Second Edition. Mosby-Year Book, Inc, Missouri, 1995.
Note: This text may assist the practitioner in the assessment and correction of biomechanical imbalances.

Appendix E
Cross Training

Basic knowledge of cross training is essential for the practitioner treating athletes and active individuals who exercise on a regular basis. Many of these patients are very reluctant to take time off from training in order to recover from an injury. However, the healing process often requires the injured patient to modify activities that aggravate the injury. That being said, it may be virtually impossible to convince a runner not to run. Your only hope may be to suggest options that don't aggravate the injury, while at some level satisfy their need for a good workout. This is where cross training fits in.

The practitioner may have to do some analysis of the location, severity, and type of injury in order to decide which activities the patient should avoid. Once that is determined, the remaining forms of exercise and activity that may be recommended will be more obvious. Telling a long-distance runner to go for a walk is not going to work – you will need to do better than that! In order to maintain the confidence of your athletic patient, the practitioner needs to be articulate with the recommendations of cross training.

If the patient has a lower-extremity injury, the swimming pool is the first place to start. Water exercises usually allow for a lower-extremity workout without stress to the site of injury. "Running in water" is an excellent alternative, and most injured athletes can do this exercise without aggravation. However, it is quite monotonous and unexciting, and the runner generally will resist this recommendation. Research water running techniques if you plan to use this recommendation; there are some "tricks" that can entice the unconvinced patient. Otherwise, there is the the obvious option of swimming. While the triathlete will not resist, the pure runner may balk at this suggestion. Water aerobics classes should not be ignored, as they offer a great workout and may be a bit more exciting.

The two major benefits of water exercises are buoyancy and viscosity. The buoyancy of water can reduce or eliminate the weight-bearing aspect of exercises, taking pressure off the injury site. The viscosity of the water acts as resistance during the activity; the faster the athlete tries to move, the more the water resists them. I have seen several elite athletes perform at a personal best after running in water for the four weeks prior to the event.

Cycling, whether on the road or a stationary bike, is another obvious alternative; that is, as long as it does not aggravate the injury. Cycling is a common cross-training exercise, and it reduces much of the impact that is incurred by running. Depending on the injury, this could be a great recommendation for the distance runner. Well-known running coach Thomas Miller demonstrated in his dissertation that runners can significantly improve 10,000 meter times with the addition of interval training on a bike. Runners who added cycling intervals to their normal training program improved their average 10K time by 8.57 percent.[1] A case can also be made that cycling may at least maintain a runner's fitness level while recovering from an injury.

Lower-extremity injuries may also require the patient to simply try upper-body exercises. There are numerous possibilities for the upper extremity; physical therapists and fitness trainers are well qualified to design such a program.

If the patient has an upper-extremity injury, obviously lower-body exercises are recommended. However, it may be possible to continue activities with the upper extremity as long as the injured muscle group or affected tissues are not actively engaged.

The following is a more complete list of cross-training activities. If you do not fully understand the mechanics involved with these exercises, refer the patient to a licensed physical therapist or a certified fitness trainer.

Cross training for the lower extremity
- Running in water
- Swimming
- Water aerobics
- Cycling, both on the road and the stationary bike
- "Spin" cycling
- Elliptical machine
- Stairmaster
- Weight lifting

Cross training for the upper extremity
- Rowing machine
- Rock climbing
- Nintendo Wii Fit[2]
- Weight lifting

REFERENCES

[1] Miller, T: *Programmed to Run*, Human Kinetics, Illinois, 2002 (page 70).

[2] *Nintendo Wii Fit probably is not going to satisfy many athletes, but it is fun.*

Appendix F
Physical Therapy

Physical therapy is recommended for many of the injuries discussed in this handbook. I have great respect for the profession, and believe that acupuncture and physical therapy, when used appropriately, comprise complementary modalities that can effectively treat most sports injuries and pain syndromes. The recommendations of a PT are so important to me, that sometimes my selection of acupuncture points is directly affected by the objectives of the physical therapist.[1]

Both the assessment of the damage and the etiology of injury are usually well-understood by the physical therapist. However, it is their expertise in the rehabilitation of sports injuries that highlights the physical therapy profession. Unfortunately, TCM diagnosis does not include these important assessments and procedures; they are essential to effectively treat an injured patient with acupuncture. My advice to the reader is to have a good referral system, with a PT you can consult with about your patients as they recover from their injury.

The practitioner of PT specializes in physical medicine, and their treatments generally help the patient recover more quickly and attain normal function following injury and trauma. The physical therapist is well educated, usually holding a master's degree, although the doctoral degree is becoming more common in the profession. All physical therapists must pass a national exam before they can become licensed. Their scope of practice may vary depending on the regulations of the state.

PHYSICAL THERAPY TREATMENT MODALITIES

Physical therapists use a wide variety of modalities with patients recovering from an injury. The following list is not complete, but includes common types of treatments used in a typical physical therapy office.

Ice (Cryotherapy)

Cryotherapy is usually used with injuries in the acute stage when inflammation is present. The purpose of cryotherapy is to reduce the inflammatory process and decrease the extent of secondary injury to the surrounding tissues caused by swelling.

Heat (Thermotherapy)

Therapeutic application of heat is usually used in the later stages of the injury when increased blood flow to the area can be beneficial. Heat is not commonly used with acute injuries, as it may aggravate inflammation, possibly increasing the secondary injury from swelling. Heat is typically used to decrease muscle spasm, increase capillary permeability, and enhance the flexibility of tissues.

Transcutaneous Electrical Nerve Stimulation (TENS)

TENS is the use of electrical current with pads on the skin, usually placed at or near the site of injury. This modality is generally used to provide pain relief. TENS is thought to work in several different ways. The "gate control" theory suggests that the electrical stimulation of large nerve fibers inhibits the transmission of small pain producing nerves. The use of electrical current may also stimulate nerves to release enkephalins and beta-endorphins to produce an "opiate-like" analgesic effect.

Ultrasound

Ultrasound is among the oldest of the physical therapy modalities. A continuous wave creates heat in the local tissues, and is similar to thermotherapy. It increases blood flow to the site of injury. A pulsed ultrasound wave does not create heat, and is believed to alter cellular permeability and metabolism. This may be important in the promotion of healing by reducing swelling and edema, pain, and muscle spasm.

Phonophoresis

Phonophoresis is the use of ultrasound to drive pharmacologic agents such as analgesics, anesthetics, and corticosteroids through the skin into the injured tissues. Some studies show that this modality can penetrate substances as far as 10 centimeters into the body.

Iontophoresis

Similar to phonophoresis, transdermal iontophoresis uses positive and negative electrical current to "push" and "pull" fluids at the site of injury. A medicated solution with positively charged ions placed under a positive lead is pushed from the positive lead and pulled toward the negative one. Iontophoresis is a modality used in many acute and sub-acute sports injuries.

MANUAL TECHNIQUES

Manual techniques, including massage and bodywork, are used by the physical therapist to treat injuries and restore normal function.

Trigger points

The use of ischemic compression (direct digital pressure, acupressure) is used to "inactivate" or release myofascial trigger points in the body. Some physical therapists now use "dry needling" to trigger points and other tissues involved with injuries and pain.

Myofascial release

This technique is used when myofacial restrictions alter the body's normal alignment or function. Deep continuous manual pressure is used to release adhesions and tension in the fascia.

Cross-friction massage

This style of massage uses friction across (perpendicular to) the fibers of muscles, tendons, and ligaments. Cross-friction massage is used to increase blood flow to the site of injury as well as break up adhesions and scar tissue. This technique is also thought to provide pain relief through the "gate control" system.

Muscle Energy Technique

Muscle Energy Technique is used to increase range of motion. This is an active form of manual therapy, where the patient contracts the muscle or muscle groups that have restricted movement. The practitioner resists the motion, either matching or overpowering the patients force of contraction.

Strain-counterstrain

Strain-counterstrain is also known as "positional release". This technique is used for musculoskeletal pain and restricted range of motion. There are 200 or more identified points on the body used in the strain-counterstrain technique.

High-velocity thrust techniques

This technique involves the application of force on an isolated joint to temporarily cause hypermobility. In theory, this allows the joint to restore its normal range of motion. This is a form of manipulation, and requires a great level of skill and should only be practiced by trained professionals.

REHABILITATION

Rehabilitation after injury plays an essential role for the complete healing of the injury. Not well articulated in TCM, the procedures of rehab are an essential component of the physical therapy profession; the acupuncturist should include these techniques after the acute stage for many injuries and pain syndromes.

Proprioceptive neuromuscular facilitation

Proprioceptive neuromuscular facilitation (PNF) is a stretching procedure that combines passive stretching and isometric contractions. It is based on utilizing the golgi-tendon apparatus to help relax the muscle being stretched. This procedure helps the patient gain greater range of motion, and thus increase flexibility.

Active stretching

With this technique the antagonist muscle (opposite to the injury site) is contracted in order to maintain the agonist (affected) muscle in an elongated position. The benefit of active stretching is that when the antagonistic muscle is contracted, the agonist receives a stimulus from the nervous system to relax, allowing greater range of motion.

Passive stretching

With passive stretching, the practitioner places the muscle into an elongated position. It is held in the stretched position for a period of time. Some muscles can be passively stretched by the patient themselves.

Range of motion exercises

Exercises that utilize range of motion are commonly recommended by physical therapists. These movements help stimulate the healing of connective tissue at and adjacent to the site of injury. These exercises also help to maintain and even increase range of motion of the joint. Range of motion exercises may be both active and passive.

Proprioceptive training

Proprioception is the "sense" of where the body is located in space. This is accomplished by afferent nerve fibers in the extremities that aid in the perception of movement and spatial orientation. Proprioceptive exercises train the body to recognize this spatial orientation, and are frequently included in post-injury rehabilitation protocols.

Strength training

This important rehab technique simply uses resistance to increase the contractile strength of a muscle. Therapeutically, it is used to increase strength, correct muscle imbalances, and speed the recovery from injury. Strength training is also used in rehabilitation after surgery. A well-trained physical therapist is able to recommend strength exercises for rehabilitation and prevention of injury as well as for enhancing basic fitness.

REFERENCES

[1] Dutton, M: *Orthopeadic Examination, Evaluation, and Intervention,* Second Edition. McGraw-Hill, USA, 2008.
Note: Most of the information in this appendix comes from Chapter 10, pages 347 to 374, of Dutton's text.

Appendix G
Orthopedic Assessment

Without adequate understanding of the etiology of an injury, it is difficult to determine a treatment plan. The simple strategy of treating local *ahshi* points may sometimes benefit the patient, but it is more likely to result in sub-par clinical results. While TCM diagnosis may give insight into the nature of a condition, most injuries require that we include orthopedic testing and other assessment procedures from the western tradition in order to provide effective treatment. Integrating these two medical systems increases the likelihood that acupuncture is directed to the primary lesion while still utilizing the other treatment principles of traditional Chinese medicine.

Assessment usually starts with the interview process. Some sports injuries may be diagnosed from the signs and symptoms of the patient. Heel pain, for instance, is most likely plantar fasciitis if it has a gradual onset and is aggravated in the morning when the patient takes their first steps. Simply knowing the signs and symptoms of an injury is a good place to start. I attempt to summarize this important information with each injury in this handbook.

There is nothing more satisfying than finding an *ahshi* point in a muscle or a sensitive distal point that serves as a guide in treatment. Acupuncturists are generally proficient in their ability to palpate. However, palpation is a static assessment. The functional assessment of the musculo-skeletal system is of equal importance, and the acupuncture profession is usually under-trained in this regard.

Range of motion is a good place to start in assessing function with the injured patient. Active movement is when the patient moves the area affected by the injury, such as flexion and extension of a joint. Passive movement is when the practitioner moves the affected area through its range of motion. Both active and passive movements are useful in assessing many sports injuries.

Manual muscle testing is another orthopedic procedure that may provide a broader diagnostic viewpoint for the acupuncturist. If manual muscle testing reveals pain and/or weakness, this usually indicates impairment of its function. Muscle testing is very specific, and it potentially reveals the site of injury as well as the meridian or meridians affected by the injury. For example, the function of the hamstring group is knee flexion. With manual muscle testing, the patient contracts the hamstrings (flexes the knee) while the practitioner provides resistance to this movement. If there is pain and/or weakness with this test, a muscle strain or tendon tear of the hamstring is likely. In TCM terms, this usually indicates stagnation of qi and blood in the Bladder meridian. Remember, pain and/or weakness with resisted contraction of a muscle is an important test to determine both the primary site of injury and the affected meridian.

There are numerous texts on manual muscle testing. My clear favorite is *Muscles: Testing and Function*, by Kendall and McCreary.[1] I prefer the older editions, which are reader-friendly. However, the latest edition is more complete, and includes a great deal of information on other orthopedic assessments.

In addition to range of motion and manual muscle testing, there are many other types of orthopedic tests used to differentiate an injury. Some involve "stress" tests to a specific ligament, while others distract ("pull apart") or compress a joint. While it is not the purpose of this book to provide a complete western assessment for each injury, I have included these tests in some of the injuries, and have listed others in Appendix H.

It would be helpful for the practitioner to have a good orthopedic text as a reference for assessment. There are many to choose from. One of my favorites is Mark Dutton's *Orthopeadic Examination, Evaluation, and Intervention*, referenced in a number of the injuries in Section II.[2]

We obviously can not ignore imaging, one of western medicine's most important forms of assessment. The technology of imaging has made enormous strides over the last twenty years, and is considered essential for the diagnosis of many sports injuries. Sometimes MRI, CT scan, and X-ray are used to determine both the cause and extent of an injury. For instance, the patient complaining of shin splints may lead the practitioner to assess strain of the anterior tibialis muscle. Only X-ray or a bone scan can definitively rule out tibial stress fracture, sometimes missed by clinical diagnosis only.

Not to be overlooked, the practitioner must know when it is appropriate to refer the patient for orthopedic assessment. Even an acupuncturist well-trained in sports medicine usually does not have the skills of an orthopedic physician or experienced physical therapist. I mention the importance of patient referral time and time again when I teach, and with many of the injuries in this handbook. Having a network of orthopedic physicians, physiatrists, and physical therapists for referral purposes is essential for the practice of sports medicine acupuncture.

REFERENCES

[1] Kendall & McCreary: *Muscles, Testing and Function with Posture and Pain,* Fifth Edition. Lippincott Williams & Wilkins, Philadelphia, 2005.
Note: The Third Edition was published in 1983.

[2] Dutton, M: *Orthopeadic Examination, Evaluation, and Intervention,* Second Edition. McGraw-Hill, USA, 2008.

Appendix H
Orthopedic Tests

LATERAL ELBOW PAIN – FOR TENNIS ELBOW

Wrist Extension

You can confirm lateral epicondylitis (tennis elbow) by testing the extensor muscles of the forearm. With your palm on the dorsal surface of their hand, have the patient extend the wrist (lift upward) while you resist with downward pressure.

You may do the same with resisted finger extension. The patient extends the fingers (again, lifting upward) while you resist with downward pressure. Both of these tests can be performed with the patient's forearm placed on a desktop or the treatment table. Pain at the lateral elbow confirms tendonitis and/or epicondylitis.

Another way to test wrist extension is with patient's arm reaching forward, parallel to the floor. Their hand is pronated (palm down). With the palm of your hand on the dorsal surface of their hand, have the patient lift their arm and forearm upwards while you resist with downward pressure. All this is done while keeping their arm parallel to the floor. Pain at the lateral elbow confirms tendonitis and/or epicondylitis.

Radial deviation

Resisted radial deviation is tested with the elbow at 90 degrees of flexion. The hand is in neutral position – it is neither flexed nor extended. This can be explained as being in the "hand-shake" position. Place the palm of your hand over the radial (thumb) side of the patient's hand, just distal to the wrist. Your fingers lie on the dorsal surface of their hand. The patient moves their hand radially, against resistance. Pain with resisted radial deviation usually confirms tendonitis and/or epicondylitis.

Hand Supination

One additional test that may be performed is for the supinator muscle, which shares the attachment at the lateral epicondyle with the common tendon of the extensors. Hold the hand of the patient's outstretched arm as if you were shaking hands. Their hand is pronated (palm down). The patient supinates their hand while you resist the motion. This is the action of turning the palm up. Pain at the lateral elbow suggests that the supinator muscle is involved, which is common in tendonitis and/or epicondylitis.

MEDIAL ELBOW PAIN – FOR GOLFER'S ELBOW

Wrist flexion

You can confirm medial epicondylitis (golfer's elbow) by testing the flexor muscles of the forearm. Place your palm on the palmar surface of the patient's supinated (palm up) hand. Have the patient flex the wrist while you resist with downward pressure. This test can be performed with the patient's forearm placed on a desktop or the treatment table. Pain at the medial elbow confirms tendonitis and/or epicondylitis.

Hand pronation

The pronator muscle shares the attachment at the medial epicondyle with the common tendon of the flexors. Hold the hand of the patient's outstretched arm as if you were shaking hands. The hand is supinated (palm up). The patient pronates their hand, which is the action of turning the palm down. You resist the motion. Pain at the medial elbow suggests that the pronator muscle is involved, which is common in tendonitis and/or epicondylitis.

HEEL PAIN – FOR THE ACHILLES TENDON

Plantar flexion

The action of the gastrocnemius-soleus group is pointing the toes, which is plantar flexion. Pain on resisted plantar flexion helps to confirm involvement of the achilles tendon.

One way to test plantar flexion is with the patient standing with a hand on a table or chair to help keep them steady. The patient rises on their toes (plantar flexion), pushing their body weight directly upward. Pain may confirm achilles tendon involvement. Be careful to note muscle weakness, as lumbar disc involvement (L5, S1 nerve roots) may be the cause.

Passive dorsiflexion

As the practitioner flexes (dorsiflexion) the patient's ankle past 90 degrees, there may be discomfort in the heel, as the muscle-tendon unit of the gastrocnemius-soleus group is passively stretched. This may help to confirm involvement of the achilles tendon.

HAND PAIN – FOR CARPAL TUNNEL SYNDROME

The Tinel sign

The Tinel sign is performed by lightly tapping on the wrist crease over the carpal tunnel at or near the acupuncture point P 7. If this produces tingling and/or numbness, inflammation of the median nerve is likely. These symptoms must be distal to the wrist in the distribution area of the median nerve for the test to be considered positive.

Phalen's maneuver

The Phalen's maneuver is performed for 30 to 60 seconds. The dorsum of the patient's hands are placed together, with the wrists in forced flexion. Increased tingling and/or numbness distal to the wrist in the distribution area of the median nerve is considered a positive test for carpal tunnel syndrome.

THIGH PAIN – FOR HAMSTRING STRAIN

Knee flexion

Test the hamstrings with resisted flexion of the knee. The patient lies prone (face down) on the treatment table. Have them flex the knee while you resist the movement with your hand on their heel. If this causes pain, the hamstring group is most likely involved. Be careful to note muscle weakness, as lumbar disc involvement (L5, S1 nerve roots) may be the cause.

HIP PAIN – FOR ARTHRITIS OF THE HIP

Passive internal rotation of the femur

Osteoarthritis of the hip will usually cause pain to be reproduced with passive internal rotation of the thigh. You can easily perform this test with the patient supine or seated at the edge of the table. With the hip and knee flexed, move the lower leg laterally, away from the center line of the body. This internally rotates the femur in the hip joint. The test is positive if it produces pain.

LATERAL KNEE PAIN – FOR IT BAND SYNDROME

Palpation

Compression of the IT band against the lateral knee with firm pressure may reproduce the pain. You may also want to compress the IT band with the patient flexing and extending the knee slightly. Pain will assist in confirming irritation and inflammation on the undersurface of the ilio-tibial tract.

MEDIAL KNEE PAIN – FOR THE MCL AND THE MEDIAL MENISCUS

Valgus challenge

By stabilizing the knee on the lateral side, and forcing the lower leg laterally, you put stress on the medial collateral ligament. This movement "gaps" the medial joint space. Joint laxity can be felt if the ligament has been stretched or torn. Pain may also be produced by this maneuver if the MCL has been sprained.

McMurray's and Apley's tests

The McMurray and Apley tests are the two standard tests to assess damage to the meniscus, ligament, and other tissues of the knee. It is beyond the scope of this handbook to describe these tests, so refer to an orthopedic text for guidance. Practitioners of acupuncture should be acquainted with the McMurray's and Apley's tests.

ANTERIOR KNEE PAIN – FOR PATELLO-FEMORAL JOINT DYSFUNCTION

Palpation

With your hand on the patella, the patient slightly flexes and extends the knee as you feel for crepitus ("creaking" or "grinding"). Crepitus can give a general feel as to the level of inflammation and dysfunction in the patello-femoral joint. If compression of the patella against the femoral groove produces pain, it also suggests an arthritic or inflamed joint. Consulting a text on these orthopedic tests is recommended.

Resisted knee extension

You can test the quadriceps muscle group with resisted knee extension. With the patient seated on the treatment table and the knee flexed, have them extend the leg forward while you resist the movement with your hand on their ankle. Pain and apprehension suggests involvement of the patello-femoral joint.

LEG PAIN – FOR ANTERIOR SHIN SPLINTS

Dorsiflexion of the ankle

You can test the anterior compartment muscles by placing your hand on the dorsal surface of the patient's foot. The patient then dorsiflexes the ankle (flexes toes and the foot upwards) while you resist the motion. Pain with resisted dorsiflexion is common with anterior shin splints.

One additional way to test dorsiflexion is with the patient standing, with a hand on a table or chair to help keep them steady. The patient lifts their foot and toes (dorsiflexion), shifting the body weight to their heels. Pain may confirm involvement of the muscles of the anterior compartment. Be careful to note muscle weakness, as lumbar disc involvement (L4, L5 nerve roots) may be the cause.

Passive stretching of the anterior compartment group

Try passive stretching of the muscle by moving the patient's foot into plantar-flexion (toe pointing). This stretches the anterior compartment muscles, which may be uncomfortable, helping to confirm involvement of this muscle group.

LEG PAIN – FOR MEDIAL SHIN SPLINTS

Dorsiflexion of the ankle

Like the anterior tibialis muscle, the posterior tibialis assists with dorsiflexion. You can test the anterior compartment muscles by placing your hand on the dorsal surface of the patient's foot. The patient then dorsiflexes the ankle (flexes toes and the foot upward) while you resist the motion. Pain with resisted dorsiflexion is sometimes found with medial shin splints.

Inversion of the foot

Inversion of the foot is probably a more important test than dorsiflexion to confirm medial shin splints. To test the posterior tibialis muscle, the patient inverts their foot, best described by turning the plantar surface of the foot inward. You hold the whole foot to resist the motion. Pain with resisted inversion confirms involvement of the posterior tibialis.

SHOULDER PAIN – FOR THE AC JOINT

Range of motion

Test the patient's range of motion as he or she stands with the arm adducted to their side. The patient then slowly abducts the arm by raising it laterally. An injured AC joint usually produces pain that starts once the arm moves above 90 degrees. Pain may continue past 120 degrees as the arm moves from the horizontal to the vertical position. Of course, if injury to the AC joint is acute, this movement may not be tolerated.

SHOULDER PAIN – FOR BICEPITAL TENDONITIS

Palpation

Palpating with internal and external rotation of the shoulder is often helpful in finding the bicepital groove. With the elbow flexed at 90 degrees, simply swing the forearm medially and laterally while you palpate. Remember, the groove is inferior and medial to the point LI 15. This movement may also reveal subluxation of the tendon, which you will feel as a "pop" or "snap" under your finger.

Yergason's and Speed's test

The Yergason's test and the Speed's test are commonly used to determine bicepital tendonitis. It is beyond the scope of this handbook to describe these tests, so refer to an orthopedic text for guidance.

Elbow flexion with hand supination

Resisted elbow flexion, which is the action of the biceps, does not consistently produce pain. However, resisted flexion of the elbow combined with hand supination (moving the palm upward) is a more reliable test for bicepital tendonitis.

Passive stretch of the biceps

The patient is usually able to perform full range of motion, but pain at the end range of shoulder extension and abduction may be found. Passive stretch of the biceps may also confirm this injury. Holding their elbow, gently pull the arm and forearm behind the patient. Pain may be produced if the bicepital tendon is inflamed.

SHOULDER PAIN – FROM FROZEN SHOULDER

External rotation

Place the arm in full adduction (to the patient's side) with the elbow flexed to 90 degrees. Stabilize the elbow next to the body with your hand. Ask the patient to swing the forearm out like a gate while you observe the movement. This is active external rotation of the humerus.

This can also be done passively. One hand holds the forearm while the other stabilizes the elbow next to the patient's body. You swing the patient's forearm laterally like a gate. Frozen shoulder usually presents with limitations to this movement, which is passive external rotation of the humerus.

Abduction

Ask the patient to raise their arm laterally. Observe the shoulder and scapula, as they may try to achieve this movement by "cheating" with shoulder movements. Limitations with abduction are common with the frozen shoulder patient.

SHOULDER PAIN – FOR THE INFRASPINATOUS

External rotation of the humerus

External rotation is the action of the infraspinatous muscle. To test this movement, place the patient's arm in full adduction with the elbow flexed at 90 degrees. Stabilize the elbow next to their body with one hand. Place your other hand on the dorsal side of the forearm just proximal to the wrist. Ask the patient to swing the forearm out like a gate, while you resist the movement. The patient must not raise the arm, so make sure you keep their elbow stabilized to the side. If there is pain and/or weakness on resisted external rotation, the infraspinatous is likely involved.

Note: There are various other methods to test the infraspinatous. They all involve external rotation with resistance. The patient's arm may be in positions other than full adduction as described above.

SHOULDER PAIN – FOR THE SUPRASPINATOUS

The "empty can" test (resisted abduction)

Abduction is the action of the supraspinatous. The "empty can" test is an easy way to evaluate this movement. With the patient standing, both arms are raised laterally at 90 degrees of abduction (parallel with the floor). The practitioner then moves the patient's arms about 30 degrees anterior, in a forward direction. Then, place their arms in full internal rotation by pointing the thumbs down. Think of this as the patient holding an "empty can" of their favorite drink! This is the position to test the supraspinatous muscle. Ask the patient to abduct (push in an upward direction) while you apply downward pressure on the forearm just proximal to the wrist. If there is pain and/or weakness, the supraspinatous in likely involved in the injury.

Note: There are various other methods to test the supraspinatous. They all involve abduction with resistance. I prefer the test described above, as it is easy and usually reliable. And you can compare the affected side with the unaffected side, noting any difference in pain and/or weakness.

The "arch of pain"

The arch of pain is simple. Have the patient stand with their arms adducted to the side. The patient then slowly abducts the arm of the injured shoulder by raising it laterally. If pain occurs with active abduction during the "arch" from approximately 70 to 110 degrees, the test is positive. When the arm is parallel with the floor, it is at 90 degrees of abduction. Pain will occur above and below this level.

Note: A painful arch suggests impingement of the supraspinatous tendon between the tuberosity of the humerus and the acromion. Remember, if pain does not start until 120 degrees, or continues past 120 degrees as the arm approaches the vertical position, other problems may exist (see Shoulder Pain – for the AC Joint).

Appendix I

Grading System for Sprains and Strains

LIGAMENT SPRAINS

A sprain is an injury to a ligament. The tissue damage ranges from a "stretch" to a complete tear. One or more ligaments may be injured at the same time. Severity of the injury depends on the extent of the tear as well as the number of ligaments involved.

Ligament sprain uses a system of grading as follows:

Grade I: Mild sprain

From a stretch without a tear to a 20 percent ligament tear

Usually no joint instability

Minimal pain and swelling

Little or no loss of functional ability

Bruising is absent or slight

The patient is able to put weight on the affected joint.

Grade II: Moderate sprain

A tear from 20 to 75 percent of the ligament

Bruising, moderate pain, and swelling

Some loss of function

The patient has difficulty putting weight on the affected joint.

Grade III: Severe sprain

From 75 percent ligament tear to a complete tear or rupture

Moderate to severe pain

Pronounced swelling and bruising

Definite loss of function

Use X-ray, MRI, or CT scan to rule out fracture

The patient is unable to put weight on the joint.

MUSCLE STRAINS

A strain is an injury to either a muscle or a tendon. Depending on the severity of the injury, a strain ranges from a simple over-stretch of the muscle or tendon to a complete tear or rupture. A tear in the belly of the muscle (muscle body) occurs in about 40 percent of cases. Tears at the muscle-tendon junction account for another 40 percent of cases. And a tear at the attachment of the tendon to the bone occurs in 20 percent of cases.

Muscle strain uses a system of grading as follows:

Grade I: Mild strain

Stretching of a few muscle fibers

10 percent or less of the muscle fibers tear

There is no palpable defect.

Grade II: Moderate strain

Partial tear of from 10 to 50 percent of the muscle fibers

There may be a palpable defect in the muscle.

Grade III: Severe strain

Extensive tear of over 50 percent of the fibers

May be a complete rupture of the muscle-tendon unit

Large palpable depression in the muscle

Normal function is disrupted.

CLINICAL COMMENTS

- Grade I and moderate grade II sprains and strains are appropriate for acupuncture treatment. Other complementary modalities may be required. Many grade II and grade III sprains and strains require orthopedic intervention. After the appropriate medical procedures are performed, acupuncture may still play a role in rehabilitation.

- With an avulsion fracture, a bony fragment tears away from the body of the bone due to acute trauma. This may be caused by a tendon or ligament that ruptures from its attachment, taking with it a portion of the bone. This is considered a complication of a grade III sprain or strain.

- In addition to acupuncture, topical medicines may be considered for sprains and strains. The site of injury is frequently close to the surface and may respond to such treatments.

- R.I.C.E. (Rest, Ice, Compression, and Elevation) are usually the typical western medical recommendations for acute sprains and strains. Heat applications may be considered after the acute phase.

- Physical therapy is often necessary in the rehabilitation of sprains and strains. This includes such modalities as strength training and range of motion exercises.

Appendix J
Electrical Stimulation

Electrical stimulation is frequently recommended in the treatments of this handbook. It is a common technique in Step Four, using it with local and adjacent points at the site of injury. However, I have suggested electrical stimulation with several other techniques in Step One and Step Two, including the shu-stream point combination and the activation of the extraordinary meridians. The following is a brief summary of the use of electrical stimulation to the inserted acupuncture needle, which usually enhances the clinical outcome.

Equipment

Electrical stimulation "machines" all have the same basic functions, but their modes and options vary. There is also a considerable range of price as well as durability of the machines. Electro-stimulators by Pantheon Research are more expensive than many Chinese and Japanese models.[1] Pantheon's machines are quite durable and provide the practitioner with the greatest amount of treatment options. There are numerous less expensive devices that hold up well with use; however, they do not always have all the treatment options available with the Pantheon machines.[2]

Micro-current versus milli-current

The first issue to consider is whether the machine treats with micro-current (microampere) or milli-current (millampere). Many of the older and less expensive stimulators from China use milliamperes. Some models, including many Japanese-made, offer only micro-current. And others, including those made by Pantheon, include both options.

Many practitioners prefer micro-current stimulation, and cite research supporting this mode. However, it is quite common to find experienced practitioners who use millampere current with good results. My clinical experience is not definitive and therefore I do not have a clear preference. I usually use milli-current, but will turn to micro-current as an option, especially in chronic cases.

Wave form and frequency

The continuous sine wave is the standard, and all machines offer this option. The only variable is frequency, which is measured in cycles per second. This is also known as "hertz", abbreviated as Hz. One hertz is one complete sine wave per second. The practitioner simply sets the frequency with a dial.

A continuous sine wave from 8 to 12 Hz is my first preference, and the starting place for all treatments. However, I vary the frequency in some cases when results are not satisfactory.

Wave form variations

Some electro-acupuncture devices will allow for variations of the wave forms. There are usually two choices. The first is known as a discontinuous wave, sometimes referred to as "intermittent". This means for one interval of time there is a sine wave, followed by an interval of time without stimulation. The second variation is the dense-disperse wave form, sometimes referred to as a "mixed" wave. The two intervals of electrical stimulation have differing frequencies. For example, the practitioner may use 100 Hz for one interval, which is a relatively high frequency (a "dense" wave). This may be followed by the second interval of 10 Hz, which is a lower frequency (a "disperse" wave).

The rationale for discontinuous (intermittent) or dense-disperse (mixed) wave forms is intriguing. These changing intervals of stimulation keep the body from accommodating to a single frequency setting. However, I rarely use these two options. If the practitioner does not have a clear point-of-view, I suggest using the continuous wave at a frequency of from 8 to 12 hertz. Use it with confidence! Refining your techniques and being more precise comes with time and clinical experience.

Amperage

Amperage is the measurement of the strength or volume of the electric current. Amperage is usually turned up to patient tolerance. My recommendation is to assure that the patient is comfortable, yet still experiencing the sensation of the electrical stimulation. If a fasciculation or contraction of the muscle is induced, it is advisable to keep it on the mild to moderate side. The patient will often accommodate to the current within five minutes. Amperage can then be turned up slightly one or two times during the treatment session.

Time or duration

There are no accepted and standard rules in relation to the time of electrical stimulation. Within the acupuncture profession, this may vary from 10 minutes to as long as one hour. Treatments using electrical stimulation usually average from 20 to 30 minutes in most acupuncture clinics, and this is the amount of time I use for treating sports injuries and pain.

Placement of the leads

The wires of most electrical machines have a red and black lead, referring to the positive and negative poles. Some machines pulse the current between these two leads, which may be referred to as biphasic stimulation. In this case, the red and black leads do not make a difference as to their placement. Generally, leads are attached to local and adjacent needles inserted at the site of injury. However, leads may combine a local point with a distal point on the affected meridian.

Most devices will have from two to six outlets. There are no accepted standards as to how many wires should be used during a typical acupuncture treatment. I never use more than two wires (four leads attached to four needles) at a time. If more than four points are to be stimulated, I will use the two wires on a second set of points. In this case, the first set of four points will be stimulated from 10 to 15 minutes, followed by the same time for the second set of four points. I never use electrical stimulation on more than eight acupuncture points per treatment.

Aggravation of symptoms

Symptom aggravation is a possible outcome of electrical stimulation. I find it impossible to predict which patient or injury will have this experience. However, post-treatment aggravation may occur with more frequency in patients over 50 years of age who present with chronic injuries. The current most likely induces too sudden a change in the local tissues, and qi and blood stagnation result. It is advisable to warn the patient that their condition could be temporarily aggravated from this modality. They should also be informed that electrical stimulation has its rewards. Significant improvement of pain and other signs and symptoms may result.

REFERENCES

[1] *Pantheon Research, Inc., Venice, California. (888) 332-3523*

[2] *The Ito IC-1107+ electro-acupuncture device (Japanese made) and the AWQ-104L (Chinese made) are examples of the lesser expensive machines.*

Appendix K

Activation of the Tendino-Muscle Meridian

Protocol for activation of the tendino-muscle meridian (TMM) with the jing-well point is discussed on page 9. This technique is used in Step One in each of the injuries of this handbook. So important in treating sports injuries and pain, bleeding the jing-well point is often the first technique I use to start a treatment. However, the activation of the TMM involves more than just treating the jing-well point. For the practitioner interested in this entire protocol, it is summarized as follows:[1]

TREAT THE JING-WELL POINT ON THE AFFECTED MERIDIAN

The jing-well point is the only acupuncture point directly shared by both the primary meridian and the tendino-muscle meridian. The following are the jing-well points of the 12 primary meridians:

Meridian	Jing-well point
Lung	Lu 11
Large Intestine	LI 1
Stomach	St 45
Spleen	Sp 1
Heart	H 9
Small Intestine	SI 1
Bladder	Bl 67
Kidney	Kid 1*
Pericardium	P 9*
San Jiao	SJ 1
Gall Bladder	GB 44
Liver	Liv 1*

There are alternate locations for Kid 1, P 9, and Liv 1. These three points do not conform to the standard jing-well location of .1 cun proximal to the corner of the nail base. See page 353 of the Appendices for these locations.

TREAT THE *AHSHI* POINTS

Most texts recommend the treatment of local *ahshi* points. When the tendino-muscle meridian is affected, these *ahshi* points are found in the superficial tissues of the muscle, fascia, and tendons. Pain is produced by relatively light palpation. Thus, superficial insertion of the needle is usually suggested. Many sources consider other techniques, such as cupping, gua sha, and massage to treat these affected tissues.

TREAT THE SHU-STREAM POINT ON THE AFFECTED MERIDIAN

Dr. Nguyen van Nghi suggests treatment of the shu-stream point to keep the pathogens in the TMM from entering the primary meridian. So important are the shu-stream points in sports medicine acupuncture, I discuss them as a separate technique in Step Two of each injury in this handbook. You can read more about the shu-stream points on page 23 of Section I.

Meridian	Shu-stream point
Lung	Lu 9
Large Intestine	LI 3
Stomach	St 43
Spleen	Sp 3
Heart	H 7
Small Intestine	SI 3
Bladder	Bl 65
Kidney	Kid 3
Pericardium	P 7
San Jiao	SJ 3
Gall Bladder	GB 41 *
Liver	Liv 3

* GB 42 may be used as an "alternative" shu-stream point for GB 41.

TREAT THE "INSERTION" OR "BINDING" POINTS

The texts refer to the "insertion" or "binding" points of each tendino-muscle meridian. This is where the TMM has a functional connection with the primary meridian at or near the three major joints of each extremity. Obviously, these points are located at the origin or insertion of the muscles, and contain significant tissues such as tendons and their rich network of afferent nerve fibers.

The insertion points of the tendino-muscle meridians are treated above and below the site of injury. For example, with extensor pain of the forearm along the Large Intestine meridian, the insertion points LI 11 and LI 5 are selected for treatment. The insertion points are summarized as follows:

Meridian	Shoulder	Elbow	Wrist
Lung	Lu 2 or Lu 3	Lu 5	Lu 9
Large Intestine	LI 15	LI 11	LI 5
Heart	H 1	H 3	H 7
Small Intestine	SI 9, SI 10	SI 8	SI 5
Pericardium	P 2 (?)	P 3	P 7
San Jiao	SJ 14	SJ 10	SJ 4

Meridian	Hip	Knee	Ankle
Stomach	St 31	St 35, St 36	St 41
Spleen	Sp 12 (?)	Sp 9	Sp 5
Bladder	Bl 36	Bl 39, Bl 40	Bl 60
Kidney	Kid 11 (?)	Kid 10	Kid 3, Kid 4
Gall Bladder	GB 30, GB 29	GB 34	GB 40
Liver	Liv 10-Liv 12	Liv 8	Liv 4

TONIFY THE PRIMARY MERIDIAN

Some texts insist that treating the primary meridian should accompany techniques used on the TMM. Tonification of the deeper primary channel will assist healing the injured tissues along the pathway of the tendino-muscle meridian.

Treating the tonification point or the yuan-source point makes sense in theory, as it strengthens the pathway where the injury has occurred. But this is a technique I rarely use when an injury is acute, as the treatment plan is to dispel stagnation of qi and blood. I consider this technique only after significant progress has been made in the healing of the injury. The tonification and yuan-source points of the 12 primary meridians are summarized as follows:

Meridian	Tonification point	Yuan-source point
Lung	Lu 9	Lu 9
Large Intestine	LI 11	LI 4
Stomach	St 41	St 42
Spleen	Sp 2	Sp 3
Heart	H 9	H 7
Small Intestine	SI 3	SI 4
Bladder	Bl 67	Bl 64
Kidney	Kid 7	Kid 3
Pericardium	P 9	P 7
San Jiao	SJ 3	SJ 4
Gall Bladder	GB 43	GB 40
Liver	Liv 8	Liv 3

TREAT THE "CONVERGENT" OR "MEETING" POINTS

The tendino-muscle meridians terminate at a specific point or "region". The texts translate this as either a "convergent" or a "meeting" point. This is where the TMM unites with the two other yin or yang meridians that traverse its extremity of origin. For example, the three leg yang muscle meridians – the Stomach, Bladder, and Gall Bladder – converge at the region of SI 18.

Some authors suggest that treatment to the convergent point "blocks" the pathogens from moving from one tendino-muscle meridian into the other two that converge at that point. However, in my experience, treatment of the convergent point rarely affects the clinical outcome, and while interesting in theory, I rarely use this technique. There are practitioners, however, who insist that treatment to the convergent point improves the results.

The convergent points of the tendino-muscle meridians are summarized as follows:

Meridian Grouping	Convergent point
Three Arm Yin (Lu, H, P)	The region of GB 22
Three Arm Yang (LI, SI, SJ)	The region of GB 13
Three Leg Yin (Sp, Kid, Liv)	The region of CV 3
Three Leg Yang (St, GB, Bl)	The region of SI 18

REFERENCES

[1] *Treatment of the Tendino-Muscle Meridians. Notes from translations of Nguyen van Nghi, MD. Publication and date unknown. However, the work of the late Dr. Nguyen van Nghi contributes to a large portion of this Appendix.*

Appendix L
Topical Applications

CHINESE TOPICAL APPLICATIONS

Topical applications of herbal formulas comprise a significant role in traditional Chinese medicine. "Die da yao", or trauma medicine, has been produced as an external application for use in sports injuries for centuries. Sometimes called "hit medicine", most acupuncturists have their favorite formula or product. While the classic texts do not provide articulate protocols for sports acupuncture, topical medicines are quite specific in their formulation. They differentiate the stages of injury from acute to chronic, from the initial signs of heat and inflammation to the cold or damp accumulation found in a *Bi* syndrome.

It is beyond the scope of this book to differentiate these stages of injury, which may be required for prescribing the correct topical application. Fortunately there are many good references. Jake Fratkin's *Chinese Herbal Patent Medicines* discusses many of the patent medicines available for sports injuries.[1] Topical applications for *Bi* syndrome are covered in Chapter 4D, and traumatic injury in 4F. Margaret Naeser's *Outline Guide to Chinese Herbal Patent Medicines in Pill Form* also has a section of products that promote blood circulation and dispel blood stasis.[2] In addition, many herbal companies have good literature on the application of their products for injury and pain.

Pay special attention to products available from Spring Wind Herbs.[3] Andy Ellis, L.Ac., is a long-time practitioner and formulator who has done a wonderful job with his various topicals, liniments, soft plasters, and compress soaks. Each is formulated for the differing stages of trauma and injury.

It would be advisable to look at internal formulas used for the treatment of trauma and pain. They may be considered with Step Three, where qi, blood, and the zang-fu organs are addressed. Equally important, these traditional formulas often form the basis of a topical application. Formulas that invigorate the blood in the treatment of traumatic injury can be found in the Bensky text *Chinese Herbal Medicine: Formulas & Strategies*.[4] Jake Fratkin references these formulas in his book in Chapter 4E.[5] Another resource is *Bi-syndromes: Rheumatic Disorders Treated by Traditional Chinese Medicine*, which might be useful for some of the chronic arthritic joint conditions discussed in Section II.[6]

350 • Appendix L *Topical Applications*

TOPICAL APPLICATIONS OF CHINESE HERBS CAN BE SUMMARIZED AS FOLLOWS

Liquids, liniments

Liquids and liniments all use common herbs to dispel stagnation of qi and blood. They differ in other aspects, including whether they are warming or cooling. Perhaps the most well known is Zheng Gu Shui, used for fractures, sprains, and other traumatic injuries. However, analysis of the formula, while well intentioned, does not assure its effectiveness. Sometimes the practitioner needs to experiment to see what works best for the patient and their specific injury.

Medicated plasters

Medicated plasters allow the patient to apply the herbal medicines as a bandage over the affected tissues. Plasters are often used for muscle and tendon injuries with swelling and bruising. They have advantages over liniments, as the plaster provides direct contact with the tissues, and the adhesive portion keeps them close to the skin. In addition, there is no liquid to spill. However, plasters can potentially irritate the skin, and don't always have the ability to penetrate into the deeper tissues.

Soft plasters

With soft plasters, herbs are combined in an "ointment-like" base. Spring Wind Herbs makes a line of soft plasters which use sesame oil and beeswax. With a little creativity, the patient can use plastic wrap and bandages to contain the soft plaster on the body and prevent it from staining clothes. Like the medicated plasters, watch for irritation of the skin.

Soaks, compresses

Herbal soaks and compresses are simple, as the herbs are boiled like any other decoction. The warm liquid is then used as a soak. If the herbs are contained in a cloth sack, it can be used as a compress. Spring Wind Herbs has a number of herbal soaks and compresses, differentiated according to the stages of the injury.

HOMEOPATHIC TOPICAL APPLICATIONS

Homeopathic topical applications should also be mentioned. Most practitioners have used the product Traumeel. It is an ointment that combines the most important homeopathic medicines used for trauma and injury. While it has its ardent users, I generally find this product unreliable. It does not interfere with other treatment protocols, so it is always worth a try.

The homeopathic tradition also offers products such as gels, salves, and oils. Arnica, hypericum, and calendula gel can be found in most natural pharmacies and health-food stores. They are generally easy to apply and do not irritate the skin. Arnica is one of the most important homeopathic remedies for injury, and is also available as an oil. Arnicated oil (or arnica oil) is very useful in acute injury and trauma to the muscles and tendons. As mentioned above with soft plasters, it can be applied to the site of injury and contained with plastic wrap and bandages. It is a quiet week in my clinic if I don't recommend Arnicated oil to a patient, either in the office or over the phone.

WESTERN TOPICAL APPLICATIONS

The western and naturopathic traditions also have their herbal topical applications. They are frequently prepared as salves, such as arnica and calendula. In addition, the practitioner should not overlook ointments containing capsaicin. Made from red chilli peppers (capsicum), capsaicin is an active component. It is approved by the FDA as an over-the-counter product for the relief of pain from minor arthritis. The ointment produces a sensation of "burning", and is sometimes useful in cases of cold (han).

REFERENCES

[1] Fratkin, J: *Chinese Herbal Patent Medicines, The Clinical Desk Reference.* Shya Publications, Boulder, 2001 (Chapter 4D, pages 370-383, Chapter 4F, pages 398-417).

[2] Naeser, M: *Outline Guide to Chinese Herbal Patent Medicines in Pill Form.* Boston Chinese Medicines, Boston, 1990.

[3] Spring Wind Herbs, Berkeley, California (510) 849-1820.
Note: The complete line of Spring Wind topicals are available through Golden Flower Chinese Herbs at (800) 729-8509.

[4] Bensky & Barolet: *Chinese Herbal Medicine: Formulas & Strategies.* Eastland Press, Seattle, 1990 (Section 3, pages 326-331).

[5] Fratkin, J: *Chinese Herbal Patent Medicines, The Clinical Desk Reference.* Shya Publications, Boulder, 2001 (Chapter 4E, pages 384-397).

[6] Vangermeersch & Sun: *Bi-syndromes: Rheumatic Disorders Treated by Traditional Chinese Medicine.* Nanjing College of Traditional Chinese Medicine, 1994.

Appendix M
Acupuncture Points
Location and Commentary

This appendix contains location and commentary on several of the acupuncture points mentioned in Section II. These are points that may not be familiar to the acupuncture practitioner, have alternate locations, or have differing clinical uses than those mentioned in the standard texts.

ALTERNATE LOCATIONS OF THREE NON-CONFORMING JING-WELL POINTS

These three alternate locations of jing-well points should be considered for the bleeding technique in Step One, Technique #1. This technique is used to activate the tendino-muscle meridian.

Kid 1 (Alternate location)

Location: On the medial side of the fifth digit (the little toe), about .1 cun proximal to the corner of the nail base.

Note: Bleeding technique at the traditional location of Kid 1 on the plantar surface of the foot is not recommended.

P 9 (Alternate location)

Location: On the radial side of the third digit (the middle finger), about .1 cun proximal to the corner of the nail base.

Note: This alternate location may be considered over the traditional point at the tip of the middle finger for bleeding technique to activate the tendino-muscle meridian.

Liv 1 (Alternate location)

Location: On the lateral side of the big toe, about .1 cun proximal to the corner of the nail base.

Note: Some texts describe the location of Liv 1 more proximal than .1 cun from the corner of the nail base. This alternate location is more advisable for bleeding technique to activate the tendino-muscle meridian.

SI 6 – LOCATION AND NEEDLE TECHNIQUE

SI 6 Xi-cleft point

Location: SI 6 is located in the cleft of the styloid process, not in the more convenient depression on its radial side. Deadman states its location on "the radial side of the high point of the styloid process".[1] He also states that SI 6 is found "in the cleft ... of the styloid process". Remember, on the bone, not in the convenient depression on the radial side of the styloid process.

Comments on needle technique: Insert at the high point of the styloid process, and with a transverse angle, thread proximally towards the elbow. I typically use a 1.5 inch needle, and thread its entire length proximally through the cleft.

POINT CATEGORY

GB 42 (Alternate shu-stream point)

Location: Between the 4th and 5th metatarsal bones, in the depression proximal to the metatarsal heads, on the medial side of the tendon of the extensor digitorum longus.[2]

Comments: GB 42 does not have a point category, instead designating the shu-stream function to GB 41. I encourage the reader to palpate GB 42, as it is frequently sensitive in pain along the Gall Bladder channel from the hip distally. Consider GB 42 as an "alternate" shu-stream point.

SPLEEN AND STOMACH DEFICIENCY

St 41 Tonification point

In the system of Korean Constitutional Acupuncture, St 41 is more important than St 36 to tonify deficiency of the Stomach and Spleen. According to four needle technique, it is the tonification point of the Stomach meridian, and is often overlooked by practitioners of TCM-style acupuncture.

St 36 Horary point

St 36 is contra-indicated in Stomach and Spleen deficiency in the system of Korean Constitutional Acupuncture. This is especially true for the patient that is lean, low body fat, and has definitive signs and symptoms of a deficiency syndrome. The point St 36, as an horary point, is used as a "mother point" in four needle technique. This Five Element inter-relationship states that qi from earth is used to tonify to metal, which is the "child" of earth. Thus, using St 36 may deplete the earth element organs of the Stomach and Spleen. It should be noted that this contra-indication is for needling, while direct or indirect moxa is permissible.

LI 11 "Earth" point, tonification point

The point LI 11 is the tonification point of the Large Intestine. As an "earth" point, it "draws" from the mother element. In Korean Constitutional Acupuncture, LI 11 is contra-indicated with Stomach and Spleen deficiency.

AURICULAR POINTS

Knee (French), Knee (Chinese)

Foot and Ankle (French)

Foot and Ankle (Chinese)

The reader should be aware than in auricular therapy, there are two locations of the lower-extremity points from the hip distally. The French system places these points in the center of the triangular fossa. The Chinese system locates them slightly higher, along the superior antihelix crus. The practitioner should use a point finder or blunt probe for palpation to determine which of these two differing locations are "active". Generally, I find the French locations to be more reliable with patients who have knee, foot, and ankle injuries.

REFERENCES

[1] Deadman, Al-Khafaji, & Baker: *A Manual of Acupuncture*. Journal of Chinese Medicine Publications, East Sussex, 2001 (page 237).

[2] Deadman, Al-Khafaji, & Baker: *A Manual of Acupuncture*. Journal of Chinese Medicine Publications, East Sussex, 2001 (page 462).

Appendix N
The Extraordinary Acupuncture Points
Location and Commentary

This appendix contains location and commentary on the extraordinary acupuncture points discussed in the treatments of Section II.

Baichongwo[1]   M-LE-34

Translates as "hundred inset burrow"

Location: 3 cun proximal to the superior medial border of the patella, in the depression on the "bulge" of the vastus medialis muscle.

Note: This is the motor point of the vastus medialis muscle.[2]

Bailao[3]   M-HN-30

Translates as "hundred taxations"

Location: On the posterior aspect of the neck, 2 cun superior and 1 cun lateral to Du 14.

Note: This point is located lateral to the vertebral body of either C4, C5, or C6, depending on the text. Bailao is the motor point for the splenius cervicis muscle of the neck.[4]

Jiankua[5]   N-LE-55

Termed "posterior" GB 29 in this handbook

Translates as "strength thigh"

Location: Midway between the crest of the ilium and the high point of the greater trochanter of the femur.

Note: This point with deep insertion reaches both the gluteus medius and the gluteus minimus muscles.

Jianqian[6]   M-UE-48

Translates as "front of the shoulder"

Location: On the anterior aspect of the shoulder joint, midway between the anterior axillary crease and the point LI 15.

Note: This point is clearly intended to treat the shoulder, accessing the joint from this anterior location. Jianneiling is another name for this point.

Lanweixue[7]   M-LE-13

Translates as "appendix point"

Location: Approximately 2 cun distal to St 36 on the right leg.

Note: This is the motor point of the anterior tibialis muscle, found on both the right and the left legs.[8]

"Outer" SI 8

This is not a defined extraordinary point in the acupuncture texts.

Location: In the depression midway between the lateral epicondyle of the humerus and the olecranon process of the ulna.

Pigen[9]   M-BW-16

Translates as "lump's root"

Location: 3.5 cun lateral to the spinous process of L1.

Note: This is the location of one of the trigger points of the quadratus lumborum muscle.[10]

Shimian[11]   M-LE-5

Translates as "insomnia"

Location: At the center of the heel on the plantar surface of the foot.

Note: This is the site of attachment of the plantar fascia to the calcaneus.

Xiyan[12]   MN-LE-16

Translates as "eyes of the knees"

Location: On the knee, in the depressions formed when the knee is flexed, immediately inferior to the patella, on both the medial and lateral sides of the patellar tendon (ligament).

Note: For patello-femoral joint syndrome, deep sub-patellar needling benefits pain and inflammation.

Yaoyan[13]   M-BW-24

Translates as "lumbar eyes"

Location: In the depression approximately 3.5 cun lateral to the lower border of L4.

Note: I locate this point as described above, which places it superior to the iliac crest. This is the location of one of the trigger points of the quadratus lumborum muscle.[14] *However, this is not how the point is illustrated in the Deadman text.*

REFERENCES

[1] Deadman, Al-Khafaji, & Baker: *A Manual of Acupuncture*. Journal of Chinese Medicine Publications, East Sussex, 2001 (page 582).

[2] Callison, M: *Motor Point Index*. AcuSport Seminar Series LLC, San Diego, 2007 (page 123).

[3] Deadman, Al-Khafaji, & Baker: *A Manual of Acupuncture*. Journal of Chinese Medicine Publications, East Sussex, 2001 (page 569).

[4] Callison, M: *Motor Point Index*. AcuSport Seminar Series LLC, San Diego, 2007 (page 31).

[5] Shanghai College of Traditional Medicine: *Acupuncture, A Comprehensive Text*. Eastland Press, Chicago, 1981 (page 363).

[6] Deadman, Al-Khafaji, & Baker: *A Manual of Acupuncture*. Journal of Chinese Medicine Publications, East Sussex, 2001 (page 581).

[7] Deadman, Al-Khafaji, & Baker: *A Manual of Acupuncture*. Journal of Chinese Medicine Publications, East Sussex, 2001 (pages 583-584).

[8] Callison, M: *Motor Point Index*. AcuSport Seminar Series LLC, San Diego, 2007 (page 130).

[9] Shanghai College of Traditional Medicine: *Acupuncture, A Comprehensive Text*. Eastland Press, Chicago, 1981 (page 378).

[10] Travell & Simons: *Myofascial Pain and Dysfunction: The Trigger Point Manual, Volume 2 (The Lower Extremities)*. Williams & Wilkins, Philadelphia, 1992 (page 30).

[11] Shanghai College of Traditional Medicine: *Acupuncture, A Comprehensive Text*. Eastland Press, Chicago, 1981 (page 387).

[12] Deadman, Al-Khafaji, & Baker: *A Manual of Acupuncture*. Journal of Chinese Medicine Publications, East Sussex, 2001 (page 583).

[13] Deadman, Al-Khafaji, & Baker: *A Manual of Acupuncture*. Journal of Chinese Medicine Publications, East Sussex, 2001 (page 572).

[14] Travell & Simons: *Myofascial Pain and Dysfunction: The Trigger Point Manual, Volume 2 (The Lower Extremities)*. Williams & Wilkins, Philadelphia, 1992 (page 30).

Appendix O
Myofascial Trigger Points

CHARACTERISTICS OF TRIGGER POINTS

According to the work of Travell and Simons, the following are the clinical characteristics of myofascial trigger points:[1]

1. Trigger points present as hyper-irritable lesions in the muscle or the fascia. As such, all trigger points are *ahshi* points. Dr. Travell uses the term "local spot tenderness". She also includes the "jump sign", which is the patient's reaction to palpation of the trigger point.

2. Trigger points present with pain, which is often the chief complaint of the patient.

3. There is a typical and predictable pain pattern referred from a trigger point.

4. Digital pressure (acupressure) may activate the pain referral pattern.

5. The trigger point may be felt as a palpable taut fascial band or fibrocystic nodule in the affected tissues.

6. The involved muscle may be shortened, taut, or guarded.

7. Manual muscle testing (resisted contraction) reveals decreased strength (weakness) of the affected muscle.

8. Manual muscle testing (resisted contraction) may reproduce the pain pattern.

9. Passive stretching of the affected muscle may reproduce the pain pattern.

10. Decreased range of motion may be observed in the affected muscle.

11. Cross-friction massage may produce a "twitch response" (fasciculation) of the muscle.

The assessment of a trigger point as the cause of a pain syndrome involves careful questioning and examination of the patient. Not all of the characteristics of an active trigger point mentioned above needs to be present to confirm the diagnosis. It is quite common that only some of these signs and symptoms are found in any individual patient or injury.

TREATMENT OF TRIGGER POINTS

Treatment of an active trigger point, which Dr. Travell calls "inactivation", includes the following procedures:

1. Injection of the trigger point

   The primary treatment modality in the early years of Travell and Simons' work was injection therapy with saline or local anesthetic. Presently, acupuncturists use needle insertion, often with electrical stimulation or needle-top moxa to activate these points. Physical therapists use what their profession terms "dry needling".

2. "Ischemic" compression

   This is simply thumb or digit pressure on the trigger points, or acupressure and tuina from the Chinese medical perspective. Dr. Travell suggests that ischemic compression produces "hypoxia followed by a reactive hyperemia". In TCM terms, this is invigorating the circulation of qi and blood in the local tissues.

3. "Spray and stretch"

   In the 1980s, Dr. Travell's system utilized vapocoolant spray along with stretching of the affected muscle group. These coolant sprays are no longer used because of the chlorohydrocarbon content.

4. Ultrasound

   Travell and Simons suggest that sustained application of ultrasound at low intensities inactivates a trigger point. This technique is still commonly used. The equivalent in the acupuncture profession is direct, indirect, or needle-top moxibustion.

5. Application of heat

   After treatment of a trigger point, moist heat is applied to release tension on the affected muscle or muscle groups.

Before concluding, what Travell and Simons call "perpetuating factors" should be mentioned. Their work includes considerable commentary on medical conditions that perpetuate a myofascial pain syndrome. This includes biomechanical imbalances such as foot pronation or supination, anatomical short leg (leg length discrepancy), and pelvic tilt or rotation. Internal metabolic considerations such as vitamin deficiencies, "stress", and other psychological disorders may also affect a trigger point and its resultant pain syndrome. Thus, while there is a precise physical medicine component to myofascial pain syndromes, the authors attempt to assess and treat each individual as a "whole" person.

REFERENCES

[1] Travell & Simons: *Myofascial Pain and Dysfunction: The Trigger Point Manual, Volume 1 (The Upper Extremities)*. Williams & Wilkins, Philadelphia, 1983 (pages 5-37).
Note: This discussion also includes seminar notes from the lectures of Janet Travell, MD, and David Simons, MD, Los Angeles, California, 1984.

Appendix P
Wrist-Ankle Acupuncture
Location and Commentary

Wrist-ankle acupuncture is an interesting and sometimes effective system of treating sports injuries and pain. There are various sources that discuss this modern technique, which is not included in the standard point location texts.[1] Wrist-ankle points may be considered when pain and other signs and symptoms of trauma affect multiple meridians. They may also be used when the site of injury is not precisely along one of the 12 primary meridians.

Wrist-ankle acupuncture has not been a treatment technique I have used consistently since I began studying acupuncture in 1976. In fact, this relatively simple system is still not widely used in the acupuncture profession. None-the-less, I include wrist-ankle treatments in some of the injuries of Section II. They are found in Step Two and are grouped with auricular therapy and microsystems.

There are 12 wrist-ankle points, six on the upper extremity and six on the lower extremity. These points are found bilaterally. In general, the six upper-extremity points are 2 cun proximal to the wrist crease. Three points are on the palmar surface, and three on the dorsal surface of the forearm. The six lower-extremity points are 3 cun proximal to the ankle crease. Three points are on the medial surface, and three on the lateral surface of the leg. Some sources suggest that the unit of measurement is two finger-breadths rather than 2 cun for the upper extremity, and three finger-breadths rather than 3 cun for the lower extremity.

Wrist-ankle points are sometimes referred to as "zones". They are needled subcutaneously with a transverse (horizontal) angle. A 1.5 inch needle is recommended, and little or no manipulation is required.

The following is a summary of the wrist-ankle zones:

WRIST ZONES OF THE UPPER EXTREMITY

Upper #1   The palmar surface of the forearm

Located 2 cun proximal to the wrist crease, along the ulna, on the ulnar side of the flexor carpi ulnaris. This zone approximates the Heart meridian.

Upper #2   The palmar surface of the forearm

Located 2 cun proximal to the wrist crease, between the tendons of the palmaris longus and the flexor carpi radialis. This zone is the Pericardium meridian, and includes the point P 6.

Upper #3   The palmar surface of the forearm

Located 2 cun proximal to the wrist crease, on the radial side of the radial artery. This zone approximates the Lung meridian.

Upper #4   The dorsal surface of the forearm

Located 2 cun proximal to the wrist crease, along the radius. This zone approximates the Large Intestine meridian.

Upper #5   The dorsal surface of the forearm

Located 2 cun proximal to the wrist crease, between the radius and the ulna. This zone is the San Jiao meridian, and includes the point SJ 5.

Upper #6   The dorsal surface of the forearm

Located 2 cun proximal to the wrist crease, along the ulna. This zone approximates the Small Intestine meridian.

ANKLE ZONES OF THE LOWER EXTREMITY

Lower #1   The medial surface of the leg

Located 3 cun proximal to the medial malleolus, on the anterior border of the achilles tendon. This zone approximates the Kidney meridian.

Lower #2   The medial surface of the leg

Located 3 cun proximal to the medial malleolus, on the posterior border of the tibia. This zone approximates the Spleen meridian, and includes the point Sp 6.

Lower #3   The medial surface of the leg

Located 3 cun proximal to the medial malleolus, along the tibia, posterior to its anterior border.

Lower #4   The lateral surface of the leg

Located 3 cun proximal to the lateral malleolus, halfway between the anterior border of the tibia and the anterior border of the fibula. This zone approximates the Stomach meridian.

Lower #5   The lateral surface of the leg

Located 3 cun proximal to the lateral malleolus, along the posterior border of the fibula. This zone approximates the Gall Bladder meridian.

Lower #6   The lateral surface of the leg

Located 3 cun proximal to the lateral malleolus, along the anterior border of the achilles tendon. This zone approximates the Bladder meridian.

REFERENCES

[1] Matsumoto & Birch: *Extraordinary Vessels.* Paradigm Publishers, Massachusetts, 1986 (pages 182-188).
Note: Dr. Zhang Xin Shu's Wrist Ankle Acupuncture (Wan Ke Zhen) is the source quoted in the text above.

Index

A

Achilles tendon
    rupture, *56*
    tendonitis, 53-62
    tendinosis, *54*
Acromial-clavicular (AC) joint, *295-302*
Adhesive capsulitis (frozen shoulder), *276*
Ankle
    inversion sprain (lateral), *75-83*
Ankle, lateral ligaments
    anterior talo-fibular ligament, 81
    calcaneo-fibular ligament, 81
    posterior talo-fibular ligamen, 81t
Anterior compartment syndrome, 102-103
Anterior tibial stress syndrome, 101-109
Anterior tibialis muscle, 102, 107-108
Anti-inflammatory medications, 323-324
Arthritis
    of the AC joint, 295-302
    of the anterior knee, 121-132
    of the first MTP joint (big toe), 85-92
    of the hip, 195-203
    of the medial knee, 153-161
    of the shoulder, 264, 276
Auricular therapy, 35-37

B

Bicepital tendon
    subluxation, 286-287
    tear, rupture, 286-287
    tendonitis, 285-294,
Biceps muscle group, 285-294
Biomechanical imbalances, 325-327
Bunion, big toe, 286
Bursitis
    sub-acromial, 250-252, 253
    trochanteric (hip), 185-194

C

Calcaneal heel spur, 64-65
Carpal tunnel syndrome, 217-226
Cervical disc syndrome, 304-305, 306

Cervical pain, 303-313
Chondromalacia, 122-123
"Climber's" elbow, 239-247
Contra-lateral treatment, 13-15
Cross training, 328-329

D

Dai mai (Waist vessel), 31-32, 34
Du mai (Governing vessel), 31-32, 34

E

Elbow pain
    lateral epicondylitis, 227-237
    medial epicondylitis, 239-247
Eight extraordinary meridians, 31-34
Electrical stimulation, 344-346
Empirical points, 21-22
Epicondylitis
    lateral (tennis elbow), 227-237
    medial (golfer's elbow), 239-247
Extensors, forearm, 228-229, 235
Extraordinary points, 356-358

F

First metatarsal-phalanges (MTP) joint, 85-92
Five antique points, 27-28
Flexors, forearm, 224, 240, 245, 246
Foot pain
    ankle sprain (lateral/inversion), 75-83
    metatarsal neuroma, 93-99
    of the first MTP joint, 85-92
    plantar fasciitis, 75-83
Four Steps, summary, 3-8
Frozen shoulder, 375-284

G

Gastrocnemius-soleus muscles, 53-55, 59-61
Gleno-humeral joint, 276, 282-283
Gluteus medius muscle, 171-173, 214
Gluteus minimus muscle, 171-173, 214
"Golfer's" elbow, 239-247

H

Hallux rigidus, 86
Hand pain
    carpal tunnel syndrome, 217-226
Hallux valgus, 86
Hamstring muscle group, 185-194
Hamstring
    strain, 176
    tendonitis, 176
Heat, application of, 320-322
He-sea points, 28
Heel pain
    achilles tendonitis, 53-62
    plantar fasciitis, 63-73
Hip
    arthritis, 195-203
    bursitis, 185-194
Hui-influential points, 29

I

Ice, application of, 320-322
Ilio-tibial (IT) band
    IT band syndrome, 163-174
    treatment techniques, 168
Infraspinatous muscle
    motor points, 264, 270
    strain, 264-265
    tendonitis, 263-273
    trigger points, 264, 270
Inversion ankle sprain, 75-83

J

Jing-river points, 28
Jing-well points, 9-11, 27
"Jumper's" knee, 133-141

K

Knee pain
    anterior, 121-132, 133-141
    IT band syndrome, 163-174
    lateral, 163-174
    medial, acute, 143-152
    medial, chronic, 153-161
    patellar tendonitis, 133-141
    patello-femoral joint, 121-132

L

Lateral (inversion) ankle sprain, 75-83
Lateral epicondylitis, 227-237
Leg pain
    anterior shin splints, 101-109
    medial shin splints, 111-120
Levator scapulae muscle
    motor points, 304-305
    treatment techniques, 303-313
    trigger points, 304-305, 310-311
Low back pain, 205-215,

Lower he-sea points, 29
Lumbar disc syndrome, 206-207
Lumbar pain, 206-207
Luo-connecting points, 28

M

Manual muscle testing, 334-335
Median nerve, entrapment, 217-226
Medial collateral ligament (MCL), 143-152
Medial compartment syndrome, 153-161
Medial epicondylitis, 239-247
Medial meniscus, 143-152
Medial tibial stress syndrome, 111-120
Metatarsal neuroma, 93-99
Metatarsal stress fracture, 94
Metatarsalgia, 94
Morton's neuroma, 93-99
Motor points, 47
Muscle testing, 334-335, 336-341

N

Neck pain, 303-313

O

Opposite extremity treatment, 17-20
Opposite side treatment, 13-15
Orthopedic assessment, 334-335
Orthopedic testing, 336-341
Osgood-Schlatter's disease, 134, 141
Osteoarthritis (see arthritis)

P

Patellar bursitis, 135
Patellar pain, 122-123, 130, 134
Patellar tendonitis, 133-141
Patello-femoral joint dysfunction, 121-132
Phalen's maneuver, 218-219
Physical therapy, 330-333
Piriformis muscle, 193
Plantar fasciitis, 63-73
Posterior tibialis muscle, 112-113, 118-119
Pronation, of the foot, 325
Pronators, of the hand, 240

Q

Quadriceps muscle group, 131
Quadratus lumborum muscle
    motor points, 206-207, 213-214
    treatment techniques, 205-215
    trigger points, 206-207, 213-214

R

R.I.C.E., 320-322
Rotator cuff injury
    of the infraspinatous, 263-273
    of the subscapularis, 276
    of the supraspinatous, 249-261

R (con't)
"Runner's" knee, 163-174

S
Sedation points, 28
Shin splints
    anterior, 101-109
    medial, 111-120
Shoulder
    dislocation, 296
    impingement syndrome, 250,251
    separation, 296
Shoulder pain
    bicepital tendonitis, 285-294
    frozen shoulder, 275-284
    infraspinatous, 263-273
    supraspinatous, 249-261
Shu-stream points, 23-25, 28
Somatic Auricular Therapy (SAT), 36
Sprains, grading system, 342-343
"Stiff neck", 303-313
Strains, grading system, 342-343
Sub-acromial bone spur, 250-252
Sub-acromial bursitis, 250-252
Sub-talar joint, 82
Subscapularis muscle, 276
Supination, of the foot, 325
Supinators, of the hand, 228-229
Supraspinatous muscle
    impingement syndrome, 250-252
    motor points, 250-251
    treatment techniques, 249-261
    trigger points, 250-251

T
Talus sinus, 82
Tendino-muscle meridians, 9-12
"Tennis" elbow, 227-237
Tensor fascia lata muscle, 164-165
Tibial stress fracture, 112-113
Tinel's sign, 218-219
Tonification points, 28
Topical applications, 350-352
Torticollis, 304-305
Traditional point categories, 27-29
"Turf toe", 86
Trigger points, 359-360
Trochanteric bursitis, 185-194

U
Upper/lower treatment, 17-20
Upper trapezius muscle, 304-305

V
Vastus medialis, 125
Vastus lateralis, 125

W
Wrist-ankle acupuncture, 361-362

X
Xi-cleft points, 28

Y
Yang Qiao mai (Yang motility vessel), 32-33
Yin Qiao mai (Yin motility vessel), 33
Ying-spring points, 28
Yuan-source points, 28

Z
Zang-fu (internal organ) treatment, 39-43

Biography of the Authors

Whitfield Reaves, OMD, L.Ac.

Whitfield Reaves is the author of *The Acupuncture Handbook of Sports Injuries and Pain.*

Whitfield Reaves began his undergraduate studies at the University of Oregon in 1969. While his first two years of study focused on pre-medicine, his interests in Asian and European history led to a Bachelor of Science degree in 1974. Whitfield first began the study of Chinese medicine in 1977 with Dr. Grace Liu, a medical doctor and acupuncturist from China. The year-long formal apprenticeship program was part of Dharma Realm Buddhist University, and he received his certificate of completion in 1978.

Whitfield moved to Los Angeles in 1978 to be part of the initial class of instruction at SAMRA University of Health Sciences. SAMRA was the first acupuncture program to be approved by the medical board in the state of California. After graduating in 1981, Whitfield was among the early practitioners licensed to practice acupuncture in the United States.

Following graduation, Whitfield's studies continued in Beijing, China. He completed an internship at three hospital clinics that were part of Beijing Medical College. Whitfield also attended the doctorate program at SAMRA University. In 1983, his thesis, entitled "Acupuncture and the treatment of common running injuries," was completed. In that year he earned his Doctorate of Oriental Medicine (OMD) degree.

In the fall of 1981, Whitfield opened his first acupuncture clinic and began practice in San Diego, California. Early in his career, a long-distance runner came to the office for treatment of achilles tendonitis, a common sports injury. After treatment, the patient competed in the Mission Bay Marathon – and won the event! Following this event in 1982, sports medicine acupuncture became Whitfield's area of specialization, and has continued to be the focus of his work for more than 25 years.

By late 1983, Whitfield had moved back to Los Angeles to be part of the 1984 Olympic Games. Working at the International Sports Medicine Institute, he treated athletes from around the world with acupuncture and traditional Chinese medicine. The '84 Olympics provided broad experience in the treatment of sports injuries, but also opened the door to a whole new clinical application of acupuncture: the enhancement of athletic performance.

After the Olympics, Whitfield continued to work with competitive athletes. From 1985 through 1988, he treated cyclists training for the 3,000 mile Race Across America. In 1989, Whitfield moved to Boulder, Colorado, where triathletes, long-distance runners, and cyclists from around the world came to train. The experience of treating these elite athletes helped to further refine his points and techniques of traditional Chinese acupuncture and their use with the athletic patient. In 2009, Whitfield completed writing and publishing The Acupuncture Handbook of Sports Injuries and Pain. It is the culmination of almost three decades of clinical experience in sports medicine acupuncture.

Whitfield lives in Boulder with his wife, Mary Saunders, and their son, Martin. Mary is also an acupuncturist, practicing in the community clinic style. Martin attends Montana State University's College of Engineering. He is a professional slalom skateboard racer, and won the North American Championships in 2008 and was the World Champion in the Giant Slalom in 2009.

Whitfield Reaves can be reached at www.whitfieldreaves.com.

Chad Bong, MS, L.Ac.

Chad Bong is a contributing writer to *The Acupuncture Handbook of Sports Injuries and Pain.*

Chad's interest in sports medicine comes from being a lifetime athlete. In high school, he competed in football, baseball, and cross-country skiing, as well as endless weight-training sessions to improve his performance on the field. His football career continued in college while he completed his Bachelor of Science degree in Physical Education in 1999.

While working on his Master's degree at Northern Michigan University, he served as the strength and conditioning coach for the college's football program. Mr. Bong also worked in the research lab, providing him the opportunity to perform sports medicine testing on various parameters of exercise physiology for numerous future Olympians, professional cross-country skiers, and biathletes. He obtained his Master's degree in Exercise Science in 2002.

Chad Bong continued his education with an 800-hour massage therapy program at The Institute of Natural Therapies. During that time, he was drawn to acupuncture and how this modality could be incorporated into his work with athletes. In 2005, he began the study of traditional Chinese medicine at Southwest Acupuncture College in Boulder, Colorado. Chad completed the program in 2008, earning his second Master's degree. His specialty internship clinics included sports medicine, the Boulder County Aids Project, and advanced Japanese techniques.

Concurrent to these studies, Chad completed a six-month apprenticeship program in acupuncture sports medicine, taught by Whitfield Reaves. He has since served as the senior assistant to Whitfield's teaching programs and seminars for the acupuncture profession. Chad has also received additional training with weekend continuing education workshops on sports medicine acupuncture with Matt Callison, MS, L.Ac., and Frank He, L.Ac.

Chad currently lives and practices acupuncture in Philadelphia, Pennsylvania. He also continues to work as a personal trainer. Chad lives with his wife, Meghan, and their dog Bailey. In his spare time, he enjoys rock climbing, kite-boarding, and reading orthopedic texts.

Chad Bong can be contacted at acusport@gmail.com